T0301665

European Fashion Law

Elgar Practical Guides

Rich in practical advice, *Elgar Practical Guides* are handy, concise guides to a range of legal practice areas.

Combining practical insight and step-by-step guidance with the relevant substantive law and procedural rules, the books in this series focus on understanding and navigating the issues that are likely to be encountered in practice. This is facilitated by a range of structural tools including checklists, glossaries, sample documentation and recommended actions.

Elgar Practical Guides are indispensable resources for the busy practitioner and for the non-specialist who requires a first introduction or a reliable turn-to reference book.

Titles in the series include:

Determann's Field Guide to Data Privacy Law
International Corporate Compliance, Second Edition
Lothar Determann

Proceedings Before the European Patent Office
A Practical Guide to Success in Opposition and Appeal
Marcus O. Müller and Cees A.M. Mulder

The World Intellectual Property Organization (WIPO)
A Reference Guide
Carolyn Deere Birkbeck

European Fashion Law
A Practical Guide from Start-up to Global Success
Rosie Burbidge

European Fashion Law

A Practical Guide from Start-up to Global Success

ROSIE BURBIDGE
Partner, Gunnercooke LLP, London, UK

Elgar Practical Guides

Edward Elgar
PUBLISHING

Cheltenham, UK • Northampton, MA, USA

Cover image: Bernhard Deckert, photographer at bernieshoots.com, 2017.

Published by
Edward Elgar Publishing Limited
The Lypiatts
15 Lansdown Road
Cheltenham
Glos GL50 2JA
UK

Edward Elgar Publishing, Inc.
William Pratt House
9 Dewey Court
Northampton
Massachusetts 01060
USA

A catalogue record for this book
is available from the British Library

Library of Congress Control Number: 2018960565

This book is available electronically in the **Elgar**online
Law subject collection
DOI 10.4337/9781788113014

ISBN 978 1 78811 300 7 (cased)
ISBN 978 1 78811 302 1 (paperback)
ISBN 978 1 78811 301 4 (eBook)

Typeset by Servis Filmsetting Ltd, Stockport, Cheshire
Printed and bound by CPI Group (UK) Ltd, Croydon, CR0 4YY

In memory of Peter Burbidge – an inspirational European lawyer, europhile, professor and parent. He had many interests – fashion wasn't one of them.

Content overview

Table of contents

PART IV THE BIG ISSUES

Figures

Preface

This book began with the realisation that while plenty of books provide an insight into the legal issues facing the fashion industry in the US, there are comparatively few that consider the European perspective. Those books that do consider European law in the context of fashion tend to do so from a more academic than practical perspective. This book aims to change that trend.

Europe is the home to three out of four of the world's major fashion weeks (Paris, Milan and London). Key global fashion movements began in these cities and they continue to influence the rest of the world. It is high time for a book which looks at European legal issues as well as those in the Americas and Asia.

There are important European legal concepts and conventions which affect both European fashion businesses and those planning to do business in Europe. For example, design protection, use of customer data and e-commerce all have specific nuances which may be unfamiliar to non-Europeans. For anyone doing business in Europe, a lack of awareness of these issues can harm reputations and lead to expensive and distracting disputes.

Before we start, I must make a confession: I am an English intellectual property lawyer. This means that this book inevitably has both an English and an intellectual property focus. However, thanks to some excellent contributors from across Europe the book escapes a narrow focus and provides some essential insights for fashion businesses and lawyers alike.

The aim and approach

The aim of this book is to set out the main legal issues that all fashion businesses need to be aware of in order to thrive in the modern marketplace. It should be essential reading for those working in the fashion business as well as students hoping to join the fashion industry and lawyers who want to better understand their clients' business needs.

I became interested in the fashion industry as a result of my work for fashion and retail clients over the last decade. In addition to working for fashion clients in a law firm, I have been fortunate enough to have two secondments to eBay and Richemont. These e-commerce and luxury businesses have been at the forefront of the technological revolutions which have shaped the fashion industry and have led some of the major European litigation into areas such as the use of keyword advertising and blocking injunctions. Consequently, in addition to the book's exploration of the key legal issues, there are occasional insights into the business practicalities as well.

Rather than consider each European country and the legal issues they face in turn, this book looks at the common legal issues throughout the European Union, European Economic Area and Switzerland. It particularly focuses on the UK, France and Italy, the homes to the three major fashion capitals. The book identifies important differences either within or between different countries. In addition to the UK, France and Italy, there is occasional insight into some of the major European markets such as Germany, Switzerland, Belgium and Poland. Overall, this book is an appetiser. It is a starting point for legal understanding rather than the end of your journey of fashion law discovery.

The aim of this book is to be as accessible to as many people as possible. It cannot answer every legal issue a fashion business may face in Europe. Instead, it highlights key issues which commonly affect the fashion industry and identifies some of the best (and worst) approaches with examples from the legal front line.

Rather than going through each legal topic in turn, such as intellectual property, employment and data protection, these issues are woven into the story of the modern fashion business. I start with a fashion design student and take them on a journey to global domination.

Thanks a million!

I am hugely grateful for the help and assistance I have received along the way from my fellow European lawyers. In particular, Charlotte

Gerrish (France) who is a woman of many talents (not least, French and English law) and has been a great support throughout the process. In no particular order, further enormous thanks are due to the contributors from across Europe: Chiara Gaido (Italy), Frederic Lejeune (Belgium), Michal Stein (England – employment), Wioletta Kulinska (Poland), Gordon Drakes (England – franchising, agents and distributors), Isabelle Pons (France), Alexandra Brenner (Switzerland), Kate Partridge (England – corporate transactions) and Hester Beuvers (Germany). Without their help this would have been a very Anglo-centric and intellectual-property-focused publication. I am immensely grateful for their time and dedication.

In addition to legal input, I have been fortunate to have had some great insights into the problems faced by new and established fashion businesses. Huge thanks are owed to Cristina Gatti (ïttag) for her practical insight into the industry – it's not every fashion owner who wants to show a lawyer around Paris fashion week! Thanks also to the glamorous Roberta Tria for providing her insights into the practical side of luxury fashion.

Thanks also to the always inspirational Marija Butkovic (Women of Wearables), Nicola Searle (Goldsmiths University) and Amit Alagh (tech and legal business guru), for their help, advice, support and proofreading. A particularly big shout out goes to Eleonora Rosati who has taken time out of her many commitments to apply her laser focus to the final draft. Any errors which remain are entirely my own fault. I would love to hear about them by email, rather than in the comments section on Amazon, although the choice, is of course, yours.

Finally, huge thanks to Edward Elgar (the publisher not the composer) and, in particular Luke Adams and Stephanie Tytherleigh for believing in me and helping me to make this happen. All websites cited in the volume were live as at 10 October 2018.

Definitions and interpretation

I have a longstanding dislike of using 'he' to represent both genders but even worse, in my view, is the distracting 's/he' or 'he or she'. Consequently, 'they' is used throughout. I studied English at university before studying law as a postgraduate so I, more than most, appreciate that this is technically incorrect. However, until a non-gendered alternative enters common linguistic use, this is the route I have adopted. Alternative suggestions are always welcome.

For those of a digital persuasion, the website associated with this book: www.EuropeanFashionLaw.com will have summaries of key issues and handy links to additional sources of information.

Throughout the book, you will see occasional images in the outer margin.

 means that a lot hangs on this point so it is worth reading carefully.

 means that this point is fairly retro and could become out of date in the near future.

 means that it is a cool practical tip but isn't strictly a legal issue.

Key terms

No matter how user friendly you try to make a law book, it is inevitable that legal jargon will sneak in. European legal issues have a distinct lexicon which is not always self explanatory. The following words will crop up repeatedly throughout the book.

Civil Law	Civil Law is the dominant legal approach in continental Europe. Civil Law is based on codified laws and does not tend to rely on a system where previous decisions inform the likely outcome of future decisions (i.e., a system of 'precedent'). Civil Law is discussed in more detail in Chapter 2
Common Law	Common Law is the dominant legal approach in the UK and Ireland. Common Law is a system of 'precedent' where each decision informs the boundaries within which the court must act in the future (unless a higher court overrules them). Common Law is discussed in more detail in Chapter 2
Data	Data can be both an intellectual property right when included in a database or consist of 'personal data'. Personal data is data which can be used to identify an individual. Data in the EU is regulated by the General Data Protection Regulation (GDPR)
Design	This refers to the intellectual property right which can be registered or unregistered and is harmonised across the European Union
Directive	This is a type of European Union law which essentially sets out minimum standards for Member States to follow. Member States typically

have two years from the date a Directive is passed by the European Union to implement it into national law

E-commerce Electronic Commerce or e-commerce is the sale of goods via the Internet. It is sometimes used interchangeably with 'distance selling' which can also include sales that are concluded over the phone. It is regulated in the European Union by several laws, in particular the E-commerce Directive

EEA Is the European Economic Area. This is an economic trading zone known as the 'single market' which includes all European Union Member States as well as Norway, Iceland and Liechtenstein

EU Is the European Union, a shared economic and political union which currently includes 28 Member States

Harmonisation One of the aims of the European Union is to provide consistency across the Union. This is achieved by a process known as 'harmonisation' and involves the creation of minimum or common standards which cover everything from trade marks to textiles

Member State The current 28 Member States of the European Union are Austria, Belgium, Bulgaria, Croatia, Republic of Cyprus, Czech Republic, Denmark, Estonia, Finland, France, Germany, Greece, Hungary, Ireland, Italy, Latvia, Lithuania, Luxembourg, Malta, the Netherlands, Poland, Portugal, Romania, Slovakia, Slovenia, Spain, Sweden and the UK

Regulation A Regulation goes one step further than a Directive and automatically applies across the European Union without the need for Member States to implement national legislation, although it is open to them to do so. The General Data Protection Regulation (GDPR) is a recent example of a Regulation

UK law

There are three different legal systems in the United Kingdom (England and Wales, Scotland and Northern Ireland). References to UK law are primarily to English law. The differences in the other legal systems tend to be more procedural than legal

PART I

Getting started

The book is split into four parts which take you on a fashion business' journey from start-up to success. This first part is about laying the groundwork for the rest of the book. Chapter 1 introduces the fashion industry and the types of legal issues that it faces both traditionally and in response to new technology.

Many aspects of the EU, EEA and wider European relationship can be hard to understand, particularly for those readers with a more Common Law background. Consequently, Chapter 2 is a handy primer on European legal concepts which includes a brief overview of the various legal structures. For those unfamiliar with the EU basics, Chapter 2 may be a section to bookmark as we will return to these issues and concepts throughout the book.

1   What is fashion law?

Before we get into the legal issues, it is worth reminding ourselves how large and important the fashion industry is for the global and, in particular, the European economy. Some of this will be very familiar for readers. If so, feel free to skip ahead to the later part of the chapter which gives an overview of some of the more current fashion law trends around intellectual property, franchising, ethical fashion, e-commerce and fashion technology.

1.1   The economics of fashion

The global fashion market is valued at US$3,000 billion (or 2 per cent of global GDP). Womenswear is the most valuable segment at US$621 billion but the men are catching up; menswear is currently worth around US$402 billion.[1] Europe is a significant contributor to this total. Indeed, five million people in the EU are directly employed in the fashion value chain and over one million people are employed in the high-end fashion and retail industries.[2]

Europe is particularly well known for its design houses. Three out of the four major global fashion weeks (London, Paris and Milan) take place in Europe. It is also an important centre for manufacturing, particularly countries in Southern and Eastern Europe such as Portugal, Spain, Italy, Romania and Turkey. Italy alone accounts for around 50 per cent of total EU footwear production with Portugal and Spain bringing the combined percentage close to 70 per cent.

Very broadly speaking, Europe tends to manufacture higher quality and more niche items e.g., sports protection clothing and footwear. Its

---

1 Data courtesy of Fashion United https://fashionunited.com/global-fashion-industry-statistics.

2 https://ec.europa.eu/growth/sectors/fashion/high-end-industries/eu_en.

main export markets are Russia and the US with increasing growth to China and the Middle East, particularly the United Arab Emirates.

Because of fashion's importance to the European economy, the EU has been at the forefront of legislating to ensure that features such as labelling of fibre names and origin of goods is clear and consumers are adequately protected from poor quality or potentially dangerous goods. Further, as technology starts to dominate all traditional industries, Europe has embraced fashion technology, particularly around smart textiles and other forms of wearable technology.

Europe's main suppliers are China (almost 50 per cent of all imports), and Vietnam but other countries such as Pakistan, Bangladesh and Sri Lanka are also very important and offer tax reliefs which make them particularly popular for the manufacture of lower value items.

1.2   Intellectual property

Although this book is focused on European fashion, most countries worldwide are connected to the fashion industry and consequently a segmented approach to fashion in a global economy is only helpful at a high level. Intellectual property rights are one of the most harmonised sets of laws worldwide, they provide fairly consistent protection over trade origin, creative works, inventions and, to a less consistent extent, product design.

Without intellectual property rights it would be virtually impossible for the European fashion industry to continue. These rights enable a business to compete knowing that it has a legal monopoly which protects the time and money it has invested into the brand. Although the European fashion industry by no means avoids counterfeits and close copies of their products, intellectual property rights enable businesses to protect their products and enforce these rights in all relevant territories worldwide. The success of enforcement varies based on strategy and budget.

While intellectual property can be a sword, most fashion businesses, at one time or another, find themselves both wielding the weapon and having it pointed at them. It is all too easy for designers to take inspiration a bit too literally and the line between following fashion trends and outright copying can be a very fine one. This can be damaging in terms of legal costs, financial compensation, internal investigation and, most importantly, reputation. The public can usually forgive a one-off instance but a pattern of infringement is much less forgivable and can substantially erode public trust.

The different types of intellectual property are discussed in Part II, they include trade marks (Chapter 3); copyright (Chapter 4); image rights (Chapter 5); designs (Chapter 6); and passing off, domain names, confidential information (Chapter 7). The methods of using these rights are discussed in an enforcement context (Chapter 20) and more specifically in relation to counterfeit goods (Chapter 24).

1.3   Franchising, licensing, distributors and agents

There are a few tried and tested methods for growing your business by working in collaboration with other businesses. Franchising, licensing, distribution or agency relationships can be used to help break into new markets or diversify into new products. For example, it is common for fashion brands to diversify from clothing and footwear into products such as perfumes, sunglasses and cosmetics which have different methods of manufacture and routes to market.

Each of these options relies on a solid contract which is easy to understand and enforce. There are two fundamental keys to making these arrangements a success. The first is taking the time to meet, learn and understand whether the proposed partner is truly the right fit for your business. The second is putting the right contracts in place to protect you if anything goes wrong in the future.

Broadly speaking franchising means licensing your brand and business to a third party who builds its own version of your business in a particular market but ultimately is accountable to you. It can offer entrepreneurial individuals the opportunity to start and run what is effectively their own business without having to spend the time developing their own brand. It offers the brand the opportunity to grow into new markets very quickly. Franchising is most commonly associated with bricks and mortar stores but it is becoming easier in the online environment and may be an attractive option if, for example, there are a lot of orders in a particular geographic region but fast fulfilment is a challenge.

The main risk of franchising is that the actions of a bad franchisee can damage a brand irreparably. Consumers do not care who the legal owner is or what contractual arrangements are going on behind the scenes. If someone behaves badly under your brand, you are ultimately going to be held accountable, if not in the eyes of the law then definitely in the eyes of social media. Consequently, quality control and regular audits are essential.

Distributors help you to break into new markets. Exclusive distribution agreements can offer comfort to distributors who are investing in your brand while at the same time enabling quick and comprehensive entry into new markets. The distribution agreement can be segmented by product and geographic area. For example, it could cover sunglasses in an entire region (Scandinavia), a European country (Sweden) or city (Stockholm). Distribution agreements can come in various forms. In some cases, they give the right to both manufacture and sell a specific product in a particular territory for a fixed period of time. More commonly, it gives an exclusive ability to sell products which you have manufactured in a territory for a fixed period of time. It is important that issues such as marketing spend and quality control are carefully set out in the agreement.

You also need to bear in mind the risks of competition law (known as anti-trust law in the US). 'Exclusivity' and 'anti-competitive behaviour' share a very porous border; you do not want to be on the wrong side. If you have a large market share (either because the market is new or you work for a very large business), you should be particularly careful and make sure you obtain legal advice on the competition law risks associated with new business strategies.

Commercial agents are an alternative (or supplemental) means of scaling a fashion business. Agents are highly regulated by EU law and not only have a dedicated Directive but also come with their own body of case law. The EU rules which govern agency agreements are particularly onerous in terms of the calculation of commission (i.e., the agent's fee) and termination of an agency relationship.

An agent is essentially an individual or business which is authorised to act on behalf of another individual or business (often referred to as the 'principal'). They are most famous in the world of celebrity but are important to all industries, including fashion. If you have authorised an agent, they can enter into contracts which bind your business, potentially without your knowledge. An implicit authorisation is sufficient for the agency relationship to arise. An agency relationship can be created without a physical contract simply on the basis of 'a course of dealing'. In other words if you treat someone as though they are an agent, even if you do not call them one, they can be treated as an agent in the eyes of the law.

This all means that an agent can be in a very powerful position. If you delegate them too much authority, they can potentially run many aspects of your business without your knowledge or permission. There are limits, for example, agents are only allowed to work with potentially conflicting clients, such as rival fashion businesses, following full disclosure and consent. Nevertheless, there are obvious risks of confidential information and know-how being inadvertently misused. The different options for agents and distributors are discussed in Chapter 11 and franchising is covered in Chapter 18.

1.4   Ethical fashion

It is no great secret that fashion leaves a large environmental and societal footprint. Some disasters such as the collapse of the Rana Plaza factory in Bangladesh garnered massive international outrage; others such as the constant pollution of water following the use of harsh dyes and bleaches currently receive far less attention.

If you are manufacturing fashion items you have a responsibility to ensure that, among many other things, the raw materials, where possible, come from sustainable sources, and the workers are treated well, given sufficient pay, breaks, paid leave and are not placed in environmental conditions which could lead to long-term health damage.

The laws around employees in Europe are discussed in Chapter 10. Ethical fashion is discussed in more detail in Chapter 25, particularly in the context of the supply chain.

1.5   The Internet

Fashion is not unique in having faced major disruption from the Internet. Fashion purchases are increasingly made via social media and from mobile phones (although the phrase m-commerce[3] never really caught on). E-commerce is expected to represent over 16 per cent of global retail sales by 2021.[4] Europe currently leads the way and is a major market for online sales.

There are all sorts of business models from the 'try now, pay later' whereby lots of products are curated and sent to potential purchasers to 'click & collect' where you can pick up and return goods from all sorts of convenient locations. The latter approach has worked particularly well in the UK for John Lewis which is able to use its Waitrose food network for this purpose. Amazon has even introduced a service whereby delivery drivers are able to open your front door when they scan a package. Another approach which deals with many of the issues associated with sustainable fashion is typified by Rent the Runway[5] (whose tagline 'buy less stuff' sums up the attitude of many so-called millennials). This business model allows you to rent high-end items on a short-term basis so you pay a fraction of the cost for an item which has a limited shelf life. There is a subscription option for regular users. Unsurprisingly, this is particularly popular for weddings and other similar events.

Although e-commerce involves significant savings in retail space and employees, it is not a complete licence to print money. In the EU, e-commerce is tightly regulated and returns of undesirable or faulty goods can be a very expensive process. Whether as a result or in spite of this tight regulatory framework, the EU has one of the most successful ecosystems for online retail in the world. The EU's consumer-focused legislation includes a two-week cooling off period following delivery. The consumer can notify the seller at any point in this two-week period that they wish to return a product. This is followed by a further two-week period in which they can arrange for the product to be returned. In other words, you may sell an item online, deliver it and find it returned in a month, following which you are obliged to reimburse the purchase price and delivery costs.

The Internet offers vast opportunities and international reach but it is incredibly important that all countries where your products are offered for sale are carefully vetted and that you comply with local laws. For

---

3 Short for 'mobile commerce.'

4 Source: Worldwide Retail and Ecommerce Sales: eMarketer's Estimates for 2016–2021, 18 July 2017.

5 https://www.renttherunway.com/. One of the UK equivalents is http://hirethecatwalk.com/.

example, it is very common for companies to receive letters claiming trade mark infringement from German and Swiss companies. Even if you have only sold a few products into Germany,[6] you may be forced to rename all of those products worldwide on the basis that the goods are available online and can theoretically be shipped to Germany. Many of these trade marks are not in use but if they are less than five years old, they cannot be easily challenged and it is often more cost effective to simply rename with an agreed sell through period.

E-commerce channels are becoming more restrictive as the European market gets more sophisticated. For example, if you are an authorised seller of luxury goods, care will have to be taken as to how and where you sell those goods online. As you will see in Chapter 11, it is now legitimate for luxury fashion businesses to prevent their distributors from selling on sites such as Amazon on the basis that sale on mainstream e-commerce sites risks damaging their 'allure.' A more detailed overview of the issues relating to e-commerce is in Chapter 17.

Another issue which can affect the producers of niche fashion products, for example luxury items made from unusual animal skins or semi-precious stones, concerns the manner in which these goods can be imported. This is a particular problem for online retail if the goods are stored outside the European Economic Area (EEA). If the UK leaves the EU Customs Union, this issue will present quite a headache for many luxury brands who will need to think carefully about the timings for shipments if they are to avoid a hold up at Customs. The issues associated with Customs are considered in the context of taxation and logistics in Chapter 22.

1.6   Counterfeit and parallel goods

Another important aspect of brand image concerns parallel[7] and counterfeit goods. It is good practice to monitor the sale of counterfeit products online, especially when they are carried out via third party sites such as eBay or via social media platforms. Even where the

---

6 Indeed, it is not unusual for the only time your product was actually purchased in Germany to be the time your opponent's German lawyer purchased it – under German law this seems to be sufficient to threaten legal proceedings.

7 Sometimes called grey goods. These are goods which are put on to the market elsewhere in the world but imported into a jurisdiction without your permission. In some limited circumstances it is possible to stop this resale.

laws are consistent, the application of those laws can vary substantially across the EU.

In France, the courts are particularly protective of rights owners, as a recent criminal case[8] concerning the sale of counterfeit copies of Adobe software on eBay demonstrates. A 'Mr X' sold almost 300 copies of the proprietary software without Adobe's consent. The French court also noted that Mr X was carrying out a commercial activity, albeit an illegal one, but had failed to register it at the French Companies House. Mr X was given a prison sentence and ordered to pay a fine of more than €600,000.

The UK's Supreme Court[9] recently went one step further and confirmed that importers of genuine goods which were brought into the EEA, specifically the UK, without the rights holder's consent (in other words, parallel imports or grey goods) could be engaging in criminal activity. Consequently, they could face both a prison sentence and a fine which could result in their assets being seized as proceeds of crime.

Many forms of intellectual property infringement can form the basis of criminal proceedings. The enforcement of intellectual property rights is discussed in Chapter 20 and counterfeit goods are considered in Chapter 24.

1.7   The rise of fashion technology

Technology is converging with all existing industries in new, exciting and occasionally disturbing ways. The fashion industry is no different. Fashion technology is part of the broader trend toward wearable technology. This includes the Fitbit, Apple Watch and jewellery which taps you when someone important gets in touch.[10] The most common fashion/tech overlaps tend to relate to fitness, social tracking and mood.[11] For example, GPS chips can be integrated into all sorts of products

---

8 See the decision of the TGI de Limoges, jugement correctionnel of 11th July 2017 (Adobe Systems Inc.c/ M. X.)

9 *R v M (appellant)* [2017] UKSC 58 https://www.supremecourt.uk/cases/uksc-2017-0006.html.

10 The current market leader in this area is probably Bellabeat https://webshop.bellabeat.com/.

11 For example, Sensoree makes various bioresponsive fashion items which provide aural, visual and tactile feedback dependent upon the wearer's emotions or mood: http://sensoree.com/.

from umbrellas[12] and suitcases[13] to bracelets and rings.[14] They could simply be used to tell you where your product is if it is lost or be triggered in a potentially dangerous situation.[15]

Fashion technology's move toward textile integration is particularly exciting. For example, fabrics which light up in the dark could save pedestrians and cyclists from injury on the roads. This is particularly beneficial in parts of the world, such as Europe, where the car is not necessarily the dominant means of transport.

One of the big issues with fashion tech is its sustainability and recyclability.[16] It is hard enough to persuade people to recycle a woolly jumper but if it is embedded with LEDs it may not be possible to recycle at all. The EU has a strict regulatory regime around electrical items. For example, the WEEE Directive,[17] set recycling and recovery targets for all types of electrical goods originally based on kilograms per head of population per annum recovered for recycling and now based on weight of electrical and electronic (E&E) products entering the market. Similarly, the RoHS Directive[18] sets restrictions upon EU manufacturers as to the material content of new electronic equipment placed on the market.[19] Both of these Directives have been criticised for failing to have an adequate enforcement mechanism and, in the case of RoHS, for penalising EU manufacturers.

---

12 See, e.g., Kisha: https://www.getkisha.com/.

13 My favourite example of this is the G-RO – it is not the most attractive suitcase but the design is certainly innovative: https://uk.g-ro.com/. For a more stylish alternative see: https://www.rebeccaminkoff.com/products/so-connected-luggage-22-lg001mblk-matte-black.

14 Teen Vogue has assembled some great examples of how wearable fashion is becoming mainstream: https://www.teenvogue.com/gallery/wearable-tech-accessories.

15 See, e.g., Nimb: https://nimb.com/.

16 Some businesses have thought this through but it is not the norm. For example, CuteCircuit's LED dresses can be washed in a regular washing machine and customers can return the dress for recycling when it reaches the end of its life: https://shop.cutecircuit.com/collections/womenswear/products/k-dress-1.

17 The Waste Electrical and Electronic Equipment Directive (WEEE) 2012/19/EU. The overall aim of WEEE was for the EU to recycle at least 2 per cent of electrical and electronics waste equipment by 2016.

18 The Restriction of Hazardous Substances Directive 2002/95/EC and updated in the RoHS 2 Directive 2011/65/EU.

19 Most famously, RoHS restricts the use of lead but it also covers nine other substances such as mercury and cadmium.

The other big trend to hit fashion is the move toward customisation.[20] This is facilitated by computer modelling and 3D printing. For example, it is possible to get a range of clothing items which match part of your unique genome or trousers which are engineered to perfectly fit you. This is important in the sporting world where tiny improvements can make the difference between first and second place. Trainer technology is leading the mainstream athleisure pack with companies such as Adidas making shoes from algae[21] and Nike manufacturing 3D printed recycled shoes.

As we have adapted to e-commerce, bricks and mortar stores have continued to suffer. However, physical stores are still important in terms of showcasing products and allowing them to stand out from the mainstream. The issues associated with commercial real estate are considered in Chapter 15, including the trend towards temporary locations and pop up stores. The connection to bricks and mortar stores may be revived again through augmented reality, smart mirrors, connected changing rooms[22] and self checkouts.[23] In the nearer future, augmented reality (AR) is likely to add a second dimension to bricks and mortar stores and may offer the opportunity to have the online experience (reviews, information and the best price) in store.[24] AR glasses are slowly moving from the ultra naff Google glass to a high fashion alternative. With the indispensable help of the fashion industry, it is likely that AR will become commonplace in the very near future. Virtual reality (VR) raises some exciting opportunities. Although market penetration of VR headsets remains low, this is an exciting possibility for the future.

Finally, blockchain or 'distributed ledger' technology is an exciting new way of ensuring that the data related to wearable devices, the sustainability journey and ownership of intellectual property rights remains accurate and secure. You can read more about the potential

---

20 A good example of this is London based Unmade: https://www.unmade.com/.

21 Arielle Pardes, Slip Into Earth-friendly Running Shoes Made of Algae, Wired 29 June 2017 https://www.wired.com/story/slip-into-earth-friendly-running-shoes-made-of-algae/.

22 Not as disturbing as it sounds. This essentially involves having a connected device in a changing room from which you can order a different size or browse a lookbook.

23 For example Amazon Go. Rebecca Minkoff has experimented with the use of this and related technology for luxury fashion, you can read the Engadget review here: https://www.engadget.com/2016/12/25/rebecca-minkoff-tech-stores.

24 Major retailers such as Zara have launched augmented reality apps.

applications of blockchain technology to the supply chain in Chapter 25.[25]

1.8   Selling your business

For many people, the ultimate prize for all their hard work on a fashion business is the sale of their business (or in corporate jargon 'exit'). What form this exit takes is very fluid and there are lots of different and related opportunities. This might mean the sale of a particular brand, a division or product line or the entire business. It could mean the sale of the business to a competitor or via a listing on a public stock exchange. Lots of factors come into play when selling a business and the more you have followed the guidance set out in this book, the easier the sale process will be. Common issues arise around important contracts, key personnel and intellectual property rights. If these cannot be easily sorted out it may affect the amount of money that your business is sold for or even if it can be sold at all.

Given that a business has a very personal relationship for the founders, it can be hard to cease all involvement and you should think carefully about whether this is something you actually want. In addition to your paycheck, you should think about the loyal employees who enabled you to build up the business. How do you plan to reward them, and keep them motivated both before and after your exit?

1.9   So, what's next?

 This first chapter gives you a flavour of what you can expect from the book itself but my hope is that the book is the beginning of a bigger conversation. The final chapter of the book looks toward the future and considers the major changes on the European fashion law horizon. These issues include Brexit,[26] the rise and importance of data and the impact of fashion technology.

Many issues could not be covered in the book due to space limitations but that does not mean that issues such as insolvency and restructur-

---

25   And also in Rosie Burbidge, 'The Blockchain is in Fashion', 107(6) *The Trademark Reporter* 1262–7.

26   'Brexit' has become shorthand for the UK's departure from the EU.

ing are not important to the fashion industry. Similarly, the case law in Europe is constantly evolving and it is important to keep on top of legal developments to avoid any nasty surprises. Fortunately for you, not only is there the associated website, www.europeanfashionlaw. com, but there is the possibility of covering these issues in future editions.

If this book can help raise awareness of legal issues and help you to avoid expensive or reputational mistakes then it will have served its purpose. While books are not famed for their interactive nature, the website can help bridge this gap. Any issues which you would like covered in more detail or European countries whose legal systems you think deserve more attention can be considered in more detail on there – just let me know. Please do get in touch with your feedback as well as any insights you can share into the fashion law issues you and your business have faced.

1.10   Instructing a lawyer

Finally, while this book will give you some general guidance on the legal issues you are likely to face, it is no substitute for legal advice. The key to getting good quality, cost effective and timely legal advice is as follows:

1.   **Don't delay** – Most legal problems become a lot more expensive if they are not dealt with up front. In some cases delay will mean that you lose a legal option altogether. It could, for example, result in the negotiation of an expensive commercial deal just so you can use your brand name in a particular territory.

2.   **Build a relationship** – Go to legal events and get to know the lawyers and paralegals who are helping you on a day-to-day basis. The more you can share with them about what you are doing and your plans for the future, the better positioned they are to put the optimum strategy in place for you.

3.   **Negotiate a good deal for you** – The main payment models for legal services are hourly rate, fixed fee or retainer. For some people a retainer model can work well, it gives the comfort of known legal spend and the flexibility to cover a range of issues. Fixed fees provide certainty but the scope of the fee must be clear up front. They

can be harder to agree for less predictable legal issues such as litigation where the full story does not tend to be known at the outset. Although people have long been predicting the death of the hourly rate, this remains the dominant method of billing for most law firms.

4. **Less is more** – If you want to avoid a nasty surprise at the end of the month, be efficient in the methods of communication with your legal team. A single clear and concise email with all relevant documents attached will take you longer to prepare but will ultimately yield better results than sending over a series of emails or unlabelled documents with little explanation. This approach gives you time to think through the issues and avoids incurring additional expense by following up with comments which can fundamentally change the legal strategy once your lawyer has started work (and fees have been incurred). It is often useful to follow up this initial email with a call to discuss the details. This call can be used to ensure that your lawyer has all relevant information and you are aware of the risks of adopting your particular strategy.

5. **Read and comment on the drafts** – You are the expert on any factual information included in any legal communication with an opponent, your landlord, the court or similar. It is therefore important that you read through all the draft legal documentation you are sent carefully and make sure it is complete and accurate before it is sent or filed. Again, it is more efficient, and consequently will save you money, if you send a single set of comments either by reference to the paragraph numbers or using tracked changes.

2   What is European law?

There are a few European legal concepts that it is important to under-stand at the outset of this book. This is by no means a comprehensive guide to European law but it should help you to understand some of the legal issues which arise in the book. For those already familiar with European law, this is a chapter you can skip!

2.1   The key political structures of Europe

2.1.1   The European Union

The European Union or EU is the political and economic union of 28 Member States[1] which has helped to shape the laws across the majority of Europe over the last 50 or so years. The EU develops new laws which affect all Member States and consequently all citizens and businesses which live or operate within the union. It is based on four fundamen-tal principles which govern the free movement of the following items around the EU:

1.   Free movement of goods

2.   Free movement of people

3.   Free movement of services

4.   Free movement of capital

There are three legislative pillars to the EU: the European Parliament, the European Commission and the Court of Justice of the European Union.

---

1 Currently the EU Member States are Austria, Belgium, Bulgaria, Croatia, Republic of Cyprus, Czech Republic, Denmark, Estonia, Finland, France, Germany, Greece, Hungary, Ireland, Italy, Latvia, Lithuania, Luxembourg, Malta, the Netherlands, Poland, Portugal, Romania, Slovakia, Slovenia, Spain, Sweden and the UK.

2.1.2   The European Parliament

The European Parliament is responsible for developing new legislation as well as supervisory and budgetary responsibilities. The European Parliament is primarily located in Brussels, Belgium but also has locations in Strasbourg, France and Luxembourg. It consists of 751 MEPs (Members of the European Parliament) who are directly elected by each Member State.

2.1.3   The European Commission

The European Commission is the EU's executive branch. Its responsibilities include:

1.   Proposing new EU laws

2.   Enforcing existing EU laws

3.   Setting spending priorities and allocating budgets

4.   Representing the EU internationally, including in treaty negotiations.

2.1.4   The Court of Justice of the European Union

 The Court of Justice of the European Union (CJEU) is often poorly understood. In most instances, it is not a 'court of appeal' in the traditional sense but more a court which is designed to clarify points of EU law. It does not make findings of fact and leaves the courts of each Member State to implement its decisions and apply EU law to the facts in each particular case in accordance with the CJEU's interpretation. Decisions of the CJEU are primarily made in response to references from the courts of Member States. However, the CJEU can also hear appeals from the General Court. In these instances there is no further appeal and the CJEU's decision is the final word on the matter.

In some cases, before deliberating the legal issues themselves, the CJEU may ask an individual, known as an Advocate-General or A-G, who has experience in the particular area of law, to provide an opinion. This opinion is not binding but in practice it is often followed by the CJEU.

Trade mark and designs law has been harmonised (i.e., made consistent across the EU). This harmonisation is both in terms of the pan-EU rights and national rights. The pan-EU rights consist of (i) the EU trade mark via the EU Trade Mark Regulation[2] and (ii) the Community Designs Regulation.[3] The legislation that harmonises trade marks and designs at a Member State level are the EU Trade Mark Directive[4] and Community Designs Regulation. The CJEU therefore is a court of reference for a wide variety of trade mark and designs issues and consequently has played an important role in shaping these rights across the EU.

2.1.5   The General Court

The General Court hears actions taken against EU institutions. It is most likely to be relevant to the fashion industry in the context of intellectual property law as appeals of EUIPO decisions regarding the registrability and validity of EU trade marks and registered Community designs can be made to the General Court. This is widely considered to be a problem as it gives up to three rounds of appeal[5] in EU trade mark and Community design validity disputes. This means that these disputes take a very long time to be resolved and undermines the value of these rights as there is a high risk of an invalidity action being filed and consequently a stay on proceedings being put in place the moment you seek to rely on the rights. Because it is harder to get a stay if there are proceedings pending before a national court, many lawyers adopt a 'file the claim first and ask questions later' approach to the litigation of these rights.

2.1.6   The European Economic Area

All Member States are part of the EEA. Norway, Iceland and Liechtenstein are also part of the EEA but not the EU. Switzerland has been invited to join the EEA but has not 'ratified', in other words, it has not passed national legislation which would confirm its membership.

This means that, for the time being, Norway, Iceland and Liechtenstein are part of the single market and are bound by the four freedoms listed above but are unable to contribute to the development of EU laws and policy. In return for this lack of involvement in EU laws, they have negotiated specific exceptions for their agriculture and fishing sectors.

---

2 EU Trade Mark Regulation or 'EUTMR' (EU) 2017/1001.

3 Community Designs Regulation or 'CDR' (EC) No 6/2002.

4 EU Trade Mark Directive (EU) 2015/2436.

5 EUIPO Boards of Appeal, General Court and CJEU.

2.1.7   The European Free Trade Association

The European Free Trade Association (EFTA) consists of the non-EU members of the EEA (i.e., Norway, Iceland and Liechtenstein) plus Switzerland. It used to be a competitor to the EU but over time, the EU has come to dominate.

2.1.8   The European Union Customs Union

The European Union Customs Union (commonly known more simply as the Customs Union) consists of all Member States together with Monaco (a sovereign city state in the French Riviera), and some island territories which are Crown dependencies[6] and not part of the EU (such as the Channel Islands of Guernsey and Jersey, and the Isle of Man).

No customs duties (i.e., taxes) are levied on goods which travel within the Customs Union. Each Member of the Customs Union is entitled to impose a common external tariff (i.e., tax) on goods which enter the Customs Union. The European Commission negotiates the terms of the Customs Union on behalf of all members of the Customs Union, regardless of whether they are a Member State. This gives the Customs Union a much stronger voice when in negotiation with the World Trade Organization (WTO).

The EU has separate customs unions with each of Andorra, San Marino and Turkey in relation to certain goods.

2.1.9   The European Convention on Human Rights

The European Convention on Human Rights (ECHR) is completely different to and separate from the EU, EEA or any of the other political structures mentioned above. The ECHR is an international treaty which was entered into in the wake of the Second World War as a means for ensuring that the human rights abuses, which were still at the forefront of everyone's minds, would not be repeated in the future. The treaty protects human rights and fundamental freedoms but recognises that many of these rights can be in competition and will need to be balanced. For example, Article 8 ECHR (the right to privacy) can

---

6   This means that they are not part of the UK but are self-governing dependencies of the British Crown. You can read more about them here: https://www.justice.gov.uk/downloads/about/moj/our-responsibilities/Background_Briefing_on_the_Crown_Dependencies2.pdf.

conflict with Article 10 ECHR (the right to freedom of expression). This is a particular issue as far as celebrities are concerned and can have an impact on advertising campaigns and publicity.

The ECHR only gives the right to take a signatory (i.e., a country) to court for non-compliance with the treaty. This can be done via the European Court of Human Rights in Strasbourg. Many signatories of the ECHR considered that this offered inadequate protection for its citizens and implemented legislation which brought the rights set out in the ECHR into national legislation. In the UK, this took the form of the Human Rights Act 1998.

2.1.10   The EU Charter

The Charter of Fundamental Rights of the European Union (the EU Charter) sets out the wide variety of rights given to EU citizens. The Charter requires the EU to legislate in accordance with certain political, social and economic rights. The EU Charter applies to all EU institutions and to all Member States when implementing EU law. The UK and Poland secured a protocol (essentially a partial 'opt out') from the EU Charter which limits the extent of the EU Charter's application to UK and Polish disputes.

2.2   European Regulations

European Regulations are EU legislation which apply to each and every Member State from the moment they come into force. They provide legal consistency across all Member States. Two of the Regulations which are particularly relevant to the fashion industry are the EU Trade Mark Regulation which is the basis for the EU trade mark and the Community Designs Regulation.[7]

2.3   European Directives

European Directives are a more flexible form of EU legislation. They set objectives for each Member State to achieve by implementing national legislation together with optional extras which Member States can choose to implement. Directives provide consistency but leave

_____

7 Council Regulation (EC) No 6/2002 of 12 December 2001 on Community Designs.

room for local nuance. For example, the Trade Marks Directive sets minimum standards for national trade marks in the EU.

2.4   Common Law vs Civil Law

The law in Europe is broadly divided between two different approaches. The first is Civil Law which is the dominant legal approach in continental Europe. The second is the Common Law which is most famously associated with English law but the system applies across Great Britain, including Scotland[8] and Northern Ireland, and also in the Republic of Ireland and Cyprus. Although Civil Law dominates in Europe, many Common Law concepts have seeped into EU law. Likewise, many Civil Law approaches, such as decisions on the papers, have now become possible under English law in some circumstances.

Civil Law in Europe derives from the Roman Empire.[9] Civil Law's philosophy is essentially that the law can only be codified (i.e., written down by government in legislation) into a single location which sets out the boundaries of what is and is not permitted by law. Under the Civil Law, the job of the judges is simply to interpret that law rather than develop it. Although the interpretation of the law given by the highest court (often known as the Supreme Court) is often binding on future decisions on the same legislation, this does not apply to the lower courts. There are three separate approaches to Civil Law in Europe which, broadly speaking, derive from France, Germany and Scandinavia.[10]

Common Law is a system of precedent where each decision informs the boundaries within which the court must act in the future (unless a higher court overrules them). This means that both the legislation and the judgments given in cases are important in understanding what the law says. It also gives judges more obvious flexibility to reach decisions which are 'equitable', i.e., fair, because they can apply various legal conventions in order to reach a just result. For example, the equitable doctrine of acquiescence means that if you wait a very long time to bring a claim (when you know that you have the right to do so) you

---

8 Scots law is a hybrid system which borrows from both the Common Law and Civil Law.

9 Specifically the Code of Justinian.

10 That is Sweden, Denmark and Norway (the other Nordic countries, Iceland and Finland, are often perceived to have inherited rather than developed the Scandinavian Civil Law system).

may be barred from pursuing someone. In any event, there will likely be a statutory bar to the amount of damages you can recover.[11]

Other Common Law systems include the US, Canada, Australia, New Zealand, Hong Kong, India and Singapore.

---

11 In England, Limitation Act 1980, s 2 states that an action founded on tort, such as intellectual property infringement, cannot be brought after six years from the date on which the cause of action accrued. However, if a tort (e.g., intellectual property infringement) is ongoing, you can still sue but only recover damages for the period of time dating back six years from the date you file the claim form.

PART II

Before you tell anyone about your new product or idea

Intellectual property rights

This part of the book considers the intellectual property rights you may want to protect at the outset of your business and how best to do so. Even if you do not take steps to obtain all of these intellectual property rights from day one, you should revisit this decision on a regular basis (at least once a year) to be certain that you are not missing opportunities to protect key products which have become a major source of revenue and/or become strongly associated with your business.

On the face of it many intellectual property rights are 'harmonised,' i.e., the laws are consistent across the EU. However, in practice the philosophical differences between each country's development of intellectual property law remain and continue to affect the approach taken by courts in each Member State. By way of example, France has traditionally approached intellectual property law from the perspective of protecting creative endeavour. This means that France is more likely to grant broader rights to creative endeavours and more likely to find that these rights have been infringed. By contrast, the UK has approached intellectual property from the perspective of protecting business interests and encouraging trade. This means that it is more careful about the scope of the monopolies that it grants to intellectual property rights holders on the basis that it does not want to unduly limit the opportunities for competition. Most other EU countries fall somewhere between these two extremes.

3   Trade marks and your brand

Brands and the trade marks that protect them are essential to the success of fashion businesses. Even companies such as Muji who avoid branding on their products rely heavily on their brand name and visual aesthetic to differentiate themselves from the rest of the market.

3.1   Clearing proposed trade marks

Before you invest a lot of time and money creating and developing your brand, it is first important to make sure that no one else got there first. Just because you do not know of a business with a similar name does not mean that there is not an earlier registered trade mark which is the same or confusingly similar to your name or logo. An earlier registered trade mark, particularly one which is still in use, can be a major problem and force you to change your name. Even if a business has not registered the trade mark, if they are already trading under the same name in one of your major markets, this can pose a problem. Conflicting unregistered rights can also limit your opportunities for growth and create confusion in the marketplace amongst your potential customers.

It is much easier to search for earlier registered rights than ever before. A quick search for 'European Intellectual Property Office trade mark search' will lead you to one of the best free search tools in the world. The European Union Intellectual Property Office or 'EUIPO' TM View search tool[1] can compare the name which you have proposed against most major intellectual property offices worldwide. If your brand name produces a lot of results you can narrow the search by thinking about which goods and services you are relying on. This cannot give absolute certainty regarding a name's availability but it is a good starting point for identifying likely problems.

---

1 https://www.tmdn.org/tmview/welcome.

For example, if you wanted to start a new fashion brand called BANAL, a search will immediately reveal 33 results,[2] some of which are 'registered' (these are a problem), 'filed' (a potential problem if they proceed to registration) or 'expired' (still potentially a problem if they can be restored to the register – the timing and conditions for restoration vary with the territory). There are a few word marks for BANAL[3] and several in Mexico which consist of BANAL plus a number e.g., BANAL-5. At least one of the marks looks as though it is for a fashion brand; it is a Korean mark for BANAL CHIC BIZARRE in stylised form. This mark is also the only registered mark for BANAL in class 25 (i.e., for clothing, footwear and headgear). If you are planning to launch BANAL as a European-based business, the coast looks fairly free. However, looks can be deceiving and you would want to do more investigation around these marks to see if they have a related fashion business, plans to launch in Europe or if there are any businesses which have a similar name but no registered trade mark as they can also pose a risk (see Chapter 20 on unfair competition and passing off). Bear in mind that while a mark in Korea may not be a huge problem when you are getting started in Europe, it can limit your expansion opportunities in the future. This does not mean you should not go for it but that you are aware of the potential risks and can plan on that basis.

Specialist intellectual property lawyers can carry out a more in depth search for a fee which varies dependent on the type of search and number of territories. This process is known as 'clearance'. The clearance process involves use of one of the paid trade mark search services to generate a report of potential issues which is then reviewed by an intellectual property expert to determine the level of risk posed by each potential mark. This is often bolstered by a search for earlier unregistered rights. Clearing a trade mark in all territories worldwide can be very expensive but it is worth doing in your core territories.

3.2 Sign?

Trade marks are a legal monopoly. Once registered they offer exclusive use of a 'sign' for particular goods and services. A sign is most commonly a word or a logo. In trade mark land, a logo is also known as a

---

2 As at 15 May 2018, more marks may have been filed since.

3 Registered in Argentina and Norway to different businesses. The latter concerns data programming and related technology.

'device.' However, a sign can be anything which is capable of telling your business apart from another business. For example, if the shape of your product is very distinctive and you have invested substantial time and money in promoting that shape as originating from your business it *may* be possible to register that shape. Similarly, it is theoretically possible to protect a colour or short musical jingle.

In order to be accepted as a trade mark, signs must overcome two key criteria. They cannot be descriptive of the goods and services for which they are registered and they must be distinctive. Apple for fruit is descriptive. However, Apple for consumer electronics is not. Similarly, the letter 'H' for hotels is descriptive but it may be possible to register a highly stylised letter H for hotels, particularly if it is widely used and there is evidence that consumers associate the stylised H with a particular business. The question of distinctiveness and the means of overcoming a distinctiveness challenge by producing evidence of acquired distinctiveness is discussed in the context of shape marks later in this chapter.

In addition, it is possible for third parties to challenge your application to register a particular sign as a trade mark if they have an earlier right for the same or a similar sign for the same or similar goods or services. If the third party can show that their mark has a reputation, for example, Coca Cola, they can even stop you from registering marks for different goods and services to their trade mark registrations. This means that you will struggle to register COCA COLA for tailor-made suits even though the Coca Cola company does not have an earlier registered trade mark which is confusingly similar.

EU law has recently changed and where previously a trade mark had to be represented graphically, it is now sufficient for a trade mark to be represented in any appropriate form provided the representation is clear, precise, self-contained, easily accessible, intelligible, durable and objective.[4] For example, an audio file is sufficient.

In practice, in order to register a non-traditional mark, you often have to rely on 'acquired distinctiveness' (more on this later in the chapter). In order to prove acquired distinctiveness, you generally need to have been trading for a long time and spent significant amounts of

---

4 For a helpful summary of the document types the EUIPO will currently accept, see here: https://euipo.europa.eu/ohimportal/en/elimination-of-graphical-representation-requirement.

marketing budget educating the public to see a more unusual sign such as shape, colour or music as originating from your business.

3.3   Goods and services?

Goods and services are separated into 45 different classes. They are known as Nice classes (after the French city not the adjective). The most important classes for fashion are:

Class 14 includes jewellery, clocks and watches;

Class 18 includes luggage and carrying bags, umbrellas and parasols;

Class 25 clothing, footwear and headgear;

Class 35 includes advertising and retail.

Other classes such as class 3 (cosmetics), class 9 (sunglasses) and class 41 (entertainment services) are also important.

The goods listed above for class 25 are known as class headings. Class headings describe the types of goods and services protected for each class. It used to be common to register a trade mark for the class heading but the level of protection granted by this application did not mean the same thing in all Member States. There were three broad different approaches: (i) registration of the class headings protected all goods and services in the class; (ii) the class headings were interpreted literally; or (iii) the class headings also included the relevant list of goods within each class as set out in the Nice classification at the time of filing.

This unsurprisingly caused a great deal of confusion and following a reference to the CJEU, the approach has changed and class headings will now be interpreted literally.[5] Consequently, you should be as specific as possible about the goods and services you apply to register.

It is important to search against the goods and services you want to register as well as those which are similar. For example, bags are protected in class 16 as 'wrapping and carrier bags', in class 18 as 'travel-

---

5   This change was as a result of the CJEU decision in IP TRANSLATOR Case C-307/10 *Chartered Institute of Patent Attorneys v Registrar of Trade Marks*.

ling bags' (this is the most important class for fashion bags), and in class 22 as 'sacks and bags not included in other classes'.

Even if there are no earlier registered trade marks on the market, if someone else is already using your brand name for a similar product, this can create problems if you try to register the mark or expand into their area in the future. As brand extensions and pop culture tie-ins become more common in a wide range of industries, this is an issue to keep under regular review. Who would have thought the DHL T-shirt would become a trend, let alone Moschino's frequent tie-ins with everyone from McDonald's to Disney?

Choosing the right classes for your business is a bit of a dark art which balances future proofing your portfolio with cost and trade mark scope. In many European territories, you have to have a genuine intent to use the mark for the relevant goods and services on the filing date. You also have to bear in mind that if you do not use the mark in Europe within five years it can be cancelled, following an application by a third party, on the basis of non-use. This non-use period is often less in non-European jurisdictions.

Many jurisdictions now have fairly helpful online trade mark filing sys- tems. This means that, for example, in the UK it is possible to file a trade mark yourself for a fairly low fee.[6] However, as with so much in life, some specialist help at the start can save lots of problems later on. Specialist intellectual property lawyers are used to identifying the best sign to register for the most appropriate goods and services. It is money well spent to seek their advice early on as once the trade mark is filed the only change you can make to the trade mark application/registration is to remove goods and services from the 'specification' (i.e., the list of goods and services for which your mark is protected). In other words, you cannot change the 'sign' or add to the list of goods and services.

3.4   Filing strategies

3.4.1   An 'international' trade mark

There is no such thing as a 'global' or 'worldwide' trade mark. However, there is an international filing system (known as the Madrid system).

---

6 Currently £170 with an extra £50 per additional class.

This is done via the World Intellectual Property Office (WIPO). The Madrid system has two main advantages. First, it has a centralised filing location which is easier to manage. Second, once you include more than three territories, the costs are *usually* lower than if you filed directly in each trade mark office. However, the Madrid system can be very risky because all international marks depend on a base mark. If that base mark is invalidated in the future (in whole or in part) all of the trade marks around the world which rely on it will also be invalidated. Further, depending on the territory, it can take longer to register your marks this way.

Whether or not the international system is worth using depends very much on your individual circumstances. For example, if you file directly with the US, UK and EU intellectual property offices you have more up-front costs but the mark is likely to proceed to registration more quickly and you will have more flexibility during the application process than if you use the Madrid system.

3.4.2   One trade mark for lots of territories

In addition to individual territories and filing via the international system, some countries have gathered together to offer a single trade mark which covers several territories. The most relevant example for a book on European fashion law is the EU trade mark which covers the whole of the EU (and therefore not territories such as Norway, Switzerland and soon the UK which are part of Europe but not the EU). Other examples include the Benelux trade mark,[7] the African Intellectual Property Organisation (OAPI),[8] African Regional Intellectual Property Organization (ARIPO)[9] and Andean Pact.[10]

The EU trade mark is particularly popular because it provides protection across a major trading block for a relatively low price. The EUIPO is increasingly efficient: this means that straightforward marks (i.e., distinctive word and logo marks) usually proceed to registration without too much fuss, assuming no one opposes the trade mark.

---

7 Which covers Belgium, the Netherlands and Luxembourg.

8 Which covers various French-speaking African countries.

9 Which covers various English-speaking African countries.

10 This pact covers Bolivia, Colombia, Ecuador and Peru. It does not provide a unitary registration but it does allow for some reciprocal rights such as use of a trade mark in one country constituting use in other member countries.

At the other end of the scale, some political territories have several trade mark offices. The most obvious example of this is the People's Republic of China which has two trade mark offices: mainland China and Hong Kong. In addition, Taiwan and Macau each have their own intellectual property offices. Consequently, if you manufacture in Taiwan and your major markets include mainland China and Hong Kong it is worth filing in all three territories (costs permitting).

3.4.3 Where to start your trade mark journey

Most fledgling fashion brands tend to apply to register a trade mark in their home country, the US, EU, China, (post Brexit, the UK) and maybe Switzerland, Canada, Hong Kong, Singapore or Australia if they are important current or potential markets. The other key territory is the one in which your brand manufactures, if it is not included in this list.

Even if you do not manufacture in China, it is likely to become an important market for your goods as your brand evolves over time. What is more, if you do not file a trade mark in China, someone else in China may well get there first. These so-called trade mark trolls identify up-and-coming brands and register them in China before the owners have a chance to do so. This can then cause significant problems if you want to sell or manufacture in China in the future. Trade mark trolls are a persistent problem in many territories; however, they have gained particular notoriety, and can cause excessive damage, in China because it is such a large market and manufacturing centre. The endgame of most trade mark trolls is to extort a large amount of money from you to facilitate the transfer of 'their' trade mark to you. Paying up may appear a cost effective solution compared to fighting a legal battle but once you develop a reputation as someone who pays rather than fights it is common to find many more trolls targeting your marks (and ultimately your pockets).

Filing a Chinese trade mark as early as possible will save a lot of money down the line. However, all is not necessarily lost if someone does sneak in there first. It is usually possible to regain control of the mark but only after significant legal costs have been expended. Michael Jordan is a recent high profile victim of this issue[11] but there are many others.

---

11 It took over four years to resolve and even now he does not have control of the English version

As your business expands, particularly if you are selling luxury goods, the Middle East and Russia are likely to be important markets as well as Mexico, Argentina, Brazil and South Africa. It is wise to consider trade mark registration in those territories as well.

Ultimately registration is a balance of risk versus costs. Focus on your main markets and revisit strategic trade mark filing decisions on a regular basis. Bear in mind that if you do not have a registered trade mark in a jurisdiction, this significantly inhibits your ability to take legal action as, in most instances, you will be forced to rely on unregistered rights such as copyright and unfair competition, if available.

3.4.4   Timing

 Unlike patents and designs you can register a trade mark at any time (even if you have an earlier mark for different goods and services). However, there are two reasons for trying to get as much coverage as possible at the start. First, it is cheaper to register in one go rather than on multiple occasions. Secondly, if you do not register in a territory or for some particular goods and services, you run the risk of someone else coming along and filing for your trade mark in the meantime. Trade marks operate on a first-to-file basis so if someone has got there before you, they will have a right which you may have to fight hard to remove. This may be a trade mark troll but it could be a completely independent third party who happens to have a similar name.

3.4.5   International strategy

 One important issue you will have to consider when registering marks around the world is how will your brand actually be used in each territory. In addition to registering the international version of your brand, it is a good idea to also register the localised version. For example, in China it is common for a brand name to be phonetically converted into Chinese characters and then transliterated into the Latin alphabet. If you just register the English mark you may find that you are not properly protected for your brand as it is actually used (whether in Chinese characters or in transliteration). Michael Jordan learnt this lesson the hard way and despite his huge international fame, he does not own the transliterated version of his name in China (Qiaodan).

---

of his transliterated name i.e., Qiaodan https://www.theguardian.com/world/2016/dec/08/ michael-jordan-scores-partial-victory-china-trademark-case-qiaodan.

There are other strategic issues to consider such as in which jurisdiction you file first (and in what name). Some countries are more liberal in terms of the approach they take to generic terms being used as trade marks. Other countries will only allow you to register a trade mark in relation to very specific goods and services (such as T-shirts, shirts, tops and blouses). The EUIPO is generally much more flexible and will allow you to register your mark in relation to broad categories of goods and services (e.g., clothing). Similarly, in some countries, particularly in Asia, you cannot register a trade mark in more than one class so you can end up incurring more administrative time and filing fees.

Confidentiality can also drive your trade mark filing strategy. This is important if you want to keep a new brand name secret for as long as possible. This can be an issue if your brand is closely followed or if you are launching a new collection in collaboration with a celebrity. For example, companies like Apple will often first register in a country such as Trinidad and Tobago which has English as its language, is close to the US, has sophisticated lawyers but no online database of trade mark filings. Because of the international priority periods, see below, this means that for six months a Trinidad trade mark filer can have potential worldwide protection for their new trade mark without having to disclose their brand strategy to the world (or at least making it very hard for the world to find out). For most businesses this extra hassle is not worth it but if your new brand name is very sensitive it may be worth the effort.

A slightly riskier alternative is to file in a different name, for example a company director or lawyer. This can create issues in many territories, such as the US, where a trade mark application is accompanied with a statement that the person filing the mark intends to use the mark in the course of trade.

3.4.6   Priority or how to get an extra six-month period of protection

The six month's protection you get after filing a trade mark in all major territories worldwide is known as the 'priority period'. It arises automatically when you register in any of the WIPO countries.[12] These countries have agreed that if you file in one of them, you have six

---

12 A complete list of the member states is available via the WIPO website: http://www.wipo.int/members/en/.

months in which to decide to register in other territories while in effect retaining the 'filing date' for the original trade mark. This might not sound important but in many cases it is the difference between being able to use your brand and being permanently prohibited from using your mark in that territory (without legal action or a negotiated agreement). The priority period means that you can file in one territory and save up for for a big trade mark splurge in six months' time. A similar regime exists for patents, where you get a one year priority period, and for registered designs.

3.4.7 Not just the core brand

In addition to registering your core brand, when it becomes relevant, you should also consider registering diffusion lines (such as DKNY or MIU MIU), key product names (such as BAYSWATER, or BIRKIN) and key hashtags to ring fence social media use. Registration of hashtags is discussed in more detail in Chapter 16 in the context of advertising. In short, the hashtag needs to be distinctive and not descriptive of fashion goods and services. This means that #fashion is not available for registration.

3.4.8 Brexit

 At the time of writing, it is not entirely clear how Brexit will affect trade marks. It is likely that there will be a period of time in which owners of EU marks can register them as UK marks but the procedure, fees and timing are not yet finalised. This issue will be covered on the accompanying website www.EuroFashionLaw.com so you can keep up with the latest developments on there.

3.5 Shape marks

It is a truth, acknowledged across the EU, that it is *possible* to register a shape as a trade mark. But how easy are they to get and how useful are they? The goalposts on shape marks have shifted so much in recent years that even experienced practitioners may struggle to keep up with the changes. In the fashion industry, where the shape of a product, particularly accessories,[13] can be its defining feature, adapting to these shifting sands is particularly important.

---

13 For example a belt buckle, shoe sole, bag clasp, necklace or perfume bottle.

Registering a shape is not easy. Because a potentially perpetual monopoly for a shape is such a valuable asset, if shape marks were handed out too easily there is a significant risk that a few companies could control the shapes for standard products and consequently limit competition. This means that the hurdle to obtain such a monopoly is very high and there are multiple criteria which need to be fulfilled. The logic behind each of these requirements is that trade marks should not be used to grant indefinite protection to shapes which should properly have been protected as patents or designs or are so commonplace that they should not be protected at all.

If you are able to get a shape mark granted it can offer you a huge competitive advantage as it prevents competitors and counterfeiters from releasing unbranded versions of your core products.

One of the major controversies around shape marks is the crossover with other intellectual property rights such as registered and unregistered Community designs which protect the shape or appearance of the whole or part of a product. This is a particular issue where the monopoly period granted by those rights has expired. If monopolies in these shapes continue indefinitely, as a registered trade mark, there is a risk of competition and innovation being stifled. Conversely, if it is less than a year since the design was made public, it should be capable of registration as a Registered Community Design. The 25 years of protection available from a Registered Community Design is ample for most businesses but many miss the boat and fail to file effective designs in time. Designs are covered in more detail in Chapter 6.

Unlike designs, shape marks can be filed at any time and potentially last forever, provided they are regularly renewed. In the EU, renewal happens every ten years. The few success stories include luxury brands such as Hermès and Fendi.[14] They also include Manolo Blahnik stilettos[15] and their associated shoe buckle.[16]

3.5.1   Position marks

Some brands have been able to register part of their products as 'position marks'. Position marks are (arguably) a subset of shape marks

---

14 See, e.g., EU trade marks 2083327: (Hermès) and 13921465: (Fendi).
15 Application No 014460455.
16 Application No 014460448.

Figure 3.1   Adidas' earlier registered trade mark

Figure 3.2   Shoe Branding's trade mark application

where a particular sign is protected when it is used on a particular part of a product. For example a stripe which bisects a tote bag has been registered but not the bag itself.[17] Position marks have been particularly litigated by Adidas which claims exclusive rights in three stripes on trainers and tracksuits (see Figure 3.1). Adidas has recently triumphed in the General Court[18] in its long-running quest against Shoe Branding which has attempted to register two stripes on trainers (see Figure 3.2) which slant in a different direction to the famous Adidas stripes.[19]

3.5.2   The Longchamp example

To understand how shape marks can work in the EU and the issues facing businesses in trying to have a single European approach, Longchamp's experience is a useful guide.

Longchamp had difficulty registering the shape of the 'Le Pliage' handbag as a trade mark, because it is a relatively simple design and consequently many trade mark examiners did not consider that the handbag had distinctive character (see Figure 3.3). It was only possible for Longchamp to successfully register the shape as an EU trade mark because either the word 'Longchamp' or the Longchamp logo was added to the trade mark

---

17 See, e.g., EU trade mark 6472898, note that the dotted lines indicate the location of the stripe on the bag but are not otherwise part of the shape mark.

18 The second line of appeal from EUIPO decisions regarding the grant or validity of EU trade marks.

19 See the General Court's decision of 1 March 2018 Case T-629/16, ECLI:EU:T:2018:108.

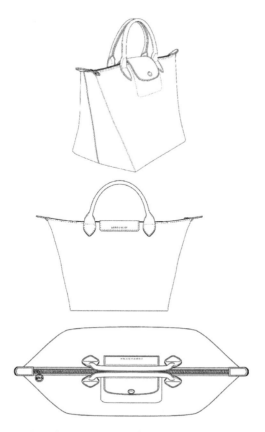

Figure 3.3   Longchamp's shape trade mark

application.[20] While this enabled them to get across the trade mark registration line, it makes it harder to rely upon the trade mark to prevent instances where the bag is copied without the word LONGCHAMP. In other words it will be of limited use in precisely the situation that the shape mark registration was intended to protect.

3.5.3   Distinctiveness

Like all trade marks, shape marks must have 'distinctive character' in order to be registered. As Longchamp discovered, this tends to be the main barrier to successful registration. This is because a trade mark in the shape of a tote bag is not a terribly distinctive sign to use for bags.

---

20 EU Trade mark Nos 014461958 and 13928528.

Distinctiveness can be a particular issue for descriptive word marks and logos and quirky marks such as colours. If a mark is not inherently distinctive, evidence that the sign you are trying to register as a trade mark has 'acquired distinctiveness' is essential.

3.5.4   How to make a shape distinctive

If the proposed shape mark is highly unusual for the goods in question, such as a belt buckle in the shape of a gaming controller, this may be sufficient for a shape trade mark to be distinctive.

It is often possible to get a shape mark over the distinctiveness line if you add another element such as a brand name or logo. This is what Longchamp did in order to register the Le Pliage bag in the EU. The downside of this approach is that you significantly limit the scope of trade mark protection and it will be hard to use the shape mark against anything other than straightforward counterfeits (where the word mark alone would be perfectly adequate). However, they can have a deterrent effect and many smaller infringers may take a view that it is not worth the fight and move on to easier targets. These marks can also be helpful in persuading Customs and online marketplaces to remove more borderline items.

Another tactic to secure registration is to register a shape mark for different goods and services to those with which they are commonly associated. For example, a Tiffany's bag and the Chanel perfume bottle have sailed through to registration for different goods. This means that the mark is only really effective against less sophisticated infringers but in many cases this may be good enough.

Succeeding in registering a shape mark can appear to be as much a matter of luck as anything else. When some fairly generic shoes and buckles sail through to trade mark registration without much fuss, it is hard to discern a coherent approach to registration shape marks. Some registries such as the EUIPO appear to be more generous in granting shape marks than, for example, the UK IPO but because so few shape marks are successfully registered across the board, the data on this is mostly perceived and anecdotal.[21] In any event, shape marks are such

---

21 An example of a recent shape mark refusal can be found here: https://trademarks.ipo.gov.uk/ ipo-tmcase/page/Results/1/UK00003109471.

valuable rights that it is worth rolling the dice and if at first you don't
succeed, it is always worth trying again.

3.5.5   How to acquire distinctiveness

If a shape mark is not inherently distinctive it may still be possible to
leap this hurdle if you can show that the mark has 'acquired distinctiveness' through its use. In other words, if you can show that you
have educated your customers to see the shape of the product as a sign
which tells them the origin of the goods for which the trade mark is
registered.

Currently, in order to prove acquired distinctiveness in the EU, you
have to provide evidence of customers relying on the particular trade
mark[22] as an indication of origin in every Member State.[23] This is controversial as it ignores the EU single market and instead treats the
EU as a series of States. The question is currently under appeal to the
CJEU and the law may well revert to the previous standard where a
substantial part of the EU was considered on a percentage basis so a
very high level of distinctiveness in one part of the EU could in theory
be sufficient to acquire distinctiveness across the EU.

Given the very different cultures and markets across the EU, proving
acquired distinctiveness in every Member State is a very high hurdle.
If this approach is approved by the CJEU it would likely, among other
things, give preferential trade mark protection to a handful of multinational companies. A bit of an own goal.

In order to have sufficient evidence of distinctiveness at the point of
filing the trade mark, it is a good idea to identify the types of data you
need to collect from the day your product launches. This is best done in
conjunction with specialist legal advice. This process includes identifying precisely the sign you intend to register, keeping track of all uses of
the sign in every country where the product is sold and ensuring that
the sign is used consistently.

Evidence of use includes invoices, licensing and distribution agreements, advertising, social media posts, mentions, likes, trending or
viral content, press mentions, influencers and bloggers, and visits to

---

22 Without taking into account other distinctive trade marks.
23 Another *Nestle v Cadbury* decision, T-112/13, ECLI:EU:T:2016:735.

websites, ideally by geographic region. If possible, it is useful to have data on the market share for your product as well as any consumer comments or other feedback. The use has to be of the intended sign as a trade mark. So if you only ever use the shape together with a logo or word, it will be much harder to succeed.

Recent CJEU decisions have confirmed that it is not necessary for the shape to be visible at the point of sale.[24] This means that shape marks can acquire distinctiveness through advertising and/or consumer use (e.g., when it is worn) however, establishing acquired distinctiveness in this way will be harder to achieve as it will be difficult to prove.

If you do not have enough evidence of the shape being used and considered distinctive across the EU, consider registering one or more national shape marks in territories where you do have sufficient recognition and evidence. This is more expensive than registering at a pan-EU level but it should be easier to obtain and retain. In practice, if your main markets are protected this is usually sufficient.

3.5.6   The Fendi example

 OHIM[25] (now renamed the EUIPO)[26] recently denied protection for Fendi's Double Baguette bag[27] and its Peekaboo bag.[28] Although the two-bags-in-one shape (see Figure 3.4) is somewhat unusual for hand-bags and the buckle is in the shape of Fendi's signature logo, the EUIPO refused the application for the Double Baguette on the basis that that square-shaped handbags are 'utterly common' and combining the bags would not necessarily be seen as a sign of commercial origin. The logo shaped buckle could not rescue the mark as the EUIPO considered that consumers would 'simply perceive the shape of the clasp as a typical design feature'.

Similarly Fendi's quirky and fun Peekaboo bag (see Figure 3.5) was denied protection on the ground that it was devoid of distinctive character. While the external appearance may not be that unusual, the

---

24 In particular *Nestle v Cadbury*, C 215/14, ECLI:EU:C:2015:604.

25 The curiously named Office for Harmonisation of the Internal Market.

26 The more descriptive EU Intellectual Property Office (although arguably still a misleading name as it only handles registered trade marks and designs not patents, copyright, trade secrets, etc).

27 EU trade mark Application No. 014792485.

28 EU trade mark Application No. 014032131.

Figure 3.4   Fendi's Double Baguette trade mark application

Figure 3.5   Fendi's Peekaboo Bag trade mark application

interior with the monster eyes and red lining is highly unusual and, in my view, inherently distinctive. This goes to show how difficult it can be to register a shape even when there are additional features such as a logo and the applicant's bags are very well known.

3.6   Other obstacles to shape mark registration

Even if you establish that the shape mark is inherently distinctive, there are specific obstacles to registration which apply to shapes and, for marks filed after 1 October 2017, to other more quirky marks such as colour marks as well. These obstacles apply to shapes which exclusively meet one or more of the following criteria.

3.6.1   Shapes resulting from the nature of the goods

If all the essential features of the shape result from the nature of the goods themselves you cannot register it as a trade mark. This obstacle applies where all of the mark's essential features are generic to products of the same category.[29] For example, watches need a face, hands and a strap so a shape mark would need more than these essential features in order to be registered.

3.6.2   No concepts allowed

Shape marks cannot monopolise an idea. This means that you cannot register a concept such as a transparent vacuum cleaner bin[30] or something which can be represented in lots of different ways such as a generic Scrabble tile.[31] The shape must be easy to identify and not require a day in court to explain! To help avoid this issue, you can put the sign into context. This is usually done using dotted lines[32] to identify the part of the mark which is not registered but is included to provide context.

3.6.3   Substantial value

A shape cannot be validly registered if the mark exclusively consists of a shape which adds substantial value to the goods for which it is registered. This is a controversial and poorly understood requirement. Although the substantial value does not include goodwill which attracts to the mark following use, it is unclear what this substantial value could be. Two shape marks (one UK and one EU) for London black cabs were recently invalidated on the basis that,

---

29 *Hauck GmbH & Co. KG v Stokke A/S* Case C-205/13 ECLI:EU:C:2014:2233.

30 *Dyson Ltd v Registrar of Trademarks* Case C-321/03 ECLI:EU:C:2007:51.

31 *JW Spear v Zynga* [2013] EWCA Civ 1175.

32 There is a lot of case law over the meaning of dotted lines (and certainty over their meaning has not yet been reached). Therefore, they should be used with caution!

among other things, the 'iconic' nature of the cabs was a substantial value which rendered the marks invalid.[33] This decision has been criticised and, on appeal,[34] one of the judges said that if the mark had not been invalidated on other grounds as well, he would have asked the CJEU for guidance on whether the 'iconic' nature of the design meant that it provided 'substantial value' in the trade mark sense. In a case closer to the fashion world, a shape mark for the jeans was refused on the basis that it consisted exclusively of a shape which gave substantial value.[35]

3.6.4   Technical result

It is not possible to register a shape which is necessary to obtain a 'technical result'. The aim of this exclusion is to prevent a perpetual monopoly in something which would more appropriately be protected by a patent (and therefore protected for a maximum 20 years). Even elements which are not visible in the shape mark itself but are used by the consumer, such as an inner fastening mechanism on a handbag, can form part of the consideration of technical function.[36] Provided that a shape mark has at least one feature which is not technical, it should be able to dodge this obstacle. However, focusing too heavily on the aesthetics to avoid a technical result objection may mean you fall into the 'substantial value' trap. So all arguments will need to be carefully considered and kept consistent.

3.7   The colour and the shape: marks in multiple categories

Colour marks can be even harder to register than shape marks. Again this is because there are significant public policy reasons for restricting the ability of a business to monopolise a colour.

---

33 *The London Taxi Corporation Ltd (t/a The London Taxi Company) v Frazer-Nash Research Ltd and Anor* [2016] EWHC 52 (Ch).

34 *The London Taxi Corporation Ltd (t/a the London Taxi Company) v Frazer-Nash Research Ltd & Anor* [2017] EWCA Civ 1729.

35 *Benetton Group SpA v G-Star International BV* C-371/06 ECLI:EU:C:2007:542.

36 In *Rubik's Cube – Simba Toys* C-30/15P ECLI:EU:C:2016:849, the proposed mark of the exterior of a Rubik's Cube was found to be an attempt to protect a technical function of the toy itself.

3.7.1   The Louboutin example

One of the more high-profile trade mark disputes of recent years concerns the red sole on the base of Louboutin shoes which was registered (or attempted to be registered) as a trade mark in various territories around the world including the US and EU. As you will see from the image of the trade mark (Figure 3.6), this is a sort of hybrid shape and colour mark where the claimed mark is the colour red on the sole of a heeled shoe (this is sometimes known as a position mark).

The registration of this mark became of particular strategic importance for Louboutin when Yves Saint Laurent brought out a range of red shoes where the sole was also red. As far as Louboutin was concerned this was clear infringement of its trade mark and it issued proceedings for trade mark infringement in the US. The US appellate court[37] was less convinced that the red sole could always act as a 'badge of origin' and limited the scope of the mark to situations where the upper shoe was of a contrasting colour to the sole. This meant that YSL was able to keep selling red shoes with red soles in the US but not red-soled shoes in other colours.

Similar issues arose when Louboutin sought to rely on its 'red sole' marks in Europe. There is a recent decision from the CJEU which concerns Louboutin's 2010 Benelux trade mark for the grey outline of a high heeled shoe with a sole in the colour red.[38] This mark is

Figure 3.6   Louboutin's colour trade mark (or is it a shape?)

---

37 *Christian Louboutin SA v Yves Saint Laurent Am. Holding, Inc.*, No. 11-3303 (2d Cir. 2013).
38 Pantone 18 1663TP to be specific.

registered in relation to 'high-heeled shoes' in class 25. The Benelux trade mark attempts to disclaim the contour of the shoe which it says 'is not part of the trade mark but is intended to show the positioning of the mark'.

Louboutin sought to rely on the mark to stop Van Haren, a Dutch shoe retail outlet, from selling shoes with red soles. The inevitable challenge to the trade mark's validity followed. The main question was whether the Benelux mark is a shape mark or a colour mark. If it was a shape mark, the additional requirements for shape marks such as 'substantial value' apply to the mark and could have meant that it is invalid. The relevant Advocate-General was asked twice[39] whether or not he thought that the mark is for a shape or a position. On both occasions he stated that, in his opinion, it is a shape. However, the the CJEU ultimately reached the conclusion that the mark was not a shape mark (an unusual departure by the CJEU from an Advocate-General's opinion and a relief for shoe aficionados).[40] The case has now been referred back to the Belgium court for a final decision.

3.8   Registering fabric and other quirky items as trade marks

In theory, trade mark protection is available for important aspects of your brand such as fabric designs or common motifs such as three stripes applied to products. However, it can be hard to prove that this is use of a 'sign' and even if it is a sign, that it is recognised by consumers as indicating the source of origin of your goods or services.

Even Adidas has run into difficulties with this issue. Shoe Branding, Adidas' long-standing shoe rival,[41] challenged the three stripes mark (see Figure 3.7) on the basis that Adidas had failed to prove that the mark had acquired distinctiveness.[42] Although Adidas had plenty of

---

39 It is highly unusual for the CJEU to ask the Advocate-General for a second opinion before making a decision. This shows the importance of this point for EU trade mark law. The role of the A-G is explained in Chapter 2.

40 *Christian Louboutin and Christian Louboutin Sas v van Haren Schoenen BV* Case C-163/16 ECLI:EU:C:2018:423.

41 See section 3.5.1 above in relation to position marks.

42 Decision of the Second Board of Appeal of EUIPO of 7 March 2017 in Case R 1515/2016-2. This decision has been appealed: http://eur-lex.europa.eu/legal-content/EN/TXT/HTML/?uri=CELEX:62017TN0307.

Figure 3.7   Adidas' three stripes trade mark

evidence to show substantial sales, sponsorship and recognition across the EU almost all of this evidence included the word mark ADIDAS and/or the Adidas logo. As the Second Board of Appeal at the EUIPO put it, the evidence of the three stripes alone being used as a badge of origin was 'paltry'.

If Adidas cannot establish that its considerable advertising investment and 'colossal sales' translate into public recognition of the three stripes mark, it will be difficult for others to do so in similar situations. Like shape marks, this does not mean that these trade marks are impossible to obtain but it requires a close working relationship between the design and trade mark/legal teams to educate the public to perceive markings as a badge of origin and stand a good chance of generating sufficient evidence for registration to be possible.

Similarly, Louis Vuitton ran into difficulty in its attempts to protect its check marks (see Figures 3.8 and 3.9).[43]

The problem that both of Louis Vuitton's marks faced was distinctiveness. The Cancellation Division and Board of Appeal of the EUIPO[44] considered that both marks consisted of a pattern which would be applied as surface decoration rather than indicating the commercial origin of the goods. The evidence that Louis Vuitton provided was not

43 *Louis Vuitton Malletier v OHIM* Case T-359/12 ECLI:EU:T:2015:214 and Case T-360/12 ECLI:EU:T:2015:215.
44 At that time the EUIPO was known as OHIM.

Figure 3.8   Louis Vuitton's first check trade mark

Figure 3.9   Louis Vuitton's second check trade mark

sufficient to show that either mark had acquired distinctive character in a substantial part of the EU.

This does not mean that registering a pattern is impossible but, as for three stripes, it is important to have sufficient evidence to show that consumers rely on the pattern itself as indicating the origin of the goods. In practice, a brand name or logo is usually used as well so this is very hard to prove.

At the retail end of the fashion spectrum, in some circumstances, it is possible to register the layout of a shop as a trade mark. The most notable example (and possibly the only example) is the Apple Store (see Figure 3.10) which has been registered as a trade mark in Germany

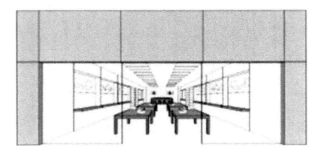

Figure 3.10   Apple's store layout trade mark

following a reference from the German trade mark office to the CJEU.[45] The value of this registration is already limited as Apple has since redesigned its stores and they do not typically look like this any longer. It is consequently at risk of a future attack on the ground of non-use.

3.9   Registering your own name

If you start a new label, it is natural to decide to use your name as the label's name. You are likely to have profile within the fashion community and as you build up your profile you are building up your business at the same time. However, this approach comes with a major risk. If you sell your business you would not be able to trade under your name ever again unless the business runs into financial difficulties and you can buy the trade mark back.[46] This is far from guaranteed.

3.9.1   The Elizabeth Emanuel example

The CJEU was asked to consider this issue in 2006. The designer of Princess Diana's wedding dress, Elizabeth Emanuel, assigned the goodwill in her name and a trade mark application for ELIZABETH EMANUEL to her company in 1996. A year or so later, she sold the company and shortly after that she left its employment. She was horrified to see that the company to which she had sold her business had applied to register a UK trade mark for ELIZABETH EMANUEL despite there being no longer being any connection between her and the business. She was concerned that the use of her name as a trade

---

45 C-421/13, *Apple Inc. v Deutsches Patent- und Markenamt.*
46 Roland Mouret was fortunate enough to be able to do just that.

mark would result in many consumers being confused. She opposed the application to register her name as a trade mark and applied to invalidate the earlier trade mark.

Her main argument was that the trade marks were of such a nature as to 'deceive the public, for instance as to the nature, quality or geographical origin of the goods or service'.[47] The CJEU acknowledged that there was a risk of confusion. However, because she had voluntarily assigned the rights in her earlier mark and goodwill in her name, there was no actual deceit. The CJEU concluded that while some customers might buy a particular product in the belief that Ms Emanuel had been involved in its design, the characteristics and qualities of the product were now guaranteed by the business that owned the rights.

3.9.2   The Karen Millen example

Karen Millen also fell into this particular trap when she sold off her eponymous fashion business in 2004. Because of the contractual terms in the sale and purchase agreement of her business, she was even more restricted than Elizabeth Emanuel, who could trade under her name even if she could not stop the business she sold trading off the earlier mark and goodwill she had assigned. Karen Millen found that over a decade later she was unable to even trade under the name KAREN alone.[48]

3.9.3   The Inès de la Fressange example

In France, the Intellectual Property Code expressly permits the registration of a personal or family name or '*nom patronymique*' as a trade mark.[49] While this is fairly common in France, see Chanel, Cartier, Karl Lagerfeld and Sonia Rykiel, it has likewise been the subject of much litigation.

The French Supreme Court considered personal name trade marks in a 2006 case between Inès de la Fressange, the model-come-stylist and designer, and her employer, the company, 'Inès de la Fressange SA'.[50]

---

47 Arts 3(1)(b) and 12(2)(b) of the Trade Marks Directive (now Art. 4(1)(g) of the Recast Directive 2015/2436).

48 *Millen v Karen Millen Fashions Ltd and Anor* [2016] EWHC 2104.

49 See Art. L. 711-1 (a) of the French Intellectual Property Code.

50 Cour de cassation, chambre commerciale, 31st January 2006 (n° 05-10.116), SA Inès de La Fressange c/ d'Urso, épouse Seignard de la Fressange.

Shortly after joining the company, Ms de la Fressange transferred several personal name trade marks to them. She was subsequently dismissed from her post, and following her dismissal, attempted to cancel the trade marks before the French courts. She argued that if they remained on the register, consumers would mistakenly purchase products which they wrongly believed to have been designed by Ms de la Fressange herself.

The French Supreme Court decided that if it cancelled the marks it would breach Ms de la Fressange's obligation to guarantee the company's use of the trade marks she had assigned to it when she was first employed by the company. This means that Inès de la Fressange SA can use Inès de la Fressange's personal name regardless of the fact that she no longer designs products for the company.

3.9.4   The Henriot champagne example

The French Intellectual Property Code allows people to trade under their name after selling an eponymous mark, provided such use is in good faith. However, they cannot register their name as a trade mark again.[51] In the Henriot champagne case,[52] the Paris Court of Appeal ruled (and the Supreme Court subsequently confirmed) that although a company, Masai, had registered various trade marks for HENRIOT, such as 'Champagne Henriot', Raymond and Serge Henriot could trade under their names as 'Champagne Serge Henriot' and 'Champagne Raymond Henriot'.[53] The fact that Raymond and Serge Henriot's use was in good faith was essential to their success.

The Henriot case is fairly unusual as the courts of Member States rarely rule in favour of a person who relies on a claim of good faith use of a personal name (commonly known as the 'own name defence'). Due to the high barrier to successfully claiming good faith in France and the low number of favourable decisions, it is high risk and expensive to rely on this provision. If you have already entered into any licence or assignment agreements relating to the rights in your name, it will be even more difficult to succeed and ultimately it is a question of what is covered in the agreement.

---

51 See Art. L. 713-6 of the French Intellectual Property Code.

52 Cour d'appel de Paris, Pôle 5 – chambre 1, 2nd June 2010, n° 08/20561.

53 Cour de cassation, Chambre commerciale, financière et économique, Arrêt n° 651 du 21st June 2011, n° 10-23.262.

3.9.5   What about Switzerland?

Under Swiss law, the registration of a natural person's name as a trade mark is permitted regardless of the type of goods or services designated in the application or the identity of the applicant.[54] This is also true for the name of real or fictional famous people, except if the name to be used as a trade mark relates to an actual person who had a major impact on the field of activity in question (for instance the name Mozart for sound recordings), in which case the application is likely to be refused.[55] This exception can be tricky to implement as it involves a fairly subjective assessment. The Swiss trade mark office may also refuse to register a name due to the general need to retain the free disposal of a particular name, the objection of the person whose name is to be registered or the misleading nature of the use of that particular name.[56] For instance, the Swiss folk hero, William Tell (*Guillaume Tell*) cannot be registered as a trade mark as there is a need to retain the free use of the name.

3.9.6   Practical points

Consequently, care should be taken to ensure that any trade mark assignment or licence is clearly drafted and covers different potential outcomes including the limitations placed on an individual bearing the name of the company (and their family) in the future. Bear in mind that just because you are registering your name does not mean that there is not a prior registered trade mark for the same name. In other words, remember that you do not have an automatic right to register or use your own name for your fashion brand.

3.10   The trade mark registration journey

You do not always get your mark through on the first try. If you apply to register a mark it must first be approved by the relevant trade mark

---

54 See trade mark guidelines of the Swiss Federal Institute of Intellectual Property: https://www.ige.ch/fileadmin/user_upload/schuetzen/marken/f/directives_marques/Directives_Marques_01012017.pdf, p 114.

55 Ibid.; see also Ralph Schlosser, Claudia Maradan, Commentaire romand de la propriété intellectuelle, *ad* Art. 3 LPM N 49, Helbing Lichtenhahn, Bâle, 2013.

56 See Schlosser, et al, ibid.; See also Jacques de Werra, LA MARQUE: ARME OU MENACE POUR LES CRÉATEURS? *in* SJ 2012 II p. 37, in which the author makes the case that the *Inès de la Fressange* French ruling could potentially be transposed in Swiss law with respect to the issue of misleading signs; for more examples of exclusions of protection see Art. 2 of the Federal Trade Mark Protection Act of 28 August 1992.

office (the 'examination' phase) and then it will be published and open to third parties who have the opportunity to 'oppose' your mark on the basis that it conflicts with their earlier rights (the 'opposition' phase).

 It is possible to resolve both issues by one or more of the following:

1. Amending the trade mark specification to reduce the number of goods and services protected.

2. Submitting evidence (for example evidence to show that your mark has acquired distinctiveness over time as a result of sustained use).

3. Purchasing an earlier trade mark to undermine an opposition from a third party.

4. Entering into a type of settlement agreement commonly known as a co-existence agreement whereby the uses to which each party can put their respective marks and extend their brands in the future are clearly delineated.

5. Changing your brand.

Sometimes even when you have entered into a settlement agreement, a trade mark office may decide that consumer confusion may result from the two marks remaining on the register and deny your application for registration. This tends to be less of an issue in the European registries but is something to watch out for and obtain local legal advice on before entering into a settlement agreement.

3.11   Assigning or licensing trade marks

 The legal principles involved in assignments and licences are covered in Chapter 9. It is important that trade mark assignments and licences (including those for 'intellectual property' generally which include trade marks) are registered with the relevant trade mark office. The amount of detail required and consequences for non-registration vary between jurisdictions. For example, failure to register could mean that the assignment or licence is not valid and enforceable (France) or that you cannot recover your costs in trade mark proceedings (UK). In some countries, you need to attach a copy of the assignment or licence to the registration request. In France, if this document is not in French, a certified French translation must also be filed.

When assigning a trade mark, it is important to remember to assign the goodwill in the marks as well. Goodwill is the attractive force which brings in custom. If you assign a trade mark without goodwill, it may be hard to rely on the mark in the future. Similarly, in a licence arrangement, it is normal for the licence to require the licensee assign back any goodwill generated from using the marks to the trade mark owner.

3.12 Trade marks and their international quirks

The above is told from a primarily European focus but thanks to various international treaties the principles and approaches set out above are broadly consistent across most major territories worldwide. The following quirks are particularly common and if you are not prepared for them, they can come with some major consequences. You have been warned.

3.12.1 The US

One of the most important features of the US system is the centrality of trade mark use to the registration process. You must file a declaration that you either have used or intend to use your proposed trade mark for all goods and services included in the trade mark specification. If you state that you 'intend to use' the trade mark, before you can get your mark registered, you will have six months from the date that the USPTO sends a Notice of Allowance in which to file a Statement of Use. Once registered you must continue to file statements of use on a regular basis in order to maintain the trade mark. Failure to provide a Statement of Use will lead to the mark being cancelled.

You can also rely on past trade mark use, to a limited extent, in order to backdate your trade marks to the first use in the US and first use in US commerce. This can create an interesting conflict where one person is claiming trade mark priority based on an earlier trade mark filing in a non-US jurisdiction and someone else is claiming prior rights in the US based on their use of the mark in commerce.

It is possible to register 'trade dress' or shape type unconventional marks in the US. The principles are broadly the same as for Europe. In other words, it may be possible to register trade dress provided that no feature of the mark applied for is essential to its use or purpose or affects the cost or quality of the article.

Finally, the US has two registers: a primary register, which is available to all, and a supplemental register, which is only available to US residents. In addition it is possible to register a State mark. In practice, the primary Federal register is the most important. For example, if the owner of a mark on the supplemental register wants to bring an action in Federal Court, they first have to prove acquired distinctiveness (a high hurdle).

3.12.2   Single class marks

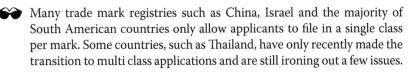 Many trade mark registries such as China, Israel and the majority of South American countries only allow applicants to file in a single class per mark. Some countries, such as Thailand, have only recently made the transition to multi class applications and are still ironing out a few issues.

3.12.3   Filing formalities

Many countries, particularly in the Middle East, Russia and parts of Asia, have specific formalities which must be completed before filing a mark, such as obtaining a power of attorney. It is wise to think about these issues long before you need to complete the relevant formality, for example the priority period ends, you need to file a new mark or assign an existing mark. In some circumstances it can take months to comply with the formalities such as to get a document notarised or apostilled.

3.12.4   Well-known marks

In many countries, if a mark is deemed to be 'well known', it can get special additional protection. This means that the mark can be used to prevent the registration or use of a trade mark for dissimilar goods and services. For example, it is likely that LVMH could prevent the registration of LOUIS VUITTON for a car showroom. In some instances this can mean that trade mark protection is extended outside of territories in which the mark is registered. Similarly, in the US in order to prevent dilution of a trade mark, it is necessary for a trade mark to be deemed 'famous'. The protection of marks where there is no likelihood of confusion is discussed in more detail in Chapter 20.

3.12.5   Trade mark renewal

In most countries worldwide, trade marks need to be renewed every
ten years. This means that if you have a big trade mark portfolio you
could face a large renewal bill at least once every ten years. It is important that you budget for this in advance. The cost will vary greatly
based on the number of marks, trade mark classes and territories. If
you do not renew your trade marks, you not only risk losing a lot of
hard-earned trade mark rights but there is a danger of opportunistic
trade mark registrations being made by third parties in the meantime.
Regular review of your trade mark portfolios can help to manage costs
and avoid the risk of important trade marks being invalidated on the
basis of non-use.

3.13   Collective and certification marks

In addition to having a trade mark which demonstrates the trade origin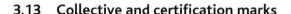
of your goods or services, in some circumstances, it is desirable to be
part of a group of companies who have obtained either a certification
or a collective mark.

A certification mark provides a guarantee that the goods or services
bearing the mark meet a certain defined standard or possess a particular characteristic. The owner of the mark (usually a legal entity
such as a trade association, technical institute or similar) will define
those standards or characteristics and ensure that anyone who it
licences to use the certification mark abides by the relevant criteria
for use. These criteria are set out in the regulations which are filed
with the certification mark and are policed by means of a licence
which all users of the certification mark will be required to sign as a
prerequisite to use.

The regulations have to include certain prescribed information such as
the characteristics to be certified by the mark, the status and compe-
tence of the applicant (the applicant cannot sell or be connected to the
sale of the goods being certified) and the dispute resolution procedure
should issues arise in the future.

A collective mark indicates that the goods or services bearing the mark
originate from members of a trade association, rather than just one
trader.

The most relevant mark for the fashion industry is probably the Woolmark (a certification mark regarding the wool content in clothing and similar items). As sustainable fashion and wearable technology become more prevalent in society, more collective and certification marks will emerge – see Chapter 25 for more details.

Currently certification marks are available in, at least, the EU, the US, China, Australia, Canada, Hong Kong, India, New Zealand, South Korea, Thailand and the UK. Like regular trade marks, certification and collective marks have a six-month priority period. This means you can file in one territory and extend certification mark protection to other territories within six months while keeping the earlier priority date.

3.14   Other ways to register your brand's name

 In addition to trade mark registration, there are some easy wins which you should secure as early as possible. They include the domain name and social media handles.

3.14.1   Domain name

Compared to the early days of the first Dot Com boom, the precise domain name that you register does not matter quite as much. This is because people's route to websites is nowadays more likely to be a result of searching or linking rather than entering a specific domain. However, domains are still a fairly cheap and flexible means of securing control over your name. There are now plenty of gTLDs (global Top Level Domains) to choose from so you do not have to worry if you cannot get the .com. However, it is worth checking the .com to see if it is selling similar products to you, in which case a name change would be wise.

Domain names are managed under a hierarchy which is headed by the IANA, the Internet Assigned Numbers Authority which is part of ICANN[57] (a non profit organisation). The hierarchy includes national registries such as Nominet in the UK, AFNIC in France and DENIC in Germany. ICANN helps to make the Internet work by coordinating the names which humans recognise (i.e., domain names) with the numbers that computers use to connect the correct parts of the Internet to each

---

57 The Internet Corporation for Assigned Names and Numbers.

other (i.e., IP addresses). ICANN offers accreditation to domain name registrars but does not get involved in ownership disputes.[58] You will purchase the domain name from a registrar such as GoDaddy or 123. reg.

3.14.2   Social media accounts

Social media accounts are usually free to register and should be secured asap. In addition to the obvious accounts such as Instagram, Twitter, Facebook, SnapChat and Pinterest, think about where your brand is heading in the future and regularly review the social media landscape for potential future registration opportunities.

---

58 Although it has adopted the Uniform Domain Name Dispute Resolution Policy (UDRP) which is
   discussed in more detail in Chapter 20 at 20.6.1.

4 Copyright and your creative works

The visual appearance of a product is essential to its success but can it be protected by copyright? The good news is that Europe has a more expansive copyright regime than many other territories. It is often possible to rely on copyright to protect the product itself, fabric patterns, logos and similar forms of surface decoration and related media such as photographs which are used in marketing and advertising campaigns. Even fashion shows themselves have been found to be protectable copyright works in certain circumstances.

Many types of copyright works are described colloquially under the general heading of 'designs'. This can be confusing when you enter the world of intellectual property law because registered and unregistered designs are also a particular type of intellectual property right. Bear in mind that when people in the fashion industry talk about 'designs', the intellectual property right in issue is usually copyright.

4.1 The copyright basics

Copyright is relatively consistent around the world due to the Berne Convention[1] and TRIPS.[2] These international agreements set minimum standards for copyright, including automatic protection of copyright works without registration. The treaty signatories offer reciprocal protection for works created by their citizens. Although most aspects of copyright have not been formally harmonised, a handful of EU

---

1 Berne Convention for the Protection of Literary and Artistic Works, 9 September 1886, revised at Paris on 24 July 1971, amended in 1979. The current list of signatories to the Berne Convention (at each stage) is available from WIPO: http://www.wipo.int/treaties/en/ip/berne/. It includes all major territories worldwide.

2 The Agreement on Trade Related Aspects of Intellectual Property Rights https://www.wto. org/english/docs_e/legal_e/27-trips.pdf, Art. 9, for example incorporates much of the Berne Convention including the requirement that copyright is not registered.

Directives directly affect copyright law, notably the 'Infosoc Directive',[3] 'Database Directive'[4] and the 'Term Directive'.[5] The 'E-commerce Directive' is also relevant but less directly as far as copyright law is concerned.[6]

Copyright protects a wide range of creative works including:

1. Artistic works such as sculptures or photographs or the original fashion drawings/CADs.

2. Literary works such as advertising or social media copy and website text.

3. Musical works such as songs integrated into fashion shows, used on websites, in clips on social media, etc.

4. Films, such as a video of a fashion show or social media posts uploaded by fans.

5. Sound recordings, such as the music used at fashion events, is likely to have copyright in the lyrics, music and sound recording itself.

6. Broadcasts (e.g., a broadcast of a fashion show).

In some countries, it has been held that copyright even protects fragrances and perfumes, but this principle has generally been quite controversial and French courts, who led the way in this broadening of copyright scope, have given very mixed decisions on this subject. Similarly, the question of whether fashion objects such as clothes and shoes can be protected by copyright is the subject of significant variation across Europe.

This goes to show that while many aspects of copyright law are consistent, the way in which the law is interpreted and applied in different countries can vary substantially. To ensure that your business is

---

3 Directive on the harmonisation of certain aspects of copyright and related rights in the information society 2001/29/EC.

4 Directive on the legal protection of databases 1996/9/EC.

5 Directive on the term of protection of copyright and certain related rights 2006/116/EC.

6 Directive on certain legal aspects of information society services, in particular electronic commerce, in the Internal Market 2000/31/EC.

protected, make sure you are aware of all applicable copyright laws in each country where you operate.

The UK operates a closed list approach to what can be a copyright work. Aside from prints (i.e., graphic works), fashion creations do not obviously fall within any of the examples of an artistic work provided in the relevant act.[7] This includes:

1.   A graphic work, photograph, sculpture or collage.

2.   A work of architecture.

3.   A work of artistic craftsmanship.

Unless there is a print or photograph on a fashion item, the most relevant category for fashion is potentially 'artistic craftsmanship'. However, it is very difficult for a fashion item to be found to be both 'artistic' and 'a work of craftsmanship' as craftsmanship implies a very small scale. This *may* apply to couture but is unlikely to extend to ready to wear.

Most other European jurisdictions adopt a more flexible approach to copyright works and simply require that a copyright work is an 'intellectual work.' Consequently, any creations that are 'original works of the mind' which reflect the personality of the author or designer are capable of copyright protection.

In Belgium,[8] fashion items are likely to be protected by copyright as 'artistic works' provided they are original (i.e., the result of their author's free and creative choices). In a famous 2005 judgment, the Brussels Court of Appeal ruled that a particular handbag was an original copyright work based on its specific shape, dimensions and unusual combination of fabrics and patterns. This followed a 2002 decision of the Brussels Court of Appeal which accepted that some of Hermès' bags and belts qualified as copyright works.

At the other end of the scale, police uniforms which were designed by a private company following a call for projects by the Belgian State were found by the Brussels Court of Appeal to be original copyright

---

7 See, Copyright, Designs and Patents Act 1988, s 4.
8 Book XI of the Belgian Economical Law Code.

works given the specific choices made by the company. The Belgian State was consequently held to have infringed the copyright works as it had used very similar uniforms without the company's permission or paying financial compensation.

These cases demonstrate that, under Belgian law, fabric, bags, belts and other fashion items are all eligible for copyright protection provided they are sufficiently original.

In France, the Intellectual Property Code expressly refers to fashion creations as being potentially protected by copyright.[9] There is a presumption that fashion creations are works of the mind and consequently copyright works.[10] The French Intellectual Property Code notes that this is because fashion items are frequently renewed in order to meet the demands of the industry. However, this does not mean that all fashion items are copyright works. French courts are often fairly strict when regarding the notion of 'originality'. Since fashion often follows trends, many new fashion creations which follow the trend may be found to not be original and consequently not protected by copyright.

Under Polish law, anybody's creative activity can be protected as a copyright work regardless of its value, purpose or form.[11] Therefore, copyright protection for fashion products is possible provided the creator can prove that it is their own creative work which is individual and original on a global scale. There is a very fine line between lawful inspiration and infringing imitation. Polish courts have ruled on numerous occasions that the creativity and individual character necessary for copyright may refer exclusively to a part or an element of a product, or a mere composition or selection of elements. For example, a collection of chef's aprons, as a whole, was said to have creative and individual character and consequently any copy of them would infringe copyright.[12]

Swiss copyright law does not have to follow the various EU Directives as Switzerland is not part of the EU. However, Switzerland is an important market for luxury fashion and if that is your business, it is worth

---

9 See Art. L112-2.14 of the French Intellectual Property Code.
10 Translation from French by Charlotte Gerrish.
11 See Art. 1 of Polish Act on Copyright and Neighbouring Rights dated 4 February 1994 ('Polish Act on Copyright').
12 Decision of Court of Appeal in Poznan, 8 May 2013, I ACa 211/13.

understanding the nuances in more detail. For example, Swiss copy-right law does not expressly refer to fashion creations.[13] However, it does not restrict copyright protection to a closed list of creations. This means that a fashion item may very well be protected by copyright in Switzerland provided it qualifies as an individual literary or artistic creation of the mind.[14]

4.2   Fast fashion in court

A common source of copyright litigation is between designer brands and high street chains which often take a slightly too literal inspiration. This is a particular issue for fast fashion where the rapid turnaround gives limited time for innovation. Because fashion designs are often inspired by past trends, claims of originality from even the most estab-lished luxury fashion houses can be defeated if the latest trend is too closely inspired by an earlier fashion design.

Designer Vanessa Bruno sued Zara on the basis that one of the fast fashion chain's blouses reproduced elements of her 2008 dress. On closer examination, the Paris Court of Appeal noted that the original elements of the dress had already featured in fashion press from the 1920s and in 1980s editions of Vogue. This meant that the design was not original and could not be protected by copyright. Consequently, Vanessa Bruno's claim was dismissed.[15]

This shows that despite France's reputation for being more copyright friendly, there is still a high hurdle for obtaining copyright protection for fashion creations. Consequently it is quite common for fashion brands in the EU to also include a design right claim such as infringe-ment of Unregistered Community Design or UK unregistered design right. This is only possible, if they file the claim within the relevant timeframe, respectively, three years or ten years from first advertising or selling the item protected by the design.[16] If the brand is fortunate

---

13 Copyright Act of 9 October 1992.

14 See Art. 2 of the Copyright Act of 9 October 1922; See also Federal Court decision of 14 February 1934, ATF 60 II 62, 70; Denis Barrelet, Willi Egloff, Le nouveau droit d'auteur, Commentaire de la loi fédérale sur le droit d'auteur et les droits voisins, *ad* Art. 2, N 18, Stämpfli Verlag AG, 2008; François Dessemontet, Commentaire romand de la propriété intellectuelle, *ad* Art. 2 LDA N 2 and 46, Helbing Lichtenhahn, Bâle, 2013.

15 CA de Paris, Pôle 5, 17 octobre 2012, n° 2011/09133.

16 The period of protection for UK unregistered design right is the shorter of 15 years from

enough to have a Registered Community Design, this makes the situation much easier as it is not necessary to prove that the design has been copied although you will still have to prove that the design is valid and that the infringing item has the same overall impression as the registered design. Registered and unregistered designs are discussed in more detail in Chapter 6.

4.3   Copyright and designs – parallel claims

The application of copyright law across the EU is slowly becoming more harmonised but significant differences remain, particularly in terms of the scope of protection. For example, the French courts tend to be more generous in terms of granting copyright protection than the English courts (although this trend is becoming less pronounced with time). As indicated above, it is common for there to be a degree of crossover in terms of copyright and designs law. Consequently it is common to rely on both rights at the same time. This could be done in the same set of proceedings and/or in parallel proceedings in different jurisdictions.

The most notable examples of the crossover between designs law and copyright in France tend to involve bags. The Versailles Court of Appeal recently considered whether copyright subsists in Longchamp's famous 'Le Pliage' bag.[17] In this case, the court held that while it is possible for copyright to subsist in a bag, infringement on the basis of copyright is appreciated by similarities and not by differences. The judges considered that the similarities between the Longchamp 1623 model and the alleged infringing bags were simply due to ordinary requirements of a bag (rectangular bottom and triangular profile). The court concluded that the differences such as the shape and dimensions of the flaps and handles, shape and size of the bags were sufficiently different that they outweighed the similarities.

Because fashion brands commonly claim both copyright and design right infringement in the same claim, the French courts have occasionally conflated the two and muddied the law. For example, in the 1990s, the French Supreme Court stated that a design right was not

---

first creation or 10 years from first marketing. In practice, in the fashion industry the 10 year period nearly always applies.

17 CA de Versailles, 1ère ch. 1ère section, 2 février 2017, n° 15/04457.

'new' since it did not reflect the personality of the author (the test for copyright).[18] This judicial confusion has been largely resolved in recent years and the courts now have more stringent requirements in order to ascertain whether a creation is 'original' for copyright purposes.

The French courts now tend to consider each right separately to avoid the risk of confusing decisions. For example, in a dispute involving sportswear, although both copyright and design right were claimed, the Paris High Court held that only design right could be relied upon as the product was not original enough to be protected by copyright.[19] This important decision marked a departure from the traditional 'all or nothing approach' to intellectual property claims. Similarly, while Ba&sh's 'distressed-style rips' on jeans were not protected by copyright because the creation was 'not a reflection of the designer's personality', the court noted that they could be protected by design right.[20] Further, while 'Soft Lady Dior' and 'Dior Soft' handbags from the Spring/Summer 2008 collection were not protected by copyright, they succeeded in their claim for unregistered Community design infringement.[21]

4.4   Can fashion shows be protected by copyright?

 Yes – in, at least, France! The Criminal Section of the French Supreme Court recently decided that fashion shows can be protected by copyright because the overall construction and arrangements, use of music, colours, lighting, the garments themselves as well as the styling of the runway as a whole are capable of copyright protection. In this case, three photographers (who were accredited by the French Couture Federation) took images of several fashion shows and posted them to an online streaming site. Usually in France, there is a legal provision which states that the monopoly conferred by copyright can be overruled if the copyrighted works are reproduced and made available online for immediate information purposes. The photographers sought to rely on this rule. However, the court considered that the publication of the images on a streaming site was not justified by an immediate need to share

---

18 Cass. 1ère civ., 11 février 1997, n°95-11.605.
19 TGI Paris, 3e ch., 1ère section., 11 janvier. 2011.
20 CA de Paris, pôle 5, ch. 1, 8 juin 2011, RG n°09/21321.
21 TGI de Paris, 3e chambre, 10 mars 2010, n° 2008/17024.

information and that the photographers' personal accreditation did not extend to publication on an unaccredited website.

The French court confirmed that the creators of the fashion shows had the exclusive right to control the copying and communication of their shows to the public. It followed that any unauthorised publication of images reproducing the fashion shows was copyright infringement.[22] This had consequences for the photographers from both financial and reputational perspectives.

Although this has not been tested in other countries, it is less likely that a fashion show would be considered to be a copyright work in more restrictive countries such as England because of English law's requirement that copyright works fall into certain specific categories. That said, a fashion show, particularly a very creative show, *may* qualify as a 'dramatic work' on the basis that it is 'a work of action, with or without words or music, which is capable of being performed before an audience'.[23] This has not yet been tested by the English courts.[24] A similar defence to that available in France applies in England for use of a copyright work for 'criticism or review' or 'reporting current events.' The defences are discussed in more detail in Chapter 21. The key is to take no more of the copyright work than is necessary. Live streaming an entire fashion show is very unlikely to meet this criterion.

This case also highlights the importance of properly defining your working relationship with employees or contractors, such as freelance photographers, particularly regarding the scope of their authority when conducting work on your behalf. This is discussed further in the context of employees and contractors in Chapter 10.

If runway shows are protected by copyright, it follows that runway models could have their performances protected by Performer's Rights.[25] If your fashion show is particularly performative, think about

---

22 Cour de Cassation, Ch. Criminelle 5 février 2008, n°07-81.387.

23 Nourse LJ in *Norowzian v Arks Ltd and Anor (No. 2)* [1999] EWCA Civ 3014. Further, movement was considered an essential component for dramatic works in *Creation Records* [1997] EWHC Ch 370; movement is certainly present in a fashion show.

24 The English courts have confirmed that a TV format is in principle capable of protection as a dramatic work so the same principle could apply to fashion shows – see *Banner Universal Motion Pictures Ltd v Endemol Shine Group Ltd & Anor* [2017] EWHC 2600.

25 Mathilde Pavis 'Runway models are not performers. Are you sure? Look closer...' http://ipkitten.blogspot.com/2018/07/runway-models-are-not-performers-are.html.

whether you have the right contractual protection in place with your runway models.

4.5 Applied art

One of the biggest sources of divergence between different countries' copyright law concerns the US concept of 'applied art' i.e., the application of art to a functional object. This is hugely important for the fashion industry because no matter how creative the design, ultimately it is designed to be worn.

The US has traditionally taken a very restrictive approach to the protection of 'functional' items such as clothing, footwear, bags, etc. In particular, the courts have been concerned about the extent to which it is possible to separate an artistic work from the functional item. This issue arises from the US Copyright Act[26] but many other jurisdictions have similar restrictions. For example, until very recently in England, any work which was replicated on an 'industrial scale' i.e., more than 50 times, was limited to a maximum term of 25 years from the date of creation.[27]

The most high-profile case to consider this issue in the US is the recent US Supreme Court *Star Athletica*[28] decision. This case considered whether cheerleading uniforms can be protected by copyright. The court essentially said 'yes', because the chevron designs (i.e., the surface decoration) could be separated from the uniform itself.

4.6 Using a copyright work

In order to rely on copyright, you must prove that you own or have the right to use the work. This could be because you created it, acquired ownership via an assignment, or hold an exclusive or non-exclusive licence.

---

26 US Copyright Act, §101 defines 'Pictorial, graphic, and sculptural works' as including: 2D and 3D works of applied art. It notes that the design of a useful article is only artistic to the extent that, the 'pictorial, graphic, or sculptural features' of the design can be (i) identified separately from, and (ii) are capable of existing independently of, the utilitarian aspects of the article. Needless to say this is quite restrictive.

27 The repeal of s. 52 of the Copyright, Designs and Patents Act 1988 has proven to be fairly controversial but so far limited evidence of the anticipated chaos has emerged.

28 *Star Athletica, LLC v Varsity Brands, Inc,* No. 15-866, 580 U.S. ___ (2017), slip op.

An assignment means that you own the work outright whereas a licence means that you have permission to use the work for particular purposes and usually in particular territories for a specific period of time. If you own the work, you have a lot more flexibility in terms of how you can deal in the work. For example, if you just have a licence, you may be restricted from licensing part of the work to someone else (known as a sub-licence). An exclusive licence means that you are the only person who is allowed to exploit the work. It is consequently fairly similar to an assignment but it will likely have a finite term, be limited to a geographical area or be subject to other restrictions.

Ownership can be established via the relevant contracts such as an employment contract or an assignment from the creator. The first owner is generally the creator and they remain the owner until the right is transferred by an assignment. An important exception to this rule applies in many European jurisdictions, including the UK, where, if the person creating the work is an employee, anything they create in the course of their employment will automatically belong to their employer.

In many countries, such as France, ownership is presumed if you exploit the work. Similarly, in countries which offer copyright registration, having a registered copyright in your name means that you are presumed to be the owner of that work. Both of these presumptions can be rebutted.

This means that even if you pay a lot of money for something, such as photographs of your fashion show, unless you have an assignment or licence with the photographer, they retain the rights in the photographs. Although a court would likely imply a licence for you to use the photographs for the purpose of the commission, this can present a problem when you do things outside the scope of an implied licence such as social media use, permanent web use or archive use. Archive use is discussed in more detail in Chapter 13.

When assigning a copyright work (or indeed any right) you must ensure that you comply with the relevant contractual formalities in order for it to be valid. For example, in the case of an assignment under English law, the assignment must be in writing, clearly state what is assigned and be signed by authorised signatories from *both* parties (i.e., the person assigning the right and the person taking possession of the right). It is possible to assign something which has not been created yet (such as a fabric pattern or a series of photographs), this is known as a 'future work'. As discussed in Chapter 10, in some jurisdictions such as England a copyright which is created in the course of employment by an employee, automatically belongs to their employee. However, as this rule does not apply to all European jurisdictions, it is a sensible precaution to also include a formal assignment in their employment contract.

In Belgium, copyright assignments are interpreted in favour of the creator so unless the contract is clear, the assumption will be that the rights remain with the creator (for example, the designer or photographer). Further, in Belgium copyright works created by employees do not normally automatically belong to the employer. Therefore copyright assignments are a requirement in all circumstances in Belgium.

Similarly, in Poland the law favours the creator and is very strict when it comes to contract formalities. For example, if the copyright assignment formalities have not been followed, what appears on the face of it to be an assignment will be deemed a licence by the court.[29] Under Polish law, an assignment agreement must be in writing and signed by both parties. Further, the subject of assignment has to be specific, this is particularly important where the assignment relates to future works. It is important to describe the ordered or expected work in as much detail as possible. If there is any doubt, the creator will retain the copyright.

A particular peculiarity of Polish law is the obligation to list the so-called 'fields of exploitation' in a copyright licence or assignment. This essentially means the ways in which the copyright works may be used. These can include the dissemination of works, their public performance, exhibition, screening, broadcasting, reproduction, marketing, etc. It is not sufficient to provide for a full assignment or licence to the 'greatest extent possible' as you have to name specific fields of exploitation.[30] As in other territories, it is possible to assign the copyright in the same work to numerous buyers, with each of them being assigned a different scope of exploitation.

---

29 See Art. 65 of the Polish Act on Copyright.
30 See, ibid., Art. 50.

Similarly, derivative rights (i.e., the right to adapt and modify works) must be considered when assigning copyright. Unless you expressly state that the acquirer is also granted the rights to derivative works, they will not be able to modify the original works.[31]

4.7 Moral rights

Moral rights are often considered as a subset of copyright. They include:

1. The right to be identified as the creator of the work (or the 'attribution right'; this tends to be the most important right for many creators).

2. The right to not have your work subjected to derogatory treatment (this concerns amendments which could damage the reputation of the creator and could potentially include a right to object to merchandising use or similar).

3. The right to object to being falsely attributed as the creator of a work.

4. The right to determine when the work is first made available to the public.

5. The right to withdraw the work from further use.

6. The right to protect the creator's reputation.

Not all of the above moral rights apply in all European jurisdictions, for example, the first three are the ones you can rely on in the UK. These rights cannot be transferred (in other words they cannot be assigned or licensed, although they can pass with a person's estate upon death). In some jurisdictions, such as the UK, they can be waived. Indeed, in the UK, if you create a work in the course of your employment, you do not have moral rights protection.

---

31 See, ibid., Art. 46.

4.8   How long does copyright last?

The length of time that a work is protected by copyright varies around the world but it is usually linked to the life of the creator plus a fixed period of time from the end of the year in which they died. In most instances, including the whole of the EU,[32] this is an additional 70 years. The notable exceptions are China, Canada and Japan (where the term is currently life plus 50 years) and Mexico (life plus 100 years).[33] Many countries also offer a fixed term of protection for previously unpublished works or unusual rules for specific works which pre-date legislation which changed the term of copyright protection in their jurisdiction.

4.9   How do you get copyright?

Throughout Europe, and indeed in most jurisdictions worldwide, copyright arises automatically upon the creation of the work. Copyright is therefore a very flexible right which has come to the rescue of many a fashion brand. For the major international copyright treaties such as the Berne Convention and TRIPS, it is an essential requirement that all signatories (in practice most countries worldwide) offer automatic protection for copyright works.

While you do not need to register a copyright work in order for it to have copyright protection, in some territories, notably the US, Canada and China, registration is a requirement in order to get full protection. For example, it can affect the amount of damages available or the willingness of Customs to take action. Consequently, in order to be able to rely upon those rights in jurisdictions which offer a registration system, it is wise to register important rights sooner rather than later. Copyright registration provides an easy way to evidence the date a copyright work was created. Some of the EU Member States such as Spain and France have various voluntary systems for copyright registration.

The main country to consider registering your copyright works is the US.[34] Importantly, if the registration is made within three months of

---

32 Thanks to the Term Directive 2006/116/EC.

33 There is an excellent map on Wikipedia which sets out copyright terms around the world:https://en.wikipedia.org/wiki/List_of_countries%27_copyright_lengths.

34 The US Copyright Office has lots of helpful information on copyright registration.

publication (or prior to infringement of a work) in addition to actual damages, statutory damages and legal costs are available. If you do not register your rights in time it may not be worth litigating in the US because the legal costs will likely outweigh both the damages and the commercial benefit associated with the injunction. Provided the copyright work is registered within five years of creation, a US copyright registration offers both proof of validity of the right and a presumption of ownership.

It can be very helpful to have copyright registration in China, particularly for important patterns and logos. Copyright protection can often be cheaper and easier to obtain than trade mark protection and in practice it can be hard to succeed in an enforcement action or in detaining goods via Customs without copyright registration.

In Argentina, unless a work is registered it can be freely used by third parties provided it is not altered and the copyright owner is correctly attributed.[35] Similarly, in Mexico copyright registration is very useful when it comes to enforcing your rights. Mexican copyright must be registered in the name of an individual, i.e., it must identify an 'author' although the copyright can be owned by a legal entity. In Canada and Brazil, while registration is not required, it is helpful evidence of the date of registration and the copyright owner which the court will accept if the copyright owner seeks to rely on it (unless an opponent can prove otherwise).

4.10   The Soleau Envelope in France

A simple and cost-effective way of protecting your ideas in France can be done via the 'Soleau Envelope'. This is a service provided by INPI, the French Intellectual Property Office. The Soleau Envelope is a way to evidence your creations and to give your ideas or projects a specific date while keeping them confidential. In a similar way to more formal copyright registration, it is a useful tool in the event of subsequent litigation as it shows when you created the work. At the time of writing, the Soleau Envelope is kept by the INPI for an initial five years, and can be renewed once for a further five years. It currently costs €15 per

---

35 Section 63 of Law No. 11,723 of 26 September 1933, which is regulated by Decree No. 41.223 of 1943. http://www.latinamerica-ipr-helpdesk.eu/sites/default/files/factsheets/en_factsheet_argentina. pdf.

filing or renewal. Even at the end of the ten year period, if you keep the envelopes unopened in your personal files, they can still prove useful for evidentiary purposes.

The creations filed in the Soleau Envelope can be artistic or technical. Those filed in connection with the fashion industry tend to concern works related to applied arts, fashion designs, audiovisual communications, graphics, shop layouts, window designs or even formats for fashion shows. Although it is possible to file an 'idea', the scope of any available copyright protection will be limited to the expression of that idea and not the idea itself. For example, if you file a coloured polka dot T-shirt, assuming the copyright work is sufficiently original, the scope of protection will be limited to the specific expression, i.e., the pattern of colours, rather than the idea of using polka dots on T-shirts.

You can also file a Soleau Envelope for technical processes or methods of manufacturing such as confidential information or potentially patentable items. While copyright arises automatically upon creation (provided that certain conditions are met), patent laws relating to technical innovations can vary around the world. Consequently, the INPI has issued specific guidance advising that the personal 'prior rights' benefit in this instance, is only valid for France.

In a practical sense, only paper evidence can be filed in the Soleau Envelope, which means that USB keys, CDs, cardboard prototypes or fabric samples are not accepted. Traditionally, this was because the evidence had to be filed in an envelope and posted to the INPI for registration. The envelope had to contain two identical copies, one of which would be returned to the creator for safekeeping once it had been stamped and recorded by the INPI. Since 2016, it has been possible to make the application online by providing an attachment of the evidence you wish to file. To make the most of the Soleau Envelope system, it is therefore important to provide a detailed written description of your idea or creation accompanied by any additional information in a 2D format (sketches, drawings, diagrams, photographs, screen shots) – the more detailed your filing, the more useful it will be if needed as evidence at a later date.

A similar system to the Soleau Envelope exists in Belgium (i-Depot), the Netherlands (via the Tax Office) and in France (again!). The Agence pour la Protection des Programmes ('APP') provides creators with the ability to confidentially file and store information related to their digital creations including the date of creation. It can also track developments and save updates of your creations over time. The fees are higher[36] but this includes unlimited storage for as long as the information is stored and for as long as you remain a member of the APP.

4.11   Blockchain verification

In the longer term, it is likely that technology will come to the rescue in terms of verifying the date on which copyright works were created. There are already businesses queueing up to show their use of distributed ledger (i.e., blockchain) technology to prove the order in which works were created.[37] In France, a Paris-based legal tech start-up called BlockchainYourIP.com offers a platform allowing the registration of a digital fingerprint of a document containing creative works (copyright) or know-how. Users can preserve the digital fingerprint of their creations (whether individual or collective works) into a blockchain.

The aim of using a blockchain is not to create independent intellectual property rights but to be able to evidence a creation date or priority date either for contractual reasons, for example, when licensing or assigning know-how, or in the event of litigation. Blockchain evidence has not yet been relied upon in court proceedings in Europe so its effectiveness remains to be seen.

4.12   Registration

The fundamental questions that all of the above recording mechanisms seek to answer is: (i) who created the work; (ii) what is the copyright work; and (iii) when was it created. If you retain clear and comprehensive business records, this is less of an issue.

Although systems like the Soleau Envelope are now fairly user friendly and blockchain is the hot topic *du jour*, there is a lot to be said for registering the work with a copyright office such as the ones in China, Canada and the US. In addition to the reasons outlined above, such

---

36 Currently €150 plus VAT per filing or per update to an existing filing.

37 For example: https://www.coindesk.com/how-block-chain-technology-is-working-to-transform-intellectual-property.

as damages available and evidence of ownership, a copyright registration can substantially improve your prospects of removing counterfeit goods using the various e-commerce platforms' online takedown processes (see Chapter 24 for more details).

5   Image rights

> [A] person's image constitutes one of the chief attributes of his or her per-
> sonality, as it reveals the person's unique characteristics and distinguishes
> the person from his or her peers. The right to the protection of one's image
> is thus one of the essential components of personal development. . . .[1]

Unlike the US where the right of publicity is considered an economic
right at the state level,[2] the majority of Europe does not have a law of
'image rights' per se. Each country in the EU has adopted a slightly different approach and unlike other intellectual property rights, there is
surprisingly little consistency in this area.

The fashion industry often talks about image rights and asks for 'image
rights waivers' or similar. There is no standalone EU right to protect
use of your image. However, it may be possible to limit usage of your
image in three circumstances based on (i) privacy, (ii) data protection
and (iii) trade mark, passing off or unfair competition law.

5.1   Privacy law

If you film or photograph in either a private place or a public area
where people would not anticipate being filmed, they are entitled to a
reasonable expectation of privacy. In these circumstances, it is possible
that the person filmed may be able to sue under privacy law.

The main European laws on privacy come from the the European
Convention on Human Rights[3] (ECHR) – a separate treaty to the EU
treaty – which includes non-EU countries such as Turkey and Russia

---

1 *von Hannover v Germany (No. 2)*, Grand Chamber judgment of 7 February 2012, at para. 96.

2 Some states have a statute while the remainder rely on Common Law. For a complete list of the
   statutes in different states see www.rightofpublicity.com/statutes.

3 http://www.echr.coe.int/Documents/Convention_ENG.pdf.

and the EU Charter,[4] both are discussed in more detail in Chapter 2. Article 8 ECHR gives a right to respect for everyone's private and family life, home and correspondence. This right is subject to certain restrictions that are 'necessary in a democratic society'. Many ECHR countries have interpreted this as a fairly broad privacy right.[5]

The European Court of Human Rights hears cases about whether the countries that signed the ECHR have complied with the law. The court is based in Strasbourg and, again, is completely separate to the EU and its court, the CJEU. The right of privacy in Article 8 ECHR has to be balanced with Article 10, the right to freedom of expression.[6] While a newspaper may be given a fair amount of latitude as far as freedom of expression is concerned, the same does not apply to fashion advertising where the justification of a campaign using people's images without their consent is unlikely to be successful.

 Claims based on privacy law can be difficult to win if the filming took place in a public place and there are appropriate signs to warn that filming is taking place. However, if the individual is recognisable in a campaign (rather than being a relatively anonymous figure in the background) they have a better chance of succeeding. Some countries such as France have a particularly strict interpretation of privacy law which creates a quasi-image right. This is discussed in more detail later in this chapter.

5.2 Data protection law

 An image rights argument based on data protection law is less conventional and the scope of this argument is still being tested by the EU courts. Data protection is a big political priority in Europe[7] and the associated laws have recently been strengthened with the General Data Protection Regulation (GDPR) so expect more image rights cases

---

4 Article 7 of the EU Charter, provides for the right to respect for family life, home and communications.

5 http://www.echr.coe.int/Documents/FS_Own_image_ENG.pdf.

6 The EU Charter equivalent is Art. 7 which gives everyone the right to freedom of expression including the right to hold opinions and to receive and impart information and ideas without interference by public authority.

7 EU Charter, Art. 8 provides EU citizens with the right to the protection of their personal data and that such personal data must be processed fairly for specified purposes and on the basis of the consent of the person who's data is being processed or some other legitimate basis which is set out in law.

based on data protection in the future. For more information on the GDPR see Chapter 14.

The data protection/image rights argument is based on the fact that someone's image is personal data from which you can tell their gender, ethnicity and possibly religion (depending on what they are wearing). Further, as image recognition software and social media become more pervasive, you do not have to have access to a government database in order to identify an individual from their image.

The GDPR confers rights on individuals regarding use of their personal information by third parties. Under the GDPR, individuals have the right to (among other things):

1. Be informed about how their personal data is used (e.g., via privacy notices).

2. Access their personal data which is held by third parties.

3. Rectify incorrect information held about them.

4. Request the erasure of their personal data.

5. Object to processing of their personal data.

Potentially each of the above is relevant if a person's image is used without their permission. This can become quite difficult and cumbersome to manage if a photograph or video which contains personal data has been integrated into an advertising or marketing campaign. Many issues can be avoided if the individual's informed consent is obtained up front. This is discussed in more detail later in this chapter and in Chapter 14.

The GDPR does not provide specific remedies related to image rights but does provide for general sanctions for breach of any of the above rights. Breaches of the GDPR obligations will be overseen by the European Data Protection Board (EDPB). On a day-to-day basis, they will be dealt with primarily by national supervisory authorities such as the ICO in the UK and the CNIL in France. These supervisory authorities are able to sanction infringing data holders by way of administrative fines or reprimands depending on the severity and nature of the breach.

When considering compliance it is worth having the worst case scenario in mind. The GDPR provides for maximum fines of up to 4 per cent of a business' global annual turnover or €20 million, whichever is higher. This is a maximum amount for very serious breaches and not a 'price tag' but it shows how seriously data protection is taken in the EU and the importance of careful compliance both in terms of image use and elsewhere. In practice, the supervisory authorities are encouraged to look at the circumstances of each individual case and award an appropriate fine depending on the individual circumstances. It is still early days for GDPR so it is difficult to say how it will work in the long term.

The GDPR states that individuals who have been subjected to a data breach have the right to seek compensation against the infringer. At the time of writing, there is no official guidance as to how this compensation should be quantified. In any event, individuals retain their right to make a complaint to their national supervisory authority or to utilise other routes for redress available at a national level, such as by recourse to local courts.

5.3   Trade marks and false endorsement

While it is possible for people to protect their likeness as a registered trade mark, in practice this is fairly unusual and only worth doing if the celebrity is trading under that precise image or one which is very similar. It is fairly easy to avoid infringing a trade mark for someone's likeness by using a different image of the same person.

Famous people can also object to their image being used on the basis that this use is a 'false endorsement'. In the UK, a false endorsement claim is brought on the basis of passing off; elsewhere in Europe they tend to be founded on unfair competition law or more generally bad faith.

French case law has long held that individuals can successfully object to their name[8] being used for commercial or advertising purposes provided the name is used in bad faith and creates a likelihood of confusion in the mind of its customers.[9] In practice, individuals who

---

8 See the French Supreme Court case: Civ.1 31 décembre 1978, Sieur de Rochechouart de Mortemart de Tonnay-Charentes c. dame Mortemard de Boisse.

9 See French Supreme Court Case: Cour de Cassation, Chambre civile 1, du 19 décembre 1967.

object to their name or image being used in relation to goods, products or services typically rely on a combination of privacy, bad faith and moral rights. The French Supreme Court has accepted the use of privacy arguments in false endorsement situations on the basis that 'the use of a person's image to promote works of art must have been authorised by that person, regardless as to whether or not that person's right to a private life had been affected or not'.[10] The French Supreme Court later clarified that 'anyone has the right to object to their image being reproduced, save when required in order to respect freedom of speech'.[11]

Further, the use of a person's image cannot go further than the limits of the authorisation that was given.[12] This means that if a celebrity has consented to their name and image being used in a press marketing campaign for a particular product, you cannot rely on the same consent to later use their name and image for clothing or accessories. The consent should clearly set out the limits of what can (and cannot) be done with a person's name or image.

5.4   The Rihanna T-shirt example

The most important English case on false endorsement in recent years concerns a T-shirt.

> The mere sale by a trader of a t-shirt bearing an image of a famous person is not, without more, an act of passing off. However the sale of this image of this person on this garment by this shop in these circumstances is a different matter. I find that Topshop's sale of this Rihanna t-shirt without her approval was an act of passing off.[13]

Rihanna is fairly ubiquitous in both pop and fashion circles. She is one of relatively few celebrities to have successfully made it into the fashion world and has lent her name and image to various high profile fashion ranges. Back in 2012, when she was on the cusp of fashion fame, she (and her manager) were understandably annoyed to see that Topshop

---

10 See French Supreme Court Ch. Civ. 1, 9 juillet 2009, Bull. 2009, I, no 175, pourvoi n° 07-19.758.

11 See French Supreme Court Case, 1re Civ., 24 septembre 2009, Bull. 2009, I, no 184, pourvoi n° 08-11.112.

12 See French Supreme Court Case 2e Civ., 4 novembre 2004, Bull. 2004, II, no 487, pourvoi n° 02-15.120.

13 *Fenty and Ors v Arcadia Group Brands Ltd (t/a Topshop) and Anor* [2013] EWHC 2310 at para. 71.

Figure 5.1   That Rihanna T-shirt – Fenty v Arcadia

were selling a T-shirt that used a very large picture of her on the front (see Figure 5.1) without her permission.

Topshop's supplier had paid the photographer for the right to use the image and the photographer had taken the image legitimately at a film shoot but Topshop did not have Rihanna's consent to use her image to sell T-shirts. Rihanna sued and the English court agreed that this sort of use was not acceptable.[14]

---

14 Ibid.

The judge reached this decision because he considered that:

1.   The fact that the photograph was taken while Rihanna was filming one of her music videos was a fairly strong indication that it could have been approved by Rihanna.

2.   There were many public links between Topshop and famous stars including Rihanna in particular. This increased the likelihood that customers would think the T-shirt was authorised by her.

3.   Although there was no explicit statement that Rihanna endorsed the product, for example on the swing tag or neck label, this absence was 'not strong enough to negate the impression the garment is authorised'.

4.   While many customers would not have thought about whether or not it was authorised, it would have mattered a lot to Rihanna's fans and the idea that the T-shirt is authorised would be part of what motivates them to buy the product.

Although the T-shirt was a high-quality product, this did not prevent the judge finding that Topshop's T-shirt was a false endorsement which damaged Rihanna's brand as she lost sales to her merchandising business and lost control over her reputation in the fashion sphere. This view was confirmed by the Court of Appeal.[15]

5.5   Statutory image rights

In France image rights are enshrined in the French Civil Code, which is founded on privacy rights. It is an exclusive right which belongs to each individual including French nationals, residents and those having their key economic interests in France. It is not always necessary to seek consent from the individual to be able to use their image, provided that the intended use does not prejudice their dignity or honour.

This means that provided the material is used for information purposes, specific consent is not required where individuals appear in photographs or footage of current events, or are filmed or photographed as part of their professional activities. However, these exceptions should

---

15   *Fenty and Ors v Arcadia and Anor* [2015] EWCA Civ 3.

be used with caution, particularly if the image is used in an advertising campaign.

 Traditionally, the French authorities are fairly strict on privacy matters. Individuals can complain directly to CNIL (the French data protection authority) which can order an injunction preventing the continued use of the individual's image and/or impose financial sanctions or official warnings on the offending party. These sanctions are published on CNIL's website and are often picked up by the wider media, creating further reputational harm for the businesses which are found to be at fault.

 Bear in mind that even if there is not a close connection with France, it is still possible that the French courts will find jurisdiction. Therefore even if France is not your primary market it is worth being aware of the French legal issues. For example, French courts have recently stated that they have jurisdiction if the:

1. images are available to the French public via a .fr domain or French publication;

2. individual's professional or personal activities are based in France; or

3. the image right breach occurred in France.

On this basis, the French courts recently held that they had jurisdiction to consider a case regarding photographs of HRH the Duke and Duchess of Cambridge (AKA Prince William and Kate Middleton) on holiday in the south of France which were featured in the French magazine, *Closer*.[16]

Germany also provides for statutory image rights.[17] This dates back to a famous incident where photographers entered the German Chancellor Otto von Bismarck's bedroom after he died in 1898 and sold the photographs that they took of his body to the highest bidder.[18] Protected images include any presentation of a person's appearance that enables

---

16 Tribunal correctionnel de Nanterre, jugement du 5 septembre 2017.

17 The Copyright in Works of Art and Photography Act 1907.

18 K. Hamacher and J. Schumacher, 'Germany's approach to publicity and image rights' 2008 September/October *World Trade Mark Review*.

them to be recognised; they therefore include, collages, sculptures and cartoons. Even the use of doppelgängers in advertising can invoke this right. For example, in 2002, the Dusseldorf Regional Court found in favour of Franz Beckenbauer, a German footballer, after they used his doppelgänger in a German advert.[19] As in the rest of Europe, German courts tend to grant more leniency to the press and less leniency to advertisers.

5.6   How to safely use another person's image

The upshot is that although image rights law varies widely across Europe, your safest course of action is to get an image rights waiver from anyone whose image you use in any form of advertising, whether on social media or otherwise. This waiver can be in the form of a model release and should be signed by the individual or, if they are under age,[20] by the individual's parents. Model releases are discussed in the context of archive material in Chapter 13.

Whether you get a 'model release' or an 'image rights waiver', essentially what you are asking for is a written consent that the subject is comfortable being filmed for specified purposes. It will consequently be difficult for them to successfully complain in the future. As a very rough rule of thumb, if you plan to focus on an individual for more than 0.5 seconds in a video or taking up more than 20 per cent of a still image, it is wise to get an image rights waiver from them.

Any consent should be obtained before the image is published and should list the specific intended uses. In many jurisdictions, such as France, an image rights waiver cannot be general or provided on a blanket basis. This means that if you plan to use photographs which were taken of someone, whether a celebrity, model or member of the public, in a new campaign (i.e., for a new purpose), you should obtain new consent from the individual for each project in which they are likely to be involved.

In many territories, including France, consent to be photographed or filmed does not equate to consent for your image to be published or broadcast (e.g., in the press or online). It is therefore important to

---

19 Regional Court of Dusseldorf, AfP 2002, 64.
20 Usually being underage means under 16 but it varies between countries.

ensure that you utilise carefully drafted image rights waivers to avoid any potential liability.

If you want to repost or share content on social media this is usually less of a problem as if someone has posted an image of themselves on social media they have usually given consent for reposting under the relevant site's terms and conditions. This does not mean that you can necessarily reuse an image someone else has posted on social media in a major advertising campaign but sharing it to your social media feed should be fine.

 To reduce the risk of a claim for breach of privacy and/or data protection rights, it is standard industry practice to place notices around any filming locations. These notices warn people that if they enter a particular area between certain hours they will be filmed and potentially used in, for example, a campaign video. Make sure you take photographs of the notices *in situ* so you can prove they were in place and visible.

In Poland, it is becoming a common practice in some industries to obtain employees' consent to photograph them and use their images on social media, for example, in order to post photos from an event. This may be a sign of things to come as awareness of the importance of controlling your image increases amongst celebrities and non-celebrities alike.

Needless to say, you should avoid using a celebrity's image without their written permission ideally in the form of a signed contract from their agent. This applies even if you have secured the copyright in that image.

5.7   Image, publicity or personality rights around the world

Some jurisdictions have a specific law of image rights. In some instances this is the product of case law encouraging particular legislation, in others, the motivation is less immediately obvious.[21] As mentioned at the start of the chapter, many US states have their own laws which protect the right of publicity including the right to prevent the appropriation of someone's name or likeness. This can be a particular issue

---

21 By way of example, the small island of Guernsey, part of the Channel Islands between the UK and France, recently created its own image rights law.

in advertising campaigns or use on social media. Unlike the situation with regards to privacy based image rights protection, the fame of the person is not relevant. The extent of protection varies on a state-to-state basis.

5.8   Criminal sanctions

Finally, in France, image rights are also governed by the French Criminal Code. If an individual considers that the publication of their image violates their right to a private life, they have six years from the publication date to file a complaint with the Criminal Court. If the court finds that there has been an infringement of someone's image rights the guilty party can face up to one year of imprisonment and a fine of €45,000. Bear in mind that simply sharing an image can be sufficient to meet the criminal law threshold.

6 Designs

Few industries benefit from design law protection more than fashion. European Union design law offers the ideal combination of protection for fashion items with a short-term unregistered right and a longer term registered right. While the unregistered right has proven popular, fashion businesses often do not take advantage of the registered right because it can appear complicated and there is a limited one year time period in which to register the design(s). Outside the EU, many countries offer design protection in one form or another, although often this is limited to registered rights.

Designs are not a single intellectual property right but rather a mixture of registered and unregistered, national and international rights (see Table 6.1). To make things even more complicated, there is substantial overlap with copyright law.

 Each option has its pros and cons as set out in more detail below.

6.1 Unregistered Community Designs

Unregistered Community Designs (UCD) cover the entire European Union.[1] UCD is an extremely flexible right. It arises automatically and can protect almost any design whether it is the whole or part of your product. For example, the whole of a bag could be protected as a UCD or just its clasp. UCD can protect shape, texture and surface decoration such as patterns or weaves on the product itself. It can even protect smaller two dimensional features such as logos. However, it does not protect internal features which are not visible in normal use. In practice this exclusion is less relevant to clothing but could apply, for example, to some types of packaging.

---

1 The EU used to be called the European Community. While trade mark law has successfully rebranded the Community trade mark as the EU trade mark, the same has yet to happen for Community designs.

Table 6.1   Designs in Europe – key points

Registered design (Community and national)	Unregistered Community Design	UK unregistered design right	Copyright
You must apply to register within 1 year of publication	Arises automatically upon publication	Arises automatically upon creation/first marketing	Arises automatically upon creation
Lasts up to 25 years (provided renewed every 5 years)	Last 3 years from publication	Lasts for the shorter of (i) 10 years from first marketing or (ii) 15 years from creation	Lasts for the life of the creator plus 70 years
Scope is set by the registration; it can include features of shape and surface decoration	Scope extends to most external product features including surface decoration provided they're new and not commonplace	Scope extends to the shape or configuration of the whole or part of a product provided it is sufficiently original It does not protect surface decoration	The work must be original/the author's own intellectual creation It can be difficult to protect 3D works using copyright
Use it to stop someone using a design with the same 'overall impression' as your registered design	Use it to stop someone copying your designs in a way which creates the same 'overall impression'	Use it to stop someone copying the whole or a 'substantial part' of one or more of your designs	Use it to stop someone copying the whole or a substantial part of your original artistic work

In order to have a valid UCD, the design must be new and have individual character. Essentially a design is new if it is not identical to an existing design. Designs are considered to be identical if the only differences are insignificant. This is interpreted fairly literally by the courts. For example, the French Supreme Court recently held that although a 'Derby' shoe design reproduced certain elements of earlier Derby shoes, it could still benefit from design right protection provided that no *identical* model had previously been disclosed to the public.[2]

---

2 J-M Weston and Manbow & Fiman Cour de cassation., civile, Chambre civile 1, 5 avril 2012, 10-27.373.

A valid UCD must also also have 'individual character'. This means that the overall visual impression that the design makes on an informed user must be sufficiently different from earlier published designs.

These limitations are important as they prevent a business obtaining a monopoly right over standard clothing items such as a vanilla T-shirt or boot cut jeans. This does not mean that you cannot get design protection for a T-shirt or jeans but the design must be 'new' and not 'commonplace' in the design field.

The designer's freedom is an important consideration which affects the scope of protection. If there is a large amount of design freedom, such as a dress, the scope of protection will be greater than a product where there is less design freedom, such as a watch.

 The major downside of UCD is that it only lasts for three years from the date that the design is first made available to the public. If the design is copied or misused before it is made available to the public such as following a trade secrets theft or computer hacking, the right is not triggered unless or until it is disclosed in its original form because you only have a UCD from the date of first public disclosure. If the design is not made available to the public, you would need to look at alternative causes of action such as misuse of confidential information or other trade secrets laws.

UCD is perfect for high-fashion items which may be out of fashion after three years. However, because the term of protection is so short, unless you act quickly and are able to get an interim injunction to remove the product from the shelves, you may only be entitled to damages (i.e., financial compensation) for the period from the infringing sales commencing to the UCD expiring.

6.2 Community and national registered designs

Accessories and classic products which tend to have a longer shelf life are best protected as a Registered Community Design or RCD. It is also a good idea to register your logo as a design as the test for design infringement is arguably wider than for trade mark infringement and it gives you a different line of attack. Registration gives you up to 25 years' protection provided renewal fees are paid every five years. You have one year to register your design from the date that you first disclose it to the public. This disclosure could be a drawing or photograph or marketing the product itself. This one year period is known as the 'grace period'.

It is possible to register designs at either the EU level (as an RCD) or the national level. As for trade marks, there is a Benelux registered design which covers Belgium, the Netherlands and Luxembourg. Because design laws have been harmonised (i.e., made consistent) across the EU, the registered design system across all current EU Member States, including Benelux, is fairly similar. The major difference is the time-frame for registration.

The same criteria for protection apply to RCD as for UCD. In other words, the design must be new and have individual character. However, the degree of attention that these requirements are given at the examination phase can vary between registries.

It is normally very quick to register a Community Design – in some circumstances, the registration can occur on the same day. This is because the EUIPO does not examine designs to see if they meet the novelty or individual character requirement. The design registries in Member States tend to examine registered designs in more detail but it is normally much faster to register a design than a trade mark.

Unlike trade marks and patents, there is no opposition period for registered designs. If you want to challenge a design, you have to either apply to invalidate it at the relevant intellectual property office or file a counterclaim to invalidate it in any court proceedings which allege that you have infringed the design. In some, but not all EU jurisdictions, it is also possible to apply to a national court for a declaration of non-infringement of a registered design. For example, this is available in England but not in France.

Overall, in England, at least, it appears to be easier to rely on unregistered designs, where the precise design can be identified once the infringement is known, than registered designs where you have to select the design in advance. This is despite the fact that, in order to succeed in an unregistered design claim, it is necessary to prove that the design was copied.

This variation in outcome between registered and unregistered design cases is largely anecdotal so may not withstand more detailed scrutiny.

The difference (if it exists) is arguably due to a lack of thought at the registration stage rather than any fundamental failing in the registered design system.

When registering your design you have to think about which features are particularly distinctive and likely to be copied as well as whether the proposed design is sufficiently new to be protected. Bear in mind that even if a design passes the new and not commonplace tests, if these features are not what someone is likely to copy then the registration is of limited use. Designs registration strategy is discussed later in this chapter at section 6.7.

There are specific limitations on design protection in various other circumstances such as where the features relied upon in the design are dictated purely by their technical function. Care must also be taken when dealing with spare parts, complex products and products which must be a particular shape in order to function. These issues are far more relevant to the car, mechanical and electronics industries than to the fashion industry but they could become more of an issue as wearables and other technologies enter the fashion mainstream.

Designs that are contrary to public order and general morality and computer programs are expressly excluded from being capable of design protection. No obscene images or binary on the designs register, please! Other restrictions on design registration include the registration of someone else's trade mark or protected symbols such as national flags.

6.3 UK unregistered design right

The UK unregistered design right sounds similar to registered designs and unregistered Community designs but it is fairly different. As the name suggests, it only applies in the UK. Unlike Community designs, UK unregistered design right (UDR) only protects the whole or a part of a product's shape and configuration. This means that UDR does not protect surface decoration, including logos and texture. Nevertheless, UDR is an important right as the UK is a fairly large market and the right lasts a lot longer than UCD (effectively ten years). It is a shame for the fashion industry that this Cinderella right is so often overlooked.

Two recent cases have considered UK UDR for clothing. The first found that there was UDR in a Superdry hooded gilet where the sweatshirt style hood could be removed from the more traditional body of the gilet using fastenings which were not visible in use.[3] The second found UDR in some G-Star RAW jeans which were made using an unusual connection of panels.[4]

In other words, even if you are limited to the shape and configuration of a product's design, UDR can still be a very useful right for the fashion industry, not least because it lasts for around seven years longer than a UCD.

A design qualifies for UDR if one or more of its designers is an EU citizen or from another qualifying country which has a reciprocal arrangement with the UK (including Hong Kong and New Zealand). This means that most European businesses can prevent infringement of the right in the UK even if they are not a UK business but US, Chinese and other international businesses may face greater difficulties.

Although UDR usually lasts for a maximum of ten years, the final five years are a licence of right period where you have to offer a licence to an infringer on reasonable market terms if they are willing to take a licence.

6.4   Designs in court

Designs cases are less regular courtroom visitors than many other rights. This may be in part because many potential litigants are not familiar with the opportunities they provide.

6.4.1   A different Karen Millen example

The CJEU confirmed that when assessing Community designs, the courts of Member States should take a fairly broad view of designs.[5] The CJEU provided this judgment following a reference from the Irish Supreme Court in relation to the sale of particular blue and brown shirts and black knit tops by Dunnes Stores in Ireland. Karen Millen Fashions Limited (a UK company) considered that the garments sold

---

3 *DKH Retail Ltd v H. Young (Operations) Ltd* [2014] EWHC 4034 (IPEC).

4 *G-Star Raw Cv v Rhodi Ltd and Ors* [2015] EWHC 216 (Ch).

5 *Karen Millen Fashions Ltd v Dunnes Stores & Dunnes Stores (Limerick) Ltd* Case C-345/13 ECLI:EU:C:2014:2013.

by Dunnes Stores were infringing copies of its UCDs. Dunnes Stores did not deny that it had copied the Karen Millen clothing but tried to claim that the tops did not have individual character on the basis of several earlier items of clothing.

The CJEU disagreed with this approach and ruled that the question of whether a design has individual character depends on whether the overall impression that the design has on the informed user is different to a *single earlier design*. In other words, you cannot pick and mix features from earlier designs in order to invalidate a design. This confirms that designs have a fairly broad scope of protection. Therefore, even if the design does not appear to be massively different to what has gone before, if a single earlier item which has the same overall impression cannot be found, it will be a valid design.

6.4.2   The French swimwear example

In a recent case before the Paris Court,[6] TRB International, the owner of the 'Vilebrequin' swim short brand brought an infringement claim against Kiwi, a clothing company based in Saint Tropez. The case concerned an RCD for a combination of lobster and pineapple images. Kiwi claimed that the RCD was invalid because it was not sufficiently new or different from earlier designs, in other words Kiwi said that the RCD lacked novelty and individual character.

The French court considered that the informed user of the design was either a professional in the fashion industry, or the end-buyer of swim wear. Because there was no combination of pineapples and lobsters in any of the earlier designs (or prior art) identified by the court and none of these earlier designs contained all of the characteristics of the RCD, Kiwi could not invalidate the design. This shows how broad the protection for registered designs can be and what an opportunity they present for the fashion industry.

6.5   Dealing in designs

As indicated above, you have *one year* from the date that you first make a design available to the public in which to register it. Bear in mind that if you release an earlier version of the design, unless the final version

---

6   TGI Paris, 3e ch., 27 mai 2016, n° 2014/18079.

is dramatically different, the clock starts ticking from the date the first design is disclosed. Keep track of these time periods and be ready to register as early as possible.

If you consider that a design has been registered in breach of: (i) your rights (such as trade marks, copyright or unregistered designs); or (ii) a legal or contractual obligation, you can make a claim before the courts to be declared as the owner. In some jurisdictions, there is a time limit for bringing this entitlement claim. For example, in France you have five years.

It is important to decide at an early stage how designs should be held, filed or transferred between a designer and a fashion company. Make sure you monitor any confidentiality agreements or potential unauthorised filings of your design.

In most jurisdictions where there is a registered right, if you assign, licence or mortgage a registered design, you must ensure that these changes are recorded on the relevant design register, such as the EUIPO, using a standard application form. This must include the contract or other official document evidencing the change. It is possible to register a short-form contract which does not set out the purchase price. As with many administrative formalities in European jurisdictions, it is often important that any original document that is not in the relevant registry's language be accompanied by a certified translation. Failure to carry out this formality can mean that any changes to the ownership would not be enforceable against third parties.

6.6 Classification of designs

You can register up to 99 designs in a single application at the EUIPO provided that they are all in the same Locarno class.[7] This a standard classification system for designs which has helped to provide consistency in the description of designs worldwide. The most relevant classes for the fashion industry are class 2 (Articles of Clothing and Haberdashery), class 3 (Travel Goods, Cases, Parasols and Personal Belongings, Not Elsewhere Specified) and class 11 (Articles of Adornment – including jewellery). Unlike trade marks, the use of the

---

7 The Locarno classification system is now in its 11th edition (last updated 1 January 2017).

class system is primarily as a search tool and design protection is not limited to designs in that particular class.

6.7   Designs registration strategy

The most future proof strategy is to register your designs at different levels of specificity. For example:

1.   a line drawing of the whole product and any unusual parts of the product such as a jacket collar or bag clasp;

2.   a CAD drawing of the same item with shading to indicate depth and tone and colour contrasts; *and*

3.   a photograph of the actual product with branding removed to protect against close copies of the design.

RCDs can cover both two dimensional and three dimensional objects. This means that a logo, patterns and textures can all be registered as two dimensional designs.

If your design is three dimensional, you will want to ensure that each possible face is registered – you can include up to seven views of a product in a design application. Registering at different levels of specificity is a more expensive approach but intellectual property offices offer economies of scale for designs so the more you register for a particular product, the cheaper each design becomes. At the EUIPO (at least) it is also possible to register a 3D CAD shape which can be moved around so that each face is visible (although you still have to select seven particular views). Overall, Community designs are fairly cheap to register and as they offer 25 years' exclusivity, they are well worth the effort for core products.

For UCD and all European registered designs including RCDs you can only protect parts of a product which are visible during the product's 'normal use' (which excludes maintenance or repair) of the product. For example, while the interior of a handbag could be protected, any features which are hidden beneath the lining could not be registered.

Unlike patents where you lose the right to register a valid patent the moment you tell anyone about your invention (outside obligations of confidence), you have one year from the date of publication in which to register a design. This one year 'grace period' applies at an EU and national level and is replicated in many international design systems.

The EUIPO does not examine RCD applications to see whether they are new and sufficiently different to other designs in the field. However, they will check the application to ensure that it meets with the core filing requirements such as a clear representation, good picture quality, etc. This means that it is very easy to get an RCD but the resulting right is open to fairly easy challenge by third parties in the future.

Finally, if a design is very commercially sensitive, it is possible to delay publication of the design for up to 30 months.

6.8   Registered designs outside the EU

Many jurisdictions outside the EU also have a registered design regime.

6.8.1   Switzerland

Switzerland has a registered design system which is very similar to RCDs. As Switzerland is not a member of the EU, if Switzerland is an important territory for your business, you need to register your design there as well.

6.8.2   Russia and Japan

Russia also requires you to file a list of the essential features which characterise the design prior to granting the right. Japan's design system only allows a six-month grace period. Therefore if Japan is an important market for you, you will need to pay close attention to the timing in order to secure protection there. It is also possible to get design patent registration in China for innovative fashion designs. This can be a useful right, particularly in terms of registering it with Customs and starting an administrative action.

6.8.3   Australia

In Australia it is possible to register a wide range of 2D and 3D designs including the patterns applied to materials such as fabric or leather as well as packaging and even the layout of a store. It is also possible to file a statement of newness and distinctiveness with a registered design. The features which are identified in this statement are given particular attention when assessing the design as a whole. This can be helpful if the rest of the design is fairly common provided the features copied by any future infringer are those identified as 'new'.

Like the EU, the Australian registration system does not require any formal examination of designs prior to registration. However, if you own an Australian registered design, it must be examined by the registry before it can be used in infringement proceedings. Indeed it is open to anyone to request examination of an Australian registered design at any time so if you are accused of infringing or want to clear a design which might block your business, it is open to you to request examination of the design.

6.8.4   The US

In the US, many types of design can be protected as design patents. Unlike the EU, it can take a long time to be granted a design patent and it is quite a lot more expensive. However, the rigorous examination process leaves you with a stronger right which can be easier to enforce against infringers.

6.8.5   Canada

Canada protects industrial designs which have been applied to a finished article. Design protection cannot exist in the abstract and has a higher threshold for protection than the EU. Unlike the EU and Australia, in order to get an industrial design in Canada, the design is examined by comparing it with pending, registered and published designs for similarities. The design will only be registered if it is sufficiently different from earlier designs.

6.9   Filing designs internationally

6.9.1   The Hague system

 Rather than registering in each country, it is possible to register across several territories[8] via the Hague system. This is an international system

---

8 At the last count 62 territories.

which is administered by WIPO (following the Hague Agreement). As for trade marks, it is possible to claim priority in the six months following the first application for a design. So if you register a design in the EU within the one year grace period you have a further six months from the date of the EU registration to claim priority in relation to a design filed elsewhere in the world. However, watch out if you want to register in Japan because of its shorter, six-month, grace period. Overall, it can be harder to claim priority under the designs system because the laws are less consistent in relation to designs than trade marks and the searches done by the various design offices can throw up very different prior designs.

6.9.2   How long does design protection last around the world?

The EU, Brazil and Russia offer the most generous term of protection – up to 25 years, provided the design is renewed by paying a fee every five years (or in the case of Brazil ten years). Most other countries have a maximum ten year term (Canada) or 15 year term (Argentina, Australia, Mexico), the US has a 20 year term.

7   Other important rights

7.1   Passing off, unfair competition and trade dress

 Even if you do not have any registered rights and you are out of time to rely on an Unregistered Community Design (UCD), you may have a remedy via the goodwill you have generated in your name and/ or the 'get up' or 'trade dress'[1] of your products (i.e., their 'design' in the industry sense of the word). This can include the packaging, appearance of products, particularly perfume bottles and bags which are often highly distinctive, and potentially even things such as your store's layout. This is particularly the case if the get up is very distinctive.

This goodwill may give you the ability to prevent a third party from using the same name or get up provided you can show that your get up pre-dates the third party, is distinctive and is relied on, at least to some extent, to tell consumers that the goods originate from or are associated with you. There must also be some form of consumer confusion or deception (the exact test varies between territories). This can be expensive to prove as substantial evidence is often required, including potentially survey evidence which is both expensive to obtain and can be risky to rely on. Consequently, you are always in a much stronger position if you have registered rights. If your product's get up is important to your brand identity, spend the time and money registering your designs as registered Community designs (RCD) within the one year grace period from first publication.

Apart from copyright, which is partially harmonised but still far from consistent, and UCD there is limited harmonisation of unregistered rights in the EU. This means that the available rights and the application of those rights can vary substantially. Some examples of the different unregistered rights are below but even where they have the same

---

1 'Get up' is the term used in the UK, 'trade dress' in the US and 'distinguishing guise' in Canada.

name in different countries (such as trade secrets), the application does not tend to be consistent and can vary even within regions.

These unregistered rights are discussed in more detail in the context of infringement of rights in Chapter 20.

7.2   Patents

One of the most expensive intellectual property mistakes you can make is to disclose a patentable invention before you have applied to register it as a patent.

Patents protect things that are new and inventive, including products and the way in which they are manufactured. New and inventive fabrics such as Gore Tex, connected clothing, skin care products, product packaging, interwoven LEDs and movement tracking accessories have been or could potentially be protected as patents. In addition to the products themselves, the method of manufacture can also be protected as a patent, again this is only if the patent is for something new and inventive. In return for the time and money spent on developing innovative new products, patent protection provides a monopoly for patent holders for up to 20 years per patented invention. There are limits to what can be patented. For example, software cannot be patented without some form of 'real world' impact – known as a 'technical contribution' or 'technical effect'. Similarly, a new business method cannot be patented in Europe, although the US is more flexible on this point.

The moment you share your idea with the public it is no longer new and therefore not eligible for patent protection. This means that if you tell people about your idea, you could lose a potential monopoly before you even get started. This often occurs when public pronouncements are made on social media or a founder or other key employee leaves taking your confidential information with them.

A patent is a legal document which sets out the context for the invention (what people are currently doing), why the invention is necessary (the problems with the status quo) and how the invention solves these problems (the solution). It is primarily a text description but there are usually diagrams or drawings which accompany the text and help to describe the invention. The important part of the patent comes from the 'claims' at the back of the patent document. The claims are a series of numbered paragraphs which set out the scope of a patent's protection. Each claim is considered separately. Usually they are structured with one or more 'independent claims' (which are very broad) followed by 'dependent claims' which limit the scope of the independent claim (for example, to a particular range).

 Patents are expensive, take a long time to be granted and, if you want global protection, you need to get separate patents in more or less every territory worldwide. The fees associated with this are huge, not to mention the large translation bill. In practice, most people register in their key current and intended markets, their place of manufacture and China. China is important to include because it is a major market and remains the global manufacturing centre so even if you do not manufacture there, it is likely that your competitors will do so.

As long as you file any foreign applications within 12 months of the date you filed your first patent application (the 'priority date'), each foreign application should get the same priority date. This is important because if two patent applications claiming the same invention are filed in the same country on different dates, the patent will be awarded to the one with the earlier priority date. Even if the patent is granted it would be fairly easy for someone to 'invalidate' (i.e., 'revoke') it in the future when you try to rely upon it.

If you do not claim the priority date after 12 months, you need to make sure that your foreign applications are filed before your first patent application is published, this usually takes around 18 months from the date you filed the first patent (the 'filing date'). If you miss this deadline, your invention will be in the public domain and any foreign applications you make will likely fail because they are not 'new'.

Patents are all about long-term returns on investment, and so they tend to work less well for fast-paced industries like fashion. However, this may change as wearable fashion and fashion technology generally becomes more mainstream.

 The most well-known patents in the fashion industry tend to revolve around sportswear and textiles. For example, an English Court of Appeal case between a patent owner, Stretchline, and H&M[2] concerned Stretchline's patent for a specific style of fusible yarn bonding

---

2   *Stretchline Intellectual Properties Ltd v H&M Hennes & Mauritz UK Ltd* [2017] EWCA Civ 199.

creating tubular fabric for use in underwired garments such as bras. The court considered whether Stretchline's patent was valid and, if so, whether H&M had infringed the patent by selling underwear containing Stretchline's technology without consent. H&M lost on both counts and had to pay damages in the form of lost royalties as well as Stretchline's legal costs.

A further example of patents being used to protect innovation in sportswear can be seen in the 'Smart Sensing Technology' utilised by Nike as part of its Nike+ Sensor range. Nike along with Asics Corp, Hexoskin and the French start-up, Cityzen Sciences, and consortium have filed several patents for the use of integrated sensors in thread fibres, T-shirts and footwear. They allow the wearer to monitor speed, heart rate and location, as well as gathering information about their blood pressure, insulin levels and body temperature.

7.3   Database right

Databases can be protected by copyright, provided they are sufficiently original. In addition, the EU has a separate standalone database right[3] which protects the investment that goes into creating a database. A database is defined as 'a collection of independent works, data or other materials arranged in a systematic or methodical way and individually accessible by electronic or other means'. This broad definition can cover a wide range of media but explicitly does not cover the computer programs which are used to create the database. Importantly, database right is separate to any rights in the data itself. For example, you may own a database of photographs which have been used in shows, on social media, in press clippings or similar but that does not mean that you own the rights in any of the photographs themselves.

The EU database right lasts for 15 years but the timer is reset every time there is a substantial modification to the database so in theory it can last indefinitely. If you own a database you can prevent other people from:

---

3 Directive 96/9/EC on the legal protection of databases.

1. copying the whole or part of the database;

2. making any adaptations or alterations to the database; or

3. sharing the database.

Database rights are increasingly important for the fashion industry and will become more of a battleground as the line between technology and retail continues to blur.

7.4   Utility models

Utility models are so similar to patents that they are sometimes known as 'petty patents' and can often be converted into patents. Like patents they protect inventions but unlike patents they tend to be restricted to mechanical features in a machine or device (rather than methods of doing something) and are only available in a few countries such as Germany, China and Japan. They are therefore of limited use to the average fashion business but are worth considering if you have some innovative packaging feature such as a perfume bottle or scarf.

Because utility models are not normally examined to check whether they are novel or inventive and last for a much shorter period of time (between six and 15 years), they are seen as of lesser value.[4]

7.5   Confidential information and trade secrets

Business ideas, new distribution platforms, product formulae, techniques and processes, key contacts, great factories which you have identified can be difficult to protect by means of the rights set out above. However, this and similar information is often critical to a business' success. If it has been kept secret, this sort of information can be protected under trade secrets law, also known as the laws of confidence. In the EU confidential information can arise automatically or following signature of a contract.

---

4 You can read more about utility models on the WIPO website here: http://www.wipo.int/sme/en/ ip_business/utility_models/utility_models.htm.

Trade secrets can be a very useful tool in terms of stopping activity which does not neatly fall within one of the more traditional intellectual property rights. It is a particularly common issue when an employee leaves a business as key information such as supplier terms or software can often disappear at the same time. It can also be helpful protection when pitching products to new businesses. It is not unheard of for a pitch to a major retailer to 'inspire' their products in next season's collection. If the designs you pitched were never made public, they will not be protected by UCD and copyright can be difficult to rely on, particularly if the design is three dimensional. It may be possible to show that the items disclosed constituted confidential information and consequently you can stop further use and claim back damages.

The law of 'trade secrets' (i.e., confidential information) was stand- ardised across the EU from 9 June 2018. Now all EU countries should define the different ways of misappropriating trade secrets and provide that reverse engineering and parallel innovation are permitted. There is also consistency in terms of the available remedies for misuse of a trade secret including stopping unlawful use and further disclosure and removal from the market of goods that have been manufactured following use of misappropriated trade secrets.

Confidential information is usually contractually protected in two ways:

1. in a specific agreement – there are lots of different names for this but they all essentially do the same thing (e.g., non-disclosure agreement (NDA), confidentiality disclosure agreement (CDA), proprietary information agreement, or a secrecy agreement); or

2. in a clause within a wider agreement such as an employment contract.

If there is a contract then the stronger the wording and greater the clarity about what is confidential, the better. It is also important that you have a clear record of precisely what was disclosed, to whom and when. No matter how robust the language of the contract if you cannot prove that something you consider to be confidential was disclosed under the contract you will struggle to start any sort of successful legal dialogue.

Even if you do not have a formal contract, if you disclose confidential information under explicit obligations of confidence then you can rely on either equitable duties of confidence (in Common Law jurisdictions) or trade secrets law to protect you.

Regardless of the method of protection, confidential information generally has certain characteristics. The following are taken from English case law but the basic principles apply to any form of confidential information:[5]

1. It must be capable of being realised as a finished product (i.e., it must be more than saying 'wouldn't it be nice if...') for example 'we could achieve X if we do Y'.

2. A simple solution to a problem can be sufficient to qualify as confidential information.[6]

3. Where the confidential information is an idea it must contain some significant element of originality, be clearly identified as an idea, be commercially attractive and be capable of actual realisation.

4. It can be disclosed by any method so an oral disclosure at a meeting is sufficient.

Once confidential information is in the public domain, it ceases to be confidential although this does not prevent a wronged party from obtaining an injunction against further use by someone who misused their confidential information.[7]

7.5.1   What if you use confidential information without knowing it belonged to someone else?

If somebody receives information that has been disclosed in breach of confidence that person is also under a duty of confidence if and when they know that the information was obtained in breach of confidence.[8] If someone alleges breach of confidence you will need to quickly establish what happened and whether the information is truly confidential.

---

5 *De Maudsley v Palumbo* [1996] EMLR 460 at 469–70.

6 *Cranleigh Precision Engineering Ltd v Bryant* [1965] 1 WLR 1293 at 1308 and 1310.

7 *BBC v HarperCollins Publishers Ltd* [2010] EWHC 2424.

8 *Campbell v MGN Ltd* [2002] EWCA Civ 1373; [2003] QB 633.

This depends on having an open and honest discussion with the people involved including staff, distributors, agents or contractors.

7.5.2   The Trade Secrets Directive

Each Member State has recently been required to implement a minimum standard of protection for trade secrets in their jurisdiction.[9] A 'trade secret' means information which meets all of the following requirements:

1. it is secret in the sense that it is not generally known among or readily accessible to persons within the circles that normally deal with the kind of information in question;

2. it has a commercial value because it is secret; and

3. the person in control of the secret has taken reasonable steps to keep it secret.[10]

This is a minimum standard so the exact level of protection offered can still vary between Member States.

7.5.3   Trade secrets around the world

There have been various attempts to make trade secrets law more consistent around the world via international treaties. TRIPS (the Agreement on Trade Related Aspects of Intellectual Property Rights) is the main source for this international legislation.[11] TRIPS has been entered into by all members of the WTO and consequently includes all EU Member States.[12] It requires all signatories to protect undisclosed information[13] provided that it has commercial value and reasonable steps have been taken to ensure that it is kept secret.

TRIPS secured minimum standards for a wide variety of rights. For example, the copyright term was set at a minimum of 50 years unless

---

9 The Trade Secrets Directive (EU) 2016/943.

10 Ibid., Art. 2(1).

11 See TRIPS, Art. 39; https://www.wto.org/english/docs_e/legal_e/27-trips.pdf.

12 For example, in most US States (47 out of 50), trade secrets are protected by the Uniform Trade Secrets Act 1985 ('UTSA'). Among other things UTSA offers remedies for misappropriation of trade secrets including an injunction to stop continued use of the trade secret.

13 Information which has not been made publicly available.

linked to the life of the author. Because WTO membership is conditional on members also signing up to TRIPS, and the sanctions for non-compliance with TRIPS are handled by the WTO's enforcement mechanism, it has been a very effective means of setting minimum standards for businesses worldwide.

7.6   Geographical indications and traditional knowledge

Champagne, Stilton Cheese, Parma Ham and Tequila are all products which you may have heard of – or even consumed! Each of these products is protected as a geographical indication or GI. If a product is protected by a GI it means that the name of the product corresponds to a particular place (i.e., the Champagne valley, Melton Mowbray, Parma and Tequila, respectively). They operate in a similar way to a certification mark, i.e., in order to apply the GI to a product, it is necessary to meet certain criteria regarding, for example the constituent parts or manufacture. The most important criterion for a GI is that the product in question must originate from a specific location. It is possible to get GIs at an EU level and from many individual countries such as France, Italy and Mexico.

 As the list above suggests, GIs are most commonly associated with agricultural products. In some countries they can also be used in relation to non-agricultural products including glass, handcrafts and some types of fabrics.[14] Currently there are no non-agricultural GIs at an EU level but there is a general movement in favour of extending GI protection to non-agricultural products so this may change in the not so distant future.

Currently, it is possible to prevent a third party using, for example, Harris Tweed or Savile Row for fabric or tailoring respectively, based on passing off, misleading advertising or unfair competition law. In some circumstances, there may be certification marks in place, or less commonly, trade marks. It will be easier to prevent this use when non-agricultural GIs are introduced by the EU.

There is a certain amount of cross-over between GIs and traditional knowledge. This is because the qualifying criteria for a GI could be the traditional artistic heritage developed in a particular geographical

---

14 For example, Murano glass is protected in Italy.

location. Therefore while GIs do not directly protect traditional knowledge, they can help to safeguard the use, name and method for future generations. This protection is important but limited as a GI cannot stop someone using the same method under a different name.

7.7   Domain names

Domain names are not technically an intellectual property right but rather a contractual right which functions in a similar way to leasing a shop, except this time the shop is online. They can be very valuable as they signpost customers to your online business and it is easy to get into a mess if you do not get your domain names in order. They are often an ancillary issue in intellectual property disputes, particularly those involving trade marks and, to a lesser extent, copyright.

Domain names are divided between global level top level domains ('gTLDs') such as .com or .net and country-code top level domains ('ccTLDs') such as .eu, .us and .co.uk. They are easy to register via third party domain registries such as GoDaddy. They are considered in more detail in Chapters 3 and 20.

7.8   Labelling

It is very helpful when it comes to infringement proceedings if you have added a label somewhere on the packaging or product which identifies at a minimum which registered rights apply to the product. This can be done by adding the ™ symbol next to the registered trade mark or the D in a circle symbol to demonstrate that there are design rights. Ideally there will also be a link to a page on your website which sets out your registered rights and/or the relevant registration number (this is particularly important for registered designs). Similarly the © symbol can be used in relation to any copyright material such as text or patterns on the fabric. This is commonly added together with the identity of the copyright owner and the date of creation.

To avoid overstating the rights position, in addition to the symbols you can say something like 'This product is protected by intellectual property rights around the world; for a full list of the rights we commonly rely on please see our website.'

Be careful when using the trade mark symbols ® and ™. In some territories, e.g., Germany and Poland, it can be an offence or breach unfair competition law to use these symbols if the mark is not registered somewhere in the EU.

7.9   What's on the horizon?

 One of the big changes to intellectual property is the long-awaited unified patent. This is a patent which covers most of the EU and consequently could save the major patent filers of the world a fortune in filing fees and open up patents to small- and medium-sized enterprises (SMEs) who might not previously have bothered. It could also open the door to many more businesses who make their money from licensing patents[15] taking a greater interest in Europe. It was conceived prior to the Brexit vote and is now subject to a constitutional challenge in Germany so its future is far from clear. If it comes into force it offers the opportunity of obtaining patent protection for most of the EU coupled with the risk of someone else using a Unified Patent to stop you selling across the whole of Europe. Patents are not often considered by the world of fashion but as wearable technology and smart fabrics take off it will become increasingly important for the industry.

7.9.1   Brexit

 Brexit, or the UK's withdrawal from the EU, is looming ever closer on the horizon. What this will entail in practice is still uncertain – and is likely to remain so for some time. In reality, even after the UK leaves the EU, it will still have to follow EU law so it is unlikely that the principles and laws set out in this book will change dramatically at least in the short term. There is more detail on what Brexit could mean in practice in Chapter 26.

---

15 These non-practising entities are often better known by the pejorative term 'patent troll'.

PART III

Getting your business started

When you are setting up a new business there are lots of competing interests for your time from finance and marketing to hiring new staff. Each of these issues has a legal angle and as with intellectual property, thinking through a few fundamental issues in advance and making strategic decisions from a position of knowledge and appreciation of the relative costs will save you money, frustration and heartache down the line. This part of the book looks at everything from company incorporation and funding to contracts and in particular agency agreements.

8 Before you incorporate your company

Most fashion businesses are founded by a special combination of creativity and business acumen. There are a few exceptional people who combine these talents in one but more often than not a fashion business is started as a team effort. This can cause tensions down the line if insufficient thought is put into the structure of the business at the outset. This chapter focuses on the key things to consider when setting up a new business. It is not a comprehensive guide and, as with everything else in this book, it is intended to give a flavour of the issues rather than set out a comprehensive list of issues to follow across the EU. It is no substitute for legal advice.

8.1 Choosing your legal structure

 There are lots of different business structures from sole trader to partnership. In purely tax terms, it can be financially beneficial to start trading as a sole trader or a partnership and then incorporate as a company down the line. A company's main benefit is that it can protect you from personal liability; it can also lend the appearance of professionalism and may be necessary to conclude some contracts. However, do not assume that incorporating immediately is essential. It is important that you work out your objectives, projected revenue and ultimate business plan and tie this into the structure that is right for you as your business evolves.

Having said that, by far and away the most common structure for fashion businesses is a limited company. Companies offer enormous flexibility in terms of share structure, decision making and the opportunity to scale up or get new cash flow easily.

The great advantage of a company is that you are not responsible for the business risk as an individual but via a separate legal entity – a company. At its simplest, this means that if your company becomes insolvent, is sued or otherwise subject to a large and unexpected liability, you are much less vulnerable to being made personally bankrupt as a result.

The company location will influence your funding opportunities, business model and potential liability. For example, in Europe, the default position is that a party is sued in their home jurisdiction. In the case of a company it is the place where they are incorporated. While you may get a tax break to incorporate in a particular jurisdiction, if you are concerned about your legal exposure and you are unfamiliar with the language or legal customs, it may not be the best location for you.

Each country in Europe has slightly different company incorporation requirements and associated costs. France, for example, has three types of company: Société à responsabilité limitée (SARL), Société anonyme (SA) and Société par actions simplifiée (SAS). Meanwhile England and Wales have two main types of commercial company: a private limited company (Ltd) or public limited company (plc). Germany has two types of private limited company, the GmbH (by far the most common) and UG (or mini GmbH). Public German companies have the suffix AG.

By and large, companies start life as the smaller and simpler type of company (such as SARL, Ltd or GmbH) and may graduate to a larger public company such as an SA, plc or AG. Many EU countries now have very fast company incorporation processes. For example, in England and Poland you can fast track your application and be incorporated in around 24 hours. It can take slightly longer, around three to four days in France. Each company type will have different requirements which will include a minimum share capital which can range from £1 or €1 for a Ltd or UG to €50,000 for an AG. The amount of regulation also varies substantially between smaller private limited companies and public companies which are listed on a stock exchange.

The taxes you are liable for will vary depending on where you have a business location. The exact nuances of the European tax system are both complex and changeable. Understand what you are signing up to, particularly if you plan to incorporate in a country with whose laws and culture you are unfamiliar.

8.2 What is a company?

A company is a new legal 'person' which has its own separate identity. At its simplest a company is used to separate personal assets from business assets but companies come into their own when looking to raise funding, working with several people and planning for a business' future. In addition, there can be significant tax benefits to incorporating a company.

Since June 2017, all EU Member States have had publicly accessible databases of companies which include the registered office, directors' names, shareholdings, articles of association (i.e., the rules which govern how the company operates) and accounts filed since incorporation.[1] Some countries such as England and Wales make this information freely available online. Others have it available in return for a relatively small payment.

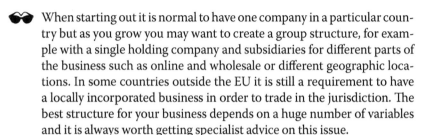 When starting out it is normal to have one company in a particular country but as you grow you may want to create a group structure, for example with a single holding company and subsidiaries for different parts of the business such as online and wholesale or different geographic locations. In some countries outside the EU it is still a requirement to have a locally incorporated business in order to trade in the jurisdiction. The best structure for your business depends on a huge number of variables and it is always worth getting specialist advice on this issue.

It is possible to have different types of share to match the many different types of potential shareholder. Consequently, shares can be voting or non-voting, be worth more or less than other shares, or can get preferential treatment if there is an insolvency. In other words, each class of share can have different levels of power and risk associated with them.

You should think about what could happen to these shares in the future. For example, what happens if:

1. someone wants to leave the business?

2. one or more of the shareholders disagrees about the strategic direction of the business?

---

1 See this website which is maintained by the European Commission for details: https://e-justice.europa.eu/content_business_registers-104-en.do.

3. you want to issue more shares to investors or as employee incentives?

4. one of the founders is considered by the others to not be pulling their weight?

5. someone wants to withdraw the assets or cash which they have invested in the business?

6. someone wants to sell the business but not all shareholders are in agreement about whether to sell, the selling price and/or the proposed purchaser?

The best way of approaching these issues is to think about them carefully at the outset and then make sure that you have a written agreement which binds everyone to the desired approach.

Bear in mind that the timing for issuing shares can be important from a tax perspective. For example, from a capital gains point of view, it is not always beneficial to issue shares at the outset as the capital gain from nothing (unless a company immediately takes ownership of assets, shares are usually worth nothing when a company first incorporates) to something will always be greater than if the shares are issued further down the line.

8.3   The 50:50 split

Where there are two co-founders the natural thing to do is for each co-founder to have 50 per cent of the shares. However, this can cause major problems in the future if there is a fundamental disagreement about the company's direction.

According to research conducted by Harvard Business Review (HBR) in 2016,[2] 'even the best of ideas can falter when the founding team neglects to carefully consider early decisions about the team: the relationships, roles, and rewards that will make the founders a winning team'. With that in mind, the timing and division of equity are important.

---

2 https://hbr.org/2016/02/the-very-first-mistake-most-startup-founders-make.

There is a temptation to agree on an equity division before you have started working together, this is particularly the case when a business is founded by friends. However, the time and significance of different people's contributions tends to not be immediately evident. In many instances, an unequal split is a fairer outcome provided it reflects the reality of everyone's contributions. According to HBR's research, the longer that founding teams spend negotiating and considering each party's contributions, the greater the likelihood of an unequal split. As they put it, 'the harder you look, the more likely you are to discover important differences' between co-founders. These differences can be extremely positive but if one person is quitting their job and dedicating 100 per cent of their time and money to a project, it can be very damaging if their 50:50 co-founder is not doing the same. HBR found that this problem is particularly pronounced where families work together.

Investors are not fans of 50:50 splits. According to HBR's research, 'companies that have equal splits have more difficulty raising outside finance, especially venture capital'. Venture capitalists invest in fewer than one out of every 100 companies, so an equal split 'can send worrisome signals about the team's ability to negotiate with others and to deal with difficult issues themselves'. HBR noted that in their research equal splits tend to be more a symptom than the cause of trouble. In other words, the concern is that an equal split indicates that there are underlying problems at the root of the company.

The best approach for most start-ups and developing businesses is an 'organic' shareholders' agreement. This involves shareholders earning their equity stake by remaining involved in the business, a sort of pre-nuptial agreement for the business. Unfortunately, as HBR notes, at the start it is hard to imagine anything going wrong and the discussion is often seen as emotionally negative rather than the opportunity to obtain clarity up front.

8.4   Government incentives

Many governments offer incentives to small businesses and/or businesses which are focusing on a particular geographic area, social problem or key growth industry. Do your research when deciding where to incorporate. Is your home territory the best place to locate? Can you locate in several territories and adopt a corporate structure which enables you to reap the benefits of all of these incentives? This is another question to add in to the mix along with where your main markets are likely located and where you plan to manufacture.

By way of example, the UK currently offers the Seed Enterprise Investment Scheme (SEIS) and Enterprise Investment Scheme (EIS).[3] SEIS provides tax relief to investors in early stage companies. The idea is that it will encourage more people to invest in these high-risk companies. If you can register for SEIS and/or EIS, it will not only make you much more attractive to investors but shows that you are a sophisticated business which takes advantage of the available investment opportunities.

The other likely shareholders of any business include friends, family and employees. While this money can be essential to starting up, you should be careful about the way in which you approach this investment as you may find yourself the wrong side of financial regulatory law. Similarly, be careful when awarding equity to employees. It can seem like an easy win – you are not giving anything but you are keeping them motivated. However, you can end up with a significant tax liability and some negative shareholders if the relationship sours in the future. These problems can be dealt with via mechanisms such as 'good leaver' and 'bad leaver' terms in employment contracts and the company's governing documents which set out the results of being a 'bad leaver' such as forced sale of shares. Adopting a share option scheme can be another way to motivate employees and protect against negative tax liability and unwanted shareholders with pre-approved tax treatment share option schemes and bad leaver terms in the share option documentation.

8.5   What funding is available?

The two most common forms of funding are equity (people paying money in return for a share of your business) or debt (someone loaning you money, usually on the basis that you pay interest on the loan and repay the amount loaned over a specified period). While these two options have not fundamentally changed, the Internet has opened up new opportunities for raising capital without necessarily

---

3 For more information see, https://www.gov.uk/topic/business-tax/investment-schemes.

giving too much away. The most well-known example of this is crowdfunding.

8.5.1   Crowdfunding

Crowdfunding is a popular method for getting a new business or product off the ground. There are two main types of crowdfunding: product and equity. The former is popularised by sites such as Kickstarter and Indiegogo.

8.5.2   Product crowdfunding

Product crowdfunding involves people paying you in advance for a product which you have not yet manufactured. They tend to offer more than just pre-ordering and can include the opportunity for fans to fully engage with your burgeoning brand. For the right price you could offer to name a product or clothing line after someone who pays you for the privilege. The following is a summary of Indiegogo's accumulated wisdom on the steps you should take in order to run a successful product crowdfunding campaign:

1.   Make sure you talk to your potential customers about what they want not just in terms of product but also pricing strategy and the value you are offering.

2.   While digital tools can help you to organise your time, do not spend too much time focused on tools at the detriment of opportunities.

3.   Do not offer too many perks as people tend to be overwhelmed by too much choice. Indiegogo suggests somewhere between two to five perks, as it gives pledgers sufficient choice and can realistically be delivered.

4.   Ask for a few large pledges, they can make the world of difference and give you an opportunity to identify your superfans.[4]

5.   You ideally want to get 25–30 per cent funded in the first few days in order to build momentum.

---

4 See Nicholas Lovell, *The Curve* (Penguin) for more information on this concept. It is reviewed by Rosie Burbidge here: http://ipkitten.blogspot.co.uk/2016/10/can-curve-combat-piracy.html.

6. Engage with the niche press and bloggers to build reputation.

7. Do not launch too early. Take the time you need to get your strategy right and the pieces in place before launching.

8. Do not assume that because someone has signed up to your mailing list they will buy your product. Indiegogo estimates around 5 per cent of all opted-in email lists convert to customers. If you cannot get to 30 per cent funded from your email list, you are launching too early.

9. Give yourself enough time to ship the product – at least 12 months. You will impress people by under promising and over-delivering, not the other way around and you'll spend less time communicating about delays which can lead to cancelled orders.

10. Set a low funding goal. Nobody pays much attention to the funding goal amount, while everyone pays attention to the funding percentage. This means that you are much better off with a lower funding goal, since your percentage will automatically be higher with every Dollar, Euro, Krona or Pound Sterling you get in. The sooner you reach 100 per cent the better!

From a legal point of view, the problems with product crowdfunding concern product liability and reputation (see below). Product crowdfunding can be an excellent means of building profile and raising finance but think carefully about your objectives and plan properly before launching. That said, it is important not to delay for too long as there are obvious advantages to being the first mover.

8.5.3   Equity crowdfunding

Another popular form of crowdfunding is equity focused. Sites such as Seedrs and Crowdcube are well established and popular forms of equity crowdfunding. They allow anyone to invest in early stage businesses in the hope of obtaining a dividend and/or the opportunity to make a profit when the shares are sold. As this form of equity crowdfunding is still in its infancy, the success stories are relatively thin on the ground. They can be a good way of building a network and developing goodwill but they come with shareholder liability and are not an easy option. At the time of writing, equity crowdfunding is particularly popular in the UK,[5] Sweden,[6] Germany,[7] Finland,[8] Estonia[9] and France.[10]

Other forms of funding include book debt funding where you sell your debts in advance of payment. This is beneficial in terms of cash flow but risky as it puts responsibility for chasing your customers in the hands of a third party who is not concerned about preserving the business relationship.

8.5.4   Debt finance

Other common forms of finance include personal loans into your business by, for example, remortgaging your home or getting help from friends and family. It is important that all loans, even ones from close family members, are properly documented as you could incur tax consequences if you fail to do so. It also ensures that you all have clarity about the terms of the loan.

Another obvious form of debt is a bank loan either as a single lump sum, or more commonly as a revolving form of debt. These sorts of loan can be very difficult to get, particularly given the difficulties facing retail and the post credit crunch approach to business debt. In order to get a sufficiently large loan to get your business off the ground, it may need to be secured against an asset, or backed up by a guarantor. It is important that everyone involved in the transaction is clear about the potential consequences as well as the rate of interest and what that can mean as the debt accumulates. Compound interest involves paying interest on accumulated interest. Even if you do not have a particularly high interest rate, you can quickly double your debt if you are not careful.

---

5 Crowdcube and Seedrs lead the way.

6 FundedByMe was one of the first platforms in the world to offer both product and equity crowdfunding.

7 For example Companisto and Seed Match.

8 Invesdor gives businesses full discretion over how they raise money and offers supplementary services such as legal advice, auditing services and branding development.

9 Estonia is leading the digital revolution in Europe with innovative developments such as digital citizenship. Its leading equity crowdfunding platform is Funderbeam.

10 WiSEED, which is available in French and English, is authorised and regulated as PSI (Provider of Investment Services) by the French Prudential Supervision and Resolution Authority (ACPR). It was the first equity crowdfunding platform in the world.

8.5.5   Equity finance

Again, friends and family are a common early source of equity finance. Other options include angel investors, high net worth individuals who invest alone or in collaboration with a few other people. Dragon's Den and Shark Tank are examples of businesses pitching to angel investors. Ideally you want an angel investor with knowledge of the fashion industry and contacts which you can use to grow your business.

Another type of equity finance is via very wealthy families, known as 'family officers'. They are somewhere between angel and venture capital investment. Essentially you get the benefit of a well-oiled business machine rather than being limited to a single angel investor but with a more personal touch than venture capital as they are investing their own money.

Venture capital is typically for larger amounts of money and they often invest in later funding rounds. It is common for several venture capital funds to co-invest as this spreads their risk and doubles the amount of potential advisory assistance available. Venture capital is interested in measurable success or 'traction' as well as the ability to 'scale' or increase in size by several multiples in a short period of time.

Private equity typically comes in for even larger transactions and is usually only available at a later stage in your business' life cycle.

Regardless of the methods of funding you use, it is normal for funding to happen in stages which are linked to the size of your business and the amount of money required at any one time. Ending up with a cash surplus which you do not require can be just as damaging as not having enough money. It is important that you plan carefully and work with dedicated finance professionals to get the best possible outcome for you and your business.

9 Before you enter into your first contract

You can create a contract without putting pen to paper but a written agreement which has been signed by all parties to the contract is a pretty good indication that you have a binding contract in place. Contracts are essential to all businesses and while a clear contract can avoid future misunderstandings, regardless of your business' size you will not have the time, money or negotiating power to dispute every single point on any given contract. Pick your battles and decide what matters to you long term and where future problems could lie.

This chapter gives you a very basic introduction to the principles behind contract law. It covers the contract basics as well as specific issues which can arise around, for example, pre-contractual liability and standard terms.

9.1 The contract basics

No matter where you operate in the world, there are some fundamental principles which govern contract law worldwide. However, contract law is far from consistent. Within the EU, each Member State has the right to create its own contract laws. This means that there can be quite a divergence in principles between the 'Common Law' of the UK and Ireland and many 'Civil Law' countries in mainland Europe such as France, Italy and Germany.

In theory, the Principles of European Contract Law, as established by the EU, can apply to contracts where the law is not stated, or if the parties have expressly chosen them. In practice, this is very rare. The European Commission is currently making efforts as part of its digital economy agenda to create harmonised contract rules in areas of digital, insurance and cloud computing, but this is still a work in progress.

Other international principles can apply to contract law, such as the Unidroit principles[1] or the United Nations Convention on Contracts for the International Sales of Goods,[2] also known as the 'Vienna Convention.' In practice, many companies choose to opt out of these international regimes and rely on national laws that they better understand, or that have a direct link to where their businesses (or legal teams!) are based.

Even if the basic contract law principles stay relatively static, the nuances of contract law are often evolving in different ways in each Member State through case law or legislation. You need to keep track of these developments in order to ensure your contracts are fully effective.

The French Contract Law regime was significantly overhauled on 1 October 2016.[3] The reform was long overdue as no significant modifications had been made to the French Civil Code since its inception in 1804! The modifications mainly served to codify principles that had already been established over the years through case law. However, as the law is so recent and some principles have not yet been tested by the courts, foreign businesses may be reticent to choose French law as the governing law of their contracts for the time being.

9.1.1   What is a contract?

Contracts are agreements which are made between two or more people or legal entities. There are two key parts to any contract:

1. An offer (such as 'if you pay me X amount of money, you can buy my product').

2. Which is accepted ('yes, please').

In addition, there must also be an intention to create legal relations and the contract must have been entered into voluntarily by legally competent persons. For example young children, heavily intoxicated people and some people suffering from mental illness may be considered to be incapable of entering into a binding legal contract.

---

1 http://www.unidroit.org/about-unidroit/overview.

2 https://www.uncitral.org/pdf/english/texts/sales/cisg/V1056997-CISG-e-book.pdf.

3 Ordinance of 10th February 2016 (No. 2016-131) on the Reform of French Contract Law modifying the general regime and evidence of obligations.

In many jurisdictions a signature is not necessary to create a binding contract. It is for this reason that many people write 'SUBJECT TO CONTRACT' at the top of emails or documents which are being negotiated. If you are not careful, in England, you can create a binding contract via something as simple as a series of emails or even text messages.

The French courts have traditionally been very reluctant to permit the existence (and therefore enforcement) of a contract in the absence of an agreement signed by both parties. However, the Reformed Civil Code states that a contract can now be formed by the mere exchange of consents, regardless of how such consent is expressed. In theory, this means that a formal written agreement is no longer necessary[4] as a contract can arise from a person's declaration or unequivocal conduct.[5] Given the past attitude of French courts, it remains good practice to obtain properly signed agreements.

In Poland, the contracts between entrepreneurs can normally be concluded in a form of an email exchange. However, as in the other Member States, some contracts, such as assignment of copyrights or an exclusive licence, must be in a single written document which is signed by both parties in order to be valid.

While everyone is usually happy when a contract is signed, what starts out appearing to be quite a simple document can become enormously complicated if one person is later unhappy with the contract (often this unhappy person is not the person who negotiated the contract but a more recent employee and may be considering it without all the relevant facts). When you return to a contract after many years it is often hard to remember the commercial rationale, context and intended meaning for certain terms. In addition, it is common for the parties to slightly vary the terms over time as new ways of working develop and are accepted by the parties.

The offer and acceptance set out in the above scenario appears quite straightforward but what if instead of 'yes, please' someone says, 'I'll buy 1,000 for 75 per cent of that price' or 'I can pay 50 per cent now and the remaining 50 per cent in two instalments' or 'I want to try before I buy.' They have indicated that they want to buy your product but they have not agreed to your terms. In other words, rather than accepting your offer, they have made you a counter-offer. It is then up

---

4 See Arts 1101 and 1109 of the Reformed French Civil Code.
5 See, ibid., Art. 1113 al. 2.

to you to either accept that offer or make your own counter-offer e.g., 'the first 100 are at full price but I can do the remaining 900 at 80 per cent' etc. Eventually you will reach a point where you are both happy to do business and someone's offer is accepted.

Acceptance means agreement to the full terms of the offer (or counter-offer) but it does not need to repeat the offer. It can be as simple as saying 'agreed' or 'where do I sign.'

9.1.2   Payment or 'consideration'

The final stage in most Common Law contracts is usually the exchange of money or a financial equivalent such as services. This is known as 'consideration.' For example, 'here's my money' or 'I can't pay cash but I can wash your dishes.'

In England, the only requirement for consideration is that it must be something you do now or in the future. The legal maxim we are taught at law school is that 'past consideration is not good consideration.' This means that, contrary to the practices in many restaurants, you cannot give something (such as bread) to someone without asking them and then later try and charge for it. This is also a surefire way to alienate your clientele.

The law will not stop one of the parties from entering into a 'bad' deal but the relative amounts that two people bring to a contract should not wildly differ (e.g., a Givenchy handbag on sale for £10 is clearly either a counterfeit or a pricing error).

By contrast, in much of the rest of Europe, the Common Law concept of 'consideration' does not exist. Prior to 2016, French law relied upon the concepts of '*cause*' and '*objet*' as the ingredients for a valid contract. (These terms will quickly become familiar if you have contractual dealings in France.) *Cause* and *objet* still apply to a contract entered into prior to the law reform. They require a contract to have a legitimate reason (*cause*) and a valid subject matter (*objet*).

From October 2016, French contracts must instead have '*lawful and certain content*'[6] to be legally binding. In order to respect these new

---

6 See, ibid., Art. 1128, which also tells us that in addition to lawful and certain content, the parties must consent to the creation of a contract and have sufficient capacity to do so.

rules for a valid contract, you basically need to ensure that your contract is not contrary to public policy and the terms concern a genuine basis for the contract. In other words, the provision of a service or the authorised sale of legitimate merchandise.

9.2 Pre-contractual negotiations

Before entering into a formal written contract, it is common to agree the commercial parameters in advance. These are often known as 'heads of terms' or may sometimes be set out in a 'letter of intent'. If they are intended to be binding as far as the formal contract is concerned, they can be signed and include a choice of law and jurisdiction clause in the event of a dispute. It is not unusual for parties to operate on the basis of heads of terms alone. This provides less certainty as to the contractual terms but is not necessarily a huge problem provided the heads of terms are sufficiently clear about the key obligations. That said, it is preferable to have a formal written contract as this process tends to identify contentious issues and provides clarity to all involved.

Many EU Member States have specific laws that govern the pre-contractual phases so even if you have not signed a document, you may still have incurred potential liability.

9.2.1 Pre-contractual liability in Italy

In Italy, pre-contractual liability[7] means that parties must act in good faith throughout contract negotiations and the contract formation process. This includes cooperation and disclosure of relevant documents during the negotiations. Pre-contractual liability is a type of tort, this means that it belongs to a subset of law which looks at conduct and does not require a contractual relationship between the parties.[8] Therefore, all rules that govern tortious liability under Italian law will apply. For instance, the limitation period is five years from the breach of the good faith duty[9] and the party invoking such liability will have the burden of proving that the tort applies and the amount of damages they should be compensated.[10]

---

7 *Culpa in Contrahendo* is governed by Art. 1337 of the Italian Civil Code.
8 Italian Supreme Court – Plenary Session – Decision No. 9645/2001 and Decision No. 10160/2003.
9 Italian Civil Code, Art. 2947.
10 See, ibid., Arts 2043, 2056 and 2059.

The duty of good faith is an objective requirement. This means that it can arise even if a party did not intentionally behave in bad faith. For example, it would apply if a party interrupted the nego-tiations without a good reason and as a result of this conduct the other party's expectations to execute the contract failed. This kind of liability will not arise if the negotiations are interrupted for a good reason.[11]

The circumstances in which pre-contractual liability will arise tend to be as follows:

1.   the parties are in advanced negotiations;

2.   the *status* of the negotiations is of such a kind that the non-breaching party has relied upon the reasonable likelihood that the contract will be executed;

3.   the breaching party interrupted the negotiations without a good reason;

4.   the declarations and/or conduct made by the breaching party led the other party to believe that the contract was likely to be executed; and

5.   there is no factual information which points against the non-breaching party's reasonable reliance on the execution of the contract.[12]

The damages that can be claimed are limited to what is called 'negative interest' meaning all losses suffered during the negotiations as well as the losses suffered due to the missed opportunity of executing a similar contract with a different party but having the same subject matter or having even more profitable conditions.[13] The non-breaching party cannot claim the damages that could be avoided and the advantages that could have been obtained if the contract had been properly executed.[14]

---

11 Italian Supreme Court Decision No. 399/1985.
12 Milan Civil Court, Corporate Division, Decision No. 4927/2017.
13 Italian Supreme Court Decision No. 8778/1994.
14 Italian Supreme Court Decision No. 1632/00.

9.2.2   Pre-contractual liability in France

The Reformed French Civil Code has now formalised certain practices which had traditionally been developed through case law, and which specifically relate to conduct during the pre-contractual stage. This includes obligations: (i) to provide pre-contractual information in certain situations, (ii) to act in good faith both during negotiations and when terminating negotiations; and (iii) to maintain confidential information exchanged during the pre-contractual phase. Each is considered in more detail below.

(A)   Pre-contractual information

If you hold information of decisive importance to another business with whom you plan to contract in France, you must inform the other party of that information if the other business either does not know about it or is reliant on it in order to enter into the contract. The same obligations apply to the other business in relation to you.

Information is of 'decisive importance' if it has a direct and necessary relationship with the content of the contract or with the status of the parties. Ultimately, this is a question for French judges. These provisions will be harder to rely on for more experienced parties.

The Reformed Civil Code adds to sanctions for failure to provide accurate information that have long existed in France. The reform also narrows the scope of the obligation to 'information actually known' and applies this obligation to all agreements.

This duty applies automatically[15] and it is not possible to limit or exclude it whether contractually or otherwise. Nevertheless, this should not be relied upon by either party and the safest course is to conduct your own due diligence before entering into contractual relations.

(B)   Acting in good faith

Like Italy, France imposes obligations to act in good faith during pre-contractual negotiations. French contracts must be 'negotiated, formed and performed in good faith.'[16] Again, these obligations

---

15 The Reformed French Civil Code, Art. 1112-1.
16 Ibid., Art. 1104.

cannot be limited or excluded by the parties. The obligation to act in good faith also applies to a party's conduct during the termination of pre-contractual negotiations. Failure to adhere to these obligations may result in cancellation of the contract and/or lead to a damages claim.

A party breaking off discussions in the negotiation phase cannot, in itself, constitute tortious behaviour or *faute* giving rise to compensation for loss (*réparation du prejudice*). In most circumstances, the best solution is likely to be simply finding an alternative business with which to contract.

Under the Reformed Code,[17] while it is possible to commence an action in relation to the negligent or tortious behaviour of a party that broke off negotiations, it is not possible to claim for the sums that would have been made had the contract been concluded (this is known as 'loss of a chance'). However, it is possible to claim for reimbursement of wasted fees spent on unfruitful negotiations or the lost opportunity to contract with another party. These sums can be significant. This can be a problem for many businesses, particularly if you are starting out and do not have much cash flow or capital to spend on legal fees for litigation or settlement sums.

When you are negotiating in France, it is therefore important to be careful about creating expectations for the other party by encouraging them to take onerous steps during the negotiation phase, such as making investments or setting up a company.

You should carefully review offer letters or letters of intent to make sure they refer to subsequent documentation and the fact that the contract will be finalised and concluded by way of a formal and separate agreement. You should also ensure that all information and documents which you provide are not misleading and do not inadvertently formalise intentions or relations.

Judges tend to be more sympathetic to the wronged party if negotiations are broken off unreasonably or in bad faith after a period of exclusivity, or if a party has taken significant steps to be bound to the other

---

17 Decisions of the Cour de Cassation, Ch. Com, of 26th November 2003, 00-10.243 00-10.949 and Ch. Civ. 3ème, of 28th June 2006, 04-20.040. This is now codified by the Reformed French Civil Code, Art. 1112.

party, for example by entering into pre-contractual confidentiality or non-compete agreements.

(C)   Confidential information

Finally, any confidential information that is obtained in the course of negotiations and is later used or disclosed without consent will give the person whose confidential information has been misused the right to start legal proceedings whether or not there is a contract such as a confidentiality agreement or non-disclosure agreement in place. In France, this misuse falls within the Reformed Code.[18] The French legislature's decision to codify this principle shows its importance to business and brings French law in line with the EU Directive on Trade Secrets referred to in Chapter 7.

Unlike the obligations of good faith and pre-contractual information which apply in many Civil Law jurisdictions, the obligation of confidentiality during pre-contractual negotiations applies across the EU.

9.2.3   Pre-contractual liability in Poland

Because French Civil Law has historically been very influential across Europe, pre-contractual liability applies in many other European countries. In Poland it applies if you counted on a contract being executed and can prove that a party conducted negotiations in bad faith, in breach of good practice and without the intention to execute the contract.[19]

9.2.4   Pre-contractual liability in Switzerland

Pre-contractual liability is not codified in Swiss law.[20] It has however been developed through case law based on the principle of good faith.[21] It is now considered to be comprised within the larger so-called liability based on trust (responsabilité fondée sur la confiance).[22]

---

18 The Reformed French Civil Code, Art. 1112-2.

19 See Article 72 of the Polish Civil Code dated 23 April 1964 ('Polish Civil Code').

20 Olivier Riske, La responsabilité précontractuelle dans le processus d'uniformisation du droit privé européen, Perspectives pour l'ordre juridique suisse – Analyse historique, comparative et prospective, in CN -Collection neuchâteloise, Helbing Lichtenhahn, 2016, p. 459, N 1216.

21 Article 2 §1 of the Swiss Civil Code.

22 Riske, supra note 20, p. 457, N 1212, p. 458 N 1214; Franz Werro, La responsabilité civile, Stämpfli Editions SA Berne, 2017, p. 111, N 357–358; Christine Chappuis, in Commentaire romand du

Generally speaking, both parties to a negotiation in Switzerland are free to end negotiations without any obligation to provide an explanation.[23] However, starting negotiations creates a legal relationship between the participants and imposes duties.[24] This includes the duty not to engage or pursue negotiations lacking the intent to actually enter into a contract. It can also include a limited requirement to provide the opposing party with the relevant information that could influence their will to enter into a contract or the terms and conditions of that contract.[25]

The legal nature of pre-contractual liability is still disputed by scholars and Swiss courts have not conclusively ruled on the matter.[26] If pre-contractual liability is found by the court, it is possible to claim compensation for damage resulting from the failed negotiations.[27] Pre-contractual liability claims in Switzerland are rarely successful because the application of the law is very restrictive.[28]

9.3   Confidentiality in practice

When discussing sensitive business secrets, strategy or your intellec- tual property rights (especially if they have not yet been registered or disclosed to the public), it is wise to include a clause in any letters or non-disclosure agreements which:

1.   Identifies the relevant confidential information.

2.   Indicates that the party receiving the information must take all measures to ensure that it remains confidential (including a potential action in negligence if this does not occur).

3.   Specifies that the individuals having access to the information are also bound by the obligations of confidentiality.

Code civil I, Helbing Lichtenhahn, Bâle, 2010, *ad* Art. 2 N 59; Decision of the Federal Court dated 10 October 1995 published in ATF 121 III 350.

23   Decision of the Federal Court dated 14 January 2011, 4A_615/2010; SJ 2002 I p. 164.

24   Ibid.

25   Werro, *supra* note 22, p. 112, N 358; Decision of the Federal Court, ibid., p. 164.

26   Decision of the Federal Court dated 6 February 1979 published in ATF 105 II 75.

27   Decision of the Federal Court, *supra* note 22.

28   Decision of the Federal Court, *supra* note 23.

4. Provides for communication to third parties in very restrictive terms (for example, limited to lawyers, accountants or judicial or administrative authorities).

5. Determines the duration of the obligations and the methods of destruction or restitution of the information conferred on the receiving party.

These practical tips could also be applicable to the treatment of confidential information exchanged between parties pre-contract or post-contract in other jurisdictions as well – however it is always prudent to check local rules just in case there are any specific points to note.

9.4   A formal written contract

The following section gives you an idea of some of the standard contractual features and terms in many formal written contracts.

9.4.1   Recitals

Recitals are included at the very start of a lot of contracts. They summarise the background to the contract and its purpose. They are an aid to interpreting the meaning of a contract but do not form part of the contract itself. They can appear under the heading 'Whereas,' 'Background' or even 'Recitals.'

9.4.2   Definitions

Definitions are the long-winded contractual glossary which often appears at the start of the contract. Because reading them can feel like reading a dictionary, there is a natural temptation to skip them in order to get to the meat of the contract (this is usually found in clauses 2 to 5 or possibly a schedule if it is a standard form contract or framework agreement).

Ignoring the definitions is a mistake as they are essential to understanding the nature of the deal into which you are entering. In many instances, a clause can fundamentally change in nature and scope depending on the definition. A definition is a means of simplifying a contract so rather than repeating, for example, the intellectual property rights which are licensed, they can be defined once and then the defined term used as a shorthand to describe the rights in the rest of the contract.

You can usually spot a defined term in a contract because it is in bold, title caps, all caps or similarly identifiable. Some modern contracts will include hyperlinks each time a defined term appears so you can see what the term means without having to return to the start of the document while reading the contract.

Important definitions include 'Intellectual Property' and 'Territory' or 'Geographic scope.' The definition of intellectual property is usually a fairly standard catch-all term but specific intellectual property rights are often separately defined. For example, 'Trade Marks' to describe any marks which are being licensed. These marks are typically listed in a schedule. The definition could be expanded to include trade marks which may be filed in the future and include a particular word for specified goods or services. The Territory in which rights are granted or obligations apply should be as specific as possible. There are still contracts being prepared which refer to the EU when they are intended to also cover the UK (and to last more than a year). This is sowing the seeds for future confusion after Brexit.

Quite often the definitions section will end with a long list of conventions to be applied when interpreting the document. For example, 'references to the singular include the plural' or 'a reference to one gender covers both genders.' These interpretation provisions are not always necessary and can add to the bulk of an agreement. Nevertheless, as with all contractual terms, make sure you have read, understood and agree with them before signing on the dotted line.

9.4.3   The operative clauses

The key parts of the contract are the 'operative clauses.' These are clauses which set out the essence of the bargain you have struck. For example, One O' One Factory is going to manufacture 2,020 products for you by 1 January 2020. Instead of (or in addition to) tangible things such as the purchase of goods, the operative clauses could concern services that you wish to procure such as distribution services in particular territories.

People are generally free to enter into any sort of commercial arrange- ment they see fit and the law will not step in to remedy a bad bargain. However, the law will be very interested in these operative clauses if they concern unlawful or illegal activity!

The most common mistakes that people tend to make in English contracts are:

1.   The inclusion of 'unfair' contract terms.

2.   The inclusion of a 'penalty' clause.

3.   Anti-competitive clauses.

4.   Misrepresenting a key part of the contract terms prior to signature.

Save for penalty clauses which are typically allowed in other Member States, Civil Law has similar but potentially broader restrictions. For example, under French law, contractual provisions that attempt to override or derogate from matters of public policy are invalid.[29]

9.5   Unfair contract terms

Although smaller companies are in a weaker bargaining position, in many European territories such as France and England, if terms are 'unfair' they cannot be relied upon by the stronger party. The French Civil Code expressly allows a party to request that certain unfair clauses be declared as 'not written,' and to claim related damages. Similarly, standard-form contracts are interpreted against the party who put them forward, whereas a bespoke contract is interpreted in favour of the party performing the obligations.[30]

The upshot is that you should proceed with caution when using standard terms, particularly in France. Ideally the other party will have the possibility to negotiate and seek amendments that go beyond price, fees and general subject matter. Evidence of pre-contractual discussions is critical to securing success in this scenario.

9.6   Penalty clauses

 A penalty clause is one which sets out an amount to be paid in the event of breach which is more than would be payable under normal

---

29 See the Reformed French Civil Code, Art. 1162.
30 See, ibid., Art. 1190.

circumstances in the event of a contractual breach. In other words, you pay a penalty for breach.

The aim of a penalty clause is to enable an injured party to seek redress without having to refer the matter to a judge. This is typically achieved by the injured party sending an invoice for the amount due.

Penalty clauses are not allowed in English contracts and any such clause will be void. It is possible under English law to have a clause which sets out a fixed amount to be paid in the event of a breach (i.e., a liquidated damages clause) but that amount cannot be a 'penalty' instead it must be a 'genuine pre-estimate of loss.' By contrast, in France and Belgium, penalty clauses are valid and frequently used. The French Reformed Code expressly allows for penalty clauses.[31]

The scope of a penalty clause varies depending on the subject matter. For example, some contracts state that a party committing a breach of a contractual term must pay a fixed amount of money to the other party to compensate for the breach. In practice, it is common to see penalties attached to confidentiality clauses for each breach of the clause. Similarly, they commonly include a daily penalty for each day in which payment or performance of a contractual term is delayed.

Under French law, a penalty clause essentially sanctions a contractual breach and is entirely independent from the actual loss suffered by the injured party (unlike a liquidated damages clause). That said, in some contexts, courts can intervene to review the clause if it is excessively onerous. For example, an excessive penalty clause in an employment contract could be considered a restraint of trade. The court can decide to increase or decrease the amount of the penalty dependent on the facts of the case.

The Belgian Civil Code states that the parties to a contract may set a lump sum amount as compensation for a specific contractual breach.[32] The benefit of including a penalty clause is that an injured party can receive compensation for loss, without having to provide any further evidence in terms of causation or quantum (i.e., they do not have to prove that the financial compensation is directly attributable to the breach of contract or show why it should be a specific amount.

---

31 See, ibid., Art. 1231-5.
32 See the Belgian Civil Code, Art. 1226.

Belgian law applies some limitations on the use of penalty clauses. The penalty clause needs to correspond to an indemnity and therefore must relate to harm that was foreseeable when the parties agreed on the clause.[33] In practice it is not always easy to predict this sort of thing in advance. If the amount of the penalty vastly exceeds the level of foreseeable harm, in a similar way to French law, the judge can (potentially of their own volition) reduce the amount of the penalty to be paid so that compensation is just and fair and does not serve to unjustly enrich the injured party.[34]

In Belgium, penalty clauses are often included in non-disclosure agreements and in non-compete agreements. This is primarily for their deterrent effect. Specific attention should be paid to the wording of these clauses as they can be easily struck out, set aside, or amended by the court. It is also wise to include a provision that any damages that exceed the foreseeable harm covered by the penalty clause can be recovered by the injured party.

 As a general rule, when drafting penalty clauses in France and Belgium, especially if the penalty is linked to a non-compete clause, it is important to bear in mind examples from case law and ensure that the scope of a penalty clause and the associated financial sanction is fair and reasonable in proportion to the protection of a party's legitimate business interests.[35]

Swiss law also allows for penalty clauses. The matter is expressly covered in the Swiss Code of Obligations.[36] According to Swiss law, the parties can set an amount that will be payable by the party at fault in case of breach or failure to perform the contract.[37] The Swiss Code of Obligations sets out two alternative presumptions in different circumstances:

1. If the penalty clause refers to breach or non-performance of the contract, it is presumed that the claimant must choose between payment of the penalty or the performance of the breached or non-performed contractual obligation.

---

33 See, ibid., Art. 1229, al. 1.

34 See, ibid., Art. 1231, §1.

35 See French Supreme Court Decision, Cour de cassation, civile, Chambre sociale, 20 février 2013, 11-22.647.

36 See Swiss Code of Obligations, Arts 160–163.

37 See, ibid., Art. 160.

2.   If the penalty clause is used to guarantee the timely performance or compliance with the place of performance, it is presumed that the claimant can request both payment of the penalty as well as requiring that the contractual obligation is met (albeit rather late).[38]

These presumptions can be rebutted by contract.

In Switzerland, as in other Civil Law jurisdictions, the full amount set out in the penalty clause must be paid irrespective of whether the breach actually causes harm to the other party.[39] If the damage exceeds the amount of the penalty clause, the claimant can request additional compensation provided it demonstrates the fault of the debtor (except if the debtor is legally liable without proof of fault).[40]

The amount of the penalty clause can be freely set by the parties.[41] However, the judge will reduce 'excessive' penalty clauses.[42] Swiss law does not define what should be considered excessive but it is more likely to apply where there is a very large difference between the amount set by the parties and the damage that actually occurred.[43]

Finally, in some extreme cases, a Swiss penalty clause can be deemed void. This could apply, for instance, if the underlying obligation is unlawful or immoral.

9.7   Anti-competitive clauses

Competition law is a huge topic which is discussed in more detail in the context of franchising in Chapter 18. Broadly speaking, you will fall foul of EU competition law if a contract prevents, restricts or distorts competition within the EU or a single Member State (each Member State has its own competition law which is similar to EU law). The classic example of anti-competitive activity is price fixing but there is a fairly long list to watch out for including the application of different conditions to similar contracts.

---

38 See, ibid., Art. 160, §1 and 2.

39 See, ibid., Art. 161, §1.

40 See, ibid., Art. 161, §2.

41 See, ibid., Art.163, §1.

42 See, ibid., Art. 163, §3.

43 Michel Mooser, Commentaire romand du Code des obligations I, *ad* Art. 163 N 7, 2012, Helbing Lichtenhahn, Bâle.

If an agreement is found to be anti-competitive it will be void and unenforceable and you may face a significant fine. In some cases it can lead to disqualification from acting as a director in the future and there may be criminal sanctions.

The good news is that there are various exemptions from competition law, many of which apply if you have a small market share. There tend to be more stringent restrictions where the contract concerns businesses at different levels of the supply chain i.e., manufacturer, supplier, distributor, wholesaler or retailer. If the contract is between businesses at the same level it may create fewer issues. If in doubt, get legal advice.

9.8   Misrepresentation

If you claim something in the course of your contractual negotiations, such as 'the manufactured product will conform to a particular specification,' and it does not in fact do so, you run the risk of a claim for misrepresentation. Again, maintaining good records and copies of any samples provided in the course of negotiations is important and will save a lot of time and hassle if a claim for 'misrep' (as lawyers like to call it) is made.

 Importantly, unlike many other contractual remedies, if a claim for misrepresentation is successful, in Common Law jurisdictions it is possible for the winning party to 'rescind' the contract. This means that the parties essentially undo the contract to the greatest extent possible. Rescission is not mandatory and simple damages may be a preferable remedy in many situations.

9.9   Good faith

 Good faith is a very important legal concept in Civil Law jurisdictions. French law has recently codified good faith. The Reformed Code now explicitly requires that French contracts must be negotiated, formed and performed in good faith.[44] Good faith provisions are an implied term in all contracts (i.e., the provisions are part of your contract even if the words do not appear on the page). You cannot use a contract to

---

44 See, the Reformed French Civil Code, Art. 1104.

exclude or limit good faith. The implied term does not apply in every European country but if a party has not acted in good faith there is usually an alternative means available to reach the same result.

The concept of good faith is particularly important in the context of the French Reformed Civil Code because the Reformed Code has created new provisions which aim to protect the economic stability of parties to a contract (including commercial parties). This means that you (or your contracting party) could potentially be saved from a 'bad bargain' if certain conditions are met further down the line. A couple of examples are below regarding the Code's intervention in areas such as price-determination and unforeseeability.

9.9.1 Price-determination in French contracts

One of the key changes in the Reformed Code is the obligation to justify a price that has been unilaterally set by one party if it is later contested by the other party. This obligation applies to both standard terms and bespoke agreements. The obligation is born out of a desire to prevent abusive behaviour by one party unilaterally setting the price. In that sense, it covers similar ground to the laws surrounding unfair contract terms.

This change is particularly important for the agreed standard terms which govern all purchase orders (also known as 'framework agreements'). In these contracts, the parties do not tend to have equal bargaining positions. The law says that 'it may be agreed that the price will be unilaterally set by one of the parties subject to the requirement that the party setting the price must provide the reason for the amount if it is later challenged.'[45] This implies that the power to unilaterally set a price must be agreed at the conclusion of the contract. It is therefore wise to save evidence relating to how the price was calculated, such as market studies and any other contemporaneous justifications for price calculations.

For one-off agreements the price can be set by the party requesting performance of the services as long they can provide a reason for the amount if it is later challenged.[46] This implies that a price may be set during performance of the contract. If the standard terms include

---

45 See, ibid., Art. 1164.
46 See, ibid., Art. 1165.

particularly unfair prices, the other party can apply to the court to have the contract set aside.

These changes highlight the importance of ensuring contract terms and price are clearly defined at an early stage and referenced in the contract as well as keeping contemporaneous evidence as to how the contract price has been set.

9.9.2   Compulsory renegotiation of French contracts

 The French Reformed Code also states that if there is a change of circumstances that could not have been predicted when the contract was made, which means that an obligation suddenly becomes excessively onerous, it may be possible to renegotiate the contract. While these renegotiations are carried out both parties must continue to perform their obligations. If the other party refuses to renegotiate or the renegotiations result in failure, the parties can either agree to terminate the contract or ask the court for help.

The new ability of the court to revise or terminate a contract[47] is one of the most complex and controversial new provisions of the updated French contract law. It changed an essential principle of French law that the forced negotiation or termination of a contract between private or commercial parties was not possible. This is particularly controversial as French judges do not have practical or commercial backgrounds, instead they train to become part of the career judiciary straight out of law school and tend to have a more academic background. Most Civil Law countries follow the same approach of career judges, by contrast, in Common Law countries like the UK and Ireland judges are usually experienced legal practitioners.

 Due to the controversial nature of this provision, the French Senate validated the first reading to amend this element of the Reform in October 2017. The draft amendments replace the notion of 'revision' by a judge with the possibility to make amendments only. For the time being, it is safest to expressly exclude the court's ability to amend the contract from all contracts until the position is clarified by the French legislator.

---

47 See, ibid., Art. 1195.

9.10   Limiting liability

One of the most contentious issues in any contract negotiation tends to revolve around who bears liability for losses (including claims made by 'third parties' i.e., people who are not party to the contract). All parties to a contract understandably want to limit their liability but neither wants to be put in a position where the other party behaves badly but there is no financial recourse available.

There are a number of ways of limiting liability, for example it may be limited by a specific cap such as the purchase price in the contract. Some types of loss, such as intellectual property infringement, are less predictable. Consequently, liability for these losses is commonly uncapped. Some types of liability cannot be limited, such as liability for death, personal injury and fraud.

9.10.1   Limitation of liability under French Law

The French Contract Law Reform codified existing principles around limitation of liability that had been established by case law.[48] The Reformed Code now expressly states that: 'Any term which deprives the other party of an essential obligation, being at the very substance of the contract, is deemed as not written'.[49]

Therefore, under French law, a cap on liability is valid unless it relates to an essential obligation of the contract and therefore deprives the contract of its essence or essential purpose. For example, in a contract for the supply of photography services, a limitation of liability relating to the quality of the photographs is not valid. However, it is possible to limit liability to direct losses and exclude liability for consequential loss. Limitations on liability can be overturned in the event of fraud, serious negligence (*faute lourde*) or intentional misconduct (*dol*) and it is very common to see liability clauses which expressly exclude loss arising from these elements from the overall liability cap.

The Reformed Code goes further than established French case law as it applies to any clause contained in an agreement. For example, the following clauses are likely to be considered invalid under the Reformed Code:

---

48 Arrêt Chronopost, Cour de cassation chambre commerciale, du 22 octobre 1996, 93-18.632.
49 See, the Reformed French Civil Code, Art. 1170, translation by author.

1. Clauses that indirectly deprive a party of their right to seek dispute resolution due to high legal costs such as an arbitration clause or a clause setting a costly jurisdiction for dispute resolution.

2. Clauses setting an extremely short deadline for performing an obligation.

3. Risk-sharing clauses which essentially exonerate one party from their contractual responsibility.

9.10.2   Limiting liability in Switzerland

In Switzerland, clauses that limit a party's liability are usually valid but are subject to certain restrictions.[50] The scope of the limitation of liability is handled differently depending on the context and the subject matter. Very broadly speaking, any clause which appears to release a party from its contractual liability in case of its own gross negligence (*faute grave*) or fraud (*dol*) will be deemed by the Swiss courts to be null and void.[51] The issue of whether civil liability can also be limited is somewhat disputed but such limitation is usually admitted, unless otherwise stipulated by law.[52] An excessive clause would still stand as valid, but only to the extent consistent with the law.[53]

Article 8 of the Swiss Federal Product Liability Act of 18 June 1993 expressly excludes any attempt by a manufacturer to limit their liability at the expense of the victim.[54] This provision does however not relate to the contractual claims.[55] In Switzerland, as in other countries, it is hard to limit liability for personal injury.[56]

---

50 Werro, *supra* note 22, p.4, N 3; See in particular Arts 19, 100 and 101 of the Swiss Code of Obligations, as well as Art. 27 of the Code.

51 See, ibid., Art. 100.

52 Werro, *supra* note 22, p.4, N 3.

53 Luc Thévenoz, *in* Commentaire romand du Code des Obligations I, Helbing Lichtenhahn, 2012, *ad* Art. 100, p. 780, N 21.

54 See Arts 2 and 8 of the Swiss Federal Product Liability Act of 18 June 1993, which defines a manufacturer as someone who either produced the product, a component part of the product or the raw material, affixed its brand, name or another distinctive sign or imported the product.

55 Werro, *supra* note 22, p.215, N 735.

56 Ibid., p.5, N 5.

9.11   Term and termination

The termination clause is one of the most important clauses in any contract and is the one most likely to be read through with a fine tooth comb in the future. This clause will tell you: Who has the right to terminate? In what circumstances? How much notice do they have to give?

When drafting the contract, think carefully about the impact of the contract being terminated in the future. How long will you need to put alternative arrangements in place? What actions will you want the other party to complete following termination? At a minimum you will likely want them to settle any outstanding bills and return any confidential information or other intellectual property in their possession.

9.11.1   Abrupt termination of established commercial relationships

In France, care must be taken when terminating an established commercial relationship. The French Commercial Code[57] includes provisions that were initially created to prevent unfair behaviour by distributors regarding their preferred supplier lists against the 'abrupt termination of an established commercial relationship.' Over the years, the scope of the provisions has widened and it now applies to all commercial relationships, whether for the sale of goods, the supply of services, subcontracting or outsourcing agreements. As mentioned earlier in the chapter, it applies to pre-contractual and informal agreements as well as formal written contracts.

In deciding whether a commercial relationship is 'established,' French case law has referred to several different conditions such as the duration of the relationship between the parties or the increase in turnover between the parties over the relationship. Most often, the duration of the relationship remains the deciding factor and this means that a contract with a long term as well as several shorter contracts over a long period or even a succession of one-off fixed term contracts can be enough to evidence the existence of an established commercial relationship.[58]

---

57 See Art. L. 442-6-I.5 of the French Commercial Code.
58 See Cass, com 15 septembre 2009, n°08-19.2009.

The concept of 'termination' includes partial termination of a commercial relationship. Total termination is usually the non-renewal or sudden ending of a contract. Partial termination can result from: (i) a change in a party's organisation and practices; (ii) a significant reduction in business; (iii) a change in applicable tariffs such as a supplier's price increase without any notice; or (iv) a unilateral and substantive change to contract terms.[59] A price increase is particularly problematic if the same supplier had special prices for its buyers.

The French Commercial Code does not set out any requirements regarding the reason for the termination as this is not important as far as the law is concerned. The key factor is whether the commercial relationship was terminated 'abruptly.' In order to be 'abrupt' the termination must be *unforeseeable, sudden and violent.* A termination is likely to be abrupt if it was done without written notice, or with no regard to previous commercial relations between the parties, common and recognised industry practices or professional agreements.

In Italy there are no specific provisions concerning the abrupt termination of commercial relationships. However, if there is an abrupt termination of an existing commercial relationship, it may be possible for the injured party to claim a violation of the good faith principle. As explained in the context of pre-contractual liability, if the termination occurs before the contract is signed, it may be possible to bring a pre-contractual liability claim.

That said, Italian law n. 192/1998 specifically governs subcontracting (*'il contratto di subfornitura'*) and has some aspects in common with the French law on abrupt termination. Article 9 states that abuse of economic dependence (*'stato di dipendenza economica'*) is prohibited. This applies, for example, to a supplier which is dependent on a particular order. Such economic dependence applies where there is an excessive imbalance of the rights and obligations.[60] This is a common issue when there is a lack of competition and the other party has no satisfactory alternatives in the market.

The law provides a non-exhaustive list of misconducts that can give rise to such kind of liability such as: (i) the refusal to sell or to buy; or

---

59 See French case law – CA de Paris, 28 octobre 2005, n° 2005-284109; Cass. Com., 6 février 2007, n° 04-13.178; CA de Paris, 12 septembre 2001, n° 99-15368.

60 See Art. 9, Sec. 1, para. 2 and 3 of law n. 192/1998.

(ii) the arbitrary interruption of commercial relationships (*'interruzione arbitraria delle relazioni commerciali in atto'*).[61] If the court finds that the there is a lack of economic independence, it will void the contract. These provisions apply to subcontracting, franchising, integrated distribution and generally to any supply agreements.[62]

9.11.2   Learn from Louboutin: terminating a French contract

The French Commercial Code provisions allow a party the right to terminate an agreement due to poor performance. For example, Christian Louboutin successfully terminated an agreement with one of its distributors, Rosenstein Chausseur Inc., with 19 months' notice. The termination was due to repeated delays for payment of the merchandise by Rosenstein. The notice period was not ultimately performed because Rosenstein failed to make payment which resulted in the cancellation of new orders. Rosenstein brought proceedings against Christian Louboutin seeking compensation based on the abrupt termination of an established commercial relationship.

The Paris Commercial Court dismissed Rosenstein's claims and ordered Rosenstein to pay all of Christian Louboutin's outstanding invoices and legal costs. The court considered that Rosenstein's failure to pay the invoices justified Christian Louboutin's decision to terminate the relationship without notice and its decision to refuse to honour any new orders was also justified on this basis. The Paris Court of Appeal confirmed the first instance decision and held that the abrupt termination of the commercial relationship during the notice period was due to the fact that Rosenstein had failed to respect one of the essential obligations in the agreement, namely, to pay Christian Louboutin's invoices.[63]

---

61 See Art. 9, Sec. 2, law n. 192/1998.

62 Scholars: Maugeri, Abuso di dipendenza economica e autonomia privata, Milano, Giuffrè, 2003, 131 ss. and also, La subfornitura, in I contratti per l'impresa, Gitti Maugeri e Notari, Bologna, Il Mulino, 2012, 228. Case law: obiter dictum of Cass. Sez. Un. (ord.), November 25, 2011, No. 24906, in Nuova giur. civ. commentata, 2012, I, 28 ss.; Taranto Court (ord.), December 22, 2003, in Danno e Resp., 2004, 424 ss.; Cass. Sez. Un. (ord.), November 25, 2011, No. 24906; Turin Court, March 11, 2010, in Giurisp. Commerciale, 2011, I, pp. 1471; Rome Court (ord.), November 5, 2003, in Riv. Dir. Comm., 2004, II, pp.1; Trieste Court (ord.), September 20, 2006, in Diritto e giurisprudenza, 2006, 568 ss. and Catania Court, (ord.), January 5, 2004, in Danno e Resp., 2004, pp. 426.

63 CA de Paris, Pôle 5, ch.4, 2 septembre 2015.

9.11.3   Notice periods when terminating a French contract

 The most risky element of the French Commercial Code provision on abrupt termination is that the notice period applicable on termination must take into account the duration of the commercial relationship. When a court decides if a notice period is sufficiently long, it will almost exclusively have regard to the length of the commercial relationship. The aim behind the notice period is to ensure that a contracting party can economically and financially prepare itself and anticipate the end of the commercial relationship by rearranging or reorganising its activities.

It is quite common that termination provisions will be fully defined in a written agreement. This means that most contracts provide for a notice period in the event of termination or non-renewal. However, even if you invoke a termination and notice clause in an agreed contract term, it is still possible that the termination will not pass the court's stringent test. If there is a dispute, the judges are not bound to accept the terms entered into by the parties and are able to decide on their own initiative whether the notice period was sufficient or not.[64] French courts often award one month of notice per year of relationship but this is a very general rule of thumb and specific advice should be sought in each individual circumstance.

When making its assessment, the court may look further than the duration of the commercial relationship. For example, at the overall circumstances such as the sector (seasonal collections in the fashion industry being less permanent in nature than a year-long commitment)[65] or the financial importance of the commercial relationship for one of the parties. The court will also consider whether there was any exclusivity agreement, whether any investments were made during the commercial relationship or the overall economic dependence of the injured party on the commercial relationship.[66] Indeed, the French Commercial Code expressly states that when a commercial relationship concerns the supply of products under the distributor's brand name, the minimum notice period should be doubled to what would have been applicable had the product not been supplied under the distributor's brand.

---

64 See CA de Lyon, 10 avril 2003, n° 2001-05067.
65 See CA de Paris, 28 juin 2004.
66 See ibid.; Cour de cassation, Ch. Comm., 7 janvier 2004, n° 02-12.437.

9.11.4   Justifying termination

A recent case from the French Supreme Court stated that the cancellation of orders resulting in the termination of a commercial relationship due to the global economic crisis was justifiable and not an *abrupt termination* of a commercial relationship.

A clothes designer had contracted with a shirt manufacturer to produce shirts in return for commission which would be calculated on the number of orders. Due to financial difficulties that the clothes designer encountered in 2008 during the 'credit crunch,' it started to reduce its orders. Two years later, the arrangement was no longer commercially viable since the clothes designer could not continue to assume the increase in costs per unit for the production of the shirts. The manufacturer had imposed this price increase in order to compensate for the reduction in the number of orders placed. As a result, the clothes designer stopped all orders.

The French Supreme Court agreed that the reduction in the number of orders was a direct consequence of a financial crisis which affected the clothes designer's sector. The reduction in orders and termination following the subsequent price increase was found to be a good reason for terminating the contract. Consequently, the designer was free from any liability arising from the termination.[67]

If an established commercial relationship is abruptly terminated, the injured party can claim damages. These damages are calculated in accordance with the length of the notice period that should have been given multiplied by the average profit that would have been made during that period.[68] In practice, French judges often award damages that go above losses arising directly from the nature of the termination. In some instances, the court may consider that compensation should also extend to related losses, such as operating costs, the cost of staff dismissals, closing premises or loss of stock.

It is therefore essential to closely manage your relationships with French suppliers and distributors as well as any other commercial relationships governed by French law. It is important that you seek legal advice to mitigate any risk if you decide to terminate an established

---

67 See French Supreme Court decision, Cass. Com., 8 November 2017, No. 16-15.285.
68 See CA d'Amiens, 15 juin 2004, n° 2004-247709.

commercial relationship in France. To put you in the strongest possible position, if a commercial relationship starts to go sour, make sure that you keep as much evidence as possible such as sales information, notice letters and other documentation to protect your position.

9.12   Confidentiality

Do you want your pricing being made publicly available or your designs to be shared before they hit the shops? A confidentiality clause is standard in many agreements. It is often linked to a definition of 'Confidential Information' and, as a minimum, usually requires that the agreement itself remains confidential, particularly the pricing. If something is particularly sensitive, it may be worth setting out the terms in a separate confidentiality agreement; for example, if you have developed a particularly innovative product which has not yet launched or have a top secret advertising campaign or celebrity endorsement for a key product.

The intellectual property rights in confidential information are discussed in more detail in Chapter 7.

9.13   Understanding 'boilerplate' clauses

 Most written contracts have some standard clauses which usually appear toward the end of document. These 'boilerplate' clauses are a common feature of most business contracts worldwide. While these terms are not essential, they can be very helpful in minimising uncertainty in the future. They are often seen as 'standard' and are therefore easy to overlook in the negotiation process. However, there are a few things which it is good to keep an eye out for . . .

9.13.1   *Force majeure*

Force majeure is an old fashioned term to describe your worst case scenario – fire, flood, terrorism, etc. A *force majeure* event is something that happens entirely outside everyone's control and could not have been predicted in advance. The paradigm examples are war or natural disasters but less cataclysmic events such as a warehouse fire or key machinery breaking may also be *force majeure* events. Think carefully about your worst case scenario and plan for how you will both approach this issue in the written contract in advance. In France, the Reformed Civil Code now contains a definition of *force majeure* together with the available solutions.[69]

Bear in mind that just because an event is bad for your business does not necessarily mean that it is a *force majeure* event. Some people unsuccessfully attempted to claim that the result of Britain's referendum on membership of the EU (commonly referred to as Brexit) was a *force majeure* event.

A good insurance policy can avoid the need to consider the contractual position and may provide a more convenient and practical solution.

9.13.2   Entire agreement

An entire agreement clause is generally along the following lines: 'This agreement constitutes the entire agreement between the parties and supersedes any previous agreements or representations.' It may go on to state something along the lines that 'each party agrees that it shall have no remedies in respect of any statement that is not set out in this agreement.' Often, parties will also include a related non-reliance clause which explicitly excludes any future claims for innocent or negligent misrepresentation based on any statement in the agreement.

The point of an entire agreement clause is to provide certainty to the parties and ensure that everyone is on the same page (i.e., the pages of the agreement). They are often relied upon where one party seeks to litigate on the basis of statements that were made before the contract was finalised (known as 'pre-contractual representations').

There are many limitations to the effectiveness of entire agreement clauses. For example, they do not prevent the parties from relying on statements or documents 'extrinsic' to the contract i.e., those documents that can be used to cast light on the meaning of the contract. Although such extrinsic documents cannot be relied on to establish a separate contractual agreement between the parties. Further, while implied terms and liability for misrepresentation cannot be excluded, some implied terms can be separately contracted out of and a non-reliance clause can exclude liability for misrepresentation (unless it is fraudulent).

---

69 Reformed Civil Code, Art. 1218.

9.13.3   Variation

Even after a contract has been signed it is always possible to vary it provided that everyone who entered into it agrees to the variation. A variation clause sets out the terms on which a variation of the agreement is possible. A variation clause may go as far as to state: 'no amendment or variation of this agreement will be effective unless it is in writing and signed by the parties.'

Consider whether this is workable in practice. For example, are any terms such as pricing or timing going to be flexible, so separate signed written agreements for each change will not work well in practice. You could, for example, limit the variation clause to specific terms of the contract.

9.13.4   Assignment

Assignment clauses are very important. They set out the circumstances in which one party to the contract can transfer or 'assign' their rights and responsibilities under the contract to a completely different party. This means that while you enter into a contract with one company, you may later find yourself locked into a business relationship with a completely different company. Of course this can happen even if the contracting parties remain the same. If key people leave or the company is taken over you may find that the relationship substantially changes in any event.

This issue can be dealt with in various ways. For example, the contract may prohibit assignment altogether or only allow assignment in certain circumstances such as all parties agreeing in writing, or the other party being given notice of the proposed alternative party (known as the 'assignee' because the contract is being assigned to them). Another alternative is to allow assignment on notice after a certain period of time. It is up to you what you agree but make sure you read it and know what you are signing up to in advance. Bear in mind that a stringent assignment clause can count against you if you want to sell your business as it may add another level of complexity to the corporate due diligence process which takes place prior to sale and in some circumstances it could reduce the purchase price.

Restrictions on assignment and change of control clauses, which give contracting parties the right to terminate the contract if the control of either party changes (usually following a share sale) can cause similar problems when it comes to selling the company. It is important to avoid these terms where possible as it could limit your options in the future. See Chapter 23 for more information.

9.13.5 No waiver

If one of the parties breaches an important term of the contract, the other party is usually entitled to terminate the contract. A 'No Waiver Clause' typically says something along the following lines: *No failure or delay to exercise any right or remedy is a waiver of that right or remedy.*

The contract may allow for a period in which the breach can be remedied (e.g., payment made or goods delivered) but some terms may be so important or 'material' to the contract that not complying with the term is an immediate breach of contract. If the 'innocent' or 'non-defaulting' party takes too long to complain or do anything about the breach then there is a risk that they have effectively said that they do not mind the breach of contract and they are no longer entitled to complain about it. In England, this is known as 'affirming' the contract.

In order to 'waive' the contract breach, you will need to have both knowledge of all the facts which gave you the right to terminate and to have given the party who is breaching the contract 'clear and unequivocal notice' that you will not be pursuing the breach of contract. A 'no waiver' clause essentially states that a failure or delay to exercise a right is not a waiver of that right. This can help to give you longer to resolve a dispute without being forced to terminate in order to preserve your legal position.

9.13.6 Severance

One of the more useful but occasionally frustrating facts about the law is that it is not static. Sometimes a change in a law or regulation can have the effect that a clause which everyone has quite happily relied upon for years becomes unlawful or otherwise unenforceable. If you have such a clause in your agreement, it is generally preferable to be able to simply delete the clause rather than rewrite the entire contract.

A typical severance clause will be along the following lines:

> If any part of this agreement is or becomes invalid, illegal or unenforceable, it shall be deemed modified to the minimum extent necessary to make it

valid, legal and enforceable. If modification is not possible, the relevant part shall be deemed deleted. Any modification or deletion shall not affect the validity and enforceability of the rest of this agreement.

A severance clause is helpful if the law changes but even if you have one, sometimes the void terms are so fundamental to the contract that you cannot simply delete them without the contract falling to pieces. Therefore while this clause can be helpful it is not a panacea for all potential contract ills.

9.13.7   Notice

It is common for longer commercial contracts to include a reference to the notice provisions to be followed. This is essentially who to notify (including their name, title, email and postal address) if something happens that requires formal notification under the terms of the contract. This could include notification of a breach of contract, desire to modify the terms or if one party wishes to terminate the contract. Bear in mind that people move jobs. Make sure that the notice provisions are flexible enough that changes in personnel will not cause any issues. In other words, try not to simply rely on an individual's email address which may not be monitored in a few years' time. Ideally a standard email address should be used which is closely monitored by you, senior management or the legal team (dependent on the size of the business).

9.13.8   Counterparts

A counterpart is a separate physical copy of a document which is signed by another party. When electronic signatures become the norm in all contracts this clause may lose importance. In the meantime, it is very helpful when signatories are not in the same physical location. One big advantage of a counterparts clause is that it is possible to have the signature pages ready in advance and then released once the final negotiations have been completed. This is therefore a useful clause to include in most contracts.

9.13.9   Further assurance

If the contract requires one of the parties to complete some paperwork in a specific time frame, a 'further assurance' clause can be very helpful. This clause is usually along the following lines: 'Each party shall execute and deliver such documents and perform such acts as may reasonably be required for the purpose of giving full effect to this agreement.' If the contract depends on third parties performing their contractual obligations as well, they can be set out here as well.

Further assurance can be particularly important where intellectual property rights are concerned because specific paperwork is often required to transfer rights and assistance may be required in the future in order to bring legal action – for example, to prove use of a trade mark or demonstrate goodwill. If a registered right needs to be transferred, it is common to include a power of attorney clause or a separate power of attorney which gives the right to transfer the rights without the other party's involvement. Powers of attorney are considered in more detail later in this chapter.

9.13.10   Third party rights

In England, the rights of 'third parties' i.e., people or legal entities who are not party to the agreement but are nevertheless affected by it are protected by the Contracts (Rights of Third Parties) Act 1999. This act gives 'third parties' the right to enforce a term of a contract in limited circumstances. The general practice has been to simply exclude the effect of the act because of the perceived risk of uncertain outcomes.

Such a clause is generally along the following lines: 'A person who is not a party to this agreement shall not have any rights under the Contracts (Rights of Third Parties) Act 1999 to enforce any term of this agreement.'

French law on the rights of third parties is not as exhaustive as the English legislation. The Reformed French Civil Code does nonetheless provide some information relating to third party rights. For example, the default position is that a contract only creates rights between the parties who entered into it. However, a third party is entitled to rely on a contract between two other parties if they need to do so for evidential purposes. For example, a supplier who granted selective rights to an authorised distributor could rely on a contract later entered into between the authorised distributor and an unauthorised third party in order to substantiate its claims.[70]

---

70 See, ibid., Arts 1199 and 1200.

Further, one party may guarantee an obligation on behalf of a third party, by promising that the third party will do something.[71] If the third party performs the obligation, the original party will be released from the guarantee, if not, the original party may be ordered to pay damages in place of the third party. This is of course a risky obligation to undertake and means that you really have to trust the third party! An example in the fashion industry could be a contract between a modelling agency and a fashion designer for the supply of a specific model. The model is not a party to the original contract but the modelling agency nonetheless undertakes to guarantee that they are available for the assignment. It is prudent to try to limit liability in these circumstances.

Further, under French law one party may make a stipulation in favour of a third party in a contract, provided that the third party can be identified or determined at the time of the performance of the contractual obligation.[72] An example of this could be seen in an agreement between a textile designer and manufacturer for the production of fabric for the benefit of an *haute couture* designer, who may not be a party to the initial production agreement.

9.13.11   Jurisdiction

If there is a dispute in the future over the contract, this clause could come back to haunt you. The jurisdiction clause determines which court can decide a future dispute over the contract.

The temptation is usually to ask for exclusive jurisdiction in your home country. However, this may not always be in your best interests. You need to think about where a breach of the contract is likely to happen and how easy it will be to get a legal remedy to that breach. It is much easier to enforce a foreign judgment in some jurisdictions rather than others. For example, it is difficult to enforce a foreign judgment in China. If this is where you manufacture, get local legal advice and consider making the agreement subject to Chinese law.

Jurisdiction can be exclusive or non-exclusive. Exclusive jurisdiction means that a breach of contract claim can only be brought in the named jurisdiction. By contrast, non-exclusive jurisdiction means that

---

71 See, ibid., Art. 1205.
72 See, ibid., Art. 1206.

a breach of contract claim can be brought in any country that can establish jurisdiction including but not limited to the country listed in the agreement. You could make some types of remedies, such as injunctive relief, non-exclusive but the remainder of the agreement exclusive. This is because you do not necessarily want to limit your options if you need to get an injunction against someone in the future.

European Union law rules[73] exist to help Member State courts to determine if they have jurisdiction in cases which involve more than one Member State. This is dealt with in more detail in the context of litigation, see Chapter 19. It is usually the court of the Member State of the party who is sued (i.e., the defendant) which will have jurisdiction. However, there are exceptions to this regime, such as exclusive jurisdiction regimes for intellectual property rights[74] and special jurisdiction[75] regimes which relate to the place of performance of a contract or where goods should have been delivered or services performed or where a harmful event occurred.

9.13.12   Choice of law

The choice of law of the contract does what it says on the tin, i.e., it sets out which country's law applies to the contract. You might assume that the law will be the same as the jurisdiction which is deciding the contract (and that is often the case), however, it is not a given. A court from one jurisdiction can consider another's law (often with assistance from local judges).

9.14   Signature

9.14.1   Authorised signatories and capacity to contract

Most agreements are regular contracts. This means they just need to be signed by an authorised signatory, e.g., a director or company secretary, in order to be legally binding.

---

73 Council Regulation (EC) No 44/2001 of 22 December 2000 on jurisdiction and the recognition and enforcement of judgments in civil and commercial matters ('Brussels Regulation').

74 See, ibid., Art. 22(4): 'In proceedings concerned with the registration or validity of patents, trade marks, designs, or other similar rights required to be deposited or registered, the courts of the Member State in which the deposit or registration has been applied for, has taken place or is under the terms of a Community instrument or an international convention deemed to have taken place.'

75 See, ibid., Art. 5.

Under French law, the Reformed Code has set out clear guidelines regarding authorised signatories and limits on a company's capacity to contract. This means that a company may only enter into contracts which are compliant and incidental with the furtherance of its purpose or object in accordance with the company's Articles of Association or '*Statuts.*'

Consequently, in France your fashion brand should only enter into contracts relating to its official activities. If you want to start entering into contracts for selling e.g., food and beverages, there is a risk that the activities would not be covered by insurance and any related contracts may be invalid. You can minimise this risk by either drafting a wide purpose when you incorporate your French company or by amending the company's purpose if you see that your activity begins to move away from what you had initially envisaged.[76]

When a company enters into a contract, it cannot physically sign itself because it is a legal entity ('*personne morale*'), and so this needs to be done on its behalf by physical representatives ('*personne physique*'). The Reformed French Civil Code states that:

> Where a duly authorised representative acts within [their] authority and in the name of the entity [they] represent, only the entity is bound to the contractual undertaking. However, where a representative states that [they are] acting on behalf of the entity, but contracts in [their] own name, only the representative is bound towards the other contracting party.[77]

It is therefore important to properly draft the signature section of your contract depending on the level of liability you wish for your signers (or the company) to have.

Italy has adopted a similar approach to France. Italian companies' legal representatives can only enter into contracts which are in accordance with the company's '*Statuto*' (i.e., the Articles of Incorporation). Consequently, drafting a wide company purpose at the time of incorporation can solve a lot of problems in the future.

Before signing a contract, it is a good idea to check the effective powers of the contracting company's legal representative. You can do this by

---

76 See, the Reformed French Civil Code, Art. 1145 al. 2.
77 See, ibid., Art. 1154, translation by the author.

carrying out an online Business Entity Search by the Italian Chambers of Commerce and requesting either a *'Visura ordinaria'* or *'Visura Storica'* (i.e., the ordinary or historic company's profile). Companies can also check data belonging to international companies through the European Business Register (Italy, France, UK and Belgium are just some of the Member States that have provided their companies' data and participate in this register).

Be aware that if your company is entering into a contract with an Italian company and the agreement is regulated by Italian law, in order to be enforceable, your company's legal representative will have to initialise all of the contract's pages as well as signing the signature block at the end of the agreement.

In Poland it is common practice to enclose an excerpt from the relevant business register (or power of attorney) which proves that the signatory is authorised. If a contract is signed by an unauthorised person it may be invalid or void until confirmation of authorisation is provided. It is therefore important to request evidence of authorisation from the counterparty.

Some agreements require a particular signing process, for example if they involve commercial real estate or the transfer of assets for less than their actual value. The latter issue can arise if you own your designs personally but want to sell your company or rely on the designs in litigation. In this case, you may have to transfer the designs to your company effectively for free. In England and many other Common Law jurisdictions you can do this by way of a deed.

The important features of a deed are: (i) it must say it is a deed – usually on page 1 and at the end; (ii) it must be in writing; and (iii) the signature process must jump through additional hoops. In England, this means that either two directors sign or one director signs with a witness to confirm their signature. If a company is particularly old school, a company seal can be used together with a director's signature instead.

The other advantage of a deed in England is that it doubles the limitation period for bringing a claim. It is 12 years for a deed and six years for a contract.

9.14.2   Powers of attorney

Powers of attorney are very important in the context of intellectual property and in a general commercial context. The French legal provisions highlight the importance of having carefully drafted powers of attorney for your nominated company representatives which clearly set out what they have the right to do on behalf of the company regardless of the applicable legal regime. For example, in France, where the authority of a representative is defined in general terms, it covers only management acts. However, a definition in specifically defined terms means that a representative may only conclude acts (and therefore ancillary or non-management acts) in the areas that have been specifically conferred on them.[78]

So what happens if a representative signs a contract that they did not have the right to sign or which covers services outside the scope of the company's purpose? The Reformed French Civil Code provides that the contract may be cancelled. This remedy depends on the knowledge of the party at the time of signing.[79] The onus is on you to verify that the representative of the other party is indeed properly empowered to conclude the act or agreement in question.[80] In other words, ask to see a copy of the Power of Attorney or company articles that they are relying upon.

9.14.3   Electronic signatures

Thankfully contracts are slowly catching up with modern technology and electronic signatures have become more common. E-signatures are fast, efficient, can be easily stored, verified and retained. There are many types of e-signature from typed to hand drawn with a stylus or a scanned physical signature. They can also be biometric data such as a thumbprint or face scan. In some fields, such as e-money, cryptographic signatures have become commonplace and this may bleed into the mainstream over time. Certainly on the face of it most e-signatures are more secure and easier to trace. In short, they have a lot of benefits.

In England, as explained at the start of this chapter, it has long been a principle of contract law that you do not need a signature to form a binding agreement – you can form a contract simply by exchanging a

---

78 See, ibid., Art. 1155.
79 See, ibid., Arts 1156 and 1157.
80 See, ibid., Art. 1158.

few texts or emails. In practice, a signature is very helpful in showing everyone concerned what has been agreed and avoids misunderstandings or confusion at a later date. The situation is similar in Switzerland where an agreement can be binding without the need of a signed document, except: (i) if Swiss law requires the document to be in a particular format; or (ii) the parties have contractually agreed that only a particular type of document will be binding e.g., a purchase order.[81]

The EU has set out the requirements for the use of electronic signatures and electronic transactions in the EU in the Electronic Identification, Authentication and Trust Services Regulation, known as eIDAS.[82] It specifically aims to strengthen confidence in new technologies and creates a set of standards for electronic signatures, digital signatures, electronic seals, timestamps and other proof of authentication mechanisms which all EU Member States are required to recognise.

There are a wide variety of available platforms which meet the eIDAS standards. The most well known are currently DocuSign and Adobe Sign. Using an electronic platform can allow users to complete approvals and agreements quickly from almost anywhere in the world and on most electronic devices. The records are much clearer and can include who signed, where (including the IP address of the computer used), their email and the exact time of signature. This is much more fraud proof and better evidence to rely on in court.

Electronic signatures also exist under Swiss law. There are several kinds, such as the qualified electronic signature with electronic timestamping,[83] the regulated electronic signature[84] or the regulated electronic stamp.[85] Only the qualified electronic signature with electronic timestamping is admissible where a formal signature is legally or contractually mandatory.[86] This type of electronic signature is only available to natural persons (i.e., not companies).[87]

In practice, it is still rare for Swiss contracts to use electronic signatures although this will likely change with time. The main purpose

---

81 See, the Swiss Code of Obligations, Art. 11.

82 eIDAS Regulation (EU) 910/2014 with effect from 1 July 2016.

83 *Signature électronique qualifiée avec horodatage électronique.*

84 *Signature électronique réglementée.*

85 *Cachet électronique réglementé.* See the Federal Act on the electronic signature of 18 March 2016 for more details.

86 See Art. 14, §2bis of the Swiss Code of Obligations.

87 See Art. 8 the Federal Act on the electronic signature.

of many of the new electronic signatures is to ensure the origin and the integrity of documents issued by authorities and legal entities.[88] However, the regulated signatures referred to above (apart from, in some circumstances, the qualified electronic signature with electronic timestamping) are not generally binding in more formal circumstances unless the parties contractually agree to use one of these new forms (and Swiss law does not prevent them from doing so).[89]

It is an open question whether deeds can be signed electronically. In theory it is possible to have a witness sign electronically as well but they will need to be in the same room and ideally on the same IP address. For the time being it is safest to get the pen out and sign deeds the old fashioned way.

The Reformed French Civil Code created several principles related to and allowing the use of electronic contracts.[90] French law also sets out requirements regarding the supply of information relating to the conclusion or performance of a contract by electronic means. For example, when using electronic contracts in a commercial, business or professional context, the applicable contractual documents must be made available so they can be saved or copied and accessed at a later stage. Further, for an electronic contract to be validly concluded under French law, the person to whom the offer is addressed must have had the possibility to verify the detail of his order, the price, and also have been allowed the possibility to correct errors.[91] It is possible to exclude this requirement or set reasonable limits on its application.[92]

In France, while a contract may be created or stored in an electronic form,[93] if a hard copy original exists the courts may still require that the 'original' be produced in court proceedings.[94] The same issue can arise in England and most, if not all, other Member States. Keep any original documents safe.

---

88 Message relatif à la révision totale de la loi sur la signature électronique (SCSE), FF 2014 957, 962.

89 See Art. 16 of the Swiss Code of Obligations; Pascal Pichonnaz, Le point sur la partie générale du droit des obligations, *in* RSJ 113/2017 p. 183.

90 See, the Reformed French Civil Code, Arts 1126 and 1127.

91 See, ibid., Art. 1127-2.

92 See, ibid., Art. 1127-3.

93 See, ibid., Art. 1174.

94 See, ibid., Art. 1379.

Finally, rules on contracts for the supply of services that are concluded exclusively by exchange of emails are much more relaxed and keeping copies of the emails should suffice. However, it is risky to rely on unsigned agreements in France given the traditional approach of French judges, so the use of a formal electronic contract (signed with an e-signature) or a traditional pen and paper copy is advisable.

9.15   Common pitfalls

9.15.1   Consequential loss

If your contract is subject to English law, make sure that you do not use the popular US legal term 'consequential loss.' In the US the term has a broad meaning which can include loss which arises as a consequence of the breach such as loss of profits or revenue. In England, it is limited to losses which were 'reasonably contemplated' at the start of the contract by at least the person who breached the contract. This can include things which are not specifically spelled out in the contract but is more limited than in the US.

For example, if you arrange for clothes to be imported from Bangladesh, it is reasonably foreseeable by the shipping company that you intend to sell them in the country you chose to ship the goods to (or at least one nearby). If there is a particular reason for getting the goods delivered before X date otherwise you lose a lucrative contract it is wise to set this out in the contract so the importance of the timing is completely clear to everyone involved. Make sure you keep records of this agreement and indeed all communication around the time of the contract.

Unlike in many Common Law jurisdictions (such as England or the US), Civil Law jurisdictions such as France define obligations as one of two categories – an obligation to provide results (*'obligation de résultat'*) or an obligation of means (*'obligation de moyen'*).

A results obligation is more stringent and means that the relevant party is obligated to achieve a predetermined result. For example, in a contract for the sale of goods, there is an obligation of results on the seller to provide the goods that he has promised. There is also an obligation of results on the purchaser who engaged to pay the agreed price.

An obligation of means occurs when a party undertakes to use resources at its disposal to accomplish the performance of an obligation, without any guarantee as to the overall result or outcome. For example, a doctor has an obligation to use their available resources to treat a patient, but has no resulting obligation to cure the patient.

This is often an area where parties or lawyers who are not familiar with Civil Law regimes can fall into difficulty. In practice it is quite common to specify in a contract (especially one for the supply of services) that the providing party is only bound by an obligation of means, or even to specify the different categories of obligations in different clauses. For example, in a contract for the supply of technical assistance, the parties may limit liability regarding breach of confidential information via third parties (i.e., staff or external consultants) to 'best efforts' or means obligations but they may agree that project delivery dates are covered by results obligations.

In some areas of law, an obligation of results is compulsory – for example, in employment law, an employer has an obligation of results to ensure the health, safety and wellbeing of its employees. It is therefore worth seeking the advice of local lawyers to ensure that the contract fully reflects your capacity to respect the obligations on a results basis, or whether you need to limit them (for example if a result depends on elements which could be difficult to control such as reliance on a third-party contractor).

The distinction between results obligations and means obligations is important when it comes to litigation. For example, in the event of breach relating to a results obligation, there is a presumption of fault on the part of the party which agreed to those results, and the burden of proof lies on that party to show that the results were indeed achieved. On the other hand, if means obligations apply, then it is for the party claiming breach of contract to show that there was contractual fault by the other party.

9.15.2 Re-using contracts

If you have spent a long time negotiating a contract, it is completely understandable that the next time the same issue comes around you simply want to get the old contract out of the box, maybe update the names and dates but essentially recycle it. This apparent environmental friendliness may come with many unforeseen strings attached.

There is a costs balance to be had here but bear in mind that what worked with one party may not work with another, not least because no two trading relationships are the same. For example, there is a risk that particular concessions which were agreed with one party can become your default. On the other hand, standard terms with suppliers can be extremely useful and are well worth the effort involved in developing and understanding them. These standard terms or framework agreements are a main contract which is negotiated in detail so that all future orders can be made on the basis of a purchase order with reference to the standard terms or framework agreement.

9.16   Consumer contracts

There are certain requirements for contracts that you enter into with consumers (as opposed to wholesalers, suppliers, etc.). This is particularly important for online sales and is set out in more detail below. Bear in mind that while consumer protection laws are becoming more consistent around the world, there can still be substantial differences between consumer protection laws in North America, Europe and Asia so a global approach is a challenge.

These global variations in consumer law have two major implications:

1.   you may be able to operate without any difficulty in your home territory but face problems if you move into new markets; and

2.   you may find that your customers expect certain terms to be offered (particularly around returns) even if in that particular territory you are not legally obliged to offer that form of protection.

Once you start to scale, think about what strategy will work best for you. Sometimes offering the higher level of protection around the world is the best bet as it provides a consistent approach and can create more customer loyalty, but this comes with a price tag.

9.17   Standard terms: what do they mean and can they be varied?

Standard terms can save a lot of time and avoid reinventing the wheel every time you want to enter into a new agreement. When you are starting out, your negotiating power is likely to be low and you are more likely to be using other people's standard terms for anything from the supply of Internet facilities to manufacturing and distribution.

Even if you do not think you have the ability to negotiate, it is still worth reading the contract and pushing back on any particularly problematic terms such as timing for delivery and payment, price, term and termination. For example, you do not want to get tied into a 12-month Internet or rental contract when you are starting out. If the company is unwilling to negotiate, shop around. There are many more options than there used to be for everything from office space to pop up shops.

Since the French Contract Law Reform, the issue of significant inequality in standard terms has been codified. Under French law, a standard-form contract[95] is an agreement for which the general conditions are determined in advance by one of the parties, without negotiation.[96] The equality between parties in cases where standard terms apply is one key innovation of the reform, the provisions are considered to be a matter of public policy and may not be limited or deleted by contract or otherwise. In theory this means that the 'weaker' party now has good arguments to avoid accepting unduly onerous pre-defined terms. The provisions of the Code state that: 'General conditions put forward by one party have no effect on the other party unless they have been brought to the other party's attention, and that party has accepted them'.[97]

If the standard terms create 'a significant imbalance in the rights and obligations of the parties,' the contract is set aside (i.e., 'deemed not written'). The assessment of a significant imbalance must not concern the main subject matter of the contract or the price relative to the performance.[98]

9.18   Licence agreements

 Licensing is hugely important for the fashion industry, it can provide access to new markets and, along with the use of franchising, distributors and agents, is an important toolkit in scaling a fashion business.

---

95 Or 'contrat d'adhésion.'
96 See, the Reformed French Civil Code, Art. 1110 al. 2.
97 See, ibid., Art. 1119, translation by Charlotte Gerrish.
98 See, ibid., Art. 1171, translation by Charlotte Gerrish.

Care should be taken to avoid over-saturating the market with branded products so try to avoid jumping on every licence deal. As with franchises, agents and distributors, it is also essential that you retain tight quality control. Make sure that you take your time during the negotiation process and are confident that your strategies, finances, infrastructures and approach are aligned before committing your business to such an important, and potentially long-term, relationship.

An exclusive licence means that only one legal entity (i.e., a person or business) has the right to use the subject matter of the licence (e.g., a trade mark) for the duration of the licence and in the licensed territory or field (e.g., sunglasses). This includes a restriction on the owner of the licensed right from using it. If you want to retain a licensed right then you need to make this clear in the contract, it then becomes what is known as a 'sole' licence. Try to avoid the words 'sole and exclusive' as this is a contradiction in terms. An exclusive licence should clearly state that it is 'exclusive.'

Exclusive licensees have more rights than non-exclusive licensees. For example, they have the right to bring proceedings in the event of an infringement by a third party. But they also tend to carry more responsibilities. If you are not sure which is best for you, get professional advice before proceeding.

Payment under a licence is typically by means of a royalty. It is important that concepts such as gross profits and net sales are clearly defined in the contract and all parties are clear about what are permitted deductions from any royalty calculation. The royalty percentage will depend on the strength of your brand and your relative licensing position. In order to assess whether the royalties are being properly paid, it is important that any licence gives some form of audit right. This is because you will not have sight of the payments which your licensee will receive directly or indirectly via retailers.

Licences commonly provide for minimum orders and fairly tight control over promotions or advertising. It can also be possible to use the licence to control the use of online sales and discount stores. This is discussed further in the context of agency agreements in Chapter 11.

Quality control is an important and ongoing issue, it can be managed by requiring a sample up front to be approved and regular checks to ensure that there has been no quality fade in later product iterations. Quality fade is where the product quality slowly deteriorates (or 'fades') over time. It is a particularly notorious problem in China. There are a few tried and tested means for reducing this risk:

1. Make sure the licence stipulates the use of a reputable manufacturer.

2. Ideally you should visit the factory at least once before signing and regularly during the course of the agreement.

3. Be as detailed as possible in your product specifications, this will assist the factory and makes it harder for the factory to move away from these requirements over time.

4. Inspect the products on a regular basis. This can be done yourself or using a third party product tester. The latter is more important if your product claims particular features, such as water resistance.

Other related commercial issues such as insurance, compliance with product safety legislation and responsibility for repairs and related customer service complaints should also be considered.

It is important in all jurisdictions, to remember to comply with the particular contractual formalities such as the requirement for exclusive licences and assignments to be in writing and signed by both parties. As we have seen, Poland has particularly strict contractual provisions which mean that where crucial issues such as the field of use are not regulated, the default position that the rights remain with the creator may apply. By way of further example, in Poland if the parties fail to specify the term for a non-exclusive licence, it will automatically expire after five years.[99]

Another important question concerns sub-licensing. If you are licensing a right you will likely want the opportunity to sub-licence it either to another company in your group or to someone else who may be better positioned to exploit the right. This makes the relationship between the licensee and the rights holder one step removed. If your rights are being licensed, this loss of control may be less than ideal. Common solutions include only permitting sub-licensing with the rights holder's prior written consent, not to be 'unreasonably withheld, conditioned or delayed.'

---

99 See Art. 66 of Polish Act on Copyright.

10 Before you get anyone new involved

In order for your business to be a success, the involvement of other people is essential. These people may be freelancers who are brought into help with a specific task; a (virtual) assistant; a designer; a sales assistant; or new business partners. Understanding and being clear about the nature of the relationship from the start is essential both from an employment (or labour) law perspective and an intellectual property point of view. Getting this wrong can have a severe impact on your reputation and may mean that you do not own all your intellectual property rights.

10.1   An employee, a worker or a contractor?

Labour laws vary substantially across Europe. If someone is your employee in France or Spain, you are taking on a potentially expensive obligation as it is difficult and expensive to terminate an employment contract in these territories. By contrast, in the UK, provided you comply with health and safety legislation and you do not discriminate, employees have limited protection for their first two years of service. Similarly, in Switzerland, employers are free to terminate employment contracts, within the contractual time constraints, provided that the underlying reason that led to the termination is not unfair – for example based on the employee's race, nationality, age or sexual orientation.[1]

Understanding the legal nature of the people who work for you is important in determining everything from the tax that they and you are obliged to pay to whether you own the intellectual property rights which they develop for you. For example, in England you automatically own copyright in works created by your employees in the course of their employment. This is easier to prove where you have an

---

1 See Art. 336 of the Code of Obligations; Rémy Wyler, Boris Heinzer, Droit du travail, Stämpfli Editions SA Berne, 2014, p.623.

employment contract in place but someone may be an employee even where some of the legal formalities have been skipped. If you have outsourced the creation process to a freelancer, in order to legally own and use the rights, you will need an 'assignment' (or at least an 'exclusive licence') of the rights which were created for you to be signed by both you and the freelancer.

In the UK and other Common Law territories, even if you have not got 'legal' ownership, provided you have paid for an intellectual property right you may have 'beneficial' ownership. This means that the court implies a term into the contract for services so that the copyright generated under that contract is assigned to the person who paid for it. This was famously an issue for Doc Martens – they had to issue court proceedings when the person who designed their logo tried to sell the copyright in the logo to a competitor! The English court was not impressed with this approach and confirmed that Doc Martens was the beneficial owner.[2] It is obviously easier to get everything in order from the start.

 In some circumstances, even if you have a document which proclaims you to be the legal owner, if the chain of title is unclear or there is someone else out there with competing rights, it may not be worth as much you might think and requires some further investigation. Chain of title is an important concept which can become an issue where older rights are concerned. It basically requires that there is a sequence of contracts from the creator of a work through to the current owner. If there is a break in the chain, because, for example a contract has been lost, it can be more risky to rely on it as you cannot guarantee that the ownership successfully transferred. This tends to be less of an issue for fashion than the music or film industries but it is worth bearing in mind when considering use of an archive design.

10.1.1   How to tell the difference

Employees in Europe typically have fairly strong rights compared to their counterparts in Asia or the Americas. However, not everyone who works for you is necessarily an employee, they could be a 'worker' or a freelancer (also known as a contractor). Working with freelancers is generally considered easier for companies as they create fewer binding contractual obligations and offer more flexibility. Whether some-

---

2 See *R. Griggs Group Ltd and Ors v Evans and Ors* [2003] EWHC 2914.

one working for you is an employee, worker or contractor will affect the associated risks and costs. This depends on the particular factual circumstances.

First, the type of employment contract (fixed term or permanent) is decisive. Under French law, a fixed term employment contract may only be used in limited situations and for a limited period (usually 18 months). Fixed term contracts cannot be used as a substitute for a job which would normally be a permanent contract. Fixed term contracts have limited grounds for termination during the employment contract such as gross misconduct.

Secondly, specific contractual clauses will impact the work relationship. For example, a probation or 'trial' period to evaluate the employee performance at the start of a contract is more typically associated with an employee relationship. Likewise, a non-competition clause to prevent someone who used to work for you competing against you in the future is commonly associated with an employee relationship.

A purported worker or contractor can challenge their legal situation and ask an employment court to classify them as an employee. This challenge is more likely to succeed when they work very closely with other employees and the business they claim is their employer is their main or only client.

In France, determining the legal nature of the people who work for you is a sensitive issue since terminating an employment contract requires a specific procedure to be followed and may be expensive. The level of damages depends on the ground of dismissal, the employee's personal situation and seniority. The recent 'Macron Ordinances'[3] implemented scales of fixed damages (minimum and maximum) for employees in case of unfair dismissal litigation. This provides more certainty for employers in terms of the potential costs.

The key is to take the time to prepare a comprehensive employment contract or service agreement and make sure this is adapted to local laws in each territory where you operate.

---

3 'Ordonnances Macron' from September 22 2017 – n° 2017-1387.

10.2   Who owns the intellectual property?

 As mentioned above, in some Member States such as England there are specific rules which govern the ownership of intellectual property rights that are created in the course of employment. This does not mean that everything an employee creates while employed belongs to their employer but it does include anything that they create in the course of their job (i.e., what they are paid to do). For example, someone in the PR team of a fashion company who designs clothes in their spare time would own the copyright and design right in those designs. However, a designer in the same company would face a more difficult task in persuading their employer that clothes which they designed out of hours did not belong to the business. This is easier to establish if the clothes are different to those made by their employer e.g., menswear rather than ladieswear and they were not specifically directed to create them.

In the US, this rule is known as the 'work for hire' doctrine. This doctrine sets out the nine specific circumstances in which a work is treated as being made in the course of employment and therefore automatically belongs to the employer. The key questions are:

1.   Was it created in the course of employment?

2.   Was it specifically commissioned by the employer?

3.   Is there a contract which stipulates otherwise?

The same broad principles apply in Europe. The most relevant contract is the employment contract which can provide for ownership of works created by employees to be broader than the default legal standard. Bear in mind that the greater the land grab you make for a designer's rights, the fewer good candidates are likely to be available. Further, such broad clauses can be difficult to enforce in some European jurisdictions.

As mentioned above, if the person creating something for your business is not an employee, unless the contract specifies otherwise, ownership of the intellectual property rights in their creation will remain with them. Even if they are an employee, in many European jurisdictions ownership remains with the employee unless the contract says otherwise. This is the case regardless of the amount of money you spend on a design, photograph or any other rights. The question of rights ownership is commonly an issue with photographs where photographers typically retain all of the relevant rights. Chapter 13 considers this issue in the broader context of fashion archives.

Bear in mind that in some jurisdictions, such as Russia, if a work which is created in the course of employment is not used by the employer within a specified period (in Russia it is three years), the ownership of the rights will transfer to the employee who created the work.[4]

Swiss law[5] distinguishes between the inventions and designs made by the employee in three different situations, namely those made:

1.   for an employer in accordance with their contractual obligations;

2.   for an employer outside the scope of their contractual obligations;

3.   outside their professional capacity and the scope of their contractual obligations.[6]

The first type belongs to the employer absolutely but the employee reserves the right to be identified as the creator. The second and third type belong to the employee. However, for the second type, an employer can contractually reserve its rights to acquire the invention or design provided it notifies the employee of that desire within six months of the rights' creation.[7] If it acquires the right, it must pay a fair compensation to the employee.[8]

Neither this provision[9] nor the Swiss Copyright Act deals with literary and artistic works save in relation to software.[10] This means that in theory a Swiss employer does not acquire any rights in the literary and artistic works created by its employee.[11] The assignment of copyright

---

4   See here for more information: https://iclg.com/practice-areas/copyright-laws-and-regulations/russia.

5   Swiss Code of Obligations, Art. 332.

6   Pierre Tercier, Laurent Bieri, Blaise Carron, Les contrats spéciaux, Schulthess Médias Juridiques SA, 5th ed., 2016, p. 402, N 2987-2993.

7   Ibid., N 2992.

8   See, Swiss Code of Obligations, Art. 332 §4.

9   Wyler, Heinzer, *supra* note 1, p. 435.

10   See, Swiss Copyright Act, Art. 17; Tercier, Bieri, Carron, *supra* note 6, p. 403, N 2995.

11   Wyler, Heinzer, *supra* note 1, p. 436.

to the employer can (and usually is) provided in the employment contract.[12] However, as in France, the creator's moral rights cannot be assigned under Swiss law.

Under Polish copyright law, any works created within the scope of employment obligations belong to the employer upon acceptance of the work. In most instances, if the employer does not explicitly reject the work, or condition the acceptance on making some specific changes, the copyright is transferred to the employer within six months. However, when it comes to software, the copyright is vested primarily in the employer.[13] The rights to a patent or 'industrial design' following employee inventions or creative innovations created in the course of employment vest automatically in the employer.[14]

10.3   Employees and moral rights

In England and other Common Law countries, it is common for contracts to include a moral rights waiver. This means that an employee agrees to waive their moral rights including the right to be attributed as the author of a work; see Chapter 4 for more information. In some European countries, such as France and Switzerland,[15] it is not possible for an employee (or any person) to waive their moral rights. This means that works created by employees (and freelancers) in these jurisdictions must be properly attributed to them and they retain at least some control over the way in which their creations are used and displayed. In practice, there are very few cases which come to court based on moral rights alone[16] but it always pays to keep people informed and involved, particularly as the court of public opinion can be just as damning and damaging as the legal system, sometimes more so.

In Poland, the author's moral rights are also not transferable; however, it is common practice for employees to undertake not to exercise their

---

12 Tercier, Bieri, Carron, *supra* note 6, p. 403, N 2995.

13 See, Polish Act on Copyright, Arts 12–13 and 74.

14 See Art. 13 of the Polish Industrial Property Law dated of 30 June 2000 ('Polish Industrial Property Law').

15 Jacques de Werra, in Commentaire romand de la Propriété intellectuelle, ad Art. 16 LDA, N 16.

16 One of the more well-known concerned cartoons which the Natural History Museum used in a smaller format than originally intended by the artist (Mr Tidy – not part of the Mr Men series) who alleged that this breached his moral right to prevent derogatory treatment. The action failed. See *Tidy v Trustees of the Natural History Museum* [1996] 39 IPR 501.

moral rights. This approach is based on contract law and does not prevent the moral rights from technically existing. It has a similar outcome to moral rights waivers.

10.4   How much should you pay?

Many countries have minimum wages which must be paid to employ- ees. These are typically calculated on an hourly rate. Remember that, even if you do not call someone an employee, if the work that they are doing for you fits a country's legal criteria for a 'worker' or an 'employee' then they will be treated as such. In addition, you generally have to pay some form of social security payment. For example, in the UK, both you and your employee have to pay 'national insurance.'

Further, many countries such as Italy, the UK and Australia (not a European country but a pioneer in pension reform) require that all employees are automatically enrolled in pension schemes. They generally require both employers and employees to add a minimum percentage into a particular pension scheme. It is possible for employees to opt out of these schemes but you need to set up the scheme first and then the employees can opt out.

In Switzerland, employees' earnings are in principle governed by contractual freedom.[17] This means that no minimum wage is set at the Federal level.[18] This contractual freedom is limited in practice by various other norms or principles aimed at preventing exploitative working conditions, such as collective agreements or prohibition of gender discrimination in employment. In some specific contexts, the issues are even more strictly regulated. For example, when entering into employment contracts with posted or foreign workers.[19]

Switzerland is divided into smaller administrative areas known as cantons. They have local control over many issues. To date, only two Swiss cantons (Neuchâtel and Jura)[20] have enacted a cantonal minimum wage. Other cantons will likely follow soon (in particular Ticino).

---

17 Wyler, Heinzer, *supra* note 1, p.135.

18 Ibid.

19 Ibid., pp.136–50.

20 See Art. 34a of the Neuchâtel Constitution and Loi sur le salaire minimum cantonal (Act on the cantonal minimum wage).

As in the UK, Swiss wages are also subjected to various mandatory and agreed social deductions, shared between the employee and the employer.[21]

10.5   Limitations on employee working hours

Most areas of employment law have been left to Member States to determine. An important exception is the Working Time Directive.[22] This Directive, among other things:

1. caps the amount of hours an employee can work at 48 hours a week (averaged over a 17-week period);

2. entitles employees to a break every six hours, a rest period of 11 consecutive hours a day and at least one rest day per week; and

3. provides a statutory right to four weeks' paid holiday per year.

It is open for Member States to exceed the holiday limit. For example, in the UK, full-time workers are entitled to a minimum of 5.6 weeks' annual leave (which includes the eight commonly observed Bank Holidays). Holiday entitlement is pro-rated for part-time workers. Except in the year in which the employment ends, the employer cannot make a payment in lieu of holiday. The rights of EU citizens continue to accrue during career breaks or sabbaticals. If an employee leaves employment in the course of a holiday year, they are entitled to be paid for the holidays that they did not take on a *pro rata* basis.

Of all the EU Member States, it is only in the UK that it is possible to contract out of the 48 hours a week cap. Many employment contracts in the UK (particularly for lawyers!) opt out of the Directive by default.

In Switzerland, a non-EU country, the situation is slightly different:

1. In most cases, working time is governed by the Swiss Federal law on labour.[23] The weekly working week is set to 45 hours for

---

21 Wyler, Heinzer, *supra* note 1, pp.176–7.
22 Working Time Directive, 2003/88/EC.
23 See Arts 2–4 of the Swiss Federal law on labour for the companies as well as types of workers excluded from the scope of this law.

employees working in industrial enterprises, office staff, technical staff and other employees in charge of intellectual tasks, as well as sales personnel of large retail businesses, or to 50 hours for all other types of employees it is for 50 hours.[24] These rules may be subject to certain exceptions and can in some cases be amended.[25]

2.   Employees are entitled to a break of at least 15 minutes in a 5.5 hour work day, 30 minutes if working a seven-hour day, and one hour if the workday lasts more than nine hours.[26] Further, employees are entitled to a daily rest period of 11 consecutive hours[27] and at least one rest day per week, usually on Sunday.[28] This is subject to exceptions.[29]

3.   The statutory entitlement to paid holiday is set at five weeks for workers aged under 21, and at four weeks afterwards.[30]

10.6   Ethical codes for models

One of the big issues which affects the fashion industry concerns model contracts. There are particular issues with models due to their age, the importance of their appearance, and the limited substitutability, particularly for celebrity models.

LVMH and Kering recently reached an agreement which prohibits the sale of clothes with a smaller size than European size 36 (US size 6 and UK size 8) and modelling for minors (i.e., anyone under the age of 16).[31] They also committed to make a dedicated psychologist/therapist available during working time.

Italy is several years ahead of the curve. A similar ethical code was adopted by *La Camera Nazionale della Moda*[32] in Italy in 2006. This

---

24 See Art. 9; Wyler, Heinzer, *supra* note 1, p.94.

25 Ibid., pp.94–6.

26 See Swiss Federal law on labour, Art. 15.

27 See, ibid., Art. 15a.

28 See, ibid., Art. 18.

29 See for instance, ibid., Arts 15a §2, 19 and 24.

30 See the Swiss Code of Obligations, Art. 329a.

31 'LVMH and Kering ban ultra-thin and underage models', *The Financial Times*, 6 September 2017: https://www.ft.com/content/a81c697e-92e6-11e7-bdfa-eda243196c2c.

32 National Chamber of Italian Fashion.

code includes a prohibition on modelling by minors and support for including larger sizes such as European sizes 46 and 48 in fashion shows and the associated fashion collections. Thanks to the cooperation between *Camera Nazionale della Moda* and the Italian Government, this code has by and large been respected in Italy since 2006.

France has recently implemented similar legal provisions in an attempt to safeguard the well-being of fashion models. Since 6 May 2017, all individual models need to obtain a medical certificate attesting to their overall general state of health with reference to their body mass index if they intend to work in France. The certificate must be provided by a medical doctor and should also set out any conditions or adjustments required as regards the model's working conditions and environment.

The medical certificate is valid for as long as the model's health is maintained subject to a maximum of two years. These legal obligations apply to all paid modelling work (whether adults or minors) and needs to be respected by all model agencies or organisers of modelling competitions whether they are based in France or the EEA (which includes the EU), should they intend to operate or carry out activities in France.[33]

10.7   Interns

Interns are often perceived as a source of free labour. You are offering them the opportunity of working in the fashion industry and in return for this experience they are giving you their time for free. On one level this may appear a fair exchange and if it is a short period of work experience or job shadowing (a week or less) it probably is not going to cause too many difficulties from a labour law point of view. However, anything above this can quickly run into problems, particularly when you give them defined responsibility for a particular task.

 Check the laws for each country in which you operate and even if the use of free interns is fine in that country, consider how long is appropriate and whether the potential public relations issues would make it worth proceeding. At a minimum, most people would expect the intern's expenses to be paid.

---

33 Arrêté du 4 mai 2017 relatif au certificat médical permettant l'exercice de l'activité de mannequin.

The courts have approached the issue of whether an intern is actually an employee by considering the factual matters surrounding their work for a fashion business. Your intern is more likely to be classified as a worker or even an employee if one or more of the following apply:

1. the intern is required to work set hours;

2. the intern's work is unsupervised (or is responsible for managing other interns); and

3. the tasks assigned to an intern would normally be given to a paid member of staff (such as responsibility for social media accounts).

Workers have fewer rights than employees and interns are, in the UK at least, more likely to be classified as workers. However, even workers are entitled to standard worker rights such as:

1. the minimum wage;

2. the statutory minimum holiday allowance; and

3. the right to take regular breaks.

So by all means hire interns but think carefully about what you want them to do and whether what you really want is an entry level worker on a short fixed term contract – in reality, many interns tend to fall into that category.

10.8   Share options – free money or a deferred problem?

It is common for businesses to award share options or even shares in return for years of service or potentially in lieu of a bonus. It is important that the implications of offering or granting these options is properly understood as they can have significant tax consequences both for your business and the beneficiary employee. For example, if shares are offered early on in a business, then any increase in value may be taxed heavily as a capital gain. Get professional tax advice if you think this is an issue which could affect you.

10.9   Social media

There are two different aspects to employee social media use which are best dealt with in two separate policies or guidelines. The first concerns the guidelines for employees who are using your social media account and using social media to represent your brand. The second concerns employees' personal social media accounts.

Any public comments associated with your business whether online or offline can end up on social media even if not posted there by your employee. Therefore good judgment and discretion should extend beyond the screen. Nobody wants to be the new meme. If your employee is the centre of a media storm you may be faced with repeated calls to 'fire' them. Bear in mind that local employment law may make such a draconian approach inadvisable (or even impossible) but it may be appropriate to take formal disciplinary action.

10.9.1   Social media guidelines for employees representing your brand

Ideally there will be clear guidelines in place for employees who are using your social media accounts.

First, it is important to be clear about who is authorised to create new social media accounts for your business. This can be a huge issue where there is a franchise or distribution arrangement. When the relationship ends, you do not want accounts and associated goodwill to be in the hands of the franchisee or distributor. The potential problems which can beset franchisee or distributor owned social media accounts are the same as those that can arise for registered trade marks (as explained in Chapter 3).

It is obviously important that employees, distributors, agents and franchise holders are engaged with and promote the brand. However, if you have not contractually engaged with the social media site itself, there is a risk that if the relationship sours a dispute may arise regarding who owns the social media accounts. Even with strong contractual protections, it is not unknown for former franchisees to attempt to leverage these accounts if a relationship sours. Retain ownership from day one to avoid these problems escalating.

A related issue is who has access to social media passwords. Make sure that they are kept secure and there are limitations on who can rename the account. There are various third party apps which provide access to a number of people who can post to an account without giving them the keys to the castle (i.e., the ability to change the account password or even delete the account). Whatever method you choose, make sure that you have the IT capability to override passwords and/or prevent access to your company social media account at very short notice. When HMV went into administration and announced plans to carry out mass redundancies, some employees took over its Twitter account, venting out their anger publicly with no one knowing how to take back control of the social media account.[34]

You also need to consider who is allowed to use social media to represent your brand and who is supervising them. It is important that there are clear guidelines for anyone who is using your official social media accounts. Likewise, guidelines should be in place for any employees who decide to launch unofficial accounts. These are not necessarily a bad thing but they should be treated with caution as there is a risk of them either becoming gripe accounts or creating a confusing or diluted brand message. Both outcomes can affect the strength of your trade marks and your ability to rely on the goodwill in a claim for passing off, unfair competition or similar.

Social media is an important part of any modern business. Make sure you have someone long term in the role and that they are fully trained and kept up to date on all major aspects of the business. Any employees who are given responsibility for your social media accounts should also have clarity regarding the parameters for responses on the business' social media accounts. You do not want your social media voice to sound contrived or artificial but neither do you want a controversial message to be sent out to followers or in response to a customer complaint. This can lead to the wrong kind of viral marketing!

It is also important to be clear about what permission is required before sharing, liking or endorsing content from other social media accounts. You could, for example, have some sources of information, such as fashion magazines, whose content is pre-approved whereas unvetted sources require approval before liking, retweeting or similar.

---

34 See https://www.theguardian.com/business/2013/jan/31/hmv-workers-twitter-feed-sacking.

10.9.2   Social media policy – personal social media accounts

Employee use of personal social media accounts can be a difficult area to regulate. In Europe, there is usually strong employee protection and the furthest you can go without causing problems is to set out standards for using social media in personal life (such as good judgement and respect in all interactions). This could perhaps be supplemented with some examples of what is considered to be inappropriate social media behaviour, for example, bullying, harassment, discrimination, threats, etc., particularly those which target fellow employees or customers.

An employee social media policy may seem like an overly formal document, however, it gives all employees, workers and freelancers certainty over what is and is not acceptable to post on to their personal social media and how any issues will be handled. As with so much in life, planning for the worst case scenario puts you in the best possible position if things go wrong in the future. The policy does not have to be overly dictatorial but it does have to be clear. You should also make sure that it is in accessible language and easily available and provided to all employees, workers and freelancers. There may be several different policies, for example one for the people handling the business' social media accounts and one for all employees regarding personal social media usage, including use while at work.

A clear social media policy should consider different types of social media use such as personal Instagram accounts, professional LinkedIn accounts and public blogs. Ultimately, the policy and its enforcement should be proportionate and balance the concerns of the company with the freedom of the employee.

10.9.3   Social media and confidentiality

The importance of not posting confidential information online has been considered in Chapter 7 but it bears repeating as it is an important issue which arises in lots of different contexts. Keeping information such as new collections and designs confidential is key to managing successful public relations. The issue of confidentiality is particularly important if the business is publicly traded or is going through an important legal change such as administration, sale, merger or similar. Training on this issue is advisable, particularly for employees with access to business critical information such as pricing, product development, human resources, legal or similar. This issue can arise either on the fashion site's social media channels or in loose comments on employee social media.

10.9.4   Social media and data protection

Any social media policy should bear in mind the major changes to EU data protection law which the General Data Protection Regulation (GDPR) brought about when it came into force on 25 May 2018. For example, the use of social media for direct marketing including to collect information for the purposes of direct marketing needs to be handled particularly carefully. Data protection is considered in more detail in Chapter 14.

10.9.5   Social media and intellectual property

Another key issue which should be incorporated into the policy and covered in regular training is the importance of not misusing other people's intellectual property – particularly images. Resharing content from social media accounts is generally covered under the terms of the social media account but using someone else's image without their permission can land you in hot water. This was an issue for Vogue Spain who posted various artists' works on Instagram without their permission or even attribution several years ago. It turned out that interns had been left in charge of the account.[35]

10.9.6   Compulsory social media disclaimers

It was once common for employers to require employees to make it clear on their personal social media accounts that the views expressed there do not represent the company. This can now appear to be quite an old fashioned approach as it is usually clear from the context that the employee and company are different. An exception to this rule concerns designers or founders, particularly if they share their name with the company. In these circumstances, it is important to be clear about what is permitted and what could be confusing both at the outset and as the relationship with the company which shares their name evolves. As for trade marks, if a social media account becomes very closely connected with the business it may become an issue in the future, particularly at the time of sale.

---

35 Read more in my blog from the time on Art and Artifice http://aandalawblog.blogspot.co.uk/2012/04/vogues-uncredited-use-of-instagram.html.

10.9.7   Social media training

It is a good idea to have training to supplement the policy and make sure that there are regular reminders (i.e., ensuring that the policy does not just get mentioned at the induction and then buried in a digital drawer). Because social media is constantly developing, it is worth revisiting this at least once a year.

10.9.8   Getting permission for your social media policy

In some jurisdictions, such as Italy, the social media policy should be agreed with the works council. If there is no works council (or you cannot reach an agreement with them) you should seek agreement from the relevant labour office. It is only once an agreement has been reached that the social media policy can be considered valid and enforceable. There are guidelines available from the Garante (Italian data protection authority) which can be a helpful starting point.

The rules governing the adoption of the company's social media policy are connected to the provisions of the Italian Labour Law (Art. 4 *Statuto dei Lavoratori*) which establish that an employer cannot exercise any kind of control over the employee's activity at work (with few exceptions such as criminal activity). Therefore, monitoring your employee's activity on social media during working hours is unlawful unless it is specifically agreed with the works councils or the competent labour office in your social media policy.

10.9.9   Implementing a social media policy: two examples

The scope of social media policies should set out the risks of failure to comply with the terms. For example, in a recent case in Belgium before the Liège Labour Courts, an employee agreed with his employer that he would not publish any content on his social media accounts which would create difficulties for his employer. The employee undertook this obligation in writing. Despite this undertaking, the employee nonetheless clicked 'Like' in respect of some damaging and controversial content about his employer. The Court of Appeal in Belgium upheld the employee's dismissal for serious fault.[36] The signed undertaking was the key to the employer's success. This case highlights the importance of seeking local legal advice on employment matters,

---

36 See the decision of the Cour du Travail de Liège, 3e ch. – Decision of 24th March 2017.

and understanding the options for enforcing rules regarding your employees.

A similar example of where it is important to monitor policies in accordance with case law can be seen in the case from 2017 between Mr Bărbulescu and his claim against Romania before the European Court of Human Rights. Mr Bărbulescu's employer was monitoring his messaging and Internet usage and used the results of this monitoring during disciplinary proceedings in order to dismiss Mr Bărbulescu.

In principle, the court held that the employer was justified to monitor Mr Bărbulescu's Internet usage, as it is not unreasonable for an employer to verify whether an employee is indeed working during office hours. However, the court considered that Mr Bărbulescu's dismissal was unfair because the employer had failed to inform its employees that their communications could be monitored. Consequently, the court ruled that Mr Bărbulescu's right to privacy had been violated.[37] For such monitoring to be lawful, employees need to be informed of this, for example, by way of a policy, before any such monitoring actually takes place. Bear in mind that the number of territories affected by the European Convention of Human Rights, on which this decision is based, is considerably broader than the EU (e.g., it includes Russia, Turkey and Ukraine).[38]

10.9.10   Social media and recruitment

When searching for potential employees, it is permissible to use social media to check the accuracy of the information they provided but the job advert should make clear what searches you will be performing. In addition, you must be able to justify decisions based on a social media profile in the usual way, particularly any suggestions that your decisions were biased or discriminatory in nature. Be careful if you decide to process third party data gleaned from social media accounts when deciding whether or not to interview or hire a candidate.

---

37 This was a breach of Art. 8 of the European Convention of Human Rights. See *Bărbulescu v Romania*, application no. 61496/08, decision of the Grand Chamber on 5 September 2017.

38 A full list of the signatories is available here https://www.coe.int/en/web/conventions/full-list/-/conventions/treaty/005/signatures.

10.10   Employee privacy and BYOD

Do your employees use the devices you provided them with to do their job for personal social media, etc.? If so, as explained above, think about the extent to which you can monitor their activities. Conversely, if you operate a BYOD (i.e., bring your own device) policy, think about the amount of access, if any, you have to data on the device as well as the security applied to the device and the social media accounts.

BYOD is a particularly common solution for start-ups who may not have the resources to pay for dedicated devices for all employees. It avoids the need for employees to carry multiple devices and can provide flexibility. In these circumstances it is common to have email operated via apps so it is self-contained and will not cross over with personal email accounts. You may want to have admin access to these apps. The important thing is that employees are clear about where they can and cannot expect privacy on their own device.

10.11   Cyber security

Cyber security is a major topic and has become a huge risk area for businesses of all sizes. The vast majority of the risks can be avoided by ensuring that all computers (including tablets, smartphones, etc.) are regularly updated and staff are regularly trained on on how to avoid cyber attacks such as phishing.

A common scam is for the scammer to submit an invoice from a known supplier, who may have been hacked. The email request will often follow the standard format and it is understandable that employees would consider the request to be legitimate and pay the invoice. To avoid this issue occurring, all purchase order requests (particularly for expensive items) should ideally be confirmed by telephone using details in an existing database and not the email from which the request was sent. Regular training on these sorts of issues can minimise the risks and will be helpful evidence to demonstrate compliance to insurers or similar. In particular, compliance with these procedures may affect your insurance premium and the likelihood of the insurer paying out.

10.12   The ePrivacy Regulation

The EU ePrivacy Regulation[39] (which has not yet been introduced) should tighten up individual privacy rights across the EU including via privacy by default in certain instances. The aim of the ePrivacy Regulation is to reinforce individual rights of online privacy and confidentiality by making online data and metadata private by default (e.g., via browsers, apps, online accounts). This would mean that you can only use this data if you have an individual's consent.

The law is likely to apply to the use of cookies and third party cookies which track user activities. This enhanced level of privacy within the EU means that in addition to complying with GDPR, companies will have to be particularly careful in relation to marketing activities which rely on social media.

The ePrivacy Regulation will likely apply to workplace privacy as well. At the time of writing, the latest report on the ePrivacy Regulation[40] includes amendments which expressly refer to privacy in the workplace, especially regarding the confidentiality of information stored in employee terminal equipment.

The report provides guidance for employers and limits the processing and collection of information from employees unless it is 'strictly technically necessary for the execution of an employee's task.' This is limited to circumstances where:

1.   the employer provides the computer equipment;

2.   the employee is the user of the equipment; and

3.   the equipment is not further used for monitoring the employee.

It is important to monitor this legislation and update your policies accordingly before it comes into force.

---

39 Accessible here http://eur-lex.europa.eu/legal-content/EN/ALL/?uri=CELEX:52017PC0010.
40 See here: http://www.europarl.europa.eu/sides/getDoc.do?pubRef=-//EP//TEXT+REPORT+A8-2017-0324+0+DOC+XML+V0//EN&language=en#title2.

10.13   Working with designers

The high end of the fashion industry has become a bit of a revolving door for big name designers in the last couple of years (Raf Simons, Phoebe Philo, Jonathan Saunders and Alber Elbaz to name but a few). This has been ascribed to a combination of increased pressure on financial returns limiting the scope of their creativity and increased pressure for designers to meet a never ending cycle of new collections, including diffusion ranges, and international markets reducing the traditional seasons approach.

As Alber Elbaz put it when he received his Fashion Group International award before leaving Lanvin:

> We designers, we started as couturiers, with dreams, with intuition, with feeling. [Then] we became 'creative directors,' so we have to create, but mostly direct. And now we have to become image-makers, creating a buzz, making sure that it looks good in the pictures. The screen has to scream, baby.[41]

This is hard work and burnout is likely if you do not set reasonable expectations. There are no easy solutions but as with all employees, happy designers tend to create a happier and more successful company.

10.14   Confidentiality

The importance and value of confidential information is discussed elsewhere. The best means of ensuring confidentiality in your business is to limit the pool of people who are aware of a particular issue. However, this can undermine your business' ability to compete as ideas which are not shared do not get the opportunity to evolve and often information can leak out anyway creating potential resentment among employees and a greater risk of the information leaving the business.

The value of confidential information and the various means of protecting it are discussed in more detail in Chapter 7. A combination of

---

41 Vanessa Friedman, 'Alber Elbaz Leaving Lanvin as Fashion's Slippery Slope Claims Another Designer' 28 October 2015 https://www.nytimes.com/2015/10/29/fashion/fashion-creates-a-slippery-slope-of-designer-departures.html.

contractual protection and regular training (not just for new employees) will put you in the best possible position. This is particularly important as far as information surrounding designs, pricing including sales and sensitive data such as mergers or acquisitions, new store locations, etc. are concerned. In larger organisations, there is a risk of insider dealing which can carry very serious consequences both for the individuals involved and for the fashion business once the information leaks out.

10.15   Avoiding discrimination

In England, whenever hiring employees, during the employment and when it comes to an end it is important to ensure that decisions and steps taken are free from discrimination on grounds of age, sex, marital status, gender reassignment, race, disability, sexual orientation and religion or belief ('protected characteristics').

Broadly speaking, the term 'discrimination' covers four categories of prohibited conduct:

1. Less favourable treatment because of an individual's protected characteristic (e.g., deciding not to hire someone because of their religion).

2. A policy, criterion or practice which has a worse effect on some people with a particular protected characteristic than others. For example, a job requirement to work full time may have a worse effect on women than men as they tend to be the primary child carers.

3. Harassment of any form.

4. Retaliation against an employee because they brought or threatened to bring a discrimination claim.

In relation to disabled individuals an additional obligation applies, which requires employers to take reasonable steps to eliminate the workplace disadvantage caused to the individual by the disability.

Employers and hirers must minimise the risk of discrimination taking place. A useful starting point is to adopt an equal opportunities and anti-harassment policy, which must be explained and communicated to all employees, freelance workers and third parties with whom the business works. Such policies set out the business' attitude to discriminatory conduct, how it will deal with complaints of harassment and possible sanctions for conduct in breach of the policy.

If an employee complains of discrimination, it is important to investigate their complaints promptly and thoroughly, while keeping the complaint and identity of the complainant confidential as far as possible, usually the matter should be discussed on a need-to-know basis only. If disciplinary action needs to be taken, this should be conducted in accordance with the code of practice issued by the relevant national authority.[42] At this point it will also be advisable to review internal procedures and learn lessons for the future.

10.16   Terminating employment

In England, broadly speaking, all employees are entitled to a minimum period of notice at the end of their employment (at least one week per each completed year of employment). Employees with two or more years' continuous employment enjoy additional statutory protections and their employment can only be terminated for certain prescribed reasons (such as redundancy).

It is usually up to the employer whether to require the employee to work their notice period in full. It is also up to the employer to decide whether or not to provide a departing employee with a reference. If the employer decides to give a reference, it must ensure it is true and accurate, as failure to do so could expose the employer to liability to the ex-employee and their new employer. For this reason, many employers often choose to only provide a 'plain vanilla' reference which is limited to dates of employment and job title.

It is customary to include in the employment contract terms which relate to events surrounding the end of the employment. Common terms include an obligation to maintain confidentiality even after the end of the employment, post-termination restrictive covenants, return of property belonging to the employer and erasure of such information from any BYODs, proper handover arrangements and more.

---

42 In the UK, this is ACAS, the Advisory, Conciliation and Arbitration Service.

Termination of employment can be more challenging in other EU jurisdictions. The rules vary between Member States and it is worth taking local legal advice before committing yourself.

10.17   Trade unions and employment law

Employees have a legal right to join (or not to join) a trade union. You cannot refuse to employ, fire or otherwise treat unfavourably an individual because of their trade union membership. In the UK, Unite is one of the biggest trade unions; it has a textile trade group with around 10,000 members. If you decide to recognise a trade union, your employees will have the right to join that union. If you do not recognise a union, employees may initiate a process which will require you to recognise one.

If you recognise a trade union, you can agree with the union the scope of the activities and areas over which you will consult with the union. Pay and benefits are the two most common areas for consultation. Often, the employees will elect trade union representatives to carry out the negotiations on their behalf. In certain cases, you are legally obliged to consult with your trade union representatives. When employees raise a grievance or are subject to a disciplinary hearing, they have a right to be accompanied by a trade union representative.

10.18   The gender pay gap and reporting obligations

For more than 40 years UK employers have had a legal obligation to provide equal pay to men and women who, broadly speaking, do 'equal work.' However, empirical evidence (including information from the Office of National Statistics) shows a lingering inequality of pay between men and women. In an attempt to combat pay inequality, new pay reporting obligations came into force in April 2017. Under these new obligations, large private and voluntary sector employers (with more than 250 employees) are required to analyse their 'gender pay gap' each year and produce and publish a report which summarises their findings each April. The pay gap in retail is below the median of 9.7 per cent but some individual fashion businesses had a very large gap. For example, the pay gap at Karen Millen was 49 per cent and at Boux Avenue it was 75.7 per cent.[43]

---

43 See http://www.bbc.co.uk/news/business-43651780.

The hope is that the negative publicity likely to result from any published gender pay gap will result in employers changing their pay practices. This has already resulted in some success, for example, the BBC, which was the subject of significant scrutiny and adverse publicity following reporting of its significant gender pay gap.

A gender pay report must contain the following information:

1. The overall gender pay gap figures for relevant employees, calculated using both the *mean* and *median* average hourly pay.

2. The proportion of men and women in each of four pay bands (quartiles), based on the employer's overall pay range. This will show how the gender pay gap differs across different levels of the organisation.

3. Information on the gender bonus gap.

4. The proportion of male and female employees who received a bonus in the same 12-month period.

Employers may include a narrative statement explaining any identified gender pay gap and the action they plan to take to tackle it. The report must be published on the employer's own website and must also be uploaded onto a government portal.[44]

Although there are no enforcement provisions or sanctions for failure to publish as required, the government has indicated an intention to run regular compliance checks.

10.18.1   Gender pay gap reporting in Germany

Germany introduced a similar form of gender pay gap reporting obligations in July 2017. If you have more than 200 employees, you can be asked by individuals for information on the criteria and procedures for salary reviews both in relation to their own pay and the pay of a comparable group of employees of the other gender.

If you have more than 500 employees, you must provide regular financial reports on the specific efforts you are making to remove

---

44 See https://www.gov.uk/report-gender-pay-gap-data.

inequality between genders. If you have not taken any measures to improve gender equality, you must explain why. You are also encouraged, but not required, to carry out internal audits to prove you are complying with the existing equal pay laws.

10.18.2   Gender pay gap reporting in Denmark

Denmark requires employers with more than ten employees to conduct gender pay audits to compare the salaries of women and men and publish annual statistics. Those statistics must then be the subject of discussion between management and employees. Significantly, a reporting failure can result in a fine and criminal prosecution.

10.18.3   Gender pay gap reporting in France

If you have more than 50 employees, you are required to either negotiate a collective agreement with measures aimed at closing the gender pay gap, or draw up an annual gender pay action plan based on an analysis of inequality in their workplaces. Failure could result in a penalty of up to 1 per cent of the total remuneration paid in the periods during which no collective agreement or action plan was implemented.

11 Before signing an agency or distribution agreement

You cannot do everything yourself. At some point, you will need to appoint an agent and/or a distributor. They help you expand into new territories and distribution channels. Although agents and distributors may appear to be the same at first glance, there is a big practical difference between the two.

11.1 Agency and distribution – what do we mean?

An agency relationship is an agreement between your fashion brand (the 'principal') and your 'agent.' In essence, you give your agent instructions and the agency agreement governs what the agent will then do, how they will do it and how they will be paid.

An agent is typically appointed for a specific territory. At a minimum, an agent will find and introduce customers to your brand. They may also have authority to enter into contracts on behalf of your fashion brand. This is clearly a position of trust with potentially major long-term financial implications so it is important that you think carefully about both who you appoint as an agent and how much latitude they are given to make decisions and bind you contractually.

A distribution relationship is an agreement between a fashion brand, which manufactures or supplies clothing and associated products and accessories, and its distributor (i.e., the person who sells the products in different territories). The distributor buys goods from your brand and the distribution agreement grants the right for the distributor to sell the goods on, either to other wholesalers or retailers. Again, a distribution agreement is often limited to a specific territory. In contrast to an agency relationship the final contract for sale of the goods is between the distributor and the end customer, so there is often no direct relationship between your brand and your customers, unless, for example, you offer a manufacturer's warranty to the end customer.

11.2   Selective distribution networks

A selective distribution network is a means by which the fashion brand can control how its distributors sell its products within the EU, without breaching EU competition (i.e. or anti-trust) laws.

A key element of a selective distribution network is that the supplier may prevent its distributors from reselling the products to other dealers outside the network, on the basis that their knowledge or retail environment does not meet the supplier's criteria.

Fashion brands supplying luxury products (such as designer handbags and high-end cosmetics) often adopt a selective distribution network to restrict the resale of their products only to approved dealers. The rationale for using such a network is that these types of products can only properly be resold to consumers by retailers with specific knowledge and expertise using appropriately trained staff, or that the sale must be from premises that are in keeping with the luxury nature of the products.

Therefore within a selective distribution network, the supplier may decide to supply its products only to those distributors that meet its selective criteria and those distributors themselves might agree to re-sell the products only to end users and other authorised dealers.

11.3   Which is better, an agency or distributor relationship?

Like so much in life, the choice of whether to use an agent or a distributor at all and, if so, in what capacity, is primarily a matter of timing. The most important thing is to work with people who you trust and have a proven track record.

11.3.1   Agency

The key attraction of an agency relationship is the ability to leverage an agent's contacts and local knowledge while maintaining a direct contract with the end customers. It can also be more efficient to delegate responsibility for many decisions. The agent never receives title and never forms part of the relationship with the end customer, they are simply there to facilitate the relationship between the fashion brand and customer.

The agency relationship is tightly regulated in the EU under the Commercial Agents Directive.[1] The Commercial Agents Directive applies to all commercial agency agreements whether or not they are written or otherwise formalised and affects all agents in the fashion industry whether they are individuals or corporate entities. The relevant law which applies to an agency agreement is the law of the country in which the agent is carrying out their activities (the default position) or another law specified by contract. If you decide to appoint an agent it is well worth investing the time in getting local law advice as there are significant differences in the way the Directive has been implemented across the EU.

 One of the most important obligations under the Commercial Agents Directive is the requirement to pay agents compensation on termination.[2] This entitles a commercial agent to commission on any post-termination commissions where either (i) the 'transaction is mainly attributable to the commercial agent's efforts during the period covered by the agency contract;' or (ii) the order was placed in the normal course of the agency relationship, and reached either the fashion brand or the agent, before the agency contract terminated. The timing for transactions which are 'mainly attributable' to the agent's efforts is also important. This is not an indefinite right for the agent and it only applies if the transaction was entered into within a 'reasonable period' after the agency contract terminated. It may not be surprising to learn that what is considered attributable to a commercial agent's effort and a 'reasonable period' are hotly contested issues.

In addition where an agent is within a territory, the fashion brand may sometimes be treated as trading there for tax purposes. This can cause problems for tax planning, efficiency and, if it was not anticipated, forecasting.

---

1 Directive on the coordination of the laws of the Member States relating to self-employed commercial Agents EC Directive 86/653.
2 Ibid., Art. 8.

11.3.2   Distributor

Distributors offer their own set of pros and cons. Fashion brands typically appoint fewer distributors than agents and consequently have fewer sources of credit risk. Over the long term, distributors are often considered to be more cost efficient due to economies of scale and, potentially, greater experience. The lack of a direct contractual relationship with the end customer is often seen as a disadvantage of the distributor model. However, this can be a positive as the brand gains from the distributor's knowledge of the local market and as more electronic data can be collected on customers even in store, subject to an appropriate data protection regime, a lot of useful customer information can still be gathered and passed back to your brand under a distributor relationship.

Although it is possible to set a maximum price under a distribution agreement, you cannot set minimum prices. Further, as the end contract for the purchase of goods is made between the distributor and the customer, unlike in an agency relationship, legal title of the goods does transfer to the distributor.

While the Commercial Agents Directive, and other associated issues, such as the tax position regarding agents, does not apply to distributor agreements, there is a risk of lower sales volumes due to the distributor adding its own markup to the goods. Further, by giving exclusivity to one distributor you are putting your eggs in one basket and risk tying the distributor's success (or otherwise) too closely to your business' success.

Distribution agreements do not escape EU law as once your fashion brand reaches a significant size (calculated as a share of your market), competition law comes into play. Distribution agreements are treated as 'vertical arrangements' under EU competition law. This means that they are given particular attention by competition authorities and the arrangements should be carefully considered in line with EU and domestic competition legislation.

11.3.3   So which option is best?

You need to weigh up the above factors and think about what your fashion brand ultimately wants to achieve from the relationship. Agency and distribution agreements give a similar outcome (the sale of your products) but via different types of relationships and with different consequences.

If your fashion brand wants to retain control over features such as the retail price and legal title to the goods an agency agreement is likely to be better.

If your fashion brand is happy only setting maximum prices in a distribution agreement, does not mind only having an indirect relationship with customers and wants the ease and experience that a distributor can often bring, the distribution model may be desirable.

11.4   What if a distributor is actually an agent?

In most jurisdictions there are no explicit laws governing the relationship between a fashion brand and their distributor. Consequently, the parties are free to negotiate and decide on the terms within an agreement. However, some European jurisdictions may provide for certain clauses to be included within the contract. This often includes specific requirements with regard to compensation on termination.

In some jurisdictions compensation is only payable where specific conditions are met, but in most, the distributor can be entitled to compensation on termination where the contract is comparable to an agency agreement. This is based on an assessment of the features of the relationship. For example, in Austria and Germany agency law is applied by analogy to certain types of distributors, such as exclusive distributors. The Austrian and German courts will look at the distribution of risk between the parties to determine the relationship and therefore the payment of compensation.

11.4.1   Agents in Switzerland

The Commercial Agents Directive does not apply in Switzerland as it is not part of the EU. In Switzerland, agency, exclusive distribution, travelling salesman and commission agreements are all closely related.[3] As in other countries, exclusive distribution contracts are not

---

3 Pierre Tercier, Laurent Bieri, Blaise Carron, Les contrats spéciaux, Schulthess Médias Juridiques SA, 5th edn, 2016, p. 740, N 5057, p.1074, N 7256.

formally regulated.[4] To avoid potential disputes, particularly in relation to remuneration and termination, you should pay close attention to the contract's terms and conditions to ensure that it will work as intended. It is important to get Swiss legal advice when starting out as terms can be implied into contracts; so even if you understand the terms which have been set out, they are not decisive.[5]

The Swiss Federal Court has ruled that agency provisions can be applicable by analogy to exclusive distribution agreements when an exclusive distributor is performing in a sufficiently similar way to an agent.[6] This closeness will be assessed in light of the distributor's integration within your marketing system and on the extent of its obligations to transfer its customer relationships (including customer data) to you.[7]

11.4.2 This is all very confusing

You are not alone. When setting up a distribution network in Europe many fashion brands find the rules imposed by European law confusing, with specific rules relating to a wide range of practices including resale price maintenance, exclusive territories, the use of transactional websites, etc. As a result, fashion brands tend to take one of three approaches:

1. They are unaware of the complex restrictions imposed by EU law and therefore impose restrictions on their distributors which unknowingly breach EU competition law, exposing the fashion brand to financial and commercial penalties.

2. They have some awareness that EU competition law prohibits certain restrictions in distribution agreements but are not fully aware of what they are permitted to do, so they err on the side of caution, imposing no or very few restrictions on their distributors, resulting in them having little or no control over how their products enter the market.

3. Ideally, they are aware of the controls they can impose on their distributors, while remaining compliant with EU competition law,

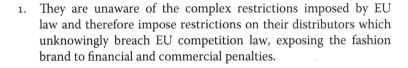

4 Ibid., p.1073, N 7250.
5 Ibid., p.740, N 5057.
6 See Federal Court decision of 22 May 2008, published under ATF 134 III 497.
7 See ibid.; Tercier, Bieri, Carron, *supra* note 3, pp.1084–5, N 7301.

and their distribution networks are set up accordingly. This option requires a bit more time to be spent up front but is worth the extra effort in terms of establishing a longer term relationship, creating a strong brand reputation and avoiding longer term costs.

The choice you make and implications of that choice is a huge topic in itself and one covered in detail by many other learned texts.[8] Your best bet is to consult a specialist lawyer in the relevant territory(ies) in which you plan to operate. You can go armed with the knowledge from this chapter with relevant questions and information about how your business operates and your intentions from the new trading relationship.

11.5   The impact of e-commerce

A major factor which affects the use of both agency and distribution relationships is the convergence of the physical and online sales channels. The EU Commission wants to create a borderless digital economy and this means that commercial arrangements which seek to control distribution could be faced with a call from the regulator. Watch out for more rules and regulations to help make this dream a reality in the future.

11.6   Restricting sales on third party marketplaces

 The CJEU recently looked at whether contractual restrictions on distributors using third party marketplaces such as Amazon and eBay are permitted under EU law. The case, *Coty Germany*,[9] is very helpful for the luxury end of the fashion industry as it confirms the status of selective distribution networks and lays out the conditions that must be met before a fashion brand can legitimately restrict sales in this way.

Coty supplies luxury cosmetics for various major fashion houses. In order to maintain its luxury image, it uses a selective distribution network in which every distributor must comply with specific criteria

---

8 *Bowstead & Reynolds on Agency* (21st edn) is the leading practitioner text, Sweet & Maxwell 6 Dec 2017.

9 *Coty Germany GmbH v Parfümerie Akzente GmbH* 6 December 2017 , Case C-230/16, ECLI:EU: C:2017:941.

including a prohibition from selling online 'via third party platforms which operate in a discernible manner towards consumers.' One of Coty Germany's authorised distributors, Parfümerie Akzente, challenged the legality of this prohibition.

There were two main issues for the CJEU to consider: (i) Are selective distribution networks permissible under EU law? (ii) If so, what criteria must be applied in order to restrict distributors in such networks from selling on third party marketplaces?

The CJEU concluded that 'luxury goods' have both certain material characteristics and an 'allure' or prestigious image which affords them an 'aura of luxury.' The CJEU considered that an impairment of that aura would likely affect the actual quality of the goods.

The CJEU explained, 'that a selective distribution system for luxury goods, designed primarily to preserve the luxury image of those goods, does not breach the prohibition of agreements, decisions and concerted practices laid down in EU law, provided that. . .'

1. distributors are selected on the basis of objective criteria of a qualitative nature;

2. those criteria must be applied equally to all potential distributors and not applied in a discriminatory fashion; and

3. those criteria do not go beyond what is necessary.

The *Coty Germany* case confirms the status of selective distribution networks including the criteria to be used when establishing them. More importantly, from an e-commerce perspective, it sheds some light on the extent to which a fashion brand can restrict its distributors from using third party Internet platforms. But the case still leaves a lot of ambiguity about when a brand is a luxury product. Price and exclusivity are obviously important but the line is sufficiently grey to give plenty of opportunity for future litigation on the subject.

Therefore, if you have a luxury brand, you can potentially restrict your distributors' ability to use third party platforms. Any permitted platforms should not have a 'discernible' impact on the end consumer and should preserve the luxury image of the goods in question.

In a recent case involving French cosmetic and beauty brand, Caudalie, the French Supreme Court held that selective distribution agreements preventing sale on third party sites are indeed lawful in favour of pre-approved sites and networks and do not infringe competition laws.

This means that a contractual clause such as the one contained in the agreement between Coty Germany and Parfümerie Akzente or in the agreement between Caudalie and its distributor, eNova Santé, prohibiting the use of certain third party platforms for Internet sales of the luxury goods can be valid. Whether or not a brand meets this 'aura of luxury' threshold will no doubt be a hotly debated issue in the future.

Finally, the *Coty Germany* case provides an opportunity for all fashion brands to revisit their European distribution models, both to ensure their current restrictions are enforceable or to introduce new restrictions which previously considered were incompatible with European law.

12 Before you post anything online

The moment you post something online it is out in the public domain. Even if it is removed immediately, a record will exist somewhere on the Internet, although how easy it is to track down this record is a moot point.

Similarly, once you offer something for sale online, you open yourself up to various laws and regulations which may apply even if you are not intentionally targeting a particular territory. There are also important data protection considerations which apply the moment you start collecting any personal data.

It is therefore important to think carefully before you post anything online and make sure that you do not open yourself up to future risks. In an ideal world, this would be considered right from the start of a new venture but do not worry if you are several years in, the principles set out in this chapter can be followed at any time and are worth revisiting on a regular basis.

12.1 Clearance of intellectual property rights

It is easy to think that because something has been posted online and has no obvious owner, it is fine to use it. As should be clear by now, this is incorrect! You do not have the right to use a work unless:

1. you own the work (e.g., because you or one of your employees created it);

2. You have been granted a licence to use the work for the purposes and in the locations where you are actually using the work; or

3. you have a contract known as an 'assignment' which transfers the rights to you.

12.1.1   Photographs

If you paid for a photograph which was used in a past advertising campaign or to illustrate your clothes or accessories, it would be understandable to believe that you have the right to use this photograph going forward. However, you do not own the rights in a photograph unless you have a signed assignment from the photographer. Depending on the scope of any licence of the photograph, which may be implied by your past business relationship even if it has not been set out in writing, you may not have the right to use it for a new purpose.

The issues related to clearing photographs are discussed in more detail in Chapter 13. The important point to remember is to keep a clear record of what was agreed, when it was agreed and, ideally, why it was agreed. The reason why you decided on specific commercial terms will not normally be listed on the contract but it is useful to keep track of the business rationale. Unless good records are maintained, a combination of time and employee changes can mean that hard won lessons are forgotten in a couple of business generations.

12.1.2   Videos

Thanks to social media, particularly Instagram, videos are increasing in importance for the fashion industry and can create more issues in terms of clearance. Live streams of catwalk shows have almost become the norm and the content created by fans and shared on social media has become an important tool for increasing brand awareness. This sort of 'user generated content' or 'UGC' generally comes with various rights via the platform's user agreement. This tends to include the right to share the content on the platform via your own social media account. However, if you want to take that content and use it elsewhere, permission will need to be sought (at a minimum) from the creator of that content.

12.2   Creative Commons

The Creative Commons (or CC) has made it much easier to use a lot of third party content. If you find something you would like to use online, it may well be made available for use under a CC licence. There are several different types of CC licence and it is very important that you check which applies to the work you would like to use. All of the CC licences require that the licensed work is properly attributed.

The most flexible CC licence is 'Attribution' or 'CC BY' which lets anyone distribute, remix, tweak, and build upon the licensed work, including commercially, as long as the creator of the work is credited. This allows for very broad dissemination of a work but is generally limited to less valuable works. At the other end of the scale is 'Attribution-NonCommercial-NoDerivs' or 'CC BY-NC-ND'. This is the most restrictive type of licence. It allows the download and sharing of the work provided that the work is credited to the creator, not changed in any way, and not used commercially.

The important lesson is that just because something has been made available under a CC licence does not mean that you can freely use it. For example, something that is only made available on a non-commercial basis cannot be used by your fashion business at all. Of course, just because something has only been made available under a restrictive CC licence does not mean that you cannot contact the creator and enter into a separate and broader licence with them directly. However, this may take considerably more time and effort than just going to an image library such as Getty or iStock which will have standard terms and pricing based on the profile of the creator, popularity of the image, locations and type of use.

Bear in mind that many photographers now regularly search the Internet for use of their photographs (something which is very easy to do thanks to Google image search). Consequently, if you use an image without permission whether on a website or a social media account, you can expect to receive a legal letter through the post at some point.

12.3   Takedowns

If someone objects to something you have posted online it is generally due to alleged intellectual property infringement or defamation. Although intellectual property infringement allegations are a more common issue for the fashion industry, any criticism of competitors, former clients, models or similar can lead to allegations of defamation.

There are two routes which people typically take when they want to get content removed from the Internet. This applies as much to situations where you want content removed as the reverse. The first is to contact the person who uploaded the content and ask them to remove it. The second is to contact the online platform (or 'intermediary') who is responsible for the content being online e.g., the online marketplace, social media site, search engine or Internet service provider (ISP).

If someone contacts you directly, it is up to you to determine whether they have a valid complaint and decide how to respond. In many instances, for example a dispute over a single social media post or use of a one-off hashtag, it may not be worth engaging in protracted correspondence and the issue can be resolved by simply removing the relevant content. Generally the more friendly and less public the communication, the more likely it is to lead to a quick resolution.

 Sometimes someone can write directly to try and resolve the issue informally but the communication gets lost in transit. It is therefore a good idea to have a dedicated method for people to communicate with you, such as an email address or online form, and make sure that these communications are carefully monitored on at least a daily basis and do not end up in a spam or junk folder.

The online takedown procedures vary between different online intermediaries. It is usually easier to persuade intermediaries to remove content that infringes copyright – particularly identical or near identical copies of photographs and videos. Removing content on the basis of trade mark law is possible where there are goods offered for sale and the person making the takedown request can show that they have the rights to a trade mark for the same goods and services. It is very difficult to make, let alone succeed, in a takedown request based on other intellectual property rights although registered designs are sometimes accepted.

If an online takeover is successful, it will usually result in the page or product listing being blocked. Where there is a complaint to an ISP website host, it can result in the entire site being removed by the ISP – although it is common for the website to simply pop up again with a new ISP hosting it. One of the most useful takedown processes is with Google. If you can get a site removed from Google's search results it may still be on the Internet but the number of visitors it will receive will greatly reduce. In general, takedowns are far easier when they are based on copyright rather than trade mark law. It is also possible to liaise with the major payment providers including Visa, MasterCard and PayPal who have a similar procedure to takedowns and in some circumstances, such as counterfeiting, may cease offering their services to these businesses.

Each of these online gatekeepers relies on the defence that they were not aware of the infringing activity in order to avoid responsibility for the content. The moment they are notified, the clock starts ticking and if they take too long, they are potentially liable together with the infringer. What is 'too long' depends on the site, media type and a range of other issues. You should not expect the takedown to be immediate but if it takes longer than two days, it may be the wrong side of the line as far as the intermediary is concerned. Either way, they should contact you to let you know their decision.

If you successfully remove someone's product on the basis of a take-
down notice but it was in fact legitimate, you open yourself up to claims of unlawful interference in trade, unfair competition, groundless threats or similar.[1] Be careful about the circumstances in which you use takedown procedures and bear in mind that something which appears to be a counterfeit good could be a legitimate resale which you cannot prevent because your rights have been 'exhausted.' See Chapter 20 for more on parallel imports and exhaustion of rights.

12.4   Google advertising

One of the major areas of contention in recent years has concerned the
use of third party adverts in Google keyword advertising. It is now clear that you can legitimately bid on a competitor's trade mark as a Google keyword provided that the advert which you serve up as a result of that keyword does not create any consumer confusion between your business and the trade mark.

A related issue has concerned the use of Google's advertising programs such as AdSense which allow third party adverts to be displayed on a website. This can be a useful source of revenue for websites such as blogs but if it creates customer confusion, it is potentially trade mark infringement.

---

1 This tends to be a particular problem in Germany. If you are contacted, get the relevant local law advice as quickly as possible.

One of the most important issues in all of the Google cases concerns whether there was 'targeting' of customers within the jurisdiction. In order to establish targeting, it is not good enough to show that someone *intended* to target your customers, you must show that customers in the jurisdiction were *actually* targeted. That said, a clear intention to target users in a particular jurisdiction will be persuasive evidence as far as the courts are concerned.

12.5   Social media and e-commerce

The intellectual property issues associated with social media are discussed in Chapter 3. The employment or labour law issues including what to include in a social media policy are in Chapter 10 and advertising in Chapter 16. However, social media creeps into all aspects of business and there are more regulatory type issues such as data protection which you need to consider both before you launch your e-commerce business and on an ongoing basis. E-commerce is discussed in more detail in Chapter 17.

13 Raiding the fashion archive

At its heart, fashion is about creative inspiration. But many of the underlying ideas are not necessarily new. Fashion archives are important sources of creative inspiration and branding; they showcase heritage designs, demonstrate the brand's longevity and extend its reach. Even if you have only just started your fashion brand, there is no harm in having one eye on the future. Perhaps one day your business will have its own museum like the Gucci museum in Florence or the Yves Saint Laurent museums in Paris and Marrakech.

It is expensive to store and display archive items, so why bother? As the world moves to digital first, physical products which can tell a story have grown in importance. They are also an investment in the same way as a painting or sculpture.

The Chanel archive in Paris is particularly famed for its pristine preservation of past collections.[1] This obsession with high-quality storage means that Chanel's designers can easily access dresses and related items which date back to the 1920s. Although a range of designers will have contributed to the archive over time, the rights to the designs (to the extent that they are not yet in the public domain) likely remains with Chanel. Further, the know-how in the designs themselves, including the stitching, weight of material, seams, etc. may not be visible from photographs and in many instances, you need the original garment to fully appreciate the craftsmanship that went into the design. By controlling the archive, Chanel remains the gatekeeper to much of this knowledge.

In addition to original clothes and accessories, it is common to retain photographs, original drawings, specification sheets, media mentions and catwalk launches. Some of these can obviously be retained in a digital archive, but be cautious about the storage medium and be sure

---

1 See Lou Stoppard, 'Fashion brands build museums as archives gain value' *The Financial Times* 22 July 2016.

to update the storage method as technology develops. You do not want to have all your key items stored on DVDs when it is hard to track down a DVD player.

13.1 Sale of an archive

Sometimes the archive may be owned by a completely different person or business (in legal speak this unconnected entity is known as a 'third party'). This can happen when a corporate group is sold separately from the archive or where designers create their own archive. This can create complications and confusion in the marketplace. Any sale contract should set out the terms upon which the archive can be accessed in the future by the fashion house and other third parties such as students, as well as how it will be funded and any rights of first refusal if it is sold in the future.

 If you decide to set up an archive for your fashion brand in addition to the curatorial concerns – storage, indexing, finance – your archive should have clear contractual parameters. These parameters include answers to the following questions:

1. What is retained in the archive? For example, what types of items and will they be limited to best sellers and notable pieces?

2. Will there be a separate digital archive? If so, how will it be backed up and kept secure?

3. Who has access to the archive?

4. Who can use the designs in the archive and for what purposes?

5. Who owns the intellectual property rights in the archive?

13.2 Orphan works

The main intellectual property rights of relevance to the use of an archive are likely to be:

1. copyright in the fashion items themselves and any associated drawings and photographs; and

2. design right in any recent designs or registered designs.

If you have clear and comprehensive contracts in place with all designers and creatives involved in your fashion brand as well as any licences of third party rights which were obtained in order to create and sell the archive item then it is likely that you will own the majority of these rights. Unfortunately, record keeping and contractual protection are often low down the priority list when fashion brands are starting up.

Another limiting factor on good record keeping concerns acquisitions. Corporate sale is common in the fashion world and with every sale, contracts can be lost together with the associated human memory. Consequently, identifying the chain of title and the owner of all intellectual property rights in an archive can be a time-consuming and challenging process.

If the owner of an intellectual property right cannot be identified, the work which is protected by that right is known as an 'orphan work.' Orphan works have long been the bane of many an archive's life. In 2012 a solution arrived to deal with the issue on a pan-European basis: the Orphan Works Directive.[2]

The Orphan Works Directive sets out rules regarding the digitisation and online display of orphan works which all Member States have been obliged to implement into their national laws.

The Directive has three main stages for using an orphan work:

1. An attempt at identification of the orphan works. Essentially, you have to show that you conducted a 'diligent search' to find the owner. Tracking the search process is important evidence to show that the search was in fact diligent. This search should include databases and registries such as the Accessible Registry of Rights Information and Orphan Works (ARROW) which applies to book publishing.[3]

---

2 Orphan Works Directive 2012/28/EU.

3 See at: http://www.arrow-net.eu/.

2.   Recognition that a work is an orphan. This is an important stage as once a work is recognised as an orphan, this status applies across the EU and organisations can make it available online in all Member States. One of the main outcomes from this recognition process was an online EU-wide database for Orphan Works. This database has been established and is managed by the EUIPO.[4] It contains information about the orphan works to enable the owners to be tracked down and the items to be used.

3.   The orphan work can be used by archives and similar cultural institutions for certain purposes. For example, they can generate revenue from the orphan works and cover the costs of digitising the work.

The Directive also provides a means for an orphan work's owner to claim ownership and terminate the work's 'orphan' status.

The UK has gone one step further and set up an orphan works licensing scheme which is useful for UK-based archives who are concerned about making orphan works in their collections accessible to the public. However, the licence only covers the UK.[5]

Many European fashion archives have now joined the Europeana digital archive project.[6] It is possible to explore past and contemporary clothing and accessories and associated design drawings as well as photographs, catalogues and videos. The materials which are used in the digital archive are taken from museums and archives across Europe.

 The Orphan Works Directive helps archives but does not help you if you want to use an orphan work as inspiration for a new line of clothing or on a website to showcase your fashion heritage. In these circumstances, the first step is to find out whether the work really is an orphan. If an owner can be identified (or potentially several owners if the works have been transferred as part of someone's estate) then you can negotiate with them. If you really want to use a work and the owner cannot be found, you can calculate the likely royalty which would be payable to use the work and retain that money in a dedicated account in case you need to pay it in the future.

---

4 See at: https://euipo.europa.eu/ohimportal/en/web/observatory/orphan-works-database.

5 You can read more about the orphan work licensing scheme at: https://www.gov.uk/guidance/copyright-orphan-works.

6 The Fashion section is available at: https://www.europeana.eu/portal/en/collections/fashion.

The bottom line is that it is best to make sure works retain their 'parents' and are not orphaned in the first place. The key to this is good record keeping and potentially registering copyright works with one of the registration systems outlined in Chapter 4.

13.3   Photographs

It is common for fashion houses to regularly review old photographs from the archive to use in social media or potentially even updated campaigns. Even if your fashion brand owns the garment and its underlying intellectual property rights, it does not necessarily own the photograph. Photographers are generally very reluctant to give up their rights and will usually agree to a limited use for any photographs shot for a campaign. The strength of their bargaining positions depends on the status of the photographer and how much you want to use them for the campaign. Whatever the case, make sure that you have the rights to store the photograph in both physical form and in a digital archive which could be made available to the public. The agreement may specify the resolution for any web images and allow limited use on social media in perpetuity.

13.4   Model release

The final right to be cleared is the appearance of the model. Usually models will have provided a 'release' before a photoshoot but you may not necessarily have a copy of that document, particularly if the archive dates back several years. A 'model release' is not always necessary but it is good to get in the habit of collecting them. Further, the release is likely limited to the original intended use, i.e., the advertisement of a particular collection or similar. It may not apply to subsequent uses.

If a model has a tattoo or another artificial feature such as distinctive piercings, these could potentially be covered by copyright as well.[7] You should require the model to provide proof of ownership of the copyright or a licence to use the image which can be sub-licensed to

---

7 The owner is likely the tattoo artist or their employer but in some circumstances e.g., where the model is heavily involved in the development of the tattoo design, they may co-own the artistic copyright.

you. The model release form normally allows for amendments to be made to the image, such as retouching, without the model's consent. A good example of a model release form is available from the Royal Photographic Society.[8]

13.5 Insurance

 As for any other type of artwork, it is important to have adequate insurance to protect the fashion archive in case of fire, flood, theft or similar. In order to obtain reasonable insurance, you will be required to put adequate safety measures in place. This can be a complicated process but it is well worth investing the time, particularly as your archive develops over time.

---

8 See for details at: http://www.rps.org/MRF.

14 Before you collect any personal data

Data is a valuable resource. It can help to target your customer's journey and experience of your products whether in store or online. Indeed this sort of focused selling has become essential to helping many e-commerce businesses to differentiate themselves, scale up and grow. However, this level of customer insight is both powerful and potentially damaging. As we know from the Spiderman franchise, with great power, comes great responsibility. Misusing or losing control of the data can lead to dire consequences both in terms of damage to reputation and fines.

The EU has some of the strictest rules on keeping and using personal data in the world. Its focus is on 'data protection' i.e., protecting individuals from having their data subjected to automated processing without their permission. This attitude is in part a product of history. Europe, and in particular, East Germany, saw first hand the effects of unfettered access to data and the damage that it can cause to society.

The European default attitude is that the processing of personal data is forbidden unless various criteria are fulfilled. The rest of the world has taken a more active and embracing approach to the use of personal data. While the European model was originally seen as overly restrictive, high-profile data scandals, such as the Cambridge Analytica fiasco, show the consequences of a relaxed approach to data sharing. This does not mean that you are unable to collect and use personal data in the EU but you do have to be careful about the approach that you take to such data collection. Because so much data processing is cross-border, even if you are not targeting a particular market, it is still highly likely that you will at least need to consider European laws. In some instances, the consequences of failed compliance can be extremely high.

Related to data protection are the concepts of 'data privacy' and 'data security'. These are concerned with protecting individuals from intrusion into their private lives including the interception of confidential information. As cyber security becomes an increasing concern for businesses across the world, data security has moved up the government and business agenda. Data security laws target particular issues such as identity theft and the loss of very sensitive personal information such as health data.

14.1   Key data protection terms

Before diving into data protection laws generally, it is important to have four key terms in mind.

The first is 'personal data'. The concept of personal data is fundamental to data protection law. In essence, personal data is any data which alone or in combination concerns an individual who can be identified. Most obviously this could be a name, email address or phone number but device IDs, IP addresses and photographs, including a photograph's metadata, can all potentially be personal data. Even a reference to the 'woman in the blue top' could be personal data if it is possible to identify the individual from the description.

The second is 'sensitive personal data'. This is personal data which, as the name suggests, is particularly sensitive. Sensitive personal data includes data regarding health, political allegiances and religious beliefs as well as race and ethnicity.

The third is 'processing'. This is a catch-all term for any activity relating to data including collecting, storing, altering, disclosing and destroying it.

The final term is 'consent'. This is consent by a 'data subject' (i.e., the person whose personal data is collected) to the processing of their personal data. This consent must be specific, freely given and informed. Europe has moved to a focus on 'opt in' consent where a data subject specifically agrees to particular types of processing of their data rather than a default acceptance from which they must take action to opt out. Even in the opt in model, data subjects have the right to withdraw their consent at any time. It is important that there are effective technical processes in place to act on any withdrawal of consent. Often this can be as simple as an 'unsubscribe' button or a 'delete my account' feature. It might sound obvious but this technology solution has to actually work, include the deletion of the relevant personal data and be implemented as quickly as possible.

The big issue with consent is explaining exactly what is happening with the personal data you have collected and/or plan to use. For example, people might be aware that you have collected their personal data but are not aware of what you have done with it including who you have shared it with. To give full consent, people need to consent both to the collection and subsequent processing of the data, ideally before that processing is carried out.

Consent is often seen as the only legitimate basis for data processing and this prompts a lot of concern about the logistics of managing so many bits of real or digital paper. In reality there are five different broad bases under which you may be able to process personal data and *consent is just one option*. The different options are set out below under the heading 14.6 'A lawful basis for processing personal data'.

14.2   The Data Protection Directive

The Data Protection Directive was the old law governing data protection across Europe. It set out the principles which must be followed when processing personal data including the requirements to only collect data for specific, explicit and legitimate purposes and only collecting and storing data to the extent that is necessary to do so. In addition, there were notification and registration requirements which, to a large extent, were not being properly implemented by businesses and required a lot of duplication as each Member State had its own data protection authority and it was necessary for businesses selling across the EU to comply with the laws of each Member State.

14.3   Cookies

One of the more frustrating aspects of the modern Internet is the regular pop ups regarding a website's use of cookies. These pop ups constantly appear whenever you browse the Internet and generally require you to click in a box to confirm you have read a notice about the use of cookies on the website and accept the position before they will disappear. These cookie notices are a direct result of data protection law.

Cookies are small text files which a website can plant on the computers of its visitors. These cookies collect information about the website's visitors, including, potentially, their names, addresses, email details, passwords and user preferences. A visitor's cookie is retrieved each time they revisit the website which planted the cookie. This can save a huge amount of time in re-entering passwords and registering each time a user visits a site and are commonly used to deliver targeted products and advertising.

Cookies also enable website owners to build up a really accurate picture of the person visiting the website by not only tracking that person's movement on their website but also tracking the pages that they visited after browsing on the website. These profiles are very valuable and can be sold on to third parties such as advertisers for a lot of money. This cookie data can be linked to individuals and their contact details so it is considered personal data and covered by data protection law.

 As annoying as they are, if you are using cookies on your website, make sure you notify people browsing the site and explain what cookies you are using and give users the opportunity to opt out.

14.4   The GDPR

 The General Data Protection Regulation or GDPR took EU data protection law a step further than the Data Protection Directive. Even if you are not an EU business, this regulation applies to you if you are processing the data of EU citizens. In practice, you will either already be doing this or be highly likely to do so in the future.

The GDPR's aim is to promote greater fairness for data subjects and greater transparency regarding what third parties are doing with personal data. The GDPR follows (broadly) the same concepts as previous data protection law but it has been tightened up and made much more streamlined across the EU (although it is still not completely consistent).

 The GDPR is equipped with some serious teeth. It allows any European data protection authority to take action against a business if they have misused data concerning an EU citizen regardless of where that business is located. If they find a breach, these authorities are able to impose fines of up to €20m or 4 per cent of the business group's annual global turnover. In other words, it pays to think about data protection from day one and to keep thinking about it on a regular basis.

The definition of personal data is now so broad that it can essentially cover anything which connects to a living being. This includes things like IP addresses which at first glance, do not obviously connect to a human. It is very unlikely that you are not collecting and/or processing personal data in your business so make sure you think about this now and if things are not already shipshape that you sort it out as soon as possible.

14.5   Data protection officers

A data protection officer is an individual who is responsible for data protection across the business. It is mandatory for companies to appoint a data protection officer if their core activities require 'regular and systematic monitoring of data subjects on a *large scale*' or consist of 'processing on a *large scale* of special categories of data'. In practice, once your fashion business gets beyond the early start-up stages, it becomes more likely that it will fall into one of these categories. In any event, there is no harm in appointing a data protection officer before you become '*large scale*' or in revisiting data protection issues on a regular basis.

One of the big practical changes with GDPR concerns privacy impact assessments or PIAs. Where the risk of a privacy breach is high, organisations are required to carry out these risk assessments in order to ensure that they have thought through the issues and are complying with the GDPR from the outset.

Although the requirements of the GDPR are stricter, it does simplify things to a large extent. For example, rather than having to comply with the requirements of all Member States, if you comply with one country's regime, you are treated as complying across the EU. It also removes the requirement to register with data protection regulatory authorities in every Member State.

The concept of consent is slightly amended under the GDPR. It is now much more important that the consent is informed and freely given for each type of processing. The consent must be active (such as ticking a box) rather than passive (having a pre-ticked box). It must be easy to withdraw consent.

One of the interesting features of the GDPR is its desire to nudge organisations into complying with data protection rights and principles. One of the core principles behind this is the idea of privacy by design. In other words, the entire processes, software and other technology must all be designed and engineered with data protection in mind. The more thought that is put into data protection by design, the safer the data will be and the lower the risk of falling foul of data protection legislation.

14.6   A lawful basis for processing personal data

In order to process personal data, you must select one of the following reasons or the 'lawful basis' for processing that data. Once you have selected this lawful basis, you must tell your customers (and any other individuals whose data you collect such as employees) about it before you start collecting their data.

 There are six available lawful bases for processing but at least two are very unlikely to be relevant for your fashion business.

1. *Consent* – This consent must be freely given and be explicit (i.e., they must have had to opt in) and for a specific purpose. This consent can be withdrawn at any point in the future at which point you must stop processing the data.

2. *Contract* – This applies to most business transactions. For example, you are entitled to retain the name and contact details of your customers so you can verify their order if there is an issue with the product in the future.

3. *Legitimate interests* – This is the most flexible lawful basis. It simply requires that the processing is necessary for someone's legitimate interests (and that *someone* could be your business). These legitimate interests can include commercial interests but they must be balanced with the interests of the individual whose personal data you have collected. This basis can be relied upon where data is used in ways that people would expect and the collection and processing have a minimal privacy impact.

4. *Legal obligation* – This applies to any legal obligations other than contractual obligations. You should keep a record of the specific

legal provision (or government guidance note) which you used as the rationale for relying on this basis.

5. *Vital interests* – This only applies if processing the data is necessary to protect someone's life. In practice, it is unlikely to affect the fashion industry apart from, potentially if there is an incident in a factory or a store. For example if someone collapses in your store and your store employee looked through their phone for any emergency medical and contact information, this would constitute a vital interest.

6. *Public task* – This is most relevant to public authorities and is highly unlikely to apply to your fashion business.

Deciding which is the most appropriate lawful basis depends on the reason why you are collecting the data and your relationship with the individual. You must first decide whether collecting the data is necessary at all. If you can reasonably achieve the same purpose without the data processing, you do not have a lawful basis.

In most cases you can change your lawful basis at a later date, although it needs a good reason in order for it to be justified. However, if your original basis was consent, you cannot change this basis in the future. If the purpose for collecting and processing the personal data changes, you may be able to continue processing under the original lawful basis if your new purpose is compatible with your original purpose. Again, this does not apply if your original lawful basis was consent.

14.7   What rights do individuals have?

The key rights under the GDPR are:

1. *Access to personal data (i.e., subject access requests).* The data provided in response to these requests must now be freely given and provided within one month. This is an existing right which has been simplified and now has a focus on quick accessibility. To avoid spending a lot of money collecting and collating data at short notice, it is wise to put automated data gathering processes in place for subject access requests to be automatically generated on request. They are very common in litigation as a means of gathering early

disclosure (or discovery) where there is a product liability issue or employment issue.

2. *Data portability.* It must be easy for a user to transfer their data from one company to another. A good example of this is fitness data. Imagine you are selling a fitness tracker. Many of your customers may prefer your design and the features you offer but be reluctant to move to your product because they do not want to lose all of the data they have accumulated with their existing fitness tracker. When building Internet-based or connected products it is therefore important to allow for user data to be easily imported into your system.

3. *Erasure of data.* This is known in the press as the right to be forgotten. It means permanent deletion of all personal data. This is not an absolute right. For example, someone cannot order some goods from you and then ask for their data to be deleted upon delivery so that they can avoid payment.

Accumulated aggregated data can usually be collected provided it is added to a sufficiently large data pool to be truly anonymised. For example, women in London visit X types of website at Y times of day. If the data is too specific, e.g., women working in intellectual property law who live in a particular postcode then the data may still be capable of identifying an individual.

14.8   Data breaches

One of the big changes brought about by the GDPR concerns the treatment of data breaches. A data breach is where you process data beyond the consent given. An obvious example is if personal data is published online but it can also cover the loss of data, including loss of the device containing the data such as a memory stick or laptop or the unauthorised deletion of data.

Businesses have 72 hours from discovering a data breach to report it to their data protection authority. The clock starts from the moment anyone working at the organisation becomes aware of the breach. This means that training and careful consideration of the technological processes are paramount.

It is very important to have a plan for how to deal with a data breach. This should include:

1. Who is responsible? There should be a clear chain of command and a plan for what to do.

2. How to detect a data breach?

3. How to investigate who is behind it (in other words, *who you gonna call*)?

4. Who you need to notify (i.e., which regulatory bodies)? At the minimum, this will be the data protection authority you have registered with in your home Member State. You may also be required to notify the relevant financial authorities if financial data was taken.

5. If the breach comes from a supplier, do you have an alternative lined up so you can minimise the breach? What does the supply agreement say? Who is liable for the financial repercussions?

6. The more steps you have taken in advance, such as employee training, the better position you will be in if anything goes wrong. This is both in terms of minimising the extent of the problem and when facing down any fine which the regulatory authorities may decide to impose.

14.9   Cyber security

Even if you have perfect data protection in place, this does not necessarily protect you or your customers from cyber security breaches.

For example, in the last quarter of 2017, around 500 of online retail site CDiscount's customers fell victim to fraudulent emails seeking bank details updates. This resulted in €300,000 of unlawful online purchases. Similarly, the CNIL (French data protection authority) recently fined Darty, a French electronics store, for its failure to secure customer personal data relating to its online after-sales customer service system.

It is nearly impossible to guarantee against a cyber security attack but the following simple steps will put you in a stronger position:

1. Use tried and tested vendors for any cloud computing. If customer data is stored away from your main servers you need to be confident that it is secure and complies with international data protection legislation including the GDPR.

2. Educate your customers about the information you will and will not ask them for and the verification process you will require them to complete before accepting payment or giving them access to their account information.

3. Do not store sensitive data in one place. If possible avoid storing financial data at all, at least until you can put in place sufficiently strong safety measures. Some sites like Shopify will take care of the transaction so that you do not have access to your customer's financial data. This reduces your risk but there is still a risk of a hack of these third party platforms affecting you reputationally even though it is entirely out of your control. There may come a time in your business' evolution when this is no longer commercially acceptable and you wish to host your own platform but it is an approach to consider when starting out.

4. Make sure your site uses secure Hypertext Transfer Protocol (i.e., https).

5. Think carefully about what information you collect on your customers. Make sure this information is secured and that any sensitive information is kept in a more secure location.

6. Have a strategy for what to do if you are hacked. This should include back up data which is stored separately and a strategy for responding to customer concerns and questions from the media.

14.10   Data protection in action

A good example of privacy and data protection rights being litigated is the Austrian case between Maximilian Schrems and Facebook Ireland. This case was referred to the CJEU by the Austrian Supreme Court in 2016 so it is based on the Data Protection Directive and not GDPR.[1] Mr Schrems is no stranger to litigation involving Facebook and pri-

---

1 Decision of the Oberste Gerichtshof (Supreme Court in Austria) 6 Ob 23/16z (2016).

vacy issues, in 2015, he was involved in a different case before the CJEU which changed the way that data flows work to the US and other jurisdictions.[2]

In fact, Max Schrems filed another dispute against Facebook and its subsidiaries, WhatsApp and Instagram, via the data protection authorities in Austria, Belgium and Germany (Hamburg) as soon as GDPR came into force in May 2018. Collectively the three complaints are worth €3.9 billion. He also filed a €3.7 billion complaint with France's CNIL at the same time regarding Google's Android operating system for smartphones.

In the 2016 case,[3] Mr Schrems claimed that Facebook Ireland violated his right to privacy and breached his data protection rights. He added seven other individuals to the proceedings as co-claimants who came from Austria, Germany and India and had assigned their claims to him.

Facebook Ireland raised several arguments in response to Mr Schrems' claims including an allegation that the Austrian courts did not have jurisdiction and that Mr Schrems could not be regarded as a 'consumer' because his professional activities were related to his various claims against Facebook. They further alleged that the seven claimants' right to commence proceedings was a personal right which could not be assigned.

The CJEU's judgment[4] largely followed the points raised by Michal Bobek, the Advocate-General in this case,[5] who stated in his opinion that:

1. Activities such as publishing, lecturing or fundraising do not result in the loss of consumer status for claims concerning one's private Facebook account.

2. 'Consumer status' depends on the nature and the aim of the contract at the time it was concluded. This means that a subsequent change in use of a Facebook page to combine professional and personal activities does not necessarily result in the loss of consumer status.

---

2 Judgment in Case C-362/14 *Maximillian Schrems v Data Protection Commissioner.*
3 Case C-498/16 *Maximilian Schrems v Facebook Ireland Ltd.*
4 See Judgment in Case C-498/16.
5 Opinion of Advocate-General Bobek delivered on 14 November 2017, Case C-498/16.

3. Jurisdictional consumer privilege is restricted to the specific parties to the initial contract.

The opinions of Advocates-General do not have to be followed by the CJEU, however, in practice it is unusual for the court to make a dramatically different decision. The CJEU confirmed that Mr Schrems could bring an individual action against Facebook Ireland before the Austrian courts but he was unable to claim consumer forum for the purpose of bringing a collective action on the basis of the assigned claims.

This gives a good indication of the way that the European courts will approach data protection and privacy more generally in the future. Although we have not seen the Austrian court's interpretation of the CJEU ruling, the Advocate-General's opinion and the CJEU judgment show the broad consumer protections afforded to EU citizens.

This case is a helpful warning of things to watch out for as your fashion business grows, in particular online. For many reasons such as privacy, brand image, employment issues, and litigation rights, it is good practice to keep private and professional Facebook pages and other social media accounts separate.

14.11   What should you do now?

 1. Build your products and brand with data in mind from the outset. If you already have an established business, take steps now to become compliant.

2. Review your existing processes and data (it is always time for an audit!). Ask yourself lots of questions, such as:

    a. Is it necessary to retain all of that data?

    b. Where did you get your marketing data from?

    c. Can you achieve the same marketing outcomes via another means?

    d. Who have you shared your personal data with?

e. Have you obtained any data on your customers or targets from third parties?

f. Do you or the people you bought the data from have the right type of consent in place? If not, get opt in consent now.

g. Have you considered the other types of personal data you may hold such as employee data?

h. Do you have an effective system for complying with a subject access request?

3. See data protection law as a positive – this is a good opportunity to tidy up your data. If people have not opted in they are probably not that interested in your product and you can focus your time and energy on your core customers who remain actively engaged.

4. Make sure you have adequate IT security systems in place, and also that you respect your data protection obligations.

5. Think carefully about what CCTV you are using in or around any premises, whether you have adequate notices up and how long that data is stored. Remember images of people can be personal data as well.

15 Before you sign a lease

Do you need to rent or own physical property? In theory it is possible to do everything remotely, and with lean manufacturing, depending on your business model, you may not need to have any office, warehouse or retail space at all. This chapter looks at the traditional approaches to bricks and mortar retail as well as the increasingly common alternatives.

15.1 Leasing retail space

It is very unusual nowadays for a shop to own the land on which it is located. Because of the high costs of commercial property coupled with the frequent changes in trading conditions, it is far more normal for fashion businesses to rent property either in the form of a standalone shop or as a concession within a larger shop or department store.

As online shopping becomes more ubiquitous, physical retail space has had to up its game. Many shops are now also destinations which include coffee bars, a theatrical element, events such as launch parties and more.[1] Some traditional fashion brands have diversified their existing retail space either by selling third party products which complement the main lines, such as homewares and soft furnishings, or essentially running a mini concession or even a co-working space within their existing store. Many of these alternative approaches require the landlord's permission and potentially permission from the relevant local authority.

Even if customers do not buy in your store as much as they once might have done, they remain an important selling point for fashion businesses. They set the tone and personality for a business and give poten-

---

1 For some good examples of this, see Alex Moore, 05.04.16 10 destination stores that chart new retail territory https://thespaces.com/2016/04/05/10-destination-stores-that-chart-new-retail-territory/.

tial customers the opportunity to experience and buy into the brand before making the financial investment of a purchase. It is increasingly possible for technology to enter the realm of the physical shop whether via beacon technology to track user movement and improve the store layout as a result or using augmented reality to add information or catwalk videos to the physical shopping experience.

A huge amount of financial and brand investment can go into stores, particularly flagship locations. In many instances, the lease can tie you in for a long time. For example, in the past it was not uncommon to take a lease for 20 years, usually with a break clause.

It is outside the scope of this book to give a detailed analysis of property law as it varies substantially across Europe. However, there are some important concepts and practical points which apply in most commercial property situations and can help you to make informed choices about where to locate and what to negotiate.

15.2   Leasehold negotiations

As noted in Chapter 9, with any business negotiations, it is common to set out the agreed parameters in advance via 'heads of terms'. In a property or real estate context, these terms set out key commercial points such as the duration of the lease, rent and rent review provisions, any restrictions on competitor businesses operating nearby (i.e., an exclusivity clause) and more detailed issues such as signage, opening hours, access for deliveries, etc. It is normal for these terms to be clearly expressed as non-binding (i.e., they alone do not create a valid lease). However, you may want to have some clauses bind you and the potential landlord at the negotiations stage. For example, it is fairly common to agree exclusivity during the negotiations and confidentiality regarding the negotiations themselves and the outcome of these negotiations.

In some circumstances, it may be necessary to involve the local council (or equivalent) in the lease creation process. The precise requirements for a valid and binding lease can vary substantially between Member States. For example, in England, a lease for more than seven years must be signed as a deed and registered at the Land Registry. In many other Member States (e.g., France) a notary is involved at regular intervals in the process. This can slow down the process and incurs additional costs.

Leases can be extremely detailed, particularly when you are taking a unit in a shopping centre where there tend to be stricter and more standard requirements. These leases can include a long list of obligations regarding the shop itself as well as the other parts of the shopping centre which are shared with other tenants (known as the 'common parts'). In addition, some information on energy usage and other technical issues associated with the property has become obligatory across the EU. By the time you add in the plans, any additional restrictions and this information, many leases can be extremely long with several annexes. Regardless of the length, make sure you and your lawyer read them thoroughly.

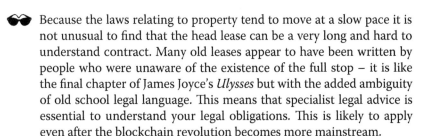 Because the laws relating to property tend to move at a slow pace it is not unusual to find that the head lease can be a very long and hard to understand contract. Many old leases appear to have been written by people who were unaware of the existence of the full stop – it is like the final chapter of James Joyce's *Ulysses* but with the added ambiguity of old school legal language. This means that specialist legal advice is essential to understand your legal obligations. This is likely to apply even after the blockchain revolution becomes more mainstream.

Planning permission can be another area which is fraught with difficulty and again requires expert involvement in order to avoid incurring the ire of local councils. If you do not seek the right permission you risk the possibility of a fine and a lot of expensive building work to restore original conditions. Any requirements which may need planning permission should be identified, and ideally resolved, before entering into a lease.

15.3   Lease terms

Rent is generally the most important term of any lease. It is usually paid in advance on a monthly basis and reviewed on a regular basis such as every two to three years. Rent review time involves a complicated negotiation between the landlord – who wants the rent to increase as much as possible – and the tenant who wants the rent to remain the same. They will usually look at the current state of the market but how this is calculated is up for negotiation. Options include an agreed percentage increase, or benchmarking to a cost of living index or even a percentage of turnover (so-called turnover rent). Getting good quality advice from innovative lawyers within the territory is essential to success.

Bear in mind that even within a Member State, property law can vary considerably. For example, the property law in Scotland is very different to that of England and Wales.

Deposits, bonds and guarantees are a common feature of leases around the world. This is usually a pot of money which will be accessed in the event that you breach the terms of a lease, for example if you do not pay your rent or damage the building. In the case of a guarantee it is someone else, such as another company within your corporate group or potentially you as an individual, who is responsible for paying the rent in the event that your business defaults on a payment.

Other important terms concern the length of the lease and your ability to assign or sublet if things do not go quite according to plan. There are more restrictions on this than in connection with residential property where issues such as competition do not arise. For example, landlord consent is typically required. Some Member States such as Italy, France and Belgium protect commercial tenants by requiring standard terms to be included in all leases which cannot be deleted by the parties (i.e., they cannot be 'contracted out'). For example, they provide more flexibility to tenants regarding leasehold renewal or similar issues.

15.4   Store fit out

Fitting out a store can be a very difficult task which involves coordinating local labour with delivery of specific items that are designed to generate a consistent in-store experience. It is sensible to run the negotiations for fit out in parallel with the lease negotiations. This avoids a substantial delay. This is particularly problematic if this is your first time in a territory or setting up a particular type of store.

It is important that the lease is clear about the extent of your freedom to contract with independent fit out consultants. Some landlords and/ or building managers will attempt to tie you into their contractors who may not necessarily offer the best price or range of options. If, for example, having WiFi available from day one is essential to the smooth running of your store, this should be a contractual requirement which is clearly set out in the lease.

Finally, at the end of the lease, there can be a long discussion over the extent to which you are liable for any damage to the property – this is known in England as 'dilapidations'. Disputes regarding damage are common and it is wise to have good insurance in place together with an emergency fund to deal with any issues which may arise. This damage tends to be the result of fit out or general wear and tear.

15.5   Pop up shops

An alternative to a long lease is a pop up shop. This is typically a shop which is only open for a few months. They offer you the opportunity to allow customers to experience your products without the financial risk of a long-term lease. There is less flexibility in these leases and they tend to be conducted on the landlord's standard terms. Nevertheless, you should consider the terms carefully, particularly as far as fit out, maintenance support and dilapidations are concerned.

A common problem is that it is not possible to get WiFi into the store in time. Ideally the company managing the store will provide high speed Internet as standard. This Internet access may be more expensive than if you make the arrangements yourself but it is usually worth the money in time, hassle and worries about access.

15.6   Concessions

Concessions give you the opportunity to have a dedicated space in a department store. They often operate on standard terms and have a set approach to issues such as fit out. However, they are usually much more cost effective than operating your own lease as you do not have to pay as much toward utilities, estate agent fees, surveyors, service charges and, where relevant, tax. All of these property costs are built into the cost of the concession itself. You also have the advantage of association with an existing brand. For example, if you are in Selfridges or Galeries LaFayette, you benefit from the cachet associated with their name.

 One of the crucial issues is termination of the concession which is usually fixed at six months. This is a long time to wait if the agreement is not going according to plan. If you do not give sufficient notice, you risk damage to your reputation as well as a damages claim from the department store for lost payments under the concession agreement.

15.6.1   Your concession's location

When negotiating a concession, look carefully at its location within the store. For example, the other concessions which are nearby and its proximity to entrances, exits and escalators. You should get as much information from the department store as possible on things such as footfall, customer purchase patterns, the types of customer as well as the technology that they use such as beacons or augmented reality.

It is also worth thinking about the practicalities such as how much storage space is available in the department store and how far away the storage facility is from your concession stand. Similarly, in some concessions, you do not have a choice over the store staff. If they are selected by the store, make sure you have time to give them dedicated training on your products, key policies and any other information which may be relevant for the sales pitch such as your sustainability credentials. In many concessions you will not have your own till. This is not necessarily a problem but locating fairly close (but not too close) to a till is important for sales.

Often department stores have an equivalent e-commerce site. You will need to think about whether you have a choice in appearing on the website. Important questions include how is fulfilment handled, what percentage is deducted by the site and how and when are you paid? This does not necessarily have to be on the same basis as the store concession agreement.

15.6.2   Payments and returns

One of the more controversial issues in concessions concerns payment and returns. Payment for a concession is typically on a commission basis. This means that around 20–30 per cent of your net receipts (i.e., the total sales of your merchandise) are paid to the store. This money is usually deducted at point of sale and the balance is paid out to you on a regular basis. There are also often base costs such as insurance, utilities, etc., which are payable regardless of the costs and variable costs such as credit card handling fees which are payable on top. You may also be required to offer staff discounts or make payments toward a reward scheme.

It is important that you are clear about how returns operate and the impact that they have on the commission you have to pay – you do not want to have to pay commission on an item which was returned (and potentially pay it a second time if the item is resold).

15.6.3   Maintaining a successful concession

The key to a successful concession is maintaining a good relationship with the store owner and fellow concessions in the same area. Ultimately you all benefit if the department store does well. Regular communication over issues which have arisen and keeping really clear and accurate records is essential.

 Good records of complaints, footfall, sales, events, brand successes, returns, concerns regarding other concessions, staffing issues, etc. will prove invaluable if you get into a dispute later on. If the store communicates with you, whether in a formal or informal way, it is important that you act quickly to rectify any concerns, even if the communication appears to be unfair. You do not want to find yourself in breach of contract.

16 Before your first ad campaign

In order to build a global brand, you need to advertise. This can range from Google and Facebook ads and working with social media influencers to full colour advertisements in glossy magazines and television or online video advertising. Sponsorship, celebrity endorsements and product tie-ins, merchandise, etc are all forms of advertising which are commonly used by the fashion industry.

When building a brand, the objective is usually to get maximum exposure in return for the least amount of money. It is not surprising therefore that many fashion businesses (at all stages) sail fairly close to the wind and sometimes end up the wrong side of the line (apologies for the mixed metaphors!)

16.1   Key elements of an ad campaign

Every advertising campaign will include some content (video, images, words, etc.) and, usually, an offer or other 'call to action.' The problems which arise in advertising campaigns boil down to either the content not being authorised for use or the offer not being entirely accurate.

This chapter first deals with the common issues which can arise with an advert's content and then the ways in which you can get into hot water with inaccurate advertising campaigns.

16.2   Google advertising

Like it or not, Google is the key to the Internet and consequently is an essential form of advertising for a lot of businesses. Keyword advertising can be very expensive so it is important to maximise the advertising spend while not infringing another's rights. (Somewhat surprisingly, in the US, many of the most expensive keywords relate to legal services!)[1]

The use of another business' company or brand name as a keyword has been extensively litigated in Europe in recent years. There was a widespread practice of people bidding on a keyword for a well-known brand such as Givenchy and then displaying an advert for a cheaper alternative. In many instances, the cheaper alternative did not make it clear that the Google ad was not connected to the known brand or deliberately created the impression that there was a connection with the famous brand.

The question of what Google keyword usage is permissible has been considered by the CJEU in several decisions following referrals from Member States on specific points of law. The keyword journey began with *L'Oréal v eBay*.[2] This dispute concerned the sale of L'Oréal's products on eBay and eBay's involvement with Google keyword advertising on behalf of its sellers.

L'Oréal sells its perfumes, makeup and similar items via a closed selective distribution network, in which authorised distributors cannot supply products to other distributors. In order to use eBay's online marketplace, both sellers and buyers must accept eBay's user agreement which includes prohibitions on selling counterfeit goods and infringing trade marks.

eBay used L'Oréal trade marks as keywords on Google's AdWords programme. This meant that every time someone searched for one of L'Oréal's trade marks it was possible that Google would display a sponsored link to www.ebay.co.uk. The Google ads would typically include the name of the product. For example:

Shu Uemura

Great deals on Shu uemura

Shop on eBay and Save!

ww.ebay.co.uk

---

1 https://blog.hubspot.com/marketing/most-expensive-keywords-google.
2 ECLI:EU:C:2011:474 Case C-324/09.

In this example, when people searching on Google clicked on the sponsored link, they were taken to a page on eBay which proclaimed: '96 items found for shu uemura' and provided links to each listing. Most of these products came from Hong Kong.

The CJEU concluded that a trade mark owner can prevent an online marketplace operator from using Google ads which do not easily enable 'reasonably well-informed and reasonably observant Internet users' to tell if the advertised goods come from the trade mark owner or someone else. With that caveat, bidding on a competitor's trade mark (e.g., a business or product name) as a keyword is fair game.

This principle was later applied to both Google ads[3] in general and listings on large marketplaces themselves. For example, an English court decided that Amazon was not allowed to use the keyword 'Lush' on its website to link to products which were similar to Lush products (particularly bath bombs).[4]

16.2.1 What keywords can you use in online advertising?

The rule now is that you can bid on a competitor's trade mark for Google ads or similar keyword search advertising, for example, on Facebook or Instagram, but you must make it very clear in the advert that your business is not connected to or authorised by the trade mark owner.

Google's policy states that: 'Google won't investigate or restrict the selection of trademarks as keywords, even if we receive a trademark complaint.'[5] However, in EU and EFTA[6] only, Google will 'in response to a valid complaint. . .conduct a limited investigation as to whether a keyword (in combination with particular ad text) is confusing as to the origin of the advertised goods and services.'

The policy further clarifies that:

> an ad can use a trademarked term in its text if either of these conditions is true:

---

3 Most famously in the *Google France* litigation, C-236/08 AC-238/08.

4 *Cosmetic Warriors Ltd and Anor v Amazon.co.uk Ltd and Anor* [2014] EWHC 181 (Ch).

5 https://support.google.com/adwordspolicy/answer/6118.

6 EFTA is a free trade agreement between the four European countries which are not currently members of the EU, namely Iceland, Liechtenstein, Norway and Switzerland | http://www.efta.int/.

1. the ad text *uses the term descriptively* in its ordinary meaning rather than in reference to the trademark
2. the ad is *not in reference to the goods or services* corresponding to the trademarked term.

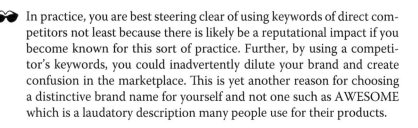 In practice, you are best steering clear of using keywords of direct competitors not least because there is likely be a reputational impact if you become known for this sort of practice. Further, by using a competitor's keywords, you could inadvertently dilute your brand and create confusion in the marketplace. This is yet another reason for choosing a distinctive brand name for yourself and not one such as AWESOME which is a laudatory description many people use for their products.

16.2.2   When Google AdWords get complicated

Complications have arisen in both France and England regarding the use of the keyword 'Interflora.' The difficulty arises because Interflora is a brand name which operates in many stores even ones such as supermarkets which you might not immediately associated with floristry. This means that if you bid on 'Interflora' as a keyword even if there is no reference to Interflora in an advert, consumers could still be confused into believing that all sponsored links following a search of 'interflora' are for shops where they can send flowers using Interflora.

Both the English and Paris High Courts[7] confirmed that provided Interflora was only used as a keyword and not in the associated message, there was no risk of confusion (and consequently no trade mark infringement). The French court noted that free access to keywords encourages competition which is essential to business success and not only struck out Interflora's case but ordered it to pay the defendant, in that case Florajet, €15,000 for abuse of process. This payment was in part because Interflora had claimed €6 million in damages but could demonstrate no loss.

An analogy to Interflora for the fashion industry applies to certification marks and textile products such as Harris Tweed. It is reasonable to assume that a sponsored link for HARRIS TWEED as a keyword would only consist of products that use Harris Tweed material but, provided the sponsored ad does not confuse customers into believing that the ad is connected to Harris Tweed, it will be permitted.

---

7 TGI Paris, 3e ch., 1re sect., 5 Mars 2015, n° 13/13092.

Subsequent French disputes regarding sellers of gothic-style clothing, confirmed that an advertiser cannot successfully sue a competitor
for not *excluding* its trade mark as a keyword (one of the options in
Google AdWords) unless the consumer is likely to be confused about
the origin of the advert. The court confirmed that the risk of confusion
based on a commercial link (in this case, they both sold the same type
of clothing) is not sufficient.[8]

16.3   Use of backlinks in bad faith

While the French courts have followed the CJEU's commercial and
liberal approach in respect of Google AdWords and link referencing,
they are not afraid to impose sanctions against parties in this area, particularly when there is evidence of bad faith. The French Commercial
Court recently held that adding 'backlinks' which diverted Internet
users visiting a company's website to its competitor's website was,
unsurprisingly, unlawful.

The defendant argued that it had no control over the actions of its
website developer and also that it had been quick to delete the links
once they had been detected. The French court was not impressed
by this argument and calculated the damages award based on the
number of visits the competitor website received during the offending period, in comparison with the usual amount of website traffic.
The judge then used this calculation to compensate the claimant
company for loss of the opportunity to sell to these potential
customers.[9]

This case serves as a helpful reminder that it is important to monitor
the actions of any service providers acting on your behalf, such as web
designers and social media managers, to ensure that they are acting
in your best interests and also within the limits of the law. This can be
best managed by entering into a contract with your service providers
setting out the scope of work and deliverables you are expecting, as
well as detailed provisions in terms of rights, obligations and liability in
the event that something goes wrong.

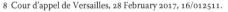

8 Cour d'appel de Versailles, 28 February 2017, 16/012511.
9 See Decision from the Tribunal de Commerce de Belfort, rendered on 17th October 2017.

16.4   Email advertising

Direct email marketing can appear to be an old fashioned way of communicating but it is still very effective, particularly when technology makes it relatively easy to personalise each email with products or promotions that are particularly exciting or useful for the recipient.

Email addresses can come from two sources. First, your customers and fans who sign up in order to receive regular updates and secondly, addresses you have purchased. If you buy email addresses you need to be very careful that you have a clear chain of title including the evidence that the email address owners actively consented to be contacted by third parties such as yourself. You should also ensure that the advert is clearly identified as promotional and gives the email recipient the ability to quickly and easily unsubscribe.

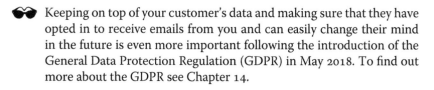 Keeping on top of your customer's data and making sure that they have opted in to receive emails from you and can easily change their mind in the future is even more important following the introduction of the General Data Protection Regulation (GDPR) in May 2018. To find out more about the GDPR see Chapter 14.

When advertisements and promotions such as discounts, bonuses, gift, competitions or promotional games are sent out by email, the recipient needs to be able to clearly identify the nature of the message as soon as it is received, ideally in the subject line but if not in the main body of the email.[10] Further, when such offers are available online, this needs to be clearly stated and must direct the consumer to the website in a clear and transparent way.

In Poland, if the material sent via electronic means could be perceived as a commercial offer, you must obtain the recipient's consent to such an offer on an opt-in basis. This consent should be separate from the personal data processing consent.[11]

---

10 See, for example, French Consumer Code, Art. L. 121-15-1 and 2.
11 Article 10 of the Act on Rendering Electronic Services dated 18 July 2002.

16.5   Sponsorship

Have you ever noticed that the first thing that happens when an athlete wins a major tournament is that they change their clothes or put on a fancy watch? Sponsorship is a huge and tightly regulated business. It has big opportunities but needs to be properly understood to be effective and avoid major pitfalls.

If you want to reach a lot of people in a particular marketplace, there are few better routes for doing so than sponsoring an event or organisation. It raises awareness of your brand across the entire marketplace and can provide a long and fruitful association between your brand and the event or a particular individual at that event such as an athlete or pop star.

There are obvious risks for both parties here. For example, if an athlete is involved in a doping scandal this can have a knock on effect on your brand. Similarly if an event is strongly associated with your brand but then you become mired in controversy (e.g., over failure to comply with modern slavery legislation – see Chapter 25) the event will be keen to cut all ties as quickly as possible. The event contracts usually stipulate what is intended to happen in these sorts of scenarios.

It is common in the early stages of a fashion business to simply send out products to people in the hope that they will use them and be photographed in public. This is a slow burn and scattergun approach which may be acceptable in the early stages of a business but carries risks in the longer term – particularly if you use these photographs in promotions. A more strategic approach to sponsorship requires negotiating an agreement with the celebrity. These agreements can be weighty documents and may need to be updated on a periodic basis.

16.6   Use of celebrities – false endorsement

If a celebrity posts a picture of themselves wearing your clothes or out and about with your bag – fantastic! They clearly like your products and you can quite happily share the fact that they are a fan. Provided you have a licence, you can also use a photograph of them wearing it. However, the position is more problematic where you try to create the impression that a celebrity has endorsed your brand or (much worse) you photoshop their image so it looks like they are wearing your hat or bag.

The pitfalls of false endorsement are best illustrated by the issues raised in connection with image rights – see Chapters 5 and 20 for more information. False endorsement is an English law concept but the same outcome is likely elsewhere in Europe based on, for example, unfair competition law.

16.7   Waivers

While in theory you do not need to get a waiver from every single person you use in advertising, in practice, it is still safer to do so, particularly if there is a celebrity in an image. Broadly speaking the risks of not clearing the image rights are a possible false endorsement claim from a celebrity or a privacy or data protection claim from anyone included in the advert (regardless of their fame). Data protection is a bigger concern following the introduction of the GDPR but remember that consent is not the only basis for processing someone's personal data, in this case their image, and you may be able to rely on, for example, legitimate interests to be able to photograph or film in a public place.

Because of the huge differences in image rights law around the world and the scope of those laws, contracts licensing image rights must be exhaustive and cover all possible outcomes which could arise from using someone's image. Bear in mind that while legal entities do not have an 'image' which can be stolen, they can be assigned the ownership of an image. This is particularly common when someone famous dies and a corporate entity or trust is created to manage that person's estate and associated rights.

16.8   Using Photoshop in your advertising

In France, pursuant to the Decree regarding commercial photography and the modification of images of the human body (known colloquially as the 'French Photoshopping Law')[12] it is a legal requirement to ensure that photographs that are taken of models for commercial purposes feature a notice stating that the 'Photograph has been modified' (or in French, *'Photographie retouchée'*) when the physical appearance

---

12   Décret n°2017-738 relatif aux photographies à usage commercial de mannequins dont l'apparence corporelle a été modifiée du 4 mai 2017 (in force from 1 October 2017).

of the model's body has been modified by image modification software (such as Adobe Photoshop) which has the effect of slimming down or augmenting certain aspects of the model's figure.

The law states that the notice needs to be placed on all commercial communications in a clearly accessible and visible way, and must be clearly differentiated from the promotional or advertising message behind the image. The application of the law is fairly wide as all images fall within its ambit regardless of whether they are made available to the public by posters, billboards, on the Internet, in the press, in advertising or even in marketing correspondence aimed at individuals.

Further, the message needs to be displayed in a way which respects the customs and good practices as defined by the French Advertising Professional Regulation Authority.[13] The advertiser is responsible for ensuring compliance with the French Photoshopping Law. Therefore if you are using an agency or a dedicated employee, you should check if all photographs obtained for commercial use, including those purchased from third party service providers, have been modified or 'Photoshopped.'[14] Breach of this law can incur a fine of €37,500 or a maximum of 30 per cent of the costs spent on the advert.

The photoshopping legislation must be complied with if you are plan-
ning any advertising campaigns in France (whether directly targeted or simply accessible in the territory). Interestingly, before the law was introduced, many key figures in the fashion world had already started to change their attitude towards 'photoshopping.' For example, Getty Images recently stated that they no longer include modified images in their image bank. Similar attitudes are being taken by companies such as Asos, and fashion brand, Monki. Both are known for their use of images of natural looking models which have not been subject to image manipulation and they have proudly incorporated this into the DNA of their respective company images and branding.

16.9   Comparative advertising

In order to demonstrate the benefits of your brand or a particular product it is common to identify the features which make it unique

---

13 Article R2133-5 of the French Public Health Code.
14 Ibid., Art. R2133-6.

compared to other products on the market. This might be in terms of your prices, quality, manufacturing process or similar. This is known as comparative advertising.

 Comparative advertising is allowed across the EU[15] provided that the advertising campaign does not go too far and either dilute the other brand's trade marks or damage their reputation. Because comparative advertising is harmonised across the EU by means of a Directive (and not a Regulation) there are some variations between Member States.

 The following approach is advised by the UK's Advertising Standards Authority and is a useful strategy to generally employ:

1. *Think about the claim you want to make.* In particular, how will consumers understand your proposed statement. If you are not sure, ask people who are not connected to your business what they think. Rethink the advert if they interpret the claim in different ways or think it may damage a competitor. Unless the statement is 'obvious puffery,' e.g., *the hippest jeans in the universe*, claims to be superior to the competition (whether or not they are named) will likely be considered to be objective and therefore require independent evidence to prove your claim.

2. *Consider how you compare your business.* Even if a competitor is not explicitly mentioned an implied connection could still be considered to refer to competitors. Consequently, adverts which compare your product to 'mainstream fashion,' 'major brands,' 'the runway' or 'couture' may all fall within the ambit of comparative advertising regulation.

3. *Are your products the same as the competitors?* The compared products must be 'the same' i.e., meet the same consumer need or be intended for the same purpose. In practice, this is less of an issue for most fashion items than some other types of product although issues may arise, for example, with technical clothing.

4. *Is the comparison legitimate?* Comparisons with identifiable competitors must objectively compare one feature of those products, for example the price. Difficulties arise when comparing features

---

15 See the Directive Concerning Misleading and Comparative Advertising 2006/114/EC (the Comparative Advertising Directive).

like 'quality' or 'convenience' as they tend to be more subjective and comparative criteria are less readily available. For the comparison to be considered verifiable you must provide enough information for the advert's audience to easily understand the comparison.

The French code[16] explicitly notes that it is forbidden to carry out comparative advertising if the aim is simply to:

1. benefit from the goodwill attached to a competitor's trade mark;

2. refer to Geographical Indications (a particular issue in France which has been at the forefront of GI protection);[17]

3. discredit the trade marks, commercial names, goods and services of a competitor; or

4. market goods or services as a copy or reproduction of those protected by trade marks or as a French commercial name.

16.10   Social media advertising

The use of social media whether for viral ad campaigns or paid advertising is essential for fashion businesses. Instagram is still the key platform for fashion but Pinterest, Snap, Facebook and Twitter are all vying for customer attention and new social media networks will no doubt pop up to supplement or replace them in due course. Social media is looked at in more detail in the context of employees in Chapter 10. The main issues for social media advertising remain the same as for other ad campaigns.

Because social media is so fast and can appear informal and ephemeral, a common issue with social media is misleading advertising. This can include promoting out-of-date deals, using hashtags belonging to other brands, posting images of a celebrity who either is not connected to the brand (false endorsement) or is paid by the brand but the connection is not made clear in the social media post.

You can minimise these risks by a clear social media advertising policy and making sure that social media promotions are given as much

---

16 French Consumer Code, Art. L. 121-9.
17 This is particularly an issue for the champagne industry.

attention as regular promotions. For example, wording along the lines of 'while stocks last' can reduce the risk of running a promotion of unlimited duration.

Bear in mind that conflicts can arise in all sorts of situations. For example, if you use the same model, or even a similar looking model or if you opt for a near identical shade of colour for your social media campaign. More importantly, make sure that all potential hashtags or other social media slogans are 'cleared' first. Clearing means checking the trade mark registers in the jurisdictions you are targeting to see if any earlier marks have been filed. If you want to further reduce your risk, you can check to see if competitors have recently used but not registered the names.

If a social media campaign is very important to your brand or a core product consider registering a trade mark to protect a key name, slogan, hashtag or any other potential trade marks used in the campaign.

16.10.1   Bloggers and influencers

As mentioned, particular care needs to be taken when engaging bloggers and other social media influencers to endorse your brand and products. It is fine to pay one of these influencers, whether by way of money, free products or a free trip as long as the influencer clearly states how they have been remunerated. On Twitter the use of #ad is considered by many authorities to be sufficient to show that a tweet is sponsored but on Instagram and longer blogs or vlogs, something clearer and more prominent is preferable as the issues of limited space do not apply to the same extent as Twitter. This gives potential customers the opportunity to assess the credibility of the endorsement.

Some countries are particularly cracking down on unclear endorsements and the related issue of reviews. For example, a fine was issued against an Australian company which allowed fake reviews to be added to its site. Similarly, the Brazilian advertising authority has been giving bloggers a great deal of attention, particularly where blog posts closely mirror a press release.

16.10.2   Hashtags as trade marks

Hashtags are increasingly being registered as trade marks. 2016 saw a major uptick (64 per cent) in registrations of hashtags as trade marks with around 2,200 trade mark applications globally.[18] Even if the hashtag itself is not registered, if you use a competitor's trade mark as a hashtag, expect a legal letter followed by potential trade mark proceedings. Not all hashtags are distinctive enough to be registered as trade marks but if they are used over a long period of time or are linked to a wider advertising campaign, such as #justdoit or #makeitcount (both Nike), even relatively generic phrases may acquire distinctiveness and consequently be eligible for trade mark registration.

The key to registration is that the hashtag must be capable of being used to identify the trade origin of the goods or services. Therefore, the more distinctive the hashtag, the better. Because hashtags are global in nature, if there are many businesses with the same name, you will face more of an uphill battle and may be better using a hashtag with a more specific association such as #BRAND_YOURLOCATION or #BRAND_TYPEOFPRODUCT.

In England, regular use of a particular hashtag where consumers are directly led to a purchase opportunity could give rise to sufficient goodwill to be able to sue for passing off and consequently stop a third party from using the hashtag. This is an untested area and would likely require substantial evidence in the first instance. As courts become more familiar with social media use, the evidence threshold may get lower.

The French Intellectual Property Office (the INPI) has provided guidance on whether hashtags can be protected as a trade mark within this scope of its *#toutsurlehashtag* (All About the Hashtag) campaign. This confirmed that a hashtag *may* be registered as a trade mark if the wording functions as a trade mark (i.e., as an indicator of the origin of the goods or services offered or sold under the hashtag). Because the INPI considers the hashtag symbol (#) to be more commonly known as a generalised graphic sign for communication purposes, it can be particularly hard to register short hashtags as trade marks.

The INPI has been particularly critical of strategic hashtag filing to prevent third parties from filing their hashtags (similar to domain name squatting). The INPI refers to this as 'hashtag squatting.'[19]

---

18 See, Claire Jones, 'Hashtag trademarks: what can be protected?' in WIPO Magazine http://www.wipo.int/wipo_magazine/en/2017/05/article_0009.html.

19 For more information regarding the INPI's advice on hashtag trade marks, see: https://www.inpi.fr/fr/valoriser-vos-actifs/le-mag/toutsurlehashtag.

16.11   Misleading claims

EU Member States take a fairly strict line against the use of advertisements which include false or misleading claims regarding the product or services, such as its existence, ingredients, composition, main qualities, uses, origin, quantity, date and method of manufacturing, price, sales conditions, conditions of use and anticipated results. It should also identify the brand, advertiser, manufacturer, or any resellers, promoters or contractors.

Failure to respect these Consumer Code provisions may lead to a court order that the advert be taken down, and the court's judgment published as well as the corrected adverts.[20] This could damage your brand image, and at a minimum, wastes your advertising investment.

16.12   Advertising complaints

Practically every Member State has its own advertisement code and dedicated organisation for ensuring compliance with the code. Where an advert does not comply with the code (or sails very close to the wind) it is common for competitors and/or the general public to complain. Each country has its own rules and procedure. For example, in the UK there is a requirement to write to the advertiser first to try to resolve the issue directly. Due to the nature of advertising campaigns, there are often quite tight deadlines for a response so be ready to act quickly in response to a complaint.

16.12.1   Advertisement arbitration in Italy

In Italy if you object to a competitor's advertising campaign, one option in response is to file a complaint before the *'Giurì'* (i.e., Jury*) of the Istituto di Autodisciplina Pubblicitaria ('IAP')*. This independent, non-judicial entity will decide whether the advertisement breaches its Code of Marketing Communication Self-Regulation.[21]

The Italian marketing code aims to ensure that marketing communication is carried out as a service to the public, with special consideration given to its influence on consumers and therefore it considers activities

---

20 See French Consumer Code, Arts L. 121-3 and 4.
21 See http://www.iap.it/about/the-code/?lang=en.

that, while legal, are in contrast with the code. The *Giurì* works as a sort of arbitral tribunal that is composed of members appointed by the IAP and chosen from among experts in law, consumer affairs and communication.[22]

Any person (whether consumers, competitors or associations) who considers themselves prejudiced by any activities that allegedly infringe the Code can file a complaint. Alternatively, the IAP '*Comitato di Controllo*' can commence an investigation of their own volition.

In order for the IAP to be able to commence proceedings, the advertiser must be a signatory of the Code. The costs of the proceedings as well as other services offered by the *Giurì* are reasonable.[23] The proceedings are fairly quick and it is not necessary to include a lawyer, although it is helpful to do so.

If an advert is non-compliant, the most common outcome is for the *Giurì* to issue a desist order. If the desist order is not complied with in the relevant time frame, the *Giurì* or its President will reiterate and publish the order is repeated and made public, including the names of the parties, via all appropriate media channels and at the expense of the non-compliant party. If this requirement is not fulfilled, IAP can request that the person who made the successful complaint pays all outstanding amounts with right of recourse.[24] The *Giurì*'s decision cannot be appealed but the *Giurì* cannot impose damages.

16.13   Other issues which may arise

16.13.1   Advertising language requirements

France has some specific requirements for advertising campaigns. In particular, all adverts must be available in the French language.[25] While the use of English slogans or phrases is common in French adverts (particularly on the Paris Metro), they are always accompanied with a French translation. For example, the McDonald's 'I'm Lovin' It' campaign was always accompanied with 'C'est tous ce que j'aime.'

---

22 See Art. 29 of the Code of Marketing Communication Self-Regulation.

23 See http://www.iap.it/2017/01/tariffeagevolateservizi/#.

24 See Arts 39 and 42 of the Code of Marketing Communication Self-Regulation.

25 See Laws No. 86-1067 of 30th September 1986 on the Freedom of Communication and No. 94-665 of 4th August 1994 on the Use of French Language as well as the Circulaire of 19th March 1996.

Similarly, any video advertising which is not in the French language is refused in favour of the French version.[26] The French authority in charge of audio visual advertising (the CSA) recently considered adverts for, among other things, Orangina, L'Oréal Studio Pro, Skittles and Streetfighter V. In many instances, the text of the French translation was too small and/or not complete, consequently the CSA liaised with the French Professional Advertising Authority[27] to enforce compliance.[28]

Similarly, in Poland, the Polish language must be used in advertising containing information on product characteristics.[29] This may be done by adding subtitles. The Advertising Ethics Commission in Poland is an independent organisation which has the power to examine advertisements following a complaint to verify their compliance with the Code of Advertising Ethics. For example, in 2014, the Advertising Ethics Commission ruled that the advertisement for Paco Rabane perfumes broadcast on TV by SiroScan constituted an act contrary to good practice and social responsibility because the voice content was not translated into Polish.[30] This perspective is likely to evolve as the English language is increasingly prevalent, particularly in online advertising in Poland.

16.13.2   Buying advertising space in France

In addition to the above issues, there are specific obligations for buying advertising space in France.[31] This means that all purchases or services relating to the publication or distribution of printed advertising can only be done by an advertising agency on behalf of an advertiser. This requires a written contract that expressly instructs the agency to carry out such activities.[32] Media consulting companies, or advertising agen-

---

26 The French Audio-Visual Council (Conseil supérieur de l'audiovisuel, or 'CSA') published a Recommendation (under reference: 2005-2 of 18th January 2005) on the use of the French language via televised and audio media. This follows earlier recommendations which date back to September 1989. The Communication is accessible in French here: http://www.csa.fr/Television/Le-suivi-des-programmes/Le-respect-de-la-langue-francaise/Publicite-televisee-l-usage-du-franc ais-est-obligatoire-la-promotion-des-films-est-interdite.

27 Autorité de Régulation Professionnelle de la Publicité, also known as ARPP.

28 See Publication of the Assemblée Plénière of 15th June 2016, available in French, at: http://www.csa.fr/Television/Le-suivi-des-programmes/Le-respect-de-la-langue-francaise/Respect-de-la-langue-francaise-dans-les-messages-publicitaires-interventions-du-CSA.

29 See Arts 7 and 7a of the Act on Polish language dated 7 October 1999.

30 Resolution of the Advertising Ethics Commission no. Nr ZO 71/14 dated 10 September 2014.

31 The Law of 29th January 1993 (also known as the Loi Sapin after the Minister who backed the bill).

32 See Art. 20, Loi Sapin.

cies which negotiate advertising space are not permitted to receive any kind of remuneration or other advantage from the seller of that advertising space.[33] The aim behind this legislation is to prevent corruption and promote transparency amongst the relevant businesses.

16.13.3   Special offers

Any advertising campaign which refers to a special offer should also refer to the dates the offer applies, the availability of stock and any special conditions.[34]

There are many other important points, outside the scope of this book, so it is worth seeking advice from specialist advertising lawyers to ensure that your advertising campaigns and purchase of advertising space are compliant with local law.

---

33 See, ibid., Art. 22.
34 See Art. L. 121-8 of the Consumer Code.

17 Before launching your e-commerce site

There is no doubt that the Internet has fundamentally changed the retail industry. The high street and out of town shopping malls are still important but they have become destinations of choice rather than necessity. This means that many businesses now start online and then move into bricks and mortar or use pop up stalls to build brand and product awareness. In many cases this move starts with a shop on a general e-commerce site such as Amazon or Etsy and then a move to a dedicated e-commerce site. Although the two can of course (and often do) occur in tandem.

There are many legal compliance issues associated with e-commerce. This chapter focuses on the most common problems that occur for the fashion industry but it does not consider the issues that can arise for specific products such as cosmetics and wearable technology. Many products have various product testing and recycling requirements which are outside the scope of this book.

17.1 Using third party 'marketplaces'

 Third party websites can give you an excellent opportunity to start trading but there are a few things you need to get right in order for your business to be successful. The most important thing is to read and completely understand the marketplace's terms and conditions. You will be entering into two contracts, one with the hosting platform and one with your ultimate customer. Make sure you understand both.

The downside of using online marketplaces is that you have much less flexibility over the appearance of the website, policies, timing and data from your customers. However, marketplaces can be a very useful means of gaining name recognition. Given that around 40 per cent of all purchases made online are made on Amazon alone, if you do not appear on these marketplaces you risk losing a huge source of revenue.

17.2   Designing your own website or app

You do not have to design your website yourself but if you engage a third party you must make sure that you are assigned ownership of the parts of the website or app which are unique to you and your business. If you do not get this assignment in place before they start work you may end up with a site which you do not own or which is difficult to update in the future. This can create problems if you fall out with the web developer in the future or you find that your competitors are using your 'unique' website features.

In addition to the design of the website, it is also essential that the content which you add to the site is owned or licensed by you. As for social media, it is common for websites to source images or videos from the Internet to promote new clothing lines or blogs. If you do not have the rights to this content you risk social media shaming and an expensive legal bill. Make sure you clear all rights used on your website in advance.

If you are only given rights by a photographer for a limited period of time, such as the length of a campaign, it is important to ensure that the images are removed from the website at the end of the campaign. You can avoid a lot of trouble down the line if you ensure that your photography contract gives you online archive rights in perpetuity.

It is also essential that your website has a good content management system (or CMS). The CMS is the bit behind the website that you use in order to upload new content on to the website. The CMS should be user friendly and able to easily integrate with other platforms and apps.

17.3   Information obligations

Europe has strict obligations regarding the information which must be included on a trading website. Usually this information is contained in the terms and conditions,[1] privacy policy[2] and often in an 'about us' link. It may also be sent by email following a purchase. This information includes the name of the individual or legal entity behind the

---

1 E-commerce Directive, Arts 5 and 10 sets out the information requirements for the website and Art. 6, the requirements for communications.

2 A requirement under the GDPR.

website with whom a customer would contract if they purchase your product as well as your contact details.

These obligations also apply to social media accounts which are associated with trading activity. A link to the relevant page on your website should be sufficient but if there is space to add this information, for example on Facebook, it is worth reducing the risk and helping out your customers by adding this information.

 Bear in mind that this information will have to be translated into the language of each territory that you are targeting. This can get expensive but it is often worth the effort as it opens up new markets.

 In addition, the EU has product labelling requirements for specific types of goods such as electrical goods[3] or breakable items such as products made of glass. In many instances you have the option to choose between a symbol or translation into multiple languages. The symbol is much simpler but it is worth adding warning wording if possible, in at least English, German, French, Italian and Spanish.

 In some European jurisdictions, notably Germany, cease and desist claims can be brought by competitors if businesses do not comply with these information obligations. This is a fairly common tactic used by many German businesses in part due to the ease with which it is possible to get an injunction in Germany and the German approach to recovery of legal costs which is on a fixed scale.

17.4   Terms and conditions

Whether you call them 'online terms,' 'T&Cs' or 'legal stuff' there is some information which you are obliged to include on your website in order to trade in the EU. This applies to any product listings you make on third party websites as well as your own website.

As mentioned above, e-commerce websites must provide general information about the business and there are also specific requirements

---

3 The CE mark is the main issue but there are obligations regarding recycling and chemicals which may apply. For more information on CE marks see at: https://europa.eu/youreurope/business/product/ce-mark/index_en.htm and more details on chemical product labelling, see at: https://europa.eu/youreurope/business/product/chemicals-packaging-labelling-classification/index_en.htm.

which must be followed before entering into a particular contract to, for example, buy some trainers. It is common for these terms to be rolled into one document but specific information relating to an individual purchase such as the delivery details can be provided separately.

You must include the information in an easily accessible format prior to consumers making a purchase via a 'remote communication medium' (this includes goods purchased by email or mobile as well as via websites). This information includes:

1.   The business name including company registration number.

2.   The relevant VAT number.

3.   Accepted methods of payment.

4.   The fact that customers can cancel their order up to 14 days after the order is delivered without giving a reason and then have a further 14 days in which to return the goods. You cannot contract out of this right even if goods are sold at a discount.

5.   A physical address – a post office or 'PO' box address is not acceptable.

6.   Other contact details, such as an email address even if you have a 'contact us' form to manage communication, you should still include a general email address.

7.   Any prices referred to on the website should state whether they include 'hidden' charges such as VAT and delivery costs and if not, clearly set out those charges.

8.   What to do if there is an issue with delivery, the product's quality or the customer wants to return the goods within the 28 day period.

All of this information must be easy to understand and be provided in a format that the customer can save for future reference, such as an email. These information requirements and associated rights come from the Consumer Rights Directive.[4]

---

4 Consumer Rights Directive 2011/83/EU.

17.5   Online Dispute Resolution

Online stores operating in the EEA are now obliged to inform the consumers about the possibility of using the so-called Online Dispute Resolution platform (ODR).[5] Both the customer and the seller can use this tool to try to reach an out of court settlement. This only applies if both the trader and customer are based in the EEA. The ODR website identifies appropriate dispute resolution bodies and then the case is decided by the selected dispute resolution body. The ODR platform explicitly relates to clothing and footwear, cosmetics, jewellery and other similar items.

17.6   VAT

 It is important to familiarise yourself with the various tax systems when selling online in Europe. Value Added Tax (or VAT), is a sales tax that applies at different rates across Europe. You have to pay VAT based on the location of the customer. This means that, by way of example, if you are based in Italy but sell products in Sweden, the taxes on those products must be charged at Sweden's VAT rate, even though it is higher than Italy's.[6] This VAT is then paid to the Swedish Government and not the Italian Government. The tax and the total price must be clearly visible to consumers. It is essential that you do not sell goods into the EU with hidden costs so the price advertised must include tax and then the total tax and delivery costs must be clearly identified prior to payment.

 If you are selling your products wholesale rather than directly to the consumer, the situation is a little different. If you are selling within a Member State, you charge the customer VAT and they can reclaim this amount from the relevant tax authority. In the UK, this VAT rebate is processed on a quarterly basis. If your transaction is from one EU Member State to another, provided they give you a valid VAT number, you do not charge the business VAT.

 If you are not based in the EEA and import products from outside the EEA, you will have to pay tax in order to clear Customs. The amount

---

5 See here for more information: https://ec.europa.eu/consumers/odr/main/?event=main.home. show.

6 This is subject to tax thresholds which apply in different Member States. You can read more about this at: https://europa.eu/youreurope/business/vat-customs/cross-border/index_en.htm.

of tax depends on the destination country and product. It is important that accurate information is provided when shipping the goods in order to avoid paying too much duty.

In addition, if there is an electrical component to your products, as is the case with wearable technology, you must make sure that you have good records of the number of items being put on the market in the EEA as well as the items taken off the market (as in the case of returns). If you do not retain these records, you are likely breaching the WEEE Regulation which is designed to manage waste in the EU.[7] You could face a significant fine as a result of breach.

17.7   Returns

Returns are the bane of the online retailer's life. They are administratively expensive and make stock management a challenge.

As mentioned in relation to the information requirements, if you sell your products online (or otherwise conclude the contract remotely such as by telephone or mail order) your customers have the right to ask you to cancel the order within 14 days, for any reason and with no justification. They then have a further 14 days in which to return the goods. In other words, the goods could be out of your control for 28 days and you are required to provide a full refund following their return (provided they are not damaged). You also have to reimburse the delivery costs for returning the goods. For higher value items, it is common to refund the original delivery costs as well, although this is not mandatory.

Unlike the position with in store purchases, you still have to give online customers their right to return goods if they are purchased on sale or as part of a promotional discount or 'outlet'. However, the rules around returns do not apply to goods such as underwear (for reasons of health or hygiene) or to bespoke or custom made items.

Importantly, if you do not inform customers of their right to cancel, they can cancel the contract at any time in the next 12 months and retain the rights set out above (i.e., a full refund and repayment of the costs of delivering the items back to you). You can reduce this period of time provided you write to them in the meantime to inform them of

---

7 The Waste Electrical and Electronic Equipment Directive 2012/19/EU.

their rights, in which case they have 14 days from the date you wrote to them.

Further, the EU offers all consumers a minimum two year guarantee on goods sold in the EU.[8] This means that a trader must repair, replace, reduce the price or give you a refund if goods you bought turn out to be faulty or do not look or work as advertised within, at least the first two years following receipt of the goods. This applies regardless of the method of purchase.[9]

Generally, the person in the best position to repair the goods is the brand. If you are a retailer, it is worth agreeing a protocol for repair of goods with the brand.

17.8   Product liability

In addition to the guarantee which is automatically granted to EU consumers, there are additional risks regarding product liability. This can arise under local tort or product liability law in each Member State or under the Defective Products Directive.[10] For example, this issue could arise if the chemicals used to treat fabric at the end of the manufacturing process are not properly washed and the resulting residue irritates the consumer's skin during wear. The risks with wearable technology are much greater as, for example, charging can cause products to overheat and batteries can contain dangerous chemicals.

17.9   Your privacy policy

As explained in Chapter 14 regarding data protection, your privacy policy is an essential element of e-commerce. You will likely have several different privacy policies as the type of data you collect and the basis for doing so is likely to vary between, at least, your employees, your website and your app.

---

8 Directive 1999/44/EC on certain aspects of the sale of consumer goods and associated guarantees.

9 There is a helpful website which explains the process at: https://europa.eu/youreurope/business/sell-abroad/client-guarantee-redress/index_en.htm.

10 Directive 85/374/EEC.

In addition, it is a good idea to have a short-form privacy notice which is automatically provided to the consumer immediately before you collect their data. This notice should state why you are collecting and processing their data. It does not need to go into a lot of detail and can cross-refer to your privacy policy if the relevant individual requires more information.

In order to prepare your privacy policy, you will need to be able to answer the following questions.

17.9.1   What types of personal data do you collect?

You will likely collect the following information directly from your customer: their full name, contact details including postal address and, potentially, their financial data. You may also use tracking software to monitor your customers' behaviour. This data, such as web log and location data, is usually collected automatically.

The privacy policy should also set out what cookies (if any) you are using and how to disable them. Cookies are small data files which most website operators add to either the browser or hard drive of their website visitor's computer. They can be used to track a website visitor's progress and create a profile of the visitor which can include their name and other identifiers.

If you receive information on the customer from other sources such as your other websites, apps or in store services (such as beacon technology or store cards), you should set that out as well.

17.9.2   How you will use that data?

This is a particularly important question if you plan to sell customer data to other people in the future or use it in advertising campaigns. Think carefully about exactly what you need now and are likely to need in the future and strike a balance. You will need a lawful basis for each type of use. Bear in mind that explicit informed consent is one option but other options are available. You can find out about these options in Chapter 14.

It can cause reputational damage if you try to collect too much data, conversely if your policy is too limited, you can miss opportunities to sell to your customers in the future. In order to comply with GDPR, you may need to obtain explicit consent for certain types of data collection and processing. This consent will likely be obtained separately from the privacy policy.

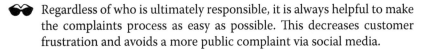 Website privacy policies are public documents so you can easily look at the approach your competitors have taken. Further, as with any contract, be careful about what you are promising and make sure you can definitely deliver the goods (so to speak).

17.9.3   Who to contact with any data protection or privacy questions or complaints?

In Europe, the contact person for all your data protection problems is known as the 'data protection officer.' It is no longer mandatory for all companies to have a data protection officer but it is nevertheless sensible to do so (and it is still mandatory for some larger or more high risk businesses). You should start thinking about how you are using personal data at an early stage and on a regular basis. Having someone at board level who is personally accountable tends to keep data on the agenda.

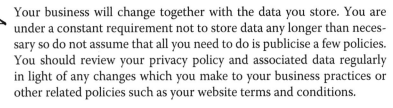 Regardless of who is ultimately responsible, it is always helpful to make the complaints process as easy as possible. This decreases customer frustration and avoids a more public complaint via social media.

17.9.4   Where will the personal data be stored?

If any of the personal data which you have collected will be transferred, processed and/or stored outside the EEA, your privacy policy should explain what data will be transferred and how the data will be used. This is a particular issue with payment transaction data. Resolving the data transfer minefield is outside the scope of this book but it is worth getting professional advice if you transfer personal data out of the EEA.

17.9.5   Future proofing

Your business will change together with the data you store. You are under a constant requirement not to store data any longer than necessary so do not assume that all you need to do is publicise a few policies. You should review your privacy policy and associated data regularly in light of any changes which you make to your business practices or other related policies such as your website terms and conditions.

Finally, while the following are not yet explicitly mandatory, they are good examples of compliance:

1. Including a short privacy notice whenever you are about to col-
    lect personal data. This should explain what data is being collected,
    such as location data, why it is being collected and give users an
    immediate option regarding collection of that data.

2. Ensuring that the privacy policy is easily accessible across your
    entire app or website.

3. Adding a section to the privacy policy regarding changes to the
    policy. This will not prevent you from seeking permission from
    users regarding changes in the future but does set out the proce-
    dure for notifying users of changes to the policy – usually by email.

17.10   Geo-blocking

The EU has been steadily moving toward a 'digital single market' where
all barriers to trade whether physical or digital are removed across the
Union. The most recent move in this direction is the Geo-blocking
Regulation[11] which applied across the EU from 3 December 2018.

Geo-blocking is common practice in the fashion industry, it consists
of blocking or otherwise limiting access to your website, app or other
online portal based on your (potential) customer's location. In some
instances, this could involve automatically redirecting the customer
to the local version of your website, etc., which often is in a different
language and has different products, prices, conditions, etc. Any differences in price, goods and services offered, etc based on the customer's
location are no longer acceptable under the Geo-blocking Regulation.

Under the Regulation, you can only redirect customers with their
explicit consent. So a French customer can access the Polish (and all
other EU versions) of a website and purchase goods from that site.
However, if you do not offer delivery to a particular country, you will
not be required to do so under the new rules. Also, payment, pricing
and other differences are still permitted provided the reason for the

---

11 Regulation (EU) 2018/302.

difference is not due to the nationality or location of the customer and can be justified for another reason.

17.11   Anti-competitive practices

Before setting up your e-commerce site take care to ensure that you are not inadvertently engaging in an anti-competitive practice. For example, luxury private sales site, BrandAlley, recently brought an action in France against its competitor, Vente-Privée.com for abuse of a dominant position.[12] BrandAlley alleged that Vente-Privée had a dominant position within the private event-based Internet sales market, and that as such, the agreements that Vente-Privée had entered into with its suppliers (well-known labels and luxury brands) which contained exclusivity clauses preventing its suppliers from selling any left-over stock to Vente-Privée's competitors, constituted an abuse of that dominant position.

The French Supreme Court noted that throughout the relevant time (2005 to 2011), there was no relevant market for event-based online sales, and so BrandAlley's claims were dismissed on the basis that there cannot be an abuse of dominant position if the market does not exist. However, the court acknowledged that this sector has seen significant growth over the last decade and the market is changing over time.

Consequently, if you are entering into supply agreements relating to an established niche market, you should ensure that you are familiar with your relative position within that market before accepting exclusivity clauses in your agreements.

17.12   Social media

The importance of social media for fashion is clear from the frequency with which it is returned to throughout this book! Social media is some of the public faces of your fashion brand. It can be the key to building reputation or, if handled badly, to brand-destruction. Currently, the most important social media platform for fashion is Instagram but fashion flirtations have occurred with rivals such as SnapChat.

---

12 See Cour de cassation, ch. com., arrêt du 6 Décembre 2017.

If you focus on one social media site it is still important to obtain some sort of presence on the other main social media sites. Not least because if you are not there, it gives your competitors and critics open season. In addition to the usual suspects such as Facebook, Twitter, Pinterest and Snapchat, think about popular Asian social media sites like Weibo, Line and WeChat.

Fashion businesses tend to use social media for one or more of the following:

1. Building brand awareness.

2. Responding to customer complaints.

3. Product or range launches.

4. Ad campaigns (often linked to new product launches).

As social media's importance has increased with time, so have the associated legal issues. These include trade mark and copyright disputes regarding account names, misleading advertising, false celebrity endorsements, e-commerce and counterfeits.

The issues associated with advertising are discussed in more detail in Chapter 16 including the impact of the Google AdWords litigation and how AdWords can be used in practice. The other big issue with social media is the sale of counterfeit goods often via private groups. This is discussed in the broader context of counterfeits in Chapter 24.

Finally, it is worth a quick reminder of design law as the first time a new design is made publicly available is often on social media. As explained in Chapter 6, disclosure of a design starts the clock ticking as far as both registered and unregistered Community designs are concerned. You have one year from the date a design is first shared to register it as a design. You also have three years from that date before unregistered Community designs expire. As mentioned above, it is wise to regularly review at least your best selling or particularly distinctive products with a view to potential registration.

PART IV

The big issues

The final part of the book looks at the various issues and opportunities you are likely to face as you grow. No two businesses follow precisely the same route to growth so you may face these problems earlier or later in your journey. This final section focuses on the major issues you are likely to face but it cannot cover every eventuality. This means that some potential issues such as restructuring, insolvency, etc which are best left to weightier tomes who can give these complicated questions the attention they deserve.

Part IV will take in the highs of international expansion and potential sale, the bigger picture of ethical fashion and sustainability as well as the inevitability of counterfeiting and risks of litigation. While it is obviously preferable to avoid expensive legal disputes, fashion can be a particularly litigious sector and if you succeed, you are likely to find yourself drawn into legal disputes to, for example, prevent competitors copying you or defend yourself against trade mark or design disputes.

18 Franchising

18.1 Why go international and why choose franchising?

The fashion market has become increasingly globalised and for many successful fashion brands, there comes a point in their growth cycle where the demand for their products and services outstrips their ability to meet that demand from their own capital and human resources.

Franchising provides a tried and tested means of extending a business' reach into new markets, allowing rapid expansion and the generation of new income streams and relationships with new customers without the need for significant capital investment and an extensive management infrastructure.

Done in the right way, the execution of your international franchising strategy can become a core asset of your business, helping to secure the long-term future as a global fashion brand and hedging the impact of economic risks in the domestic market. Indeed, a number of established European fashion brands rely increasingly on international business to drive growth, given the low rates of growth seen in their respective saturated and competitive domestic markets.

18.2 How to structure an international franchise

The key to franchise success is a strong business concept, which can be operated as a franchise system and successfully adapted to each target market. In addition, it is necessary to ensure that the overall structure adopted is one that suits your business.

There are five options when it comes to structuring an international franchise: master franchising, direct franchising, multi-unit development, subordinated equity and joint ventures. Each option is considered in more detail below.

18.2.1   Master franchising

In a master franchise arrangement, your fashion brand, 'the franchisor,' grants a third party (the 'master franchisee') the right to either operate a franchise of your business themselves and/or grant sub-franchises to third parties. This usually occurs within a substantial territory. Your master franchisee effectively takes on your role and responsibilities (i.e., becomes the franchisor) for the territory covered by the Master Franchise Agreement. The master franchisee operates their business as well as recruiting, training and managing a network of sub-franchisees. This may be appropriate where the concept is suited to multiple units and low levels of entry cost.

 Master franchising is not a common model for the fashion industry, except for where the geography of a market (such as Russia or China) requires the master franchisee to develop key regions itself and appoint sub-franchisees in more remote locations.

18.2.2   Direct franchising

In this model, your brand (the franchisor) grants another business (the franchisee) the right to operate a single site business themselves.

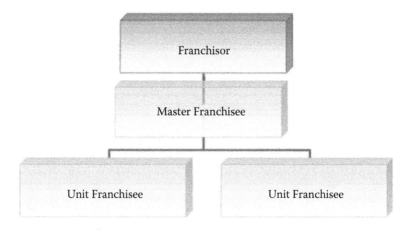

Figure 18.1   A master franchisee structure

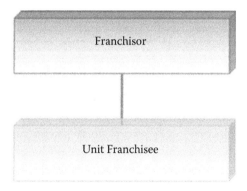

Figure 18.2 A direct franchising structure

This structure may be appropriate where your concept is not suited to multiple units (e.g., luxury fashion) or where you prefer to have a direct relationship with multiple operators in a single territory.

18.2.3   Multi-unit developer franchising

Under this model, your fashion brand, 'the franchisor,' gives the 'developer' the right to exploit a designated territory by opening outlets and/ or providing services themselves. This is known as the 'Development Structure.' In order for this approach to be successful, the developer needs to have considerable financial and other resources.

This structure is commonly used in fashion retail franchising.

You can enter into a development agreement with the developer that either:

1. incorporates both the development schedule/targets and provisions relating to the operation of the outlets; or

2. only sets out the development schedule/targets (with a separate unit franchise agreement or 'operating agreement' that sets out the provisions relating to the operation of the outlets).

18.2.4   Subordinated equity or joint venture franchising?

Most people are familiar with the concept of a joint venture or 'JV', where two businesses join forces to achieve a particular business

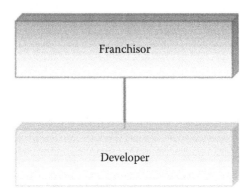

Figure 18.3   A multi-unit developer franchising structure

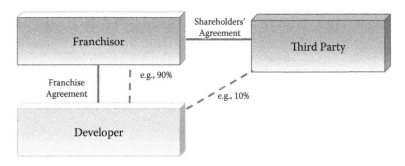

Figure 18.4   A joint venture structure

goal. Joint venture arrangements are usually relatively short lived and their only strategic aim tends to be establishing a presence in a target market.

 Subordinated equity arrangements are less well known and are far more nuanced. They tend to be one piece of a longer term strategy. This mechanism is becoming increasingly popular among fashion retailers.

Subordinated equity agreements can be used as a 'sequenced market entry strategy'. This means that your brand (the franchisor) contracts with a third party operator (the franchisee) to establish its brand in the target market with the stated aim of that business being transferred to you, as the brand owner, in the future (if you want purchase it) at a pre-agreed and formula-based price.

This structure can be attempted by way of a contractual provision in the main franchise agreement. However, this approach often causes confusion in the negotiations and there tends to be a lack of clarity on the final agreement. It also results in the acquisition of a company that is not necessarily culturally attuned to your expectations and can become difficult to integrate into your global group. This structure can also be attempted by way of a joint venture, but again this can be too blunt an instrument to address the differing levels of control and interest involved.

Under a subordinated equity franchising arrangement, all of the financial, brand and quality assurance obligations are contained in the franchise agreement. The Subordinated Equity Agreement is a standalone agreement which deals only with how the equity in the franchisee should be apportioned and valued and does not focus on detailed issues around corporate governance. This approach delivers much greater clarity, better protects your brand and related income streams and avoids you becoming embroiled in the day-to-day management of the franchisee company while also preserving the option to acquire the entire business in the future.

The intention of the subordinated equity approach is to let a third party set up the franchisee business and prepare it for you to take over ownership and operations in the future. This takeover can be in one or more markets after an agreed period of time. It is therefore of the utmost importance that the franchisee business is set up and organised so that the strategy and culture will be implemented in line with your business from day one. This will facilitate a smooth ownership transfer in due course.

This approach is often used together with a multi-unit developer structure where your brand (i.e., the franchisor) wants to own a shareholding in the developer. It may be adopted for many reasons including where there is a need to obtain third party investment.

In order to make both the joint venture and subordinated equity models work, your brand and the local business need to co-create a new company, known as a special purpose vehicle or 'SPV.' The SPV is granted the right to exploit a particular territory by opening and running franchises.

The key difference between a joint venture and the subordinated equity structure is your level of control and day-to-day involvement in the management of the business. You will generally be fairly involved in a joint venture. By contrast, subordinated equity structures are designed for minimal franchisor involvement (apart from key brand protection and quality control issues). Regardless of the model selected, it is important to retain some oversight over a subordinated equity structure as you will want to retain the option to buy back the entire issued share capital of the SPV at a later point in time.

The subordinated equity structure at Figure 18.5 involves a two-layered relationship:

1.   The first layer of the relationship is a licensed one under which the SPV is granted the right to open and operate stores in the target territory (this is the traditional franchise model).

2.   The second layer of the relationship is based on the equity ownership of the SPV. The 'development partner' finances and operates the SPV; however, both you (i.e., the 'franchisor') and the development partner take a shareholding in the SPV.

The equity layer of the arrangement is subordinated to the licensing layer, hence its name.

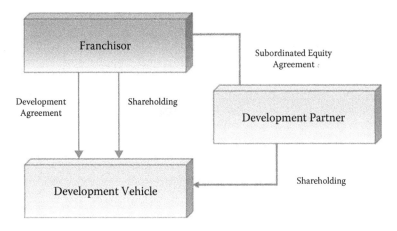

Figure 18.5   A subordinated equity structure

Subordinated equity arrangements differ from traditional joint venture arrangements in that they do not involve your brand (the franchisor) either investing capital in the franchisee's SPV or taking a role in its day-to-day operations. A further point of difference is that there is an agreed objective for the enterprise which will cease to exist once the objective has been achieved.

This set-up is arranged so that the development partner can make an investment of its operational experience, capital and other resources in a high value brand in return for an appropriate return on investment (the 'ROI'). As no level of return can be guaranteed, the ROI must be verified by the development partner based on its experience of operating businesses in the markets in question.

In return for the development partner making the required investment into your brand, you[1] allow the development partner to participate in the generation of a strong income stream with a predetermined fixed-term exit strategy on an agreed valuation coupled with a release of its written down capital investment.

This is generally a win-win situation. The development partner sets up a number of stores in the chosen territory through the dedicated company or SPV then at a point in the future, which has been agreed in advance, you can buy the development partner's share in the SPV for an agreed price.

18.3   How to choose the right structure

As indicated above, certain types of business are suited to particular structures but there are a few other points to consider which can guide the decision making process.

18.3.1   What resources do you have?

If your business has a large reserve of manpower that is experienced in franchising matters and plenty of cash to throw at the project, direct franchising might be safer and more cost effective in the long run in certain jurisdictions. If you have much more limited resources, then a master franchise or multi-unit developer approach may suit you best.

---

1 The franchisor.

18.3.2   What is the target market?

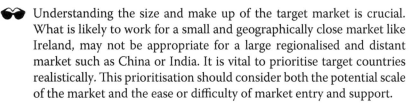 Understanding the size and make up of the target market is crucial. What is likely to work for a small and geographically close market like Ireland, may not be appropriate for a large regionalised and distant market such as China or India. It is vital to prioritise target countries realistically. This prioritisation should consider both the potential scale of the market and the ease or difficulty of market entry and support.

18.3.3   Who is your ideal partner?

If you are aiming for a large blue chip partner, it is likely that the multi-unit developer or subordinated equity or JV route will be most appropriate. However, if the partner is a smaller, more entrepreneurial organisation, a master franchise approach may be more appropriate.

It is vital to establish a partner recruitment process which selects the right candidate for the business. The first few international franchisees will be ambassadors for those who follow – for better or for worse!

18.3.4   Is there enough margin for you and the franchise partner?

It is important to understand how your business can make money out of international franchising. Is it related to the supply of goods? Is it linked to the ongoing supply of support or central services? Is it merely attached to the use of the brand and know-how? Different answers will lead to different conclusions as to the most appropriate structure.

18.4   The legal challenges of going global

Regardless of the structure you adopt, your international strategy should be designed to identify the regulatory and legal hurdles at an early stage.

18.4.1   Brand protection

You should invest prudently to ensure that each target market will be underpinned by, at a minimum, appropriate registered trade marks, patents or design rights (if appropriate), social media accounts and domain name registrations. This can be a costly exercise, but the cost of dealing with counterfeiters, copycats and cyber squatters or claims from local third parties with prior rights far outweighs the upfront protection costs.

Bear in mind that trade marks should be registered both as used and in likely counterfeit equivalents. For example, Chinese trade marks should be registered for all relevant classes of goods and services in the original script and ideally also in Chinese characters known as hanzi (or kanji in Japan) and in transliterated form. See Chapter 3 for more detail on an international trade mark strategy.

18.4.2   Pre-contractual protection

Before you sign the franchise agreement, you and the other party will inevitably exchange sensitive information. You should only disclose this information under the protection of a robust confidentiality agreement. However, the best way to protect confidential information is to keep disclosure to a minimum until you have both signed on the dotted line.

Your franchise's manual is the 'crown jewel' of any franchised brand, and this document should not be disclosed until the franchise agreement has been signed.

In addition, it is your brand as the franchisor, who will incur legal costs leading up to the signing of the franchise agreement. Therefore, at the stage of either signing the confidentiality agreement or agreeing heads of terms, you should request a deposit, which will be deducted from any upfront fee under the agreement. If it is not possible to reach an agreement, you can deduct your costs from the deposit and return the balance to the franchisee.

18.4.3   International regulation

Franchising is regulated in a significant number of countries that have franchise specific laws. Some countries impose a complex and challenging regulatory environment through more general commercial laws; these laws regulate the franchise sales process, the content of the franchise agreement and some require that the documentation be filed on a public register. These compliance issues can impact on commercial timelines for doing deals and opening sites. Therefore any local regulatory issues should be identified at the planning stage.

18.4.4 Regulation of the sales process

Countries such as the US, Canada, Australia and China require set-form pre-contractual disclosure during the franchise negotiation. Key issues include how and when the disclosure must be made, mandatory cooling off periods before the deal can be finalised and the scope of the content of the sales and disclosure documentation.

The consequences of a failure to comply with disclosure requirements vary. Non-compliance generally entitles the franchisee to walk away from the agreement without restrictions provided it acts within a reasonable period of entering into the agreement. The franchisee can also sue you for damages and some jurisdictions may impose fines.

18.4.5 Regulation of contractual terms

Some countries impose mandatory contractual terms in the franchise agreement. These often include clauses such as a minimum term, a duty of good faith, restrictions on termination and the extent to which competition between former franchise partners can be limited post termination. These mandatory provisions may impact on your proposed business model and change the terms of the commercial deal on offer.

18.4.6 Registration requirements

Some jurisdictions require you, as the franchisor, to register only relevant details while others require registration of all the franchise documentation. In some countries, there are multiple registration requirements. For example, franchisors in China who sell franchises in just one province, must file the information at the local office of the MOFCOM (Ministry of Commerce) of that province, whereas for cross-province franchising the papers have to be filed with the central office of MOFCOM.

18.4.7 The impact of general commercial laws on franchising

Franchising is also regulated by a variety of general laws such as the duty of good faith, competition (also known as anti-trust) law, unfair competition law, agency law and consumer law, all of which vary slightly between jurisdictions and must be taken into account.

18.5   Current trends and issues in European franchising

18.5.1   EU competition law

The European Commission, through its development of EU competition law, is committed to creating a borderless economy within the EU. Commercial agreements or businesses practices which seek to control distribution in the EU are currently in the crosshairs of the regulators both at a national and EU level. Resale price maintenance, restrictions on advertising prices online, price parity clauses and outright online sales bans have received particular focus.

Internet policies must be carefully reviewed to ensure that they not only secure the desired commercial aims but also comply with the law such as the information and geo-blocking requirements set out in Chapter 17. Failure to comply with the law may expose businesses to fines (which could be as much as 10 per cent of annual worldwide group turnover), unenforceable agreements and potentially even criminal sanctions.

18.5.2   European Parliament Resolution on franchising in the retail sector

The European Parliament's Resolution on franchising in the retail sector cites statistics from a recent study on the regulatory framework for franchising in the EU. This study argues that franchising is underperforming in the EU compared with other countries. This underperformance is attributed to inconsistent legislation between Member States and an absence of any EU-level mechanism to collect information on potentially unfair contract terms in franchise arrangements. These gaps were identified as creating technical barriers that may discourage both franchisors and franchisees from expanding across borders.

The European Parliament's Resolution calls on the European Commission and Member States to introduce measures to deal with these issues, including non-binding best practice guidelines on franchising contracts, and more systematic data collection about franchising in the EU, particularly in relation to unfair trading practices. The Resolution notes that given the growing importance of online sales for franchises, specific model terms should be included in franchising contracts.

The Resolution asked the European Commission to open a public consultation in order to obtain unbiased information as to the real situation in franchising, and to produce non-legislative guidelines. It also invited the Commission to complete an analysis of existing self-regulatory and legislative practices of Member States, including recommendations on how to further develop the franchising sector in the EU.

 Finally, the Commission was asked to review the application of the Vertical Agreements Block Exemption Regulation[2] to franchising agreements across Member States and consider whether it should be revised. This is important because the block exemption currently allows franchisors and franchisees to contract without worrying about whether the agreement has as its 'object or effect the prevention, restriction or distortion of competition within the internal market.' (The internal market is another way of referring to the single market which consists of the EU plus Switzerland and the additional EEA countries of Norway, Iceland and Liechtenstein.)

The relevant legislation[3] includes various examples of this sort of distortion such as fixing purchase or selling prices or any other trading conditions and limiting or controlling production, markets, technical development or investment. These are all common terms in a franchise agreement.

18.5.3   European Consultation on barriers to establishing and operating retail outlets within the EU

 The European Commission regards a competitive retail sector as being essential to the EU economy. In 2017, following increasing concerns about the persistent lack of growth in the European retail sector (especially when compared with the less-regulated US market) and the possible negative impact of national restrictions on the sector as a result of the growing importance of e-commerce, the European Commission adopted a *Roadmap on Best Practices on Retail Regulation*. The roadmap proposed that Member States adopt a set of voluntary best practices to guide them when assessing and modernising national rules in order to make it easier for retailers to become established and reduce the operational restrictions they face when expanding into new ter-

---

2 330/2010/EU.

3 Article 101 of the Treaty on the Functioning of the European Union.

ritories or increasing operations in those territories where they already had a presence.

The roadmap identified the information that the Commission would need to formulate this guidance and launched a public consultation in order to start the information-gathering process. This latest consultation is intended to complete the fact-finding phase of the Commission's initiative and focuses on the implications of the growing importance of e-commerce and changing consumer habits for the retail sector and its regulatory framework and on the opportunities and obstacles for the integration of the EU retail market. The consultation sought input on a number of specific issues such as the most significant barriers to entry into the retail sector and the impact on regulations such as opening hours and sales promotions as well as any issues in the enforcement of existing regulations.

18.6   How should you approach franchising?

There is no 'one size fits all' solution to international expansion. Such ventures need to be carefully structured to reflect the needs of the business, the target market and the franchise partner. The most appropriate structure needs to be determined at the outset, as restructuring an international franchise is a complex, costly and time-consuming exercise. Consequently, it is crucial that the business has 'bought into' franchising at the board level.

Whether you are new to franchising or manage a wide range of international franchises, choosing to work with experienced legal counsel who have walked down this path before and can manage the international compliance on your behalf can be the difference between success and failure.

Once the strategy and structure are in place, rolling out the franchise strategy internationally can be a relatively low-risk/high-reward venture and one which over time will generate significant income and ultimately a paradigm shift in the way the business operates. With the power of the franchise in your hands, you can evolve from a domestically focused business with an international presence into a truly global brand.

19 Resolving disputes

With business success comes an increased likelihood of lawsuits. These may be due to contractual issues such as non-payment for goods or non-contractual issues such as product liability or intellectual property infringement claims.

In order to resolve a dispute you generally have two main options, either:

1. fight the dispute via the courts or a similar dispute resolution mechanism such as arbitration; or

2. reach a negotiated settlement.

This chapter sets out the general legal principles to be aware of in terms of dispute resolution, and Chapters 20 and 21 consider specific issues in the context of intellectual property rights. The first part of this chapter looks at the practical issues you need to consider at the outset. The remainder of the chapter gives an overview of the main legal options which are available via the different European court systems and the road to trial or dispute resolution. Many of the legal remedies were harmonised by the Enforcement Directive but there are significant differences in the implementation of this Directive.

19.1 Practical issues

 Before getting into the procedural detail, it is worth thinking about the practical steps you can take. First and foremost, understanding the strength of your legal position depends on the facts and consequently tracking down the relevant documents, emails, texts, photographs, etc. is essential. The start of a dispute is the time to start gathering all of the relevant information together. A lawyer can help you to identify what information they require to help you but the sooner you can get hold of it, the better. Once your lawyer has a handle on the facts, they can advise you on the best strategy for handling the dispute. This could include writing a letter before action, filing a claim or a counterclaim or making a settlement proposal.

The best approach depends on your commercial position as much as the facts so it is also worth thinking carefully about your ultimate objective and how much money you are willing to spend in order to get there. A related question is whether you can salvage any pre-existing business relationship (or have a desire to do so)!

19.1.1   Are you in time?

Many countries set a limit on the period in which it is possible to bring a claim – this is known as a limitation period. This time limit is designed to provide business certainty and ensure that records do not have to be maintained indefinitely.

Bear in mind that if an issue, such as intellectual property infringement, is ongoing, the limitation period does not kick in until the infringement stops (although in this instance, the period in which damages is available is capped at the limitation period). So, for example, if the limitation period is six years[1] then provided the intellectual property infringement is continuing, even if it has lasted more than six years, the limitation period has not yet kicked in and it should still be possible to bring a claim.

In some countries, if you take a very long time to take action it is possible that the court will not permit you to bring a claim for a different reason. For example, in England there are equitable doctrines such as 'acquiescence' which could apply if you take too long to take action.

19.1.2   Attorney client privilege

People and businesses need to be able to speak freely with their law- yers in order to understand the legal claim against them. This includes obtaining legal advice at meetings, by phone or email and providing the lawyers with internal documents to help them understand the legal issues in dispute. As a result, actual and potential litigants are entitled to a particular form of protection known as attorney client privilege. While attorney client privilege is not a form of confidentiality, it is a

---

1 This is the limitation period in England and Wales.

good legal analogy as the outcomes are similar. Essentially, any documents which are subject to attorney client privilege cannot be disclosed to the court or to the other parties in the dispute except in very limited circumstances.

Attorney client privilege is particularly important in Common Law jurisdictions like England and Ireland where there is a possibility for wide-ranging disclosure and witness evidence. By contrast, Civil Law jurisdictions tend to focus on paper documents which the parties choose to provide to support their case.

In order for attorney client privilege to apply, you usually need to have a lawyer involved in the relevant meetings and emails. The lawyer has to at least be asked to give some form of advice so just copying a lawyer in on your internal emails is unlikely to be sufficient.

Legal privilege is subject to different national regimes in each Member State. For example, countries such as England, Belgium,[2] the Netherlands, Portugal and Poland allow legal privilege to apply to lawyer who works directly for your business (commonly referred to as an 'in-house lawyer'). Other countries such as France and Germany do not extend privilege to cover in-house lawyers.

In competition law proceedings, the CJEU has decided that communications with in-house lawyers working for a company are not covered by legal privilege. The CJEU reached this decision on the basis that in-house lawyers are employees and consequently they 'do not enjoy the same degree of independence' as a law firm.[3] This means that exchanges between in-house lawyers and their 'internal client' can be scrutinised by the European Commission regardless of the location where the document was prepared or email was sent and even if the in-house lawyer was registered with a national Bar Association which affords legal privilege to exchanges with all lawyers including those working in-house.[4]

 As there is no overarching rule relating to attorney client privilege in Europe, it is safest to assume that this form of legal privilege does not apply when working with an in-house lawyer.

---

2 Provided that they are registered with the Institute of Belgian Company Lawyers (the IBJ). The Belgian law of 1 March 2000, modified by the law of 19 May 2010, created the IBJ.

3 *Akzo Nobel Chemicals Ltd v Commission of the European Communities* Case C-550/07.

4 In this case, the Netherlands.

19.1.3   Insurance and litigation funding

Insurance is not necessarily the first thing people consider upon receipt of a legal letter but thinking about insurance can be a good habit to get into! Legal insurance is fairly common now so the moment you get a hint of a possible dispute it is worth checking your insurance policy to see if you are covered.

Even if you are not protected it can still be possible to obtain specialist insurance once you are aware of the issue. This insurance is known as After the Event or ATE insurance. ATE insurance is much easier to obtain if you are the claimant (or counter-claimant) and have a large potential money claim and good prospects of success. This is because the underwriter is assessing both your likelihood of success-fully defending the claim and offsetting it against any potential costs payments which may have to be made along the way.

ATE insurance is still relatively new and with a lack of competition, the premiums can be fairly large. It is generally only worth getting ATE insurance if the amount in dispute is above a fairly high threshold or the dispute itself is high risk for your business. However, in those circumstances it is likely to be hard to get the insurance.

Insurers often insist that the legal team you appoint to conduct the action operates under some form of delayed payment basis. In England, this is either a conditional fee agreement or a damages based agreement.

A conditional fee agreement or 'CFA' is where a percentage of the law firm's fees is delayed until after either a negotiated compromise is reached or you have won the dispute. A CFA will only cover the law firm's fees and not expenses such as the barrister and court fees. In return for taking a risk on their fees, law firms require an uplift which is capped at a maximum of the percentage they have risked. For example, if the law firm is operating under a CFA where they get 70 per cent of their fees paid now but 30 per cent of their fees are delayed, if success-ful, the maximum they would be entitled to is 130 per cent of their fees.

In theory it is possible to get a 100 per cent CFA. This means that all of the lawyer's fees are deferred but most commercial law firms are unwilling to accept that level of risk. Many law firms are wary of oper-ating under this model at all and, like an insurer, will carefully assess the risks of the case before determining how to proceed.

In the UK and Ireland, in addition to solicitors who run the case day to day, a court case usually also involves barristers who are specialists in advocacy. Barristers have also been known to work under a CFA but this tends to be the exception rather than the rule.

A damages based agreement or 'DBA' means that the law firm takes the whole or part of its fee as a percentage of the damages. The percentages that a law firm is entitled to from the damages award are capped depending on the type of loss and the nature of the dispute. DBAs are still comparatively rare in England as they are a relatively new innovation and carry a high level of risk.

Finally, it is now possible to get litigation funding for many disputes. As for ATE insurance, the potential financial up side and prospects of success have to be above a certain threshold in order for third party funding to be available. There are still comparatively few funders to choose from and the amount that the funder deducts may mean that it is not economically viable for you. When making your decision, it is sensible to look at the funder's track record and to check their status from a financial regulatory standpoint.

Elsewhere in Europe, ATE insurance and third party funding are seen as a very 'Anglo-Saxon' concept. Indeed, compared to the US and the UK, litigation before European courts *can* be relatively inexpensive because the trial length is *usually* shorter and disclosure and evidence are much more limited in scope. Further, adverse costs awards are relatively low in comparison with other countries. Consequently, countries such as France have been reluctant to officially recognise or provide access to litigation funding and companies tend to account for litigation risk and cost as part of their annual provisioning.

That said, there are some tentative steps toward introducing litigation funding for international arbitration which is often a more costly form of dispute resolution than the courts. The Paris Bar Association has formally authorised the use of third party funding and ATE insurance by litigants using private dispute mechanisms such as arbitration.[5]

---

5 See Resolution of the Paris Bar Association adopted on 21st February 2017 available in French at: http://www.avocatparis.org/system/files/publications/resolution_financement_de_larbitrage_par_les_tiers.pdf.

19.1.4   Litigants in person

The high-profile disputes which reach the newspapers tend to be between big brands. Even in a stereotypical David versus Goliath type dispute, David usually has a lawyer. Unrepresented litigants or 'litigants in person' are a common issue for most businesses at some point in their lifetime. They can be individuals or unrepresented companies. In theory litigants in person are treated in the same way as parties with legal representation but in practice they involve significantly more work.

In many instances, cases brought by unrepresented litigants are without merit or at least fail to properly articulate the legal basis for the claim. This can lead to a lot of wasted time and costs trying to understand the true source of the complaint. They often allege vastly inflated sums by way of damage and allege fraud or other serious criminal conduct which does not tend to be relevant. However, litigants in person are often given more leeway regarding legal procedure and the amount of costs involved can spiral quite quickly.

If you are sued by a litigant in person, a common tactic in some juris- dictions, such as England, is to require them to provide security for costs (provided they are a business rather than an individual).[6] This is essentially a bond which is paid into court to protect against the litigant in person becoming liable for your costs but unable to pay them.

In most jurisdictions, larger disputes can only be heard by courts where use of a lawyer is mandatory (e.g., the District or Paris High Courts). In France, parties are only able to represent themselves before Commercial Courts,[7] or before the district First Instance Courts (*Tribunaux d'instance*). For matters before the French District High Courts (*Tribunaux de Grande Instance*), where the value of disputes exceeds €10,000, party representation by a lawyer is mandatory. This is the same for appeal courts or the French Supreme Court.

---

6 It is much harder to obtain security for costs against an individual or a company which is based outside the jurisdiction.

7 I.e., as a representative of the company involved in the dispute, for example, a director or president or pursuant to a power of attorney.

19.2   When delay is not an option – emergency relief

In most instances, you have to wait to have your day in court but some-times, the damage caused to your business is so great that you may be entitled to 'emergency' remedies from the court. This sort of relief can also be referred to as 'interim,' 'interlocutory,' or 'preliminary' relief. The best known form of emergency relief is an interim injunction. This is usually only available where the damage that is being caused is not capable of financial remedy.

 It may be possible to get emergency relief if, for example:

A.   Your goods are being held in a warehouse under a spurious inter-pretation of a retention of title clause. If you cannot get hold of the stock, your business will go insolvent.

B.   Your former employee has just launched a rival business which uses a similar name, near identical designs and your database of contacts. You need to take action immediately before your brand is irreparably damaged.

The ease with which you can get emergency relief varies substantially between Member States. For example, it is much easier to get an interim injunction in Germany than the UK.

 Emergency relief is usually only available if you take action quickly after being put on notice of the issue. As a rough rule of thumb, if you take longer than a month from finding out about an issue to applying to the court for emergency relief, you have probably waited too long. However, this approach varies both between jurisdictions and even courts within that jurisdiction.

19.2.1   Interim injunctions

Where there is an intellectual property infringement, the reputational damage to your brand may not be capable of being quantified or com-pensated by money paid in the future. In these circumstances, you are likely to want an interim injunction. This is an injunction which pre-vents further infringement pending trial. A lot depends on the jurisdic-tion and the particular circumstances but it can be difficult to persuade a court to grant an interim injunction as it usually causes significant damage to the other business.

In Common Law jurisdictions, the key limbs which need to be established in order to get an interim injunction are:

1. there is a serious issue to be tried;

2. you would suffer irreparable harm if the infringing activity does not stop pending trial (i.e., money alone could not compensate you); and

3. on the balance of convenience, it is fairer to grant the injunction than allow the infringing activity to continue.

Common Law courts tend to be keen to maintain the status quo as much as possible so if the infringing activity has only just begun (or has only just been threatened) you are much more likely to succeed in getting your interim injunction. An injunction is normally only granted if the other party has the opportunity to turn up to court and present the counter arguments. However, in some instances there is a risk that putting the other party on notice will lead to them taking action such as destroying evidence. In these circumstances, the court may grant an injunction on the basis of evidence and arguments from only one party. This is known as an *ex parte* basis.

By contrast, it appears to be surprisingly common for businesses to get an interim injunction on an *ex parte* basis in many Civil Law jurisdictions, such as Germany and Poland. This does not mean that they can be easily obtained as you have to justify your claims and show that they are highly probable. If the injunction is granted, the decision is usually served and enforced by a bailiff in accordance with the court's order. After an interim injunction is awarded, you have 14 days to either reach a settlement or file a claim otherwise the injunction order expires. When used wisely, this can be a very useful tool for rights holders.

In both Civil and Common Law systems, there is recognition that an interim injunction could cause significant harm to the recipient as they are required to stop selling an important product, close their store, or similar. It is common for the court to order that the injunction can only be awarded on the basis that a security deposit or 'bond' is lodged at the court or a cross-undertaking is given to pay the damages occasioned by the injunction if the court ultimately finds that there has been no infringement.

If you have delayed taking action, you may still be entitled to an injunction if there has been a major change in the other party's behaviour. For example, they were originally using your name on bags but are now using it for T-shirts and caps which is much closer to your trade mark registration.

As with so much in law, your success in obtaining an interim injunction depends on the arguments and individual circumstances together with an element of luck. The important message is that if an issue causes you significant concern, do not delay getting legal advice.

19.2.2   Pre-action disclosure

In intellectual property claims, identifying who is responsible for infringing activity is a common problem online where infringers are able to hide behind false identities. In this scenario, the information regarding the person's identity is in the hands of a third party, usually an Internet Service Provider (ISP) but potentially a courier or other third party such as Google.

It has long been a feature of the Common Law that it is possible to get some types of disclosure from third parties before commencing proceedings. This can be very helpful in identifying the correct infringer and related information such as the extent of the infringing activity. In England and Ireland, this court order is often known as a *Norwich Pharmacal* order. Essentially, it compels the recipient to provide information such as a customer's name, address and other contact details. This court order overrides any data protection obligations.

Thanks to the Enforcement Directive, all Member States, must now provide a means for potential litigants to get information on their potential opponent before they issue a claim.[8] Each Member State must have a process by which a court can (in response to a justified and proportionate request) order that information on the factory of origin and distribution networks of infringing goods or services be provided by the infringer and/or any other connected person such as someone found in possession of infringing goods on a commercial scale or involved in the production, manufacture or distribution of the goods.

---

8 This is possible under Art. 8(1) of the Intellectual Property Enforcement Directive 2004/48/EC.

This information can include the names and addresses of the producers, manufacturers, distributors, suppliers and other previous holders of the goods or services, as well as the intended wholesalers and retailers and information on the quantities produced, manufactured, delivered, received or ordered, as well as the price obtained for the goods or services in question.

This right was explained by the CJEU following a referral from the Czech Supreme Court.[9] The CJEU confirmed that this right to information was not limited to intellectual property infringement proceedings and consequently it was possible to apply to the court to have this information provided after a trial on liability had taken place so that a more accurate assessment of damages could be reached.

Some Member States, such as Poland, may grant an order which compels an individual or business to provide the court with a document that is in its possession and is deemed essential to the potential case.[10] This is particularly useful when an invoice has to be shown for the purpose of calculating damages or an account of profits (also known as 'undue benefits').

19.2.3   Subject access requests

A less obvious form of pre-action disclosure is the 'subject access request.' This is the right to be provided with all personal data which an organisation holds on an individual. Under the GDPR,[11] this right is available to all EU citizens (regardless of where their data is held in the world). If a subject access request is made, the recipient of the request has a maximum of one month in which to respond, free of charge. This is a common tactic in employment and consumer claims but can have wider application.

19.3   Evidence preservation – search and seizure orders

A search and seizure order is at the more draconian end of the legal remedies scale. It essentially gives the successful applicant the right to enter a named property, search it and seize any infringing goods or

---

9 *NEW WAVE CZ, a.s. v ALLTOYS, spol. s r. o.,* Case C-427/15, ECLI:EU:C:2017:18.

10 Article 248 of the Polish Civil Code dated 17 November 1964.

11 See Chapter 14 for more details.

materials relating to the infringement. Because this is quite a major invasion of privacy, in order to obtain a search order you need to demonstrate that there is a genuine legal claim and a risk that the materials relating to the cause of action will be destroyed if you put the other party on notice of the infringement. The threshold for both the genuine claim and risk of destruction varies between European jurisdictions.

The key to a successful search order application is to do your homework. In advance of making the application, you need to identify the best locations for carrying out a search and seizure, such as factories, storage units, warehouses, or offices. Where more than one location is targeted, it is common to have simultaneous execution of the search order so that you keep the element of surprise and avoid any destruction of evidence.

19.3.1   *Anton Pillar* orders – England and Ireland

In England and Ireland, search and seizure orders are commonly known as *Anton Pillar* orders after the case which originally established the right to a search order. The procedure is now set out in the English Civil Procedure Rules and the Irish equivalent.

Once you have a search order it needs to be executed within a fixed amount of time by a court appointed 'supervising solicitor' who is identified and paid for by the applicant. The search party quickly grows in size from there as it typically includes at least two lawyers from your legal team, investigators and computer forensics experts. Investigators can watch additional entrances and exits and will often have been involved in identifying the infringing activity in the first place so have particular knowledge of the infringers' patterns and activities. The forensics experts are on hand to image (i.e., copy) any electronic storage devices which may be seized on the premises. As you can imagine, with so many professionals involved, usually on hourly rates it can all get expensive quite quickly.

After you have executed the search order you then have a set amount of time to review the documents and other materials obtained from the search. By far and away the easiest means of doing this is via an e-discovery platform for the digital materials. In practice it is now rare for there to be substantial physical records so any hard copy records can usually be reviewed in conjunction with the supervising solicitor on the day of the search.

For both types of document, the supervising solicitor first reviews the document to ensure that it is not legally privileged (i.e., contains legal advice). Any privileged documents are set to one side and cannot be considered further. The remaining documents are reviewed for relevance. Any relevant documents such as supplier lists, or electronic communications regarding the infringing activity are then made available to the applicant so that they can be used in the case against the infringer.

After a fixed amount of time – around ten days depending on the court's calendar – everyone returns to court for the 'return date.' By this time, the defendant will usually have legal representation and the extent to which the materials seized during the search can be used will be determined by the court. If any further search of the remaining electronic documents is necessary, this will have to be agreed by the court.

19.3.2   Saisie contrefaçon – France and Belgium

A similar right to *Anton Pillar* orders exists in France[12] and Belgium although the procedure to be followed there is fairly different. *Saisie contrefaçons* (or *saisie* for short) are a very effective means of obtaining further information in relation to known infringements of intellectual property rights but they should not be used as a 'fishing expedition' i.e., where you only have a suspicion of potential infringement. The scope of *saisies* and the locations which can be searched tends to be broader but less thorough than *Anton Pillar* orders. This is because the search is conducted by an independent bailiff rather than your legal team under the supervision of the supervising solicitor.

In France, only the Paris High Court has jurisdiction to hear *saisie* applications including those regarding patents,[13] EU trade marks and Community designs.[14] Some French regional specialised High Courts can grant infringement seizures based on artistic and literary copyright, and French designs, trade marks and geographical indications.[15]

---

12 This right is codified. In France, the part of the Code depends on the infringed right (for Patents – see Art. L. 615-5, for Trade Marks – see Art. L. 716-7, for Design Rights – see Art. L. 521-4, for Copyright – see Arts L. 332-1–3 and for Software, see Art. L. 332-4).

13 Article R. 615-2 of the French Intellectual Property Code (See Decree – 2008-624).

14 Article R. 522-1 of the French Intellectual Property Code and Art. R. 211-7 of the Judicial Organisation Code.

15 Article D. 211-6-1 of the Judicial Organisation Code.

They are based in Bordeaux, Lille, Lyon, Marseille, Nanterre, Nancy, Rennes, Strasbourg and Fort-de-France.

 It is more common and easier to get *saisies* in France and Belgium than *Anton Pillar* orders in England and Ireland. However, they are more vulnerable to subsequent challenge as a result. In order to avoid a legal challenge, it is important that the application contains sufficient detail to both convince the judge to grant the order in the first place and avoid future legal liability from the *saisie*'s target. The *saisie* application must include evidence that you are the owner of the relevant intellectual property rights, potentially including evidence that any royalties or fees are paid and are up to date, and details of any assignments or pledges against the right.

As for the *Anton Pillar* order, the execution of the *saisie* commonly includes a fairly large group of people including the bailiff who will carry out the order, independent lawyers, computer experts, as well as specialist patent or trade mark attorneys, depending on the right. For reasons of independence, it is not recommended that your lawyers, employees or other representatives attend the *saisie*.

During the *saisie*, the bailiff needs to ensure that they follow the correct procedure including serving a copy of the application and the order on the alleged infringer, identifying themselves and any other members of the search team and distinguishing between any bailiff comments and any *constats* (factual statements). Only items listed in the order can be seized. Where documents are purportedly confidential, the alleged infringer can request that these be placed in a sealed envelope, and then it will be for a judge to rule on the contents at a later stage. The summary of the infringement seizure should be signed by all parties in attendance, including the alleged infringer, and a copy should be provided to the alleged infringer.

Following a *saisie*, the applicant must commence infringement proceedings within 31 calendar days. Failure to do so means that the seizure could be invalidated by the court. If the alleged infringer contests the seizure, they can commence emergency withdrawal proceedings so that the infringement seizure is cancelled, as if it had never occurred (known as a *référé en rétractation*). Alternatively, they can ask for the infringement seizure to be annulled once infringement proceedings are commenced (known as a *demande en nullité*) or seek civil remedies on the basis that the seizure was carried out in bad faith or in an abusive or injurious way.

19.3.3   Sworn Bailiff Statements

An alternative to the *saisie* in France is the sworn Bailiff Statement (or *Constats d'Huissier*). This is a sworn document carried out by a bailiff in accordance with specified rules (as to performance and presentation of content). It allows a party to provide evidence of a situation or infringement at a particular date.

Essentially, the bailiff provides a sworn statement as to a fact or a situation (e.g., 'On this date, I saw those items being sold in that store. I purchased two of them, and here is the receipt'). They can also be used to confirm the validity of a document such as certified copies of website printouts. Care has to be taken to ensure that the French civil procedure rules are closely followed to ensure that the validity of the bailiff's acts are not called into question by your opponent. This issue recently arose in a dispute before the Paris High Court[16] on the validity of Bailiff Statements in a trade mark infringement case between JM Weston and Coach.

JM Weston alleged that Coach had been marketing a belt under JM Weston's name on its French website, and in its concession at the large department store *Printemps Hausmann* in Paris. JM Weston sought to bring an action against the French division of Coach, as the offending acts occurred in France, and in respect of the online sales, the belt was available online via a website directed at the French public (France. coach.com).

In order to provide evidence of the alleged unlawful sale and marketing of its product, JM Weston carried out a Bailiff Statement both at the *Printemps Hausmann* concession and online. Coach sought to refute the validity of the Bailiff Statement as it had been carried out in the presence of a trainee lawyer when the usual procedure is that the lawyer is fully qualified.

The Paris High Court found the Bailiff Statement to be valid but did not find that there had been any infringement of intellectual property rights by virtue of the sale of the belt in *Printemps Hausmann*.

---

16 See TGI Paris, Judgment rendered on 1st December 2017.

Nonetheless, they held that Coach had infringed JM Weston's registered trade mark on its French website.

Although JM Weston was the right side of the line on this occasion, it is important to seek specialist advice and respect local procedural rules when relying on Bailiff Statements.

19.3.4   *Descrizione* in Italy

In Italy there is a similar procedure called '*procedimento di descrizione.*' In Italy, it is difficult to start proceedings on an *ex parte* basis unless there is a risk that the other party will destroy or hide evidence if they are put on notice. Therefore, it is unusual to start a dispute against an infringer by filing a request for *descrizione.*[17] Normally, you start with a cease and desist letter. If it is not possible to resolve the issue in writing or you do not get a response from the alleged infringer, then you can seek an order of *descrizione.*

A rights holder can obtain the *descrizione* by itself or together with the seizure of the infringing goods.[18] If there is a seizure, this can only take place after the *descrizione* has been executed. The seizure can concern not only the infringing goods but also the means of production used by the infringer as well as any other evidence supporting the unlawful conduct. *Descrizione* it is not limited to counterfeiting, although this is the most common scenario.

In order to obtain *descrizione* on an *ex parte* basis, you must prove to the court that delays in obtaining such measures could cause you irreparable harm or that there is a high risk of evidence being destroyed.

Like *saisies*, enforcement of the *descrizione* is left to the bailiff. Experts, together with parties' attorneys, can participate in the proceedings and technical instruments can be used as well.

Finally, in order to have the *descrizione* order confirmed, modified or revoked by the court, the judge will have a second hearing to discuss the results of the search and any necessary amendments to the order. This is broadly the same procedure as in England.

---

17 I.e. one of the specialist intellectual property courts which have exclusive jurisdiction on this matter.
18 Articles 129 and 130 of the Italian Intellectual Property Code.

19.4 The Enforcement Directive

The *Anton Pillar, descrizione* and *saisie* systems were used as the basis for Article 7 of the Enforcement Directive which concerns measures for preserving evidence. Among other things, Member States are required to provide rights holders who come armed with compelling evidence of infringement with 'prompt and effective provisional measures to preserve relevant evidence in respect of the alleged infringement, subject to the protection of confidential information.'

The Directive suggests that the measures imposed by Member States could include taking a detailed description of the infringement, samples, physical seizure of the infringing goods as well as the materials and documents associated with the infringing activity. The Directive expressly allows for these hearings to be heard on an *ex parte* basis if appropriate and in particular where any delay is likely to cause irreparable harm to the rights holder or where there is a demonstrable risk of evidence being destroyed.

19.5 Freezing orders

A freezing order is available if you can persuade the court that there is a high risk of the infringer disposing of assets or leaving the jurisdiction. A freezing order blocks a party's ability to access or use their assets (including but not limited to money). This is a very draconian order so your evidence must be more than a mere suspicion. For example, evidence of past behaviour can be very useful evidence. This may require quite a lot of time and money in investigation to establish.

19.6 Blocking orders

Across the EU, intermediaries such as ISPs are able to avoid liability for hosting, caching or transmitting infringing content provided they are not aware of the issue.[19] In practice, this means that once an intermediary is put on notice of an infringement, it has a limited amount of time in which to remove the content, i.e., take it down. It is as a direct result of this and similar laws around the world that the 'takedown' process came into being. This is a semi-automated process for removing

---

19 This right comes from Directive 2000/31/EC (the E-commerce Directive).

infringing content and is common on most major technology websites including e-commerce platforms. The aim of the E-commerce Directive was to provide a consistent approach to the treatment of intermediaries across the EU. Because it is a Directive, each Member State has some flexibility over the way in which they implement the Directive into their national law.

In the UK, it is possible to get a court order which requires the major Internet service providers of the jurisdiction to prevent their subscribers from, for example, accessing sites which allow illegal downloads of copyright works or sell counterfeit goods. The French Supreme Court[20] and Swedish Supreme Court[21] also reached a similar conclusion.

Blocking orders were first made popular by the content industries, particularly music and film. This is because some jurisdictions have specific legislation which states that it is possible to obtain a blocking injunction in relation to copyright infringement.[22]

It was unclear whether blocking injunctions could apply to trade mark infringement in England because there was no equivalent legislation. The High Court of England and Wales determined that it was possible to apply the same principles based in part on the intention behind Article 11 E-commerce Directive and also the judicial discretion which is available thanks to section 37(1) of the Senior Courts Act 1981. This approach was endorsed by the Court of Appeal and was not appealed to the UK's Supreme Court. However, the Supreme Court did overturn the position with regard to who should meet the costs for technically implementing the blocking process.[23] This has now been passed to the rights holders, at least as far as trade marks are concerned.

19.7   Jurisdiction or where to sue?

The question of which court has jurisdiction to hear a claim is often complex. Even if the country with jurisdiction has been correctly iden-

---

20 Cour Cass, Civ 1, 6 July 2017, *SFR and Others v Association of cinema producers and others*, (16-17.217, 16-18.298, 16-18.348, 16-18.595) ECLI:FR:CCASS:2017:C100909.

21 Svea Högsta Domstolen 2017-12-22 B 2787-16.

22 Copyright, Designs and Patents Act 1988, s. 97A. The first blocking injunction in the UK is known as "Newzbin2" *Twentieth Century Fox Film Corporation and Others v British Telecommunications plc* [2011] EWHC 2714 (Ch).

23 *Cartier International AG and Ors v British Telecommunications plc and Anor* [2018] UKSC 28.

tified there may be related issues concerning which court within the country should hear the claim.

In Europe, jurisdiction is regulated by the 'Brussels regime' which is a series of treaties between the EU and other ETFA nations.[24] There are entire books dedicated to the question of jurisdiction but broadly speaking the location depends on the location of the defendant and whether or not there is a written contract. If there is a contract, the action usually has to be brought in the jurisdiction which was chosen by the parties unless the contract only provides for non-exclusive jurisdiction or carves out jurisdiction for emergency relief such as an interim injunction.

If the dispute is non-contractual, proceedings are usually brought in either the place where the defendant is located, or the place where the infringing act first occurred. There are obvious exceptions, for example, if the dispute concerns a national intellectual property right, the dispute must be brought in the country where the rights are located. This means you cannot sue for infringement of a French trade mark in Spain. The exception to this exclusive jurisdiction is where the legal question to be considered is not validity or infringement but, for example, ownership of a right. In this scenario, courts of another Member State could have jurisdiction.[25]

There are specific requirements for jurisdiction where a pan-EU right such as the EU trade mark is concerned. One of the important questions is where the initial act of infringement was committed. For online infringement, this means where the offer was placed online[26] (usually this is the same as the defendant's home location or 'domicile').

19.8   Which court to choose?

Once you know which jurisdiction applies, the next question is which court to choose. In some Member States you may not have an option but in many there are now optional streamlined procedures or

---

24 The (Recast) Brussels I Regulation on jurisdiction and the recognition and enforcement of judgments (Regulation (EU) No 1215/2012) has applied to the EU since January 2015.

25 See, e.g., C-341/16 *Knipping* which concerned a German company that owned a Benelux trade mark.

26 See CJEU C-24/16 and C-25/16 *Nintendo* for details.

specialist courts. Even if you do not have a choice in the matter, it is important that you start your case in the right court.

 Some jurisdictions have embraced the opportunities afforded by the Internet. For example, England also has a means of commencing small claims for money using 'money claim online.'[27] This is a simple government website which allows individuals or businesses to start legal claims by filling in an online form (and paying the inevitable fee). It is a useful service for small debt claims but can be misused by litigants in person who try to start a variety of claims for non-monetary relief using the portal. Bear in mind that if you start a claim in this way you may find that the dispute escalates out of your control quite quickly. For example, it is common for the defendant to issue a counterclaim and before you know it, you are embroiled in expensive proceedings.

19.8.1   Specialist intellectual property courts

Many countries in the EU have one or more specialist courts which are dedicated to intellectual property rights. A few of the more notable examples are below.

In France, the civil and commercial courts (*tribunaux d'instance* and *tribunaux de grande instance*) are most likely to be the first instance courts which would hear any disputes arising out of the activities related to your fashion business. The commercial courts hear disputes between businesses and commercial companies, and the civil courts are able to hear a variety of private disputes.

In France, court proceedings must usually be commenced in the court for the region where the defendant has their registered office or usual residential domicile. However, intellectual property disputes have an extra level of complexity as they can only be heard in specific courts due to their intricacy and specialist nature. Which particular intellectual property court is appropriate depends on the type of intellectual property right and whether the application concerns infringement seizures.[28] This reform has generally been positive as it provides litigants with certainty as to where disputes may be heard and also means that

---

27 See https://www.moneyclaim.gov.uk/web/mcol/welcome.

28 A map of the specialist Intellectual Property Courts in France is available at: http://www.justice.gouv.fr/publication/atlas_judiciaire/C_09_TGI_ProprieteIntellectuelle.pdf.

the judges in these specialist courts are well versed in the issues arising out of intellectual property disputes.

Further, decisions from the French intellectual property office (INPI) can only be heard by specific courts. For example, appeals against INPI decisions on the grant, rejection or maintenance of French registered design rights and trade marks can only be heard by a handful of courts.[29] A similar, but not identical list of French courts, have jurisdiction to hear cases on copyright, designs, trade marks and geographical indications.[30]

Only the Paris High Court has jurisdiction to hear *saisie* applications regarding patents and EU intellectual property rights (i.e., EU trade marks and Community designs). The regional specialised High Courts can also grant *saisie* applications relating to copyright and French rights.

In Italy, the *Sezioni Specializzate in materia di Impresa* have exclusive jurisdiction for civil actions concerning intellectual property rights and unfair competition (provided the claim relates to intellectual property rights in some way). Italy first introduced specialist intellectual property courts in 2003,[31] there are now 21 courts across the country which roughly correspond to each Italian region. These courts include a specialist Court of Appeal. The final level of appeal is to the Italian Supreme Court.

England and Wales have several different courts which are dedicated to intellectual property disputes of different sizes. Large cases (usually ones which are complex and/or have a value of over £500,000) are dealt with by the Intellectual Property Court which sits within the Chancery Division of the High Court. Lower value and/or less technically complex disputes are heard by the Intellectual Property Enterprise Court or 'IPEC.'[32] IPEC has a simplified procedure which involves much more active case management by the judge. This means that disclosure

---

29 Douai, Nancy, Versailles, Colmar, Paris, Rennes, Bordeaux, Lyon, Aix-en-Provence, Fort-de-France. See Art. D.311-8 of the Judicial Organisation Code and Arts R.411-19 and D.411-19-1 of the Intellectual Property Code.

30 Bordeaux, Lille, Lyon, Marseille, Nanterre, Nancy, Paris, Rennes, Strasbourg and Fort-de-France. See Art. D. 211-6-1 of the Judicial Organisation Code.

31 They were introduced with the Legislative Decree No. 168/2003 (and modified with Law No. 27/2012 and Law No. 9/2014).

32 See https://www.gov.uk/courts-tribunals/intellectual-property-enterprise-court.

and witness evidence are not guaranteed and when they are ordered they have to be justified and limited to set parameters. For example, two witnesses per side is the norm.

The main consequence of this simplified procedure is that costs in IPEC are a lot less, typically around 80 per cent less than the High Court although the fixed costs recovery (set at a maximum of £50,000) is often also less than the costs which are actually incurred. The cases are also usually heard and decided more quickly, nine to 12 months compared to the High Court's 12–18 months.

 IPEC also has a small claims track for very simple and low value disputes (under £10,000). As it is not possible to recover more than £260 in legal costs in this track, it tends to be used directly with minimal external legal assistance, although this can be a mistake as complex issues can arise on even seemingly straightforward cases.

The lessons from IPEC have been applied to much larger value disputes and it is possible to have much more active case management and streamlined procedure in even multi-million pound disputes via the Shorter Trials Scheme and Flexible Trials Scheme.

19.8.2   International intellectual property courts

Specialist intellectual property courts are by no means a solely European phenomenon. For example, China has established specialist intellectual property courts in the three major cities for intellectual property: Beijing, Shanghai and Guangzhou. These courts have become very sophisticated and the damages awards have substantially increased over time. They have been so well received that the same approach has been rolled out in a further 15 cities across China.[33]

19.9   Who to sue?

Choosing the right defendants is not as straightforward as it may first appear. Some businesses have very opaque corporate structures which means it is very hard to identify who is responsible for the infringing activity. Further, some infringers hide themselves behind fake

---

33 'When it comes to IP enforcement, Chinese IP maths: 3 + 15 = more than 18?' Michael Lin guest post for IPKat http://ipkitten.blogspot.co.uk/2018/05/when-it-comes-to-ip-enforcement-chinese.html.

identities online. As mentioned earlier in this chapter, it is possible to apply for pre-action disclosure if you can identify someone such as an ISP who is likely to have access to the relevant information. This can add a significant expense at the start of an action.

19.9.1   Vicarious liability

In some situations, even if you did nothing wrong, you can be held liable for the actions of third parties such as agents or employees. This is known as vicarious liability. In an employee situation the liability concerns actions which the employee committed during their employment including harassment, bullying or copyright infringement. For example, a UK supermarket was recently found vicariously liable for their employee's deliberate disclosure of personal data on many of their colleagues.[34] You can reduce the likelihood of both these actions occurring and being held liable for the actions by having a rigorous recruitment process, regular workplace training and having clear policies which set out acceptable behaviour in the workplace.

19.9.2   Contractual liability

A similar situation where you are liable for someone else's actions can arise via contractual terms. For example, a department store's terms of business may require you to share liability for any issues which arise in your concession, such as trip-and-slip litigation. This can apply even if the cause of the fall was outside your control such as it being the result of the actions of a department store employee. In some situations, the contractual power imbalance is such that you cannot always agree to different terms but it is important that you know what you are signing up to and have taken all reasonable steps to reduce the likelihood of liability arising.

19.9.3   Sharing liability – joint tortfeasance and common design

At the outset of many intellectual property proceedings, the potential claimant does not have any direct knowledge of how the infringement occurred or who was directly involved in the infringing activity. This can create difficulties and means that claimants may have to make a best guess in the absence of better information.

---

34 *Various Claimants v WM Morrisons Supermarket plc* [2017] EWHC 3113 (QB).

Sometimes there is only one infringer (or only one which is worth suing) but more often there are several legal entities involved in an infringement. For example, you may have different companies manufacturing, importing and selling. If there is a very small business infringing, it may be that one or more of the company directors is taking such an active role in the infringing activities that they could also be liable. In bigger operations, companies often divide responsibility for online and in store sales between different corporate entities. Each of these businesses is a separate legal person and if you want to stop the infringement across the board, get full financial compensation and receive comprehensive disclosure of the extent of the infringing activities, you will often have to sue more than one company.

In England, the key question for whether there is shared liability is *did each party make the infringing act their own?*[35] This includes 'active co-operation' to help bring about the infringing activities.[36] In England, at least, it has recently become easier to make company directors liable as joint tortfeasors with their company on this basis, particularly where they are a sole director and sole shareholder.

19.9.4   Landlord liability

 The CJEU recently confirmed that the same principles under which ISPs can be liable for the sale of counterfeit goods on websites once they are put on notice of the same can also apply to physical marketplaces. In other words, in the EU, it is possible to sue a landlord for the actions of the tenant. This particularly arises in the context of intellectual property disputes.

This CJEU decision followed a referral from the Czech High Court in Prague and concerned the sale of counterfeit goods from Tommy Hilfiger, Lacoste, Burberry and other well-known brands.[37] Although landlord liability does not yet extend to damages and costs, if the injunction is breached, the landlord is in contempt of court – which typically carries criminal penalties such as imprisonment or a fine.

---

35 *SABAF v MFI* [2004] UKHL 45.

36 *Sea Shepherd UK v Fish & Fish Ltd* [2015] UKSC 10.

37 *Tommy Hilfiger Licensing LLC and Others v DELTA CENTER a.s.* Case C-494/15. ECLI:EU: C:2016:528.

19.10   The road to trial

There are various steps which are completed on the road to trial. Disputes normally begin with correspondence to try to resolve the dispute without issuing a claim. If correspondence fails then the court process begins. However, as discussed in Chapter 20 there may be tactical reasons for suing first in some intellectual property cases.

The claim is prepared by the claimant's lawyers. The level of detail involved at this stage depends on the legal issue in dispute, jurisdiction and court. Broadly speaking, Civil Law jurisdictions tend to include more detail in their claim. For example, in France the claim (known as the *assignation*) must include a list of the supporting evidence upon which the claimant relies. It is therefore fairly detailed and can be time consuming and expensive to compile.

An important first stage in the court process is service of the claim on the defendant. The claimant is usually responsible for service in Common Law jurisdictions. In many Civil Law jurisdictions, the court (e.g., in Germany) or a court-appointed bailiff (e.g., in France) serves the claim. This can add a delay and creates uncertainty as to when service actually occurs. However, it avoids many of the service issues which occur in jurisdictions such as the US where process servers are required. In England, hand delivery and post are all acceptable forms of service. In some circumstances an English court has even allowed service by more modern forms of communication such as Twitter. If the defendant is not based in the same jurisdiction, service is more complicated.

The defendant will then have the opportunity to file a formal response to the claim. The time available for filing this response can vary considerably. For example, in England's IPEC, if there has not been any correspondence before the claim is filed you can have up to 70 days[38] to file and serve a response (which is known as a defence) whereas the norm for other High Court proceedings is 28 days. In any event, in England, it is essential that an acknowledgement of service is filed within 14 days of service.

The timetable up to trial is then fixed either by the court alone or following representations from the parties. Some countries have

---

38 See Civil Procedure Rule 63.22.

a docketing system whereby the case is assigned to a specific judge. In France, the supervising judge for the District and High Courts is referred to as a *juge de la mise en état*, and before the Commercial Courts, a *juge rapporteur*. England has had a recent trial of an optional docketing system which has been very successful and is likely to become a permanent feature.[39]

19.10.1   Disclosure or discovery

In Common Law jurisdictions such as England and Ireland there is a fairly detailed 'disclosure' process (known as 'discovery' in the US). This essentially involves identifying and handing over all documents which are relevant to your case because they either help or hinder you or your opponent.

 Once you are aware of a potential claim, in most countries, you are under an obligation to retain all relevant documents because they either need to be disclosed or used in evidence. For example, in a design claim this includes your original design, the inspiration for that design, internal emails and text messages about the design and external communications, e.g., with the manufacturer. Once you become aware of a dispute, the safest course of action is to immediately preserve all documents, particularly those which may be on personal employee phones. It is a good idea to review the most likely relevant documents immediately so you can get a good feel for how big a risk the dispute is for your business and consequently how to approach any settlement negotiations.

Often just because you disclose a document in one jurisdiction does not mean that you have to disclose it in another jurisdiction. This is a common concern if you are engaged in parallel litigation across multiple jurisdictions. However, once your opponent is aware of the document's existence, they will inevitably take steps to ensure it is provided in the course of other proceedings. Further, as soon as a document has been considered by a court and referred to in a judgment, the judgment itself is in the public domain.

In Civil Law jurisdictions such as France and Germany, the documents you may have to disclose tend to only relate to the positive aspects of your case (unless they are uncovered as part of the *saisie*). This means

---

39 See Civil Procedure Rules Practice Direction 51N – Shorter and Flexible Trials Pilot Schemes.

that you are able to substantially limit the documents which you share with the court and your opponent. An exception to this is if you refer to documents but later change your mind about the wisdom of handing them over. If you have referred to a document in your court submissions, you leave yourself open to the judge ordering you to provide the missing documents. Failure to comply with this court order can result in financial penalties or 'adverse inferences' being drawn by the judge (i.e., the judge becomes a lot more suspicious of your case and is less likely to rule in your favour).[40] Similarly, a judge can take any measures they consider necessary to avoid anybody destroying evidence.

The fact that you are not obliged to provide harmful documents to your opponent does not necessarily mean that a party is able to fully 'hide' evidence from another party. For example, the *saisie* is a powerful tool which allows a party claiming to be the victim of infringement of its intellectual property rights the possibility to seek an order from a judge to seize evidence from an alleged counterfeiters' premises. Further, the French Code of Civil Procedure[41] states that if a party has evidence in its possession, the judge may order that it be produced in the proceedings if requested by the other party, providing that there is no legitimate reason for not doing so. Confidentiality is unlikely to be a valid argument, as courts will often allow redaction of documents, or will rule separately on such arguments.

In practice, the judge does not always have to wait for an application of one of the parties. The investigative role of a French judge means that they also have the right to act on their own initiative and can order the production of a document that has not already been submitted in the proceedings if it appears that such evidence is genuinely necessary in order to properly decide the dispute between the parties. A party can also ask the judge to order production of a document from a third party, but which it does not have in its possession[42] (this is similar to a *Norwich Pharmacal* order in England).

It can be very uncomfortable to have your business information dissected in a courtroom or pored over by junior lawyers in the course of disclosure. Therefore, from the moment a dispute is contemplated it is helpful to imagine that everything you and your staff write to each

---

40 See Arts 133 and 134 of the French Code of Civil Procedure.

41 See, ibid., Art. 11.

42 See, ibid., Art. 138.

other, your opponent and any related parties could one day be read out in court. Is this text message or email something you would feel comfortable being included in a court judgment? If not, find a more neutral way of expressing the same issue. In fact, regardless of whether litigation is contemplated, this is a helpful habit to get into. Make sure that your staff have regular reminders so they are similarly careful about the way they express themselves.

 A French law, commonly known as the 'French Blocking Statute'[43] protects French citizens and residents (including companies) by allowing them to 'block' any requests to supply economic, commercial, industrial, financial, or technical documents or other information which could be used as evidence in legal or administrative proceedings outside France, unless otherwise authorised to do so under an international treaty.

This law can be quite troublesome for an opposing party when a French company is involved in legal proceedings abroad, particularly in the US or England (countries with wide discovery and disclosure obligations). Foreign judges tend to be unwilling to indulge refusals from French parties to provide evidence, including those founded on the French Blocking Statute. In England, a recent case held that when French parties have agreed to submit to the laws of England (e.g., under a contract), then they need to adhere to the English Civil Procedure Rules, which include the right to seek full disclosure of evidence.[44]

The US courts have often drawn a similar conclusion when faced with a French party's refusal to adhere to discovery obligations. For example, the US Supreme Court held that the French Blocking Statute does not 'deprive an American court of the power to order a party subject to its jurisdiction to produce evidence even though the act of production may violate that statute.'[45]

A Delaware court also recently held that the French Blocking Statute could not overrule US discovery rules. The court stated that the party seeking discovery could overcome the French Blocking Statute by rely-

---

43 See French law 68-678 of 26 July 1968, as amended.

44 *National Grid Electricity Transmission plc v ABB Ltd and Others; Secretary of State for Health v Servier Laboratories Ltd and Others* [2013] EWCA Civ 1234.

45 *Société Nationale Industrielle Aerospatiale v US District Court for the Southern District of Iowa*, 482 U.S. 522 (1987).

ing on Hague Evidence Convention procedure (to which France has been a party since 1970).[46]

The French courts are in disagreement with these foreign rulings which seek to circumvent its legislation, and actually take offence to the term 'Block,' as for the French courts, this statute is a fundamental right to protect against overzealous document requests. In 2014, the Nancy Court of Appeal stated that the aim of the French Blocking Statute is to protect parties from any abusive disclosure or discovery obligations. The French court considered that placing requests for cross-border document production in the hands of judges is a breach of public policy which cannot be overcome by a contractual provision (such as a dispute resolution clause). The Nancy Court of Appeal[47] further considered that requests for documents pursuant to US pre-trial discovery rules far outweigh the scope of the Hague Evidence Convention and ignore France's reserve at Article 23 which expressly excludes so-called fishing expeditions.

Therefore, while a non-French party can potentially get their hands on French documents, cooperation from the French company or judicial authorities is unlikely. Further, the document request procedure under the Hague Evidence Convention is much more onerous and expensive than under national civil procedure rules.

19.10.2   Evidence

Overall, the Civil Law systems (i.e., mainland Europe) focus more on documentary evidence, which may include written witness statements, whereas the Common Law systems (such as England and Ireland) focus more on oral witness evidence where witnesses can be cross-examined regarding their written testimony.

In practice cross-examination is rarely as exciting as it appears on television. It tends to involve a series of relatively formulaic questions based on the witness' statement. In England, you need to put your positive case to the relevant witness. This can result in a fairly drawn out process. However, the enormous benefit of cross-examination is that it enables each side's case to be properly interrogated and witnesses who have embellished their position or cut corners in their written testimony are usually found out.

---

46 See *Activision Blizzard Inc, Stockholder Litig*, 86 A.3d 531 (Del. Ch. 2014).
47 See Decision of the Nancy Court of Appeal of 4th June 2014, no 1335/14.

Trials in Civil Law jurisdictions such as France tend to be limited to a review of the facts and arguments rather than involving lengthy oral submissions or cross-examination of witnesses. It is nonetheless fairly common for a party to submit witness statements or expert reports as exhibits to their pleadings. In theory a French judge can decide to hear and question the author of a witness statement but even on the rare occasions when this occurs, they do not have the same level of scrutiny as in Common Law cross-examination.[48]

Although witness statements must be made in accordance with strict requirements, including an acknowledgment that a false statement may incur criminal charges, in practice, because the witness is not cross-examined, French judges apply less weight to such evidence compared to judges in Common Law jurisdictions. Further, if an employee makes the statement, or a party commissioned its own expert report, judges review such evidence as less impartial.

To overcome this hurdle in respect of expert evidence, the court can order its own expert report if it considers that it needs further clarification regarding technical issues in a case.[49] Usually, the expert is nominated from a list of designated experts and is limited to one sole expert, unless the complexity of the case requires more. The use of experts is particularly common in patent cases.

 In global disputes between the same parties, or in respect of the same intellectual property rights, it is common to closely monitor the arguments submitted in the course of foreign proceedings. This is done to ensure that contradictory arguments are not advanced by your legal team (or are identified if raised by your opponent).

In addition, it can be persuasive for judges, particularly those in Civil Law jurisdictions, to have sight of an expert report or witness statement that has been filed in a Common Law jurisdiction and been tried and tested in open court through cross-examination. Even more persuasive can be the inclusion of a foreign judgment as an exhibit which makes direct reference to that court's favourable opinion as to the credibility or the validity of statements made by a witness or an expert, or which simply finds in your favour overall. No matter how persuasive they may be, ultimately judges are not bound to follow judgments from foreign courts.

---

48 See Art. 203 of the French Code of Civil Procedure.
49 Ibid., s. IV.

19.10.3   Trial

Although it is possible to have final decisions made solely on the papers, this tends to be in relation to lower value claims or specific applications. Decisions on the papers are more common in Civil Law jurisdictions but when the claim is higher value the trial procedure is usually oral. In all oral proceedings, written submissions are normally sent to the judge before the hearing so that they have the opportunity to understand the salient points in advance.

At trial, a judge will review and assess the written court file, which contains all the evidence set out and exchanged by the parties. Lawyers tend to take the judge through the case in order to draw their attention to key elements, arguments or documents, there may also be cross-examination of witnesses depending on the jurisdiction. The time this takes can vary considerably. For simple cases in France, a 30-minute trial is sufficient. In extremely complex (and rare!) cases, the court will set aside a full day, or even up to three days to allow the lawyers to express the arguments orally. It is exceptional for a French case to take more than three days. The judge will usually take the opportunity at this stage to seek oral clarification from the lawyers on points which are unclear or need further explanation. This is a very different process to the UK and US where legal argument and cross-examination typically takes days or even weeks.

The judge will then deliberate on the matter in their chambers and provide a date on which the final written judgment is likely to be available to the parties. Usually the judgment is handed down around one month after the hearing date.

19.10.4   Summary judgment or strike out

Some jurisdictions, such as England, have a very helpful process for quickly disposing of spurious claims via an application for summary judgment or to have the claim struck out. Even in countries such as France where there is no specific system enabling a party to summarily dismiss proceedings, it is possible to raise lack of jurisdiction or invalidity of procedural documents in order to quickly dispense with a case. In France, arguments need to be raised together and must be filed before any defence on the merits is submitted.

In Germany, the court is required to issue a final decision as soon as it has sufficient information to do so. This could be after the first exchange of written briefs if the claimant has not issued a valid claim. Similarly, if a valid defence is not submitted, the court may order judgment in default. This produces a similar result to a successful strike out or summary judgment application.

19.10.5   Preliminary non-binding opinions

 Another useful means of potentially dispensing with a dispute early on is a preliminary non-binding opinion. This is where the court is given an overview of the issues in dispute and provides an initial view on the likely outcome should the case proceed to trial. This can be particularly helpful if the dispute is against someone who does not have professional legal support (i.e., a litigant in person). This is because litigants in person are more likely to take a judge's word that their case is bad than your lawyers! The danger is of course that the opinion could go against you and consequently put you in a very bad position for settlement.

19.11   Legal remedies

19.11.1   Financial compensation

In EU Member States, there are three different approaches to calculating the financial compensation which is available for intellectual property infringement.

Damages

 Damages are based on the loss to your business. This could be the amount you would have charged for your intellectual property right if it had been licensed (a so-called 'reasonable royalty') or the damage caused to your business in lost sales or similar. Lost sales can be hard to prove so the reasonable royalty is generally preferable.

Sometimes it is possible to add in an amount to compensate for the goods which would have been sold at the same time (convoyed goods). For example, if only a bikini top was found to infringe, you may also be able to recover damages for the matching bikini bottoms on the basis that the top and bottoms are commonly sold together.

It is also possible to get damages instead of an injunction if the court considers that this approach is appropriate.[50] This may be relevant if the infringement was unintentional and an injunction would cause disproportionate harm.

Account of profits

This remedy is an account of the profits which the infringer made from the goods. An account of profits is usually an alternative to damages. Again, you will not be entitled to all of the infringer's profits as they are entitled to deduct expenses including general overheads (within reason). It is unusual for an intellectual property infringement to be the sole factor driving the sale of an infringing item. For example, some people may have bought a shirt which includes an infringing logo because they liked the cut or the pattern. Identifying a fair percentage of the net profits associated with an infringement is carried out on a 'broad brush' basis and is usually somewhere between 40 and 60 per cent.

The extent of permitted deductions in account of profits calculations was recently considered by the English courts.[51] The sales of shirts under an infringing logo came to just under £1.3 million (including VAT). Before applying a percentage to the net profits, House of Fraser (the unsuccessful defendant) was able to deduct VAT, the cost of goods, written-off stock and a percentage of overheads which included a percentage based on the costs of employees, property, asset depreciation and advertising. However, some deductions were not permitted for unspecified expenses, such as consultancy fees, on the basis that they were exceptional expenses and not general overheads.

Additional damages

The third and final form of damages in the EU is 'additional damages.' The power for courts to award these damages comes from Article 13 of the Enforcement Directive.[52] Article 13 requires that EU Member States ensure that the damages associated with infringement take into account both the economic consequences and 'in appropriate cases, elements other than economic factors, such as the moral prejudice caused to the rightsholder by the infringement.'

50 Article 12 Enforcement Directive.

51 *Jack Wills Ltd v House of Fraser (Stores) Ltd* [2016] EWHC 626.

52 Directive 2004/48/EC on the Enforcement of Intellectual Property Rights.

In some non-EU jurisdictions, such as the US, it is possible to award statutory damages which fix the financial harm done at a certain level and punitive damages which punish the infringer beyond the actual harm caused.

The CJEU has considered whether the additional damages introduced in Article 13 of the Enforcement Directive created a type of punitive damages for the EU.[53] The referral to the CJEU came from Poland whose Copyright Law introduced the option to claim double or even triple the amount of damages based on a notional licence fee[54] provided that that the infringement was intentional. This approach enables easy calculation of damages but there was concern that the triple damages offered under the Copyright Law was closer to punitive damages than the drafters of Article 13 had intended.

The Polish Supreme Court requested the CJEU's ruling on whether Polish law had complied with Article 13 of the Enforcement Directive. The CJEU stated[55] that there was nothing in EU law which expressly prohibited punitive damages, consequently, the scope of 'additional damages' remains unclear.

In the meantime, the Constitutional Tribunal of the Republic of Poland ruled that triple damages was unconstitutional because it contradicted the right to proprietorship, the rule of social justice and proportionality.[56] The availability of double damages for infringement was not considered by the Polish court or CJEU and consequently rights holders can still claim double damages before the Polish courts in copyright cases.

19.11.2 Non-monetary compensation

In addition to financial relief, it is possible to get non-monetary relief such as an:

1. injunction to prevent further infringement;[57]

2. order that the infringer sends (i.e., 'delivers up') all infringing

---

53 *OTK v SFP* Case C-367/15 ECLI:EU:C:2017:36.

54 Also known as a reasonable royalty, see Art. 79 of the Polish Act on Copyright.

55 Judgment C 367/15 dated 25 January 2017.

56 Decision of the Constitutional Tribunal of the Republic of Poland SK 32/14 dated 23 June 2015.

57 See Art. 11 Enforcement Directive 2004/48/EC.

products to you or destroys the goods providing independent evidence of the same; or[58]

3. order for publication (i.e., advertisement) of the decision at the infringer's expense.[59]

19.11.3   Pan-European injunctions

Permanent injunctions are usually awarded by a court on a national basis which means that they restrict activities within that court's territory. For example, an injunction which is awarded by a Spanish court will only restrict the unsuccessful defendant from continuing its activities in Spain.

An important exception to this is where the rights involved are pan-EU such as an EU trade mark or registered Community design. In these situations it is possible to get an injunction which covers the whole of the EU provided that the claim is brought in the infringer's home Member State. If the court is selected because it is where the infringer has been selling infringing products (assuming that is not the same as the infringer's home territory), it is only possible to get an injunction for that particular territory.[60]

An exception to the exception applies for some trade marks. A pan-European injunction cannot cover parts of the EU where use of a sign would not amount to trade mark infringement because the linguistic approach of one or more Member States is such that there would be no likelihood of confusion.[61] In the *Combit/Commit* case, the CJEU took the view that English-speaking Member States would be able to easily distinguish between Combit and Commit and consequently the pan-European injunction should not apply to those Member States.

19.11.4   Delivery up or destruction

You do not necessarily want to have thousands of infringing products delivered to your door and destruction of products can be

---

58 Ibid., Art. 10.
59 Ibid., Art. 15.
60 *Nintendo Co. Ltd v BigBen Interactive GmbH*, Cases C-24/16 and C-25/16.
61 *Combit Software GmbH v Commit Business Solutions Ltd*, Case C-223/15.

environmentally damaging and may result in negative publicity if it becomes public. A middle ground can be to arrange for the destruction to be by recycling rather than incineration. Another option which may be available is to have infringing branding removed and the underlying product donated to charities.

19.11.5   Publication of the judgment

If you win your case, in addition to the common remedies such as damages, legal costs, an injunction and delivery up of infringing items, you can ask the court for an order to publish the judgment online (e.g., on the infringer's website) and/or in the press.[62] This approach was endorsed by the Court of Appeal for England and Wales in the infamous *Apple v Samsung* litigation. The court was very critical of Apple's attempt to bury the bad news that Samsung did not infringe its registered Community design for the iPad's shape and ordered that a prominent notice was displayed on its website.[63]

Although publication of the judgment is a potential remedy, it is discretionary and you do not necessarily have complete freedom to publish a decision yourself. The French Supreme Court recently explained that publishing a favourable judgment online, without the court's permission, could constitute an act of bad faith or unfair competition in France.[64]

Unlike the majority of judgments in Common Law jurisdictions, French and other Civil Law judgments are not automatically made public and do not tend to include detailed reasoning as to how the decision was reached. Consequently, the French Supreme Court held that while it is not forbidden for an injured party to publish copies of favourable decisions at their own cost, this does not give a right to publish simple extracts of the judgment if this renders the overall publication and decision misleading. The common way to avoid this issue arising is to present the proposed form of wording to the court for approval.

---

62 See Art. 15 Enforcement Directive.
63 *Apple v Samsung* [2012] EWCA Civ 1430.
64 See decision of the Cour de Cassation, ch. com., 18th October 2017.

19.12   Costs

The recovery of legal costs can prove to be a very important factor in any legal dispute. If you secure your injunction and damages but are left with an enormous legal bill which cannot be recovered from the losing party your victory can appear to be somewhat pyrrhic in nature. Across the EU, the general rule is that Member States must ensure that reasonable and proportionate legal costs and other expenses incurred by the successful party are paid by the unsuccessful party unless it would be unfair to do so.[65]

Despite this general principle, set out in the Enforcement Directive, the amount of costs incurred and way in which they are awarded varies considerably across the EU. In England, a winning party tends to incur more costs but can expect to recover the majority of their costs – usually over 70 per cent. By contrast, Germany has a fixed approach to costs recovery based on the stage of the proceedings and the value of the claim.[66] This can result in recovering the majority of your legal costs if you are early in an action but the case may become less economic as it proceeds as the difference between the scale costs and actual costs incurred tends to increase with time.

Each jurisdiction has good and bad points in terms of costs. Civil Law jurisdictions such as France and Germany have shorter hearings and tend to focus more on written documents. This reduces trial times and consequently the overall costs tend to be lower. However, this is not always the case. For example, in Germany, it is common for courts in different cities to hear different parts of the same action which can increase travel and coordination costs. Further, in France, there can be last-minute court hearings scheduled which tie up your lawyer's time.

In Common Law jurisdictions such as England, it is normal to instruct both a solicitor who handles strategy and the day-to-day issues and a barrister who prepares the formal legal submissions and appears in court to present the arguments and cross-examine the witnesses. There are big advantages to this approach as you have a team which includes your solicitor who understands your legal strategy and business together with an expert in both advocacy and the specific legal issue at hand. However, it tends to be more expensive.

---

65 See Art. 14 Enforcement Directive 2004/48/EC.
66 German Act on Lawyer's Remuneration.

19.13   Timing

 The court process is frequently criticised for taking a long time. The quickest trial I have ever been involved in was a patent trial which took just over three months from the initial letter to trial. This speedy trial is, sadly, not the norm. All European jurisdictions have made considerable leaps forward in recent years and have embraced the time savings offered by technology. However, a combination of a large caseload, limited numbers of specialist judges and procedural issues means that most disputes take around a year to get a first instance decision and potentially one or more years for an appeal.

Italy was once notorious as a jurisdiction where cases would go to slowly die but it has revolutionised its court system and whilst the cases are still not determined quickly it is now a matter of months (although often more than 12 months) rather than years until the first instance decision is provided.

Even within a jurisdiction, the timing of a case is greatly affected by the court in which the claim is started. For example, there can be considerable differences in timing and approach between Milan and Rome or Frankfurt and Berlin.

When the intellectual property registries are involved, it can take even longer. For example, it is common for it to take over five years to get a final decision if the validity of an EU trade mark or Community design is challenged at the EUIPO. This is because there are three rounds of appeal, the last of which is to the CJEU.

19.14   Failure to comply with a court order

If you obtain judgment against someone but they fail to comply with the court's decision, the available methods for encouraging them to comply vary between jurisdictions. The use of fines is quite common in French and other Civil Law court proceedings, and acts as a deterrent to parties who consider non-compliance with court orders. These fines are a bit like the English concept of contempt of court where non-compliance with a court order can result in imprisonment in severe cases.[67] Generally you

---

67 By way of example, Anthony Knight repeatedly failed to comply with the judge's order in a dispute with Dame Vivienne Westwood OBE regarding use of her trade marks. Consequently, Mr Knight

will need to draw the failed compliance to the court's attention as they will not make an order of their own volition.

19.15   References to the CJEU

The CJEU can appear to operate as an appeal court as its rulings bind all EU courts including the national courts of each Member State. However, in most instances the CJEU is not there to decide on an appeal in a particular case but rather to clarify points of EU law which may not be clear or where the application of the law to particular factual circumstances has not been considered before.[68]

Any Member State's court can apply to the CJEU for a reference at any time in the proceedings including before a first instance decision has been given. A reference is essentially one or more questions which the court wants the CJEU to answer. In some jurisdictions this can happen following an application and before the first instance trial, in others it only tends to happen on appeal.

The CJEU will consider the question and in some circumstances an Advocate-General will be given the task of first considering the question and providing their opinion. A-G opinions are a helpful tool as they tend to go into quite a bit of detail. Because an A-G's opinion comes from a single individual rather than a panel, they can be clearer and less focused on achieving consensus. While they do not bind the CJEU, in practice the CJEU will often follow the gist of an A-G's opinion.

The CJEU has been criticised for not providing clear answers and not always answering the questions that have been referred. However, given the difficult task the court faces of finding consensus in EU laws between Member States with long-established but very different legal structures, principles and processes, they have achieved a remarkable amount of consistency. Admittedly, it has taken a while to get to this point.

---

served a period of time at Her Majesty's pleasure. The judgment where Mr Knight was committed is not reported but the earlier decision where Mr Justice Birss confirmed that he was entitled as a judge of IPEC (as he then was) to issue a bench warrant for Mr Knight's arrest is *Westwood v Knight* [2012] EWPCC 14.

68 The exception to this is appeals from the EUIPO, where the CJEU is the final court of appeal after the Board of Appeal in the EUIPO and the General Court.

Because CJEU decisions have to be agreed by all judges there are no dissenting or minority judgments. However, unlike some Civil Law judgments, CJEU judgments are all published and accessible online.

The CJEU's working language is French and consequently all documents, pleadings and judgments are translated into French. Beyond that, the rules on translation differ depending on the nature of the proceedings. The EU has 23 different languages (for its 28 Member States). CJEU decisions tend to raise issues of general importance for all Member States so it is important that preliminary ruling requests, A-G opinions and the court's judgments are translated into all 23 languages. As you can imagine, it can take a long time for all of the translations to be made. English has often been a priority language because it is spoken in the UK, Ireland and Malta and is a common second language across the EU. However, this may change following Brexit.

19.16   Appeals

A first instance decision is not the end of the litigation journey: there are appeals to contend with! In many European jurisdictions, an appeal is often granted for a first instance decision and in exceptional circumstances a further appeal can be granted. Because appeals tend to focus on points of law and not evidence they usually take less time to be heard (e.g., a day or two in England rather than a week or two at first instance). However, because appeal courts often have high workloads, the time from lodging the appeal to the judgment being handed down can take a long time.

In France, the parties have a guaranteed right to a second hearing if they are not satisfied with the outcome of the first instance proceedings. This means that a first appeal in France can be reviewed in relation to both factual and legal findings. The court also allows parties to refine their arguments and submit additional evidence. You have one month from being notified of a judgment to file an appeal (or two months if you are based outside France).

This approach both delays a final decision and increases the risk of the first instance decision being overturned on appeal. This can be reassuring for a losing party as a case which was initially decided by a judge with no professional legal experience is reviewed on appeal by a career professional judge. However, it is obviously annoying if you won at first instance. This is particularly frustrating because an appeal suspends any judgment and the resulting court order such as an injunction against selling particular goods unless the court specifically orders otherwise. Similarly, any monies obtained by a winning party should be kept in a separate account, usually a secure account held by a lawyer in accordance with Bar Association Rules. This is important because if you lose on appeal, you may have to return those monies to the other party!

The relative ease with which appeals can be obtained is particularly problematic in terms of managing litigation risk and budgets, as the second bite at the cherry approach of the French appeal system means that it is an attractive option for losing parties, especially as legal fees are not as expensive in France as in other countries. Consequently, it can take twice as long for you to get certainty on your dispute (assuming the dispute is not escalated further to the Supreme Court or *Cour de Cassation*).

19.17   Settlement

The great advantage of settlement is that it is a final decision which provides business certainty. It is also possible to be much more creative in identifying a form of compromise than the fairly blunt instrument of the court. Importantly, settlement is possible across multiple jurisdictions so it can operate on a global level resolving several parallel strands of a dispute at once. Settlement agreements are important contracts which require time and effort to negotiate and conclude. Like any contract, even if an agreement has been through several rounds of negotiation, it is still worth a careful final read through to ensure that it still makes sense and no major issues have been overlooked.

Settlement agreements that have been validly entered into cannot be disclosed to any third parties except on strict grounds such as to a party's auditors or legal advisers. Similarly, if a party has breached the terms of a settlement agreement and separate legal proceedings are required the settlement agreement could then be disclosed for use in evidence.

If a settlement agreement is entered into during the course of court proceedings, then there are certain formalities that must be followed to withdraw the claim and advise the court that a settlement has been reached. This does not involve revealing the terms of the settlement to the presiding judge and does not imply an admission of liability by either of the parties.

 Settlement negotiations in Common Law jurisdictions are typically conducted on a 'without prejudice' basis, this means that they cannot be disclosed to the court unless there is a breach of the settlement agreement in which case these discussions may form part of the 'factual matrix' of a dispute regarding the agreement's terms. Any settlement discussions in France cannot be brought to the attention of the courts provided that all exchanges between the parties went through external lawyers. This is because of the legal privilege which is attached to external lawyer negotiations, from which in-house counsel cannot benefit. In other jurisdictions, settlement discussions are not formally protected but are not typically disclosed to the court or otherwise made public.

It is common to settle trade mark disputes with a co-existence agreement. The issues that can arise in those sorts of agreements are considered in more detail in Chapter 20.

19.18   Alternative dispute resolution

The courts are a familiar dispute resolution mechanism but there are many alternatives. Most forms of alternative dispute resolution or ADR can resolve a dispute on a binding, final and global basis. Often ADR is a supplement to litigation which can be used as a tool to put pressure on both parties in order to reach a settlement.

 ADR is commonly used in France, Germany and the UK both for national and for international disputes. Paris and London pride themselves on being an international hub for ADR. They are both home to the International Chamber of Commerce (ICC) and have local centres for mediation and arbitration.[69]

19.18.1   Arbitration

Arbitration is a confidential procedure whereby independent arbitrators consider a dispute and decide on the outcome. It bears many

---

69 E.g. the CMAP in Paris, at http://www.cmap.fr/our-offer/arbitration/?lang=en.

similarities to court procedure and can be provided as the dispute resolution mechanism in a contract. It tends to be a popular choice for sensitive disputes where confidentiality is important. It is also often easier to enforce internationally than a court judgment. However, there are a number of significant downsides. For example, it can be a lot more expensive than the courts. Further, the experience of arbitrators in particular areas of law can vary significantly and arbitration limits the ability to use other forms of ADR such as mediations.

Paris and London are both parties to the UN Convention on the Recognition and Enforcement of Foreign Arbitral Awards 1958 (the 'New York Convention').[70] This arbitration-friendly environment provides parties with comfort that local courts will look favourably on arbitral proceedings and enforcement of awards. Italy has also adopted the New York Convention.[71]

Consent is generally required in order to submit a dispute to arbitration. This is usually by including an arbitration clause in a contract, or by entering into a separate agreement where the parties agree to resolve a pre-existing dispute by arbitration. The existence of a written agreement is compulsory for arbitration between French parties[72] and is common in practice in other arbitration disputes.

19.18.2   The *Giurì* in Italy

The Italian concept of *Giurì* or Jury was first referred to in Chapter 16 in the context of advertising. There are *Giurì* for other areas of law in Italy. For example, the *Associazione del Design Industriale* (ADI) has its own *Giurì* which aims to ensure that the creations of industrial design are original and do not involve any unfair conduct. They adjudicate based on a self-regulatory code which is binding upon the signatories.

The ADI *Giurì* is composed of 11 members including producers and a designer appointed by each of *Confindustria* and ADI as well as experts on market problems and consumer problems and at least three lawyers. It is a fast procedure which cannot be appealed.

---

70 France also has many arbitration-friendly provisions in the French Code of Civil Procedure.

71 Articles 839 and 840 of the Italian Civil Procedure Code regulate the recognition of foreign arbitration awards in the Italian system.

72 See Arts 1443 and 1507 of the French Code of Civil Procedure.

19.18.3   Mediation

 Mediation is probably the most flexible form of ADR and is commonly used as a precursor to settlement. Essentially a mediation is a settlement meeting which is supervised by an independent mediator who brings the parties together and listens to each party separately with a view to facilitating a negotiated settlement.

Parties can use mediation either during court proceedings, or before proceedings have been issued. There is no limit on what kinds of dispute can be resolved by mediation. Parties to a dispute cannot be forced to resort to mediation but courts will commonly encourage settlement discussions including by way of mediation. In some Member States such as France, the court can directly appoint a mediator, provided the parties agree.

France has recently made ADR much more accessible to parties and more actively promotes settlement via amicable methods, such as mediation.[73] While no party can be forced to mediate, claimants are typically under an obligation to first try to resolve a dispute without using the court system. They may be penalised if they fail to do so unless there was a legitimate reason such as the urgency of the dispute or potential destruction of evidence.[74] Any failure by the parties to try to resolve their dispute amicably may result in a judge imposing a compulsory conciliation period which can delay resolution of the dispute.

19.18.4   Internet operator disputes

 A final form of dispute resolution concerns the mandatory dispute resolution mechanisms which are provided in many online platforms' terms and conditions. They are typically a hybrid of mediation and very simple arbitration. Basically, each side has the opportunity to put forward their case and evidence such as proof of delivery and then the operator concludes on the facts whether, for example, the goods did not arrive at all or were damaged on delivery. They then make a decision which typically concerns either repayment of the goods and/or delivery costs. Many sellers consider these dispute resolution mechanisms to be biased toward the buyer but ultimately they save a lot of

---

73 Law No. 2016-1547 of 18 November 2016 on the modernisation of justice for the 21st century.
74 See Art. 56, Code of Civil Procedure.

time and money in legal fees and do provide a quick and satisfactory resolution to most issues.

Online takedowns are another form of dispute resolution mechanism. They are available on many e-commerce and social media sites and are discussed in more detail in Chapter 20 in the context of online marketplaces.

19.18.5   Litigation through social media

Many individuals and smaller brands are choosing to take justice into their own hands via social media. This has two major downsides.

First, the court of public opinion is fickle and it is easy to end up on the wrong side even if you start the conversation. This negative publicity can be much more damaging to the business than the original issue.

Second, it does not guarantee you what you actually want, whether that is a competitor to stop copying you and withdraw their product from the market and/or financial compensation. Worse, it can mean that you show your hand so that if you do need to start a legal claim you are in a less favourable position. The worst case scenario is that you could provide someone with sufficient ammunition to start defamation or unfair competition proceedings.

19.19   Criminal liability

An alternative to bringing proceedings yourself is to encourage the state to intervene. This may be possible if a parallel criminal offence has been committed. For example, in counterfeiting situations, the state can sometimes be persuaded to step in and take action. This is particularly common in Southern European countries such as Spain and France. The downsides of the state taking over are that you lose control of the proceedings, they may ultimately decide not to prosecute and you are less likely to get any information on the counterfeiting supply chain which you would ordinarily want to rely on in order to stop the entire counterfeiting operation.

The threat of criminal liability can be a useful tool in the intellectual property arsenal but it can also be wielded against you if you infringe someone else's right. Many other areas of law such as competition, tax, fraud, modern slavery and product liability can all give rise to criminal liability.

 Generally criminal action is only possible where infringement is very blatant, usually an exact copy or counterfeit or a very close match. It tends to be available only for trade mark and copyright infringement. Criminal action on the basis of registered Community designs (RCDs) may in theory be available, however, it can be hard to persuade the authorities to take action. This is because RCDs are not so well known and there is a common perception that they are weaker than other registered rights as there is no substantive examination before an RCD is granted.

In order for the state to bring criminal proceedings in many countries, particularly those in Northern Europe, you often have to convince the relevant authorities that you have sufficient evidence to prove that the infringer had an intention to commit the relevant infringing activity 'beyond reasonable doubt.' This is a high hurdle and may require the investment of significant time and money investigating the infringers first.

When the state brings criminal proceedings, even though the prosecution concerns your rights, you will not necessarily be that involved or gain access to relevant information unless it comes out in court. You will also not be entitled to any damages or reimbursement of your legal costs.

Because counterfeiting is linked to the fight against organised crime and terrorist activity, if a case proceeds to trial the sanctions can be very serious. For example, in France infringement accompanied by aggravating circumstances, such as a link to terrorism or human trafficking, could be punished by up to seven years' imprisonment and/or fines up to €750,000.[75] Further, because the monies made from infringing activities are proceeds of crime, it is possible for the authorities in some countries such as England to seize high-value assets including real estate, cars or luxury goods if they can been linked to the infringing activities.

By comparison, in France 'normal' intellectual property infringement can be punished by up to three years' imprisonment and/or a fine of

---

75 The Law of 3rd June 2016 (No. 2016-731).

up to €300,000.[76] If the infringer is a company (*personne morale)* then other sanctions are also applicable including company dissolution, closure or being placed under surveillance.[77]

In some countries, including England, it is possible to bring a private prosecution against someone who has committed a criminal act but the state has elected not to prosecute. This means that you take on the role of the state and prosecute someone under the criminal law. This is very expensive. Consequently, private prosecutions are rare.

19.20   Social media disputes

Before you start any legal dispute (whether on social media or otherwise) make sure you have all the facts. In many instances, when a social media dispute first arises, the best option is to try to resolve it directly with the individuals concerned (but not too informally). It is always worth seeking legal and, potentially, PR advice before making first contact to ensure you are not weakening your position. If your complaint concerns a social media post, before starting a claim try to resolve it first via the social media site's complaints process.

It is useful to think in advance about the sorts of issues that are likely to arise and how you plan to respond. In the heat of the moment, it is easy to get this wrong so considering how to deal with social media disputes in advance can be very helpful. Leaving aside customer complaints (which you should respond to as quickly as possible) and trolls (who are usually best ignored or reported to the relevant site), the main conflict areas tend to be:

1.   Counterfeit goods.

2.   Trade mark infringement.

3.   Parody accounts.

4.   Overzealous fans.

---

76 This can be increased to five years' imprisonment and/or fines of up to €500,000 if there is a link to organised crime, health and safety risks, or there is a link to public online communication networks.

77 See Arts L.335-2, L.335-4, L.343-4, L.521-10, L.615-14 and L.716-10 of the French Intellectual Property Code and Arts 131-38 and 39 of the French Criminal Code.

Options range from a friendly direct message to use of the social media website's reporting tool or, in more extreme cases, a legal 'cease and desist' letter. A friendly message that sets out your intellectual property rights and requests that they stop infringing them can often go a long way to solving the dispute. Be prepared for any communication that you send to be posted on social media so ensure that your staff are trained to always be polite even if heavily antagonised.

It is always worth first considering whether you need to do anything at all. In some instances such as fan or parody accounts, provided there is no confusion, the use may not be an infringement or a breach of the social media platform's policy. In these instances, monitoring the accounts on a regular basis may be the best course of action.

Also be careful that you are the right side of unfair competition law and/or have not left yourself open to a claim for groundless threats (see Chapters 20 and 21 for more).

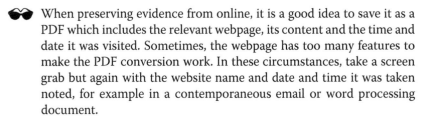 To help catch issues as early as possible, you should actively monitor social media sites for trade mark and copyright infringement. This should be outsourced as early as possible to a dedicated paralegal, supervised by a specialist lawyer, using appropriate monitoring software. The worst case scenario is someone misrepresenting themselves as you and either damaging actual or potential customer relationships or diverting trade to their site.

Once an infringement is identified you should:

1. preserve as much evidence as possible;

2. review the social media site's relevant intellectual property policy and try to resolve the matter with them; and

3. if that does not resolve the issue, consult a lawyer.

When preserving evidence from online, it is a good idea to save it as a PDF which includes the relevant webpage, its content and the time and date it was visited. Sometimes, the webpage has too many features to make the PDF conversion work. In these circumstances, take a screen grab but again with the website name and date and time it was taken noted, for example in a contemporaneous email or word processing document.

Make sure you carefully review the social media site's intellectual property policy. These policies are often divided between trade mark, copyright, privacy and other issues. This is known as a 'takedown' policy because it governs the conditions under which a social media platform will take down (i.e., remove) content. Follow the process set out in the policy to the letter. Be sure to set out accurate and complete details of your rights and avoid any emotive language. Focus on the facts. This is because: (i) it is much more likely that the site will consider your request quickly; and (ii) most social media sites publish their notice and takedown notices in one form or another. If you repeatedly make extreme allegations, this will be picked up by someone on the Internet and can be reputationally damaging.

If the social media site denies your request, consider the reasons. If you do not think they are accurate or they have not considered something important, contact a lawyer.

While most sites are responsive to communications regarding removal of infringing material, others may not always respond to takedown requests particularly quickly or may make it difficult to find a point of contact to correspond with regarding intellectual property infringement. A legal letter tends to reach the relevant people more quickly.

As mentioned above, you always need to bear in mind that your email, letter or similar could be published online. It is useful to think of it as a press release and give it the same degree of attention. You can have standardised letters and emails but be careful to tailor them appropriately. Make sure it is not a wholly automated process.

20 If someone copies you

It can be a heart-stopping moment if you see your design on display in someone else's store or a rival business using your trade mark online. Infringement of intellectual property rights can be a huge problem for fashion businesses. If you are an emerging designer, the problem often stems from larger retailers, particularly those in fast fashion, being a little too inspired. If you are a major brand the issue is more often counterfeiting. Counterfeits and their close cousins, knock-offs, are discussed in more detail in Chapter 24.

Sometimes the copying can be as blatant as a business sending your product to a factory with instructions to make an unbranded copy. Other times, it is a bit more subtle. The good news is that you have lots of options but in all instances the sooner you act the better.

 The key to all intellectual property disputes is to ask yourself what your objectives are up front and not lose sight of them. In most cases, the main objective is to get someone to stop using your intellectual property rights. However, once someone has agreed to stop, the focus often shifts to financial compensation. Bear in mind that if you pursue a case to trial, the legal fees can be substantial, although funding and insurance may be available in some circumstances. This means that you could end up out of pocket even if you ultimately win the dispute. This is not necessarily a bad outcome if you stop a competitor and send a clear message to the market that your brand is not to be trifled with. However, you need to be clear up front that this is a good result and avoid focusing on the spreadsheet.

There are many different types of copying, different intellectual property rights can help with some or all of these issues. For example, a copyright infringement claim is often brought together with a claim for infringement of trade marks and registered and unregistered Community designs, assuming these rights are all relevant and available.

20.1   First things first

20.1.1   Make sure you own the rights

It might sound obvious but in order to be able to enforce intellectual property rights, you need to have them in the first place. Chapters 3–7 set out the different rights which may be available and how to find out if they are available to you.

Even if the rights exist, you may not necessarily own them. This may be an issue if, for example, the right you want to rely upon was created by a contractor and either there is no written contract or the contract does not include an intellectual property assignment or exclusive licence. Chapter 10 considers the relationship between employees and intellectual property ownership.

By way of reminder, timing is important both in terms of the intel- lectual property rights' duration and whether it is available in the first place. In summary:

Patents: You cannot get a patent if you have publicly told people about the idea with enough detail for an expert in the relevant technology to be able to implement it.

Designs: If more than a year has elapsed since you first published (i.e. shared) a design, you will not be able to register a valid Community design. If more than three years have elapsed since that first disclosure, unregistered Community design right will have expired.

Trade marks: Although trade marks do not suffer from the same timing concerns as designs and patents, if you delay filing your trade mark there is a risk of another business including a trade mark troll (or wily competitor) applying to register the mark before you. Therefore, before making a public statement about a new product or brand name it is always worth considering whether there is a trade mark which could be registered. You have six months from the date of first filing a trade mark in which to apply to register the same mark for the same goods and services in other jurisdictions whilst retaining the original filing date. This is known as the priority period.

Copyright: Copyright lasts for the life of the creator plus 70 years. For older rights, identifying the creator and the current owner of the rights can be a challenge.

 For unregistered rights such as designs and copyright, you will also need to consider whether the right meets the qualifying criteria. This may involve discussions with the designer of the work and potentially a review of earlier works to determine the extent of 'originality' or 'individual character.'

 It is common for people to think that they can register intellectual property rights themselves but often this comes with a price tag down the line as they may miss important procedural requirements or opportunities. Further, in some jurisdictions it is simply not possible to register a right without the assistance of a specialist lawyer, particularly if you are not based in the jurisdiction.

20.1.2   Have you kept your registration details up to date?

 It is important that every time you are assigned or enter into an exclusive licence regarding registered rights you update the relevant intellectual property registries with the new owner or licensee information. Rather than recording the entire licence agreement which will include commercially sensitive terms, such as the price, it is possible to register a short form version of the licence.

 The penalties for failure to keep the register up to date vary between territories as does the time period for notifying them. If you are not careful, you may find that you are not entitled to sue for infringement or, if you are, that you cannot recover your legal costs either at all or until the registration details have been updated. There may also be tax consequences. The approach to registration can vary substantially between territories, for example, in Germany it is not possible to register a licence at all.

20.1.3   Have you taken too long?

 Most countries have a limited time period for bringing a claim (this is known as the limitation period). In some jurisdictions if the infringing activity is continuing the limitation period only starts when the infringing activity stops but damages can only be recovered for the length of the limitation period.

Similarly, if you take a really long time to complain about something such as the use of a trade mark you may not be able to complain about it in the future. This is because a court may decide that your failure to take action was a tacit approval of the infringing activity.

You obviously need time to assess the level of risk, costs involved in taking action and risk to your business but if you leave the issue for too long you can end up with a much bigger and more expensive problem.

20.1.4   Exhaustion of rights (AKA first sale doctrine)

Exhaustion of rights is a very important concept for the fashion industry as it affects the conditions under which goods can be resold. These resale goods are known as 'grey' or 'parallel' goods. Resale goods are often a concern for rights holders as it is common for brands to sell the same product at different price points around the world.

This means that resellers can buy your product in a cheaper juris- diction and resell in a more expensive jurisdiction, undercutting your distribution networks. If the intellectual property rights in your goods have been exhausted, there may be nothing you can do about this.

The rules surrounding parallel goods in the European Economic Area (EEA) may at first seem straightforward: once a product has been placed on the market in the EEA by the trade mark holder (either directly or with its consent) the trade mark holder's right to distribute the product is 'exhausted' and it cannot prevent resale of that product elsewhere in the EEA. Intellectual property rights are rarely that straightforward.

The principle of exhaustion of rights is essential to one of the four fundamental principles of the EU: free movement of goods. However, intellectual property owners are keen to retain as much control over their rights, and in particular their brand, as possible. There have therefore been a large number of disputes (usually about perfumes, pharmaceuticals or consumer electronics) which have been referred by the courts of Member States to the CJEU on this issue.

The principles of trade mark exhaustion apply where the owner of the trade mark in the importing state and the owner in the exporting state are the same or economically linked.[1] There is an economic link between: (i) a manufacturer and its distributor; (ii) a licensor and its licensee; or (iii) companies belonging to the same corporate group. However, it is important that the economic link is considered in its context and that the licensee who placed the goods on to the market did not exceed their authority when they did so.[2]

An economic link can also be found if the people exploiting the trade mark share the same centre of interests and coordinate their commercial policies including over the goods to which the mark can be affixed and the quality of these goods. If one of these people puts goods on to the market, the brand's rights are exhausted unless the goods are changed following resale.[3]

Exhaustion of rights can get complicated if the goods are changed prior to resale or do not comply with local laws. It is common for a product to be localised, often in the form of a change to packaging or product information, to comply with local laws or customs. For example, cosmetics have very specific requirements as far as testing is concerned. In the EU, cosmetics cannot be put on to the market if the ingredients were tested on animals anywhere in the world after 11 March 2013. (By contrast, in China, all cosmetics and skincare products must be tested on animals in order to be sold in China.) Resellers do not always alter the goods to ensure that these local law requirements are met.

 It *may* be possible to prevent resale of your goods if they have been altered,[4] repackaged,[5] rebranded or even advertised.[6] For example, if perfume bottles are first sold as a set but resold separately in new packaging, their kind and quality have changed so the resale could be prevented. Separate rules on exhaustion apply for other rights but

---

1 *IHT Internationale Heiztechnik v Danziger*, C-9/93, EU:C:1994:261.

2 This was one of the issues raised in *Parfums Christian Dior v Evora*, C-337/95, ECLI:EU:C:1997:517.

3 *Schweppes SA v Red Paralela SL*, C-291/16, ECLI:EU:C:2017:666.

4 If, e.g., something is added to the package *Sony Computer Entertainment v Tesco Stores* [2000] ETMR 104.

5 *Bristol Myers v Paranova* C-427/93, ECLI:EU:C:1996:282 if the repackaging affects the original condition of the product, the repackager is not clearly identified or the product is poor quality or otherwise defective and/or the repackager does not first provide a specimen of the repackaged product, exhaustion is unlikely to apply and the trade mark owner can prevent further sales.

6 *Parfums Christian Dior v Evora, supra* note 2.

it is not possible to rely on a different right, such as copyright, to get around trade mark exhaustion.[7]

If the goods do not originate from the EEA and were not placed on the market in the EEA by the trade mark owner (or with their consent), the rights in the goods have not been exhausted across the EEA and it is possible to prevent further sale.[8]

20.1.5   Primary or secondary infringement?

Most countries, including the EU Member States, differentiate between primary and secondary liability for intellectual property infringement.

Primary infringement is carried out by infringers who were directly involved in the infringing activity. For example, copying a copyright work or affixing an infringing sign (i.e., adding someone else's registered trade mark) to a product are both types of primary infringement. If somebody is liable for primary infringement, it is not necessary to show that the infringer knew that they were infringing.

Secondary infringement is carried out by people who are not so directly involved in the infringement but knew that they were involved in intellectual property infringement. This could include possessing an infringing copy in the course of business. The fact that they knew they were infringing is essential to establishing that they are legally liable but it can be hard to prove.

Bear in mind that some activities may be a primary infringement in one scenario but secondary in another scenario. For example, in England, importing is primary infringement in relation to patent infringement[9] but secondary infringement in relation to copyright.[10]

20.1.6   Which rights to rely on?

As noted at the start of this chapter, it is usually possible to bring a claim based on multiple rights. For example, if someone sells a counterfeit version of your bag they have usually infringed your trade mark

---

7 Ibid.
8 *Silhouette International Schmied v Hartlauer Handelsgesellschaft*, C-355/96, ECLI:EU:C:1998:374.
9 Patents Act 1977, s. 60(1)(a).
10 Copyright, Designs and Patents Act 1988, s. 22.

as well as, possibly, your registered and unregistered designs and maybe even copyright. Rather than bringing several different sets of proceedings based on each right, you can usually bring one set of proceedings which includes them all.

- You do not necessarily want to rely on all of the available rights. For example, if you have a strong trade mark claim, then unless you have good prospects of success or want to leverage the other rights in order to get a broader settlement agreement, there may be little benefit including rights such as unregistered designs, which require more time and money to prove their existence and that they have been copied, or rights which are fairly vulnerable to an attack on their validity such as registered Community designs. Similar considerations apply to shape marks.

- It is always open to you to agree wider settlement terms than would be granted by the court in the proceedings. For example, if you have only sued based on trade mark infringement, you could insist that they also agree not to infringe your designs as a prerequisite for settlement.

20.1.7   Taking down online infringements

- If someone is selling items that infringe your rights online, it is possible to notify one or more of the online intermediaries of your rights. These intermediaries include Apple, Etsy, eBay, Facebook and Amazon (who can remove digital and physical products and associated adverts from their websites), Google (who will remove pages from search rankings in certain circumstances), PayPal, Visa and Mastercard (who can suspend the infringer's ability to take payments) and the infringer's Internet Service Provider if they use a hosted website.

The technology businesses involved are usually willing to remove clearly infringing content, including product listings, as the alternative is that they may be fixed with secondary liability (often referred to as intermediary liability). However, they will be very reluctant to remove borderline infringements.

- A practice has developed of registering rights which are commonly counterfeit such as trade mark misspellings. This is to improve the chances of the takedown being successful. However, this tactic is a bit controversial if there is no genuine intent to actually use the misspelled mark. Similarly, although copyright does not have to be registered in order to be protected around the world, obtaining a copyright registration in the US, Canada and/or China can be very helpful in persuading online businesses to remove infringing content. This is particularly useful with Alibaba in China.

It is possible to notify these intermediaries directly (most of them have online reporting tools) or via a legal letter from a lawyer. There are lots of tools for semi-automating these takedowns but care must be taken to have a trained expert review these takedowns to avoid targeting genuine goods whose rights have been 'exhausted' such as parallel imports or second hand goods.

Many of these platforms also enable you to upload your rights and then they will filter content which may infringe your rights before it is posted. These systems are not foolproof but they are a helpful starting point and it is well worth investing the time in getting your rights registered with each of the major websites.

Online takedowns work particularly well for trade marks and copyright but are much less successful for designs, passing off and unfair competition. This is because these rights tend to be more legally complex, less well known and in the case of unregistered rights, less well defined.

If the infringement is happening on a mass scale, it is possible to get a blocking order based on trade mark or copyright which prevents access to an infringing website within a defined territory. See Chapter 19 for more details.

Takedowns typically happen across all versions of the site and are consequently more of a cross-border remedy than you would typically be entitled to from the court. They are also much cheaper and quicker. Usually the takedowns will work on all versions of the website but in some instances, these takedowns will only happen to the European version of the site. For example, the right to be forgotten is available to all EU citizens under the GDPR[11] but Google is, at the time of writing, stating that it will not remove search results from its algorithm (i.e., de-list) unless it is a European top level domain.

If online takedowns are unsuccessful, the more traditional approach of investigation into the infringer followed by legal correspondence and, if necessary, infringement proceedings is always possible.

---

11 Article 7, The General Data Protection Regulation (GDPR) (EU) 2016/679.

20.1.8   Administrative enforcement

Administrative enforcement is a common dispute resolution mechanism in parts of Asia. It is conducted by an administrative government department as opposed to a law enforcement agency or court. This type of enforcement is available for many but not all rights and is best suited to counterfeit goods. It is only available where the infringement causes 'damage to the public interest.' The authorities are generally only willing to take action where the issues are both substantial and simple. This makes it a less useful dispute resolution mechanism for smaller scale infringers or cases involving non-identical copying.

 This approach to intellectual property infringement is particularly useful in China where a rights holder has two options for administrative enforcement. The first is via a complaint to the Administration for Industry and Commerce ('AIC'). AIC can order an injunction, delivery up or destruction of the counterfeit goods and fine the infringer. The second is applicable where the goods are 'fake and inferior.' In this scenario, the Technical Supervision Bureau ('TSB') can get involved.

20.1.9   Criminal proceedings

The merits of using criminal proceedings to resolve disputes are discussed in Chapter 19. Bear in mind that the criminal courts do not tend to be filled with intellectual property specialists so a criminal action is usually best left for situations where there is very clear infringement. Consequently criminal action is usually only appropriate for 'double identity' trade mark counterfeits where there is use of an identical sign for identical goods and services or copyright infringement claims where exact copying has occurred.

20.2   Trade mark infringement

In some jurisdictions having a registered trade mark is a defence to trade mark infringement. This defence is obviously lost if the trade mark turns out to be invalid but it puts trade mark owners in these territories in a stronger negotiating position. There is no equivalent provision for EU trade marks.

20.2.1   Groundless threats

Groundless threats law is not consistent across the EU. In England, Ireland, Australia and other Common Law territories, a claim for 'groundless threats' can be made in response to any threat to sue for infringement of a registered trade mark apart from if the alleged infringer has: (a) applied the trade mark to goods or their packaging; (b) imported these marked goods; or (c) supplied services under the trade mark.[12] If the recipient of the threat does not fall within one of these three criteria, the threat to sue may be 'groundless' if the person making the threat cannot establish that the alleged infringer did in fact infringe the trade mark.

Although groundless threats sound dramatic, and they are often threatened, it is rare to see groundless threats the focus of judicial attention. The remedies for groundless threats are: (i) a declaration that the threats were groundless; (ii) an injunction against making further threats in the future; and (iii) any damages caused by the threat. The damages are often hard to prove but if, for example, a manufacturer refused to continue working with you, or a distributor pulled out of a business relationship, they could be substantial.

This lack of harmonisation was brought into sharp focus in a recent English case for groundless threats which was brought by NVIDIA, the graphics processing unit (GPU) maker.[13] This case considered whether a letter sent in the English language from a German company to a US parent company regarding infringement of an EU trade mark could constitute a threat to bring trade mark infringement proceedings in England and Wales.

An EU trade mark can currently be used as the basis for a claim for groundless threats if the proceedings are threatened in the UK.[14] In the *NVIDIA* case, the court found that the letter from the German company was clearly a threat to sue but the threat was of proceedings in Germany so English law did not apply. Whether it was a threat to sue in England depended on what a reasonable person, who received the letter and had all of the background knowledge of the dispute would have understood the letter to mean.

---

12 Trade Marks Act 1994, s. 21.

13 *NVidia Corporation and Ors v Hardware Labs Performance Systems Inc* [2016] EWHC 3135.

14 *Best Buy Co Inc and Anor v Worldwide Sales Corporation Espana SL* [2010] EWHC 1666 (Ch) and on appeal [2011] EWCA Civ 618.

In practice, groundless threats are usually only an issue if you have written legal letters to someone such as a manufacturer who ceased trading as a result. The damage this would cause to a business is such that it is worth the time and expense of suing.

20.2.2   Co-existence agreements

A popular means of resolving trade mark disputes around the world is the co-existence agreement. This is an agreement which defines the circumstances in which each party can use their trade mark and/or a particular sign. For example, it may be divided by territory or by type of use. As part of a co-existence agreement, each party may have to withdraw from certain activities in the future even if they go against their basic economic interest. This is the *quid pro quo* for long-term settlement and avoiding persistent legal fees.

 Co-existence agreements can be a very effective means of resolving trade mark disputes but it is hard to predict where brands will move to in the future and, as technology and business practices change over time, clear delineation regarding use in particular territories may become less clear cut. This means that even with a co-existence agreement in place, it is not always possible to avoid disputes in the longer term.

The High Court of England and Wales has recently considered a 1970s co-existence agreement where precisely this issue arose.[15] The agreement set out clear territorial restrictions on use of the word 'Merck' but while it was fairly easy to divide trade on a territorial basis in the 20th Century, the agreement had not predicted the rise of the Internet and the consequent blurring of international borders.

The Merck business began as a German apothecary shop in 1668. By 1889 Merck was operating internationally, including in the US. The US and EU businesses separated at the end of the First World War but they managed to trade in parallel under an informal agreement until the 1970s when they had a legal tussle and ultimately entered into a co-existence agreement under German governing law. German law takes a less literal approach toward contract interpretation than English law and considers the true intention of the parties in the context of the agreement as a whole. In this case, the English judge (following sub-

---

15 *KGaA v Merck Sharp & Dohme Corp and Ors* [2016] EWHC 49.

missions from expert witnesses on German law) identified the 'objective intention' of the parties to be a combination of resolving historic conflicts and building a co-existence framework for the future which would enable both businesses to grow.

By considering the pre-Internet features which were defined in the agreement and identifying their modern day equivalents, the English court prevented the US Merck's attempt to broaden its reach into Europe and the rest of the world via social media and its various websites.

This is a salutary lesson for all future co-existence agreements: you can try to future proof them as much as possible but ultimately this is close to impossible. If the co-existence is with a significant competitor, particularly one which used to be part of the same business, the best investment may be to keep the relationship going via regular meetings between the businesses. This flushes out issues when they arise and means that there can be a joint strategy over issues such as counterfeiting or third party infringement which affect both parties.

20.3   Copyright infringement

As explained in Chapter 4, other than printed fabric, it is hard to protect fashion designs as copyright. This is a particular issue in England which only protects specific types of 'work' and the US which offers even narrower protection for copyright works that, even if they meet the requirements for copyright protection, essentially have to be registered in advance.

The first thing you need to do when you find out that your work has been copied is to identify the copyright work. In England, the most relevant types of copyright work for the fashion industry are a 'graphic work'[16] and a 'photograph'.[17] Three dimensional artistic works are much harder to protect. There have been valiant attempts to classify iconic fashion pieces as 'works of artistic craftsmanship' but even

16 A graphic work includes 'any painting, drawing . . . or similar work.'
17 A photograph is defined as 'a recording of light or other radiation on any medium on which an image is produced or from which an image may by any means be produced, and which is not part of a film'. See Copyright Designs and Patents Act 1988, s. 4.

if they are one of a kind and have been exhibited at internationally famous design museums such as The Victoria and Albert Museum, the English court has been reluctant to see these items as 'works of artistic craftsmanship.'[18]

 Following various referrals to the CJEU, in order to be protected by copyright a work must be the creator's *own intellectual creation*.[19] A referral was recently made by the Arnhem-Leeuwarden Court of Appeal (the Netherlands) to the CJEU regarding the protection of more unusual types of copyright (in this case the taste of cheese).[20] Although the Advocate-General, in this case A-G Wathelet, indicated that he did not consider that the taste of cheese was capable of protection as a copyright work under the Infosoc Directive,[21] the CJEU has not yet reached a decision.

The door remains open for the CJEU to broaden out the protection of works beyond the closed list approach adopted by the English legislation. Although Brexit is on the horizon, the UK will likely be bound by the CJEU's decision in this case.[22] This case could have important implications for perfume and similar fashion accessories which rely on other senses such as touch and smell.

20.3.1   Photographs

Because of the ease with which photographs can be taken, they can face a higher hurdle before copyright will be recognised. For example, in France, a photograph attracts copyright protection if it is original and carries the 'imprint of the personality' of its author. What this means in practice is that the court will look at a combination of the image's exposure, lighting, composition etc to determine whether a work is sufficiently original.

Germany has a two-tier approach to photographic protection. 'Personal intellectual creations' which meet the European test for copyright

---

18 See, e.g., *Merlet v Mothercare* [1985] EWCA Civ 19 where a baby cape was not considered artistic and *Guild v Eskandar* [2001] FSR 38 which reached the same conclusion for sweaters displayed in the V&A.

19 *Infopaq International A/S v Danske Dagblades Forening* Case C-5/08.

20 *Levola Hengelo*, C-310/17.

21 2001/29/EC.

22 Rosati, Eleonora Is there copyright in the taste of a cheese? Sensory copyright finally makes its way to CJEU at: http://ipkitten.blogspot.com/2017/05/is-there-copyright-in-taste-of-cheese.html.

protectable photographs[23] are awarded the title of 'photographic work' and protected for the entire copyright term of the life of the artist plus 70 years. By contrast, a simple 'photograph' or 'snap' with no creativity or artistic quality is treated as a 'relative right' and protected for 50 years from the date of publication.

20.3.2   Fashion designs and copyright

A copyright work can potentially be a garment's design drawing. Even if a design document has copyright protection articles made to that design do not necessarily have copyright protection.[24] This issue was considered by the English Court of Appeal in a case about tracksuit tops.[25] One important reason for this limitation is that otherwise, fairly simple designs could potentially be used to restrict design innovation for the life of the creator plus 70 years.[26] This would present significant problems for the fashion industry as it could lead to 'copyright trolls' dominating a relatively small number of designs.

The one area where copyright is usually fairly easy to establish for fashion concerns two dimensional prints which are used on fabric. These are protected across Europe, including England, provided they are not completely generic (e.g., Breton stripes). Woven fabric is a more controversial topic under English law as it is technically not a flat two dimensional surface (even if it can appear that way). Therefore it is not a 'graphic work' and in theory it is entitled to less copyright protection than a printed fabric with the same appearance.

An English case managed to sidestep this issue when it considered whether tweed could be protected by copyright. Because the tweed fabric designers are so specialist, the court considered that the loom instructions (i.e., the 'ticket stamp') could be either a literary work or an artistic work on the basis that when an expert designer read the written instructions, an image of the finished fabric would be generated in the designer's mind![27]

---

23 I.e. include the artist's intellectual creation in terms of angle, focus, colour, etc.
24 Copyright, Designs and Patents Act 1988, s. 51 at: https://www.legislation.gov.uk/ukpga/1988/48/section/51.
25 *Lambretta Clothing Company Ltd v Teddy Smith (UK) Ltd and Anor* [2004] EWCA Civ 886.
26 This is the full term for copyright in the EU.
27 *Abraham Moon v Thornber* [2012] EWPCC 37.

As fashion becomes more technology focused, it may be easier to succeed in copyright litigation. For example, 3D printed designs can be protected based on literary copyright in the source code. If that code is copied then it will be possible to sue on the basis of literary copyright rather than worrying about whether the 3D item the code produces is a copyright work. Similarly, wearable technology incorporates a wide range of intellectual property rights including copyright in the software and potentially patents or trade secrets. Further, even if the physical item is hard to protect, the smartphone app may be protectable based on literary copyright in the source code.

20.3.3   Practical steps

 The quickest way of stopping any infringement is usually to write to the person who has copied you either directly or via a lawyer. This letter should put them on notice of your rights. This can be done nicely (the Jack Daniels way)[28] if it appears to be an honest mistake or more formally if it is serious and potentially damaging to your business. In addition to asking the infringer to stop, this letter will often ask for financial compensation, information on their manufacturer or suppliers (to go after the rest of the supply chain) and the number of products sold (in order to calculate the damages). It is often possible to reach an agreement without spending too much time or incurring too many legal fees.

Writing to an infringer before issuing proceedings is an important feature of Common Law procedure but this approach is less strictly adhered to in Civil Law jurisdictions.[29] In order to meet these 'pre-action' requirements, the letter should clearly state the right(s) relied upon, the owner(s) of those rights, the reason for the dispute and the desired remedy.

Regardless of the jurisdiction, writing is not necessary if there is a high risk that it will lead to evidence being destroyed. In these circumstances, you must act quickly when you are put on notice of the problem. This means that you have to convince the court to give you

---

28 A lawyer for Jack Daniels sent a famously polite cease and desist letter in 2012, see at: http://www.abajournal.com/news/article/jack_daniels_cease-and-desist_letter_goes_viral_for_being_exceeedingly_poli/.

29 In Civil Law jurisdictions, it is not uncommon for a party to receive a judgment in default or preliminary injunction without any warning. This is particularly an issue if you are based outside the jurisdiction.

the ability to obtain access to the relevant premises (see Chapter 19 regarding search and seizure orders, *saisies* and similar).

In some situations, writing to put an infringer on notice of a dispute creates the risk that they will apply to invalidate the right. Once a right's validity has been challenged by an intellectual property office, it is common for a court to stay proceedings until validity has been determined. This tends to be more of an issue for registered designs. Therefore, in some circumstances it can be wise to issue proceedings without a substantial delay.

20.3.4   Was it copied?

An important question for both copyright and unregistered designs is – was it copied? Sometimes this can be fairly straightforward. Often, if you check your sales records, you will have a record of your item being bought by the business that copied you. If the designs are near identical and you have evidence of the infringer purchasing your product, there is a strong inference of copying! In other instances, if your product was widely available and there are substantial similarities between it and the infringement, it may be possible to persuade the court to infer copying.

To establish copying, there are two sliding scales to consider. The first looks at how 'original' your copyright work is and the second looks at how much of your copyright work has been incorporated into the copy.

If you have a very original or distinctive copyright work, it is usually easier to establish an inference of copying because the court will be less likely to believe that the alleged infringing copy was made without the defendant having access to your work. If you have a very simple artistic work, such as a series of geometric shapes, it will be harder to show that someone copied your work as they could have been inspired from a similar starting point.

20.3.5   Extent of copying

This is a very important point to understand and the source of many copyright misconceptions. You do not compare the two works side by side (i.e., your work vs the copy) but rather you look at whether the whole or a *substantial part* of your work was included in the copy. This may sound like splitting hairs and in many cases it does not matter, but sometimes it is crucial. For example, imagine that someone copies your signature logo and uses it as one of many logos on a printed dress. Even though, when considered as a whole, the print on the dress is not similar to your logo, the whole of your logo was copied when it was printed on the dress.

 The copying does not have to be that precise and in some cases copyright infringement has been found even when the substantial part of the copyright work which was taken was closer to a concept. The most important English case to consider this issue concerns soft furnishings, a world which is increasingly linked to fashion. Designers Guild, a well-known 'posh' British design brand, was not happy when it saw its competitor Russell Williams selling a fabric which used the same colours, flowers and stripes to one of its designs. The dispute went right the way up to the House of Lords[30] (then the highest court in the UK and now replaced by the UK Supreme Court). The copied features included:

1. '. . .vertical stripes, with spaces between the stripes equal to the width of the stripe, and in each fabric flowers and leaves are scattered over and between the stripes, so as to give the same general effect.'

Designers Guild	Russell Williams

Note: These are the original case materials from the House of Lords archive, at: https://blogs.loc.gov/law/2015/06/house-of-lords-case-records-become-microfilm-stars/.

Figure 20.1   Comparison of the Designers Guild and Russell Williams fabrics

---

30 *Designers Guild Ltd v Russell Williams (Textiles) Ltd* [2000] UKHL 58.

2. '. . .a similar neo-Impressionistic style. . . a brushstroke technique, i.e., the use of one brush to create a stripe, showing the brush marks against the texture.'

This approach has been considered and adopted in several further cases. For example, in Australia,[31] the Federal Court found that there was infringement of Seafolly's copyright even though it was primarily

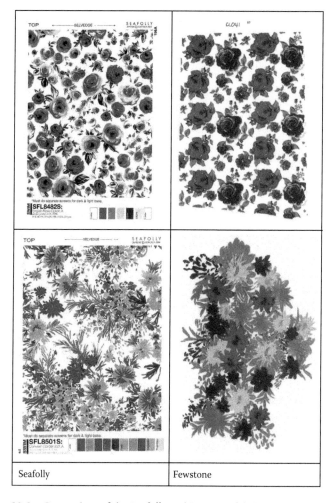

Figure 20.2   *Comparison of the Seafolly and Fewstone fabrics*

---

31 *Seafolly Pty Ltd v Fewstone Pty Ltd* [2014] FCA 321.

the design elements such as the layout and style which were taken and there were many substantial differences. Examples of some of the works in dispute are set out in Figure 20.2.

This Australian case is probably on the outer edges of what would be considered copyright infringement and part of the reason why the court found infringement was the clear evidence that Fewstone had copied. It is possible to copy without infringing the copyright in a work if you do not take a 'substantial part' of it. However, if there is a good evidence of an intention to copy, the court, particularly one in a Common Law jurisdiction, is more likely to apply the legal principle that 'what is worth copying, is worth protecting.'[32]

Another case at the edge of copyright protectability concerns the iconic London red bus. The predecessor to the English Intellectual Property Enterprise Court[33] decided that an image of a red bus on a black and white background had been copied when the photograph was of the same subject matter (Westminster Bridge) and reproduced the same idea (a black and white photograph with a red bus in the foreground). It was particularly relevant that the copied images had been manipulated to look more like the original. For example, the type of bus in the first image no longer travelled over Westminster Bridge so they had to insert a photo stock image in order to recreate the effect. This concerned many commentators for a while but it was a decision by a lower court (so not binding) and does not appear to have led to the drastic overhaul of copyright law that some people predicted. In circumstances where there is not such blatant copying, it is less likely to be an issue.[34]

Whilst this case was considered at the fringes of copyright protection in England, the courts in France and Germany would likely have reached the same conclusion.[35] France's test for copyright infringement is very broad and is general enough to include cases where '*characteristic and original elements*' have been taken. Germany specifically prevents both reproduction (i.e., a direct copy) and adaptation (which

---

32 *University of London Press Ltd v University Tutorial Press Ltd* [1916] 2 Ch 601.

33 The Patents County Court.

34 *Temple Island Collections Ltd v New English Teas Ltd and Anor* [2012] EWPCC 1 see more at: http://aandalawblog.blogspot.co.uk/2012/01/red-bus-suggests-copyright-law-is-not.html.

35 R. Burbidge, summarising a talk by Brigitte Linder, at: http://aandalawblog.blogspot.co.uk/2012/02/would-germany-and-france-find-red-bus.html.

includes alterations of an existing work and potentially a reimagining of that work).

The test for infringement of unregistered UK design right is also a *'substantial part,'* so the same principles apply as for copyright. For registered and unregistered Community designs, the question is do the same designs have the same overall impression on the informed user. The two tests often lead to the same outcome.

20.3.6   Copyright infringement around the world

In *China* it is hard to succeed in a copyright claim if you have not registered the copyright work in China. It is possible to lodge a complaint with the relevant local administrative body. The local enforcement body can then take administrative action including ordering an injunction against further infringement, confiscating infringing goods and the income associated with past sales of infringing goods and, sometimes, the tools used to infringe the rights, e.g., the plates for printing infringing fabric.

If you want more direct involvement, you can apply to the People's Court for an interim injunction followed by, hopefully, a finding of infringement. The damages are calculated based on the actual losses incurred. Where such losses are difficult to calculate, statutory damages of up to RMB 500,000 (around €65,000) are available.

As noted in Chapter 4, *the US* only offers very limited protection for fashion items. This may soften following the US Supreme Court's decision in *Star Athletica*.[36] Following that case, it is now clear that at least the surface decoration which is applied to clothing can be protected. However, it is unlikely that the US's restrictive approach to the protection of 'functional' items such as clothing, footwear and bags will fundamentally change any time soon.

As in China, while your copyright work may technically be valid and enforceable without registration in the US, in practice it is essential that you register a copyright work in order to be able to prevent third parties from infringing it.

36 *Star Athletica, LLC v. Varsity Brands, Inc.*, 580 U.S. ___ (2017).

In *Canada*, if a copyright work has been incorporated into a useful article, such as clothing or a bag, which has been reproduced more than 50 times, you lose the right to rely on copyright in court proceedings. In practice, copyright is therefore of limited use to the fashion industry.

If infringement is established, it is possible to get both damages for the loss you have suffered and an account of the infringer's profits. As an alternative, it is possible to claim statutory damages but these damages awards are typically much lower. It is also possible to obtain 'aggravated damages' if the infringer's activities injured your feelings of dignity and pride and, in some circumstances, 'punitive damages' where general and aggravated damages would be an inadequate remedy or the infringer's conduct is so egregious that they need to be taught a lesson.

20.3.7   Exceptions to copyright infringement

The most well known defence to copyright infringement is 'fair use.' This is a US legal concept which provides a legal defence to use of a copyright work in the US for a limited and 'transformative' purpose (such as commentary, criticism, parody or similar). The question of what is a 'transformative' use is not particularly clear-cut and often appears to require judicial guidance in order for the parties to a dispute to know where the line falls in their particular case. This gives a large amount of flexibility at the expense of legal certainty.

Fair use does not apply in Europe.

In Europe, the two main 'defences' (which are more properly characterised as exceptions to copyright infringement) concern 'fair dealing' (e.g., UK, Ireland) and 'free use' (e.g., France, Germany).

Fair dealing comes from a similar philosophical background to fair use but is a closed list approach. In other words, in order to qualify for the fair dealing exception, it is necessary to show that the use is for one of a small number of narrow categories such as 'criticism or review.' Even if your use falls into one of these categories, you must show that the amount copied was no more than necessary. This varies with the type of work. For example, you do not need to reproduce a book in order to review it; a few quotations will be sufficient. By contrast, you may need to reproduce an entire artwork in order to adequately comment on it.

In practice, fair dealing is rarely a relevant exception for the fashion industry.

Free use is essentially a freedom of expression defence. In order to qualify for the defence the new work must be so separate from the original that the first work 'fades' in comparison. This exception has recently been considered in the context of artwork but is less likely to be available for fashion. There is currently some debate as to whether free use goes further than the copyright exceptions permitted in EU copyright law. The German Federal Court of Justice has referred the issue to the CJEU in connection with the use of music sampling by the German dance music icons Kraftwerk.[37]

20.4   Passing off and unfair competition

Passing off is essentially a right to stop a third party trading off your goodwill. It is quite evidence heavy and is often included as part of a registered trade mark claim. In order to establish passing off you have to show each of the following elements:

Goodwill: This is the *'attractive force which brings in custom'*[38] to a business. The goodwill must be in the thing you are trying to claim goodwill in. For example, if you are claiming goodwill in the get up, it is not good enough to show that you have goodwill in your name, you must be able to show goodwill in the get up itself. In order to succeed in an action for passing off in, at least, England, the goodwill must exist in the relevant territory and it must be more than mere reputation.[39]

Misrepresentation: This means that your competitor's actions lead to consumers being 'deceived' into believing that their product is authorised by or somehow connected with you.

Damage: This could be your lost sales, the lost opportunity to charge a licence fee for the competitor's use or the profits that the competitor

---

37 See the press release at: http://juris.bundesgerichtshof.de/cgi-bin/rechtsprechung/document.py?G ericht=bgh&Art=pm&Datum=2017&Sort=3&nr=78496&pos=1&anz=87.

38 Lord Macnaughton in *IRC v Muller and Co's Margarine* [1901] AC 217 at 223.

39 *Starbucks (HK) Ltd and another v British Sky Broadcasting Group (No 2)* [2015] UKSC 31; [2015] 1 WLR 2628, Lord Neuberger at para. 47: 'In other words, I consider that we should reaffirm that the law is that a claimant in a passing off claim must establish that it has actual goodwill in this jurisdiction. . .'.

has made from using your goodwill. Usually if goodwill and misrepresentation are found, it is fairly easy to establish that there has been damage (although the level of damage could be quite low).

20.4.1   Get up

 It is theoretically possible, but usually very difficult, to rely on passing off to stop someone using a product with the same get up. This is because it is hard to prove that sufficient goodwill resides in the get up alone (i.e., without the brand name or logo). Although the tests are different, the fundamental difficulty with proving passing off in relation to get up is similar to the difficulty in obtaining shape mark protection (see Chapter 3 for details).

The cases where a claimant has successfully established passing off in relation to get up alone tend to be where the product is very distinctive and popular and there is enough evidence to show that consumers buy the product based on the 'get up' and not, for example, the brand name.

20.4.2   False endorsement

False endorsement is a type of passing off which only applies if the person in the image is famous (i.e., has goodwill). While image rights are not available in the UK, false endorsement can create a similar sort of protection to image rights – see Chapter 5.

There have been two prominent English cases on false endorsement in recent years. The first concerned a UK radio station which photoshopped its logo into an image of a famous racing car driver (Eddie Irvine) and then used it in advertising.[40]

The second case concerned Topshop's use of an image of Rihanna on one of its T-shirts.[41] Although Topshop's supplier had the right to use the copyright in the photograph, they had not asked for Rihanna's permission to use it on the T-shirt. This case is discussed in more detail in Chapter 5.

---

40 *Irvine and Ors v Talksport Ltd* [2003] EWCA Civ 423, this photoshopping was found to be a false endorsement.

41 *Fenty and Ors v Arcadia Group Brands Ltd and Anor* [2015] EWCA Civ 3.

In short, Rihanna was able to persuade the court that by using her
image on the T-shirt, Topshop and its supplier were incorrectly telling
the public that she had approved or otherwise endorsed the product.
In reaching this decision, it was important that Rihanna is well-known
in fashion circles and that Topshop had tried to establish a connection
with her in the past, for example tweeting about her coming into their
flagship London store. The upshot of this case is that you should be
careful when using celebrity images on clothing.

20.4.3   Unfair competition and parasitic copying in France

Passing off is a very Common Law affair. Elsewhere in Europe, the
same types of disputes are dealt with by the law of unfair competition.
Unfair competition can be much broader and covers scenarios such as
employee poaching which, in the UK and Ireland, tend to be dealt with
by contract law or by the tort of inducement to breach contract.

In France, 'unfair competition' is not limited to intellectual property
disputes.[42] It includes any actions which have the aim or effect of
adversely impacting another person's business – this is usually, but not
necessarily, due to a competitor's actions. The usual remedy for unfair
competition is payment of a financial sum to compensate for the harm
caused including loss of clients or employees, loss of chance, or moral
harm such as reputational damage.

In order for your unfair competition claim to succeed: (i) the potential
defendant must have committed a *faute* (a tort); (ii) you must have suffered a *préjudice* (harm or loss); and (iii) the harm or loss suffered must
have resulted from the *faute*.

Unfair competition claims usually concern one or more of the following
kinds of *faute*:

Disorganisation: A business' actions disrupt the proper functioning
of your business (e.g., headhunting entire teams or key employees in
bad faith).

Damage to reputation (*dénigrement*): A business discredits another
by creating doubt as to the honour of the company or its managers, its
expertise or its financial status. If the statements are true, you can still

---

42 Reformed French Civil Code, Arts 1240 and 1241.

be caught by the tort if they are made in bad faith (this is similar to the English law of malicious falsehood).

Economic hijacking (parasitisme économique): A business benefits from a competitor's resources when it has not had any involvement or provided any contribution to the creation of those resources (in practice this often overlaps with intellectual property infringement).

Confusion: A business holding itself out in a way which is likely to cause confusion in the minds of its competitor's clients (this is the most similar to passing off).

In practice, unfair competition is often combined with other claims, particularly intellectual property infringement, although this is not necessary.

 Unfair competition claims can often push the boundaries of what is possible under intellectual property law. For example, Zadig & Voltaire was able to stop a competitor, Berenice, from recreating the layout, design and various 'visual codes' of its store on the basis it is likely to create confusion in the minds of customers between the two businesses.[43] While it is in theory possible to register a store layout as a trade mark this is very difficult to obtain and even harder to enforce.

If you claim unfair competition in order to reinforce an intellectual property infringement action, the unfair competition claims must be based on different facts. Failure to do so is the most common reason an unfair competition claim fails.[44]

20.4.4   Parasitic copying – *parasitisme*

Over time, the French courts have developed the general *faute* of economic hijacking (which applies to all kinds of commercial activities) to a specialist branch of 'parasitic copying,' or *parasitisme* which is a *faute* involving the close copying of another person's ideas, image, brand, product and essentially hijacking the goodwill, investment and noto-

---

43 See Cour d'appel de Paris, Pôle 5 – Chambre 2, 16 Avril 2010, n° 09/00407.

44 In the Decision from the Tribunal de grande instance de Paris, 3e chambre 1re section, 13 Avril 2010, n° 08/15883, registered design right in swimwear was found to be infringed, but as the facts constituting faute were the same to unfair competition, that action failed.

riety. The idea is that by doing so, the competitor is acting a bit like a parasite (hence the name).

Parasitic copying is a particular problem within the luxury goods industry. A high-profile decision in this area concerned L'Oréal and Cartier[45] and shows how broad the scope of parasitic copying can be in France. L'Oréal's advertising campaign for Opium perfume[46] featured a leopard together with red, gold and black jewels, all of which were very similar to Cartier's branding. Cartier alleged that L'Oréal copied its branding in order to benefit from Cartier's image and reputation.

Cartier won at first instance and L'Oréal appealed the decision on the basis that it effectively gave Cartier a monopoly right regarding the use of feline animals with particular colours and jewels (i.e., much broader scope than copyright protection) and consequently, the judges had used the theory of economic hijacking and parasitic copying to substitute rights which should be limited to the field of intellectual property. L'Oréal also argued that it breached the fundamental right to freedom of expression.[47]

The Paris Court of Appeal confirmed that parasitic copying had occurred on the basis that 'parasitic copying involves a company unjustly benefiting from the notoriety of a brand which has been acquired through legitimate investments.' The judge noted that unlike other unfair competition claims, parasitic copying depends on 'an overall appreciation of different elements, independent from any risk of confusion.' Any deliberate intention to copy was unnecessary and unintentional copying was sufficient.

In other words, parasitic copying can give very broad scope of protection even when there is no likelihood of confusion, direct copying or bad faith. In other European countries, particularly England, such a broad scope of protection is very controversial.

To add further insult to injury, L'Oréal was ordered to pay €1 million damages on the basis that four different advertising campaigns had been run over a two year period and this sum was required to compensate the harm Cartier suffered to its reputation, together with the

---

45 Decision of the Cour d'appel de Paris, 21 Octobre 2015, n° 13/08861.
46 L'Oréal had the right to exploit Yves Saint Laurent's perfumes.
47 European Convention of Human Rights, Art. 10.

communication costs which it had to incur in order to reinstate its visual identity.

 Consequently in France, parasitic copying can be easier to prove than intellectual property infringement (depending on the right) and offers a much broader scope of protection. There is no need to consider a right's validity, the technology involved or actual infringement. This means it is a very powerful tool in the armoury but also a weapon which can be wielded against you when doing business in France.

Many fashion designers rely heavily on unfair competition claims for this reason. Starting a claim on the basis of unfair competition can be a useful strategy as it reduces the risk of any counterclaims to invalidate registered intellectual property rights.

More recently, the Paris High Court held that unfair competition existed in a case involving a mobile gaming app which had been largely copied (i.e., cloned) by a competitor. The court considered that the copying of the overall get-up, look and feel of the app itself was close enough to create 'confusion in the minds of users between the competitor and the originating company,' without needing to delve into whether the copyright in the source code behind the app was valid or had been infringed. This saved both parties and the court a lot of time and expense but meant that a much more broad brush approach was given to the case and arguably a much broader scope of protection awarded than is necessary in order to stimulate competition.

20.4.5   Unfair competition and *concorrenza parassitaria* in Italy

 Under Italian law,[48] unfair competition claims can arise in similar situations to France, namely:

1.   use of a competitor's trade mark or other distinctive sign in order to create confusion;[49]

2.   slavish imitation of a competitor's products or means of presenting its services;[50]

---

48 Italian Civil Code, Art. 2598. The provisions regulating unfair competition in Italy are considered to be a specific application of the so-called '*neminem laedere*' established by, ibid., Art. 2043.

49 Ibid., Art. 2598 No.1.

50 Ibid., Art. 2598 No. 1, second para.

3. discrediting or appropriating a competitor's products or business/activity;[51] and

4. directly or indirectly, using any other means that is not in line with the principles of professional fairness.[52]

Parasitic copying is covered by the third and fourth types identified above.[53] To be caught by parasitic copying, you need to engage in repetitive conduct which considered together represents the repeated and continuous copying of a competitor's initiatives. This type of conduct is deemed to constitute the systematic unlawful exploitation of the competitor's work and creativity.[54] This can apply even if, taken alone, each example of parasitic copying could be considered lawful.

In order to claim parasitic copying, there must be evidence that the alleged infringer has adopted a continuous and repetitive path of copying your initiative. Because repetitive conduct is an essential component, even if there is a single egregious act of copying, that is not enough to establish parasitic competition and the related claim will be rejected.[55] Getting adequate evidence together to prove repetitive copying in court is very difficult. Consequently, Italian courts are reluctant to recognise this type of unfair competition.

Copying is considered parasitic in the following circumstances:

1. if it takes place within a short period of time from the competitor's use (this is called *sincronic* parasitic competition); or

2. from the competitor's latest and most significant initiative if multiple examples have been taken (i.e. *diacronic* parasitic competition).

The Italian Supreme Court has clarified that 'short period of time' means the time frame during which the competitor expects to receive

---

51 Ibid., Art. 2598 No. 2.

52 Ibid., Art. 2598 No. 3.

53 This is considered an 'open' provision which includes types of unfair competition conducts that are not expressly codified in the previous provisions.

54 Italian Supreme Court decision No. 5582/1984.

55 Italian Supreme Court decision No. 9387/1994.

revenues from their initiative. It is also includes the time period when the initiative is advertised and actions are taken pre launch.[56]

20.4.6 Parasitic copying in practice – *Gucci v Guess*

Parasitic copying was an important part of the famous dispute between Gucci and Guess. This saga saw Gucci battling Guess worldwide, starting in the US. This litigation ended in Italy and a global settlement was reached in early 2018.

The dispute began in 2009 when Gucci sued Guess and one of its online retailers, Zappos, for trade mark infringement and unfair competition, including parasitic competition. This claim was based on sales in Italy of two pairs of Guess shoes which Gucci considered to be a 'slavish imitation' of its shoes. Guess denied all of the claims and counter claimed to invalidate Gucci's trade marks on the basis that they were not distinctive and, in relation to one mark,[57] had not been used.

The Court of Milan,[58] at first instance, denied all of Gucci's requests including its unfair competition claim. The Milan court went on to invalidate several trade marks[59] and reject the remaining counterclaims. Gucci appealed. The Court of Appeal[60] found Guess liable for parasitic copying. The court considered the techniques and actions adopted by Guess overall. While individually they were probably the right side of the line, when considered in combination, there appeared to be a continuous copying of Gucci's trade marks.[61] The court noted that Guess sold very similar products which specifically recalled Gucci's shape, colours, materials, graphics and decorative elements.

 Therefore, regardless of the risk of likelihood of confusion, due to Guess's continuous conduct which the court considered systematically exploited Gucci's creativity and commercial initiative, Guess was

---

56 Italian Supreme Court decision No. 13423/2004.

57 Italian trade mark No. 331121.

58 Court of Milan, decision No. 6095/2013 adopted on January 10, 2013.

59 Trade marks 105760, 940491, 1057600, 940490, 971291, 4462735, 5172218.

60 Milan Court of Appeal, decision No. 3308/2014 adopted on September 15, 2014. This decision is also interesting because the court affirmed having personal jurisdiction over Zappos, Inc a US company with no branch in Italy and which carries out its business only through e-commerce, mainly in the US market. The court based its decision exclusively on the fact that the alleged tort (i.e., the selling of a pair of shoes infringing the plaintiff's trademarks) occurred in Italy.

61 In breach of Art. 2598, No. 3 of the Italian Civil Code.

found liable for parasitic copying. The determination of damages for such unlawful conduct was then left to a separate proceeding through the help of experts (*'Consulenza Tecnica d'Ufficio'*).

By contrast, Gucci's claims based on trade mark infringement failed based on very few small existing differences between the Gucci and Guess marks. This shows the strength of an unfair competition claim and how much more flexible it can be than trade mark infringement.

20.5   Designs

The key issue with registered Community designs (RCDs) is that because they are not examined for validity, they can be very easy to invalidate in response to someone alleging infringement of the right. This is often on the basis of earlier similar designs that the design owner previously advertised or sold. It is possible to challenge validity in response to an infringement claim in any court of a Member State which has been designated a Community Design Court. If you are threatened with infringement proceedings, it is also possible to file a pre-emptive application at the EUIPO to invalidate the registered Community design. In most instances, national courts will not consider the design until the question of validity has been decided by EUIPO. It is therefore important to file a protective claim before writing to a potential infringer. You do not necessarily need to serve this claim (depending on the procedural rules in the relevant jurisdiction) but filing the claim will protect your position.

The question of the scope of a design is very important when considering infringement. A design that is very unusual will have a much larger scope of protection than a fairly standard design which makes only minimal changes from the norm. This issue is discussed in more detail in Chapter 6.

The difficulty that many unregistered design owners face is getting the right balance between claiming a broad enough scope so that the court finds that the copied design infringes without unintentionally invalidating the design by including earlier designs, or 'prior art,' which are used to challenge the design's validity. This needs to be handled with care and requires careful thought and legal expertise to get it right.

Even if a design is found to be valid and infringed (because the copy has the same overall impression as the design), there may be a defence if artistic expression is in issue.[62] This issue came up in a dispute between an artist, Nadja Plesner, and Louis Vuitton which was heard by the District Court of the Hague. Ms Plesner created an artwork called Darfurnica which included images of starving children holding Louis Vuitton bags. Louis Vuitton sued on the basis of their RCD for the LV print. This was no doubt selected as unlike copyright, there is no statutory defence of freedom of expression in the Community Designs Regulation.

Nevertheless, the Dutch Court concluded that Ms Plesner's overall right to freedom of expression under the European Convention on Human Rights trumped Louis Vuitton's design rights and noted that the average viewer of the painting would not conclude that Louis Vuitton was actually involved in the conflict in Darfur. The court suggested that owners of well-known brands had to accept critical use to a higher degree than others.[63]

Similar issues apply to unregistered Community designs (UCD). There is more flexibility in terms of identifying and selecting the design but the right must be correctly identified at the outset and take into account the risk of earlier designs with the same overall impression invalidating the design.

The worlds of fast fashion and UCDs recently collided in the Milan Court of First Instance which confirmed the validity of an interim injunction in favour of Diesel and Marni's parent company against Zara.[64] This case is important as it confirms the availability of pan-EU injunctive and other relief in relation to Community designs.

 The case also noted that when assessing design freedom in relation to clothing, the important question is not so much the functional aspects (which are dictated by the shape of the human body) but rather the 'extremely crowded character of the clothing sector (in particular, jeans).'[65] Consequently, there can be a valid UCD in relation to small differences provided they are 'perceived by the informed user as different from already known shapes.'[66]

---

62 Under ECHR, Art. 10.

63 ECtHR, 15 February 2005, NJ 2006, 39, *Steel and Morris v UK*, para. 94, known as the 'McLibel' case.

64 Decision 5390/2018.

65 Translation from the Italian by Eleonora Rosati.

66 Eleonora Rosati, 'Milan court applies Nintendo v Big Ben in fast fashion lawsuit against ZARA', at: http://ipkitten.blogspot.com/2018/07/milan-court-applies-nintendo-v-big-ben.html.

UK unregistered design right takes a slightly different approach to Community designs. The essential question for UK unregistered design right is has a '*substantial part*' of the design been copied? Evidence, usually from a designer, is the key to success. Again, any earlier examples of highly similar designs can either invalidate the claimed right or significantly limit the scope of protection.

20.6   Domain names

The process for domain names is a little more complicated. As mentioned above, they are not really an intellectual property right but are governed by a contractual agreement. For gTLDs you have three options: the UDRP, URS or a lawsuit in the relevant national court. Other ccTLDs such as .co.uk have their own dispute resolution procedures.

20.6.1   UDRP

The UDRP is the Uniform Domain Name Dispute Resolution Policy. It sets out the basis on which you can challenge the registration of a gTLD domain name (e.g., a .com) and have it transferred into your name or cancelled. This is usually on the basis of prior trade mark rights. The process is like a mini arbitration and can be slow[67] so if you are concerned about counterfeit goods being sold via the website associated with the domain name, relying on the UDRP alone is unlikely to yield satisfactory results. Bear in mind that if your trade mark is a normal word or name it is not possible to stop someone else registering the mark as a domain unless you can establish that they registered it in bad faith. For example, someone registering Apple.org for an organisation dedicated to apple farming is legitimate and could not be stopped by the technology giant.

20.6.2   URS

This is the Uniform Rapid Suspension system. As the name suggests, although it is much faster than UDRP, it does not lead to the domain name being transferred or cancelled but rather suspended indefinitely. This is a helpful process where the domain name in question is not commercially valuable but is causing problems by diverting custom.

---

67 ICANN aims to have a decision within 60 days of an application but it can take longer.

20.6.3   The national court

 If you are taking action against an infringer, such as trade mark infringement, it makes sense to add the domain name into the action. The court can order that the domain name is transferred or cancelled. This is helpful where you have multiple domain names or use of an infringing domain name is one of several issues which have arisen in relation to an infringer.

21 If you are sued

This chapter is primarily written from the point of view of being sued for intellectual property infringement. This is because intellectual property is so important to the fashion industry, and many fashion law disputes centre on intellectual property. However, in practice a wide range of disputes can arise. By way of example, disputes over supply contracts, leasehold or other real estate issues,[1] negligence,[2] product liability,[3] termination of employment, agency or franchise relationships, discrimination, etc.

The procedural options set out in Chapter 19 and issues set out in Chapter 20 apply here as well, in some cases from the opposite perspective. For example, in some jurisdictions you may be able to argue that the threats are 'groundless' and claim compensation if they have caused you any damage such as scaring off a customer or a supplier.

If you are defending a claim, it is important to find out exactly what happened as quickly as possible and then get legal advice on the relative merits of the claim. You will also need to consider whether the person claiming the infringement has proven ownership of the rights. This is usually fairly simple with registered rights where it is possible to simply refer to the relevant register (unless they have failed to register an exclusive licence) but it can be less straightforward with unregistered

---

1 In addition to obvious issues such as non-payment of rent, issues such as being a nuisance to neighbouring residents and businesses and structural defects created during the fit out stage can also arise.

2 A heartbreaking recent example of this concerns a mirror in a retail park which was not properly secured and fell onto a small child. Hugo Boss, who operated the store, was fined £1.1million for breach of health and safety regulations, see at: https://www.healthandsafetyatwork.com/risk-assessment/hugo-boss-fine-bicester-village.

3 If your products cause harm to your customers, e.g., death, personal injury or material damage to personal belongings (exceeding €500), you are at risk of a claim. This is more likely to be an issue with accessories such as jewellery and with related product ranges such as perfume, cosmetics and skin care.

rights such as copyright and unregistered designs. If anything, such as the ownership position, is unclear, you are entitled to ask for more information. Similarly, if a very short deadline is set, you are entitled to request an extension to obtain legal advice and respond.

 In some instances, your businesses' knowledge of the infringement may be relevant. For example, if you are simply importing or dealing in goods which infringe copyright you are likely to be a secondary infringer and consequently, it is necessary for the rights owner to establish that you knew about the infringement in order for you to be liable. You will be fixed with knowledge from receipt of the letter.

If the issue concerns copyright or design infringement, speak to the design team and find out what was used as the inspiration or if they relied on fabric or a design from a third party such as a factory. Design teams are under a lot of pressure and with the best will in the world, it is not unknown for them to stray toward the wrong side of the inspiration/copying line. Another common issue arises if you source the designs and/or fabric from a factory. It is not unknown for these fabrics to have been copied from online images or other existing fabric designs. Do your due diligence as quickly as possible. Your legal strategy in defending a claim can only succeed if you have all of the relevant information.

21.1 The validity torpedo

If you are threatened with a lawsuit on the basis of some registered rights such as trade marks, designs or patents, it may be possible to threaten and, if you have good grounds, commence proceedings to invalidate or revoke the right. Invalidity actions essentially argue that the right should not have been granted in the first place because it did not meet the relevant qualifying criteria. For example, if the right is a trade mark you might argue that it was devoid of distinctive character at the time it was filed.

 Similarly, if a mark has not been put to genuine use for five years (for some or all of the goods and services for which it is registered), it is possible to apply to have the mark revoked for non-use.[4] It is possible

---

4 It is possible to revoke all trade marks for non-use, the period in the EU and in Member States is fixed at five years. Other countries have a shorter period for non-use.

to revoke the whole of a mark or only part of it if use can be proven in relation to some of the goods and services for which it is registered.

If you commence invalidity or revocation proceedings at the relevant intellectual property office,[5] this can mean that it is not possible to sue on the basis of the right until after the invalidity decision and any appeals of that decision have been exhausted. This can take several years.

Filing an invalidity action is known as 'torpedoing' the rights as it kicks the claim into the long grass. This is particularly useful in fashion claims where the subject of the claim will often be old news by the time the relevant intellectual property office has determined whether the rights are valid. However, it can be very frustrating if it is your right which is torpedoed. For this reason many businesses adopt a 'file the claim first and ask questions later' approach to infringement proceedings.

21.2   Make the most of any prior warning

Most disputes do not come as a complete surprise as businesses tend to prefer to try to reach informal settlements before involving the lawyers. This is perfectly sensible but you need to be careful about what you say before proceedings are initiated.

Different European countries have different conventions on how much notice they are required to give of a potential claim and the procedure for settlement. By way of example, in Germany, it is common to file a claim before raising the possibility in correspondence. This is because it enables the claimant[6] to choose the court and 'seize jurisdiction'. This has an important tactical advantage because it prevents the defendant from using the torpedo tactic.

In England, it is more normal to write a letter before action which gives the other party a fixed amount of time (which must be reasonable) to respond. However, it is possible to file a claim without serving it and write a letter in the meantime if you are concerned about the risk of a torpedo or running out of time for the limitation period. What is reasonable varies, depending on the complexity of the dispute, a simple

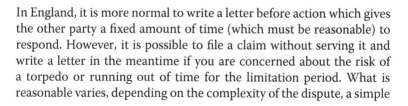

---

5 Such as EUIPO.

6 Also known as the 'plaintiff'.

money claim will require less time to investigate than a complicated intellectual property rights dispute. The letter before action is sometimes followed by a 'without prejudice save as to costs' letter. This is a private settlement proposal which can only be made available to the court if there is a dispute over costs after the claim has been decided by the court. This system is available in Ireland but not elsewhere in Europe where settlement negotiations can potentially be raised in future proceedings.

As mentioned in Chapter 19, it is possible that the first time you hear about potential proceedings is when the court bailiff, supervising solicitor or a similar expert enters your premises and tries to record the alleged infringements by seizing stock and other documents. This process can be quite distressing for your staff so it is worth warning personnel and having a procedure regarding who should be called (both in terms of management and lawyers) if the issue arises.

21.3   Responding to a legal letter

If you do get some warning before the claim is filed, there are various things that you can do but they boil down to three options:

1. Instruct a lawyer.

2. Respond yourself.

3. Do nothing.

It can be a stressful experience to receive a legal letter and the temptation is to go for the first law firm you come across. You can get lucky with this approach but it is an important decision and worth some serious research before committing. This can be as simple as asking friends or business connections such as your accountant (if you have one) for referrals but it is worth following up with your own research. Who are their clients? What is their charge out rate? Where are their offices? How responsive are they to your initial email or phone call?

 Sometimes it is possible to resolve the issue yourself without involving a lawyer. However, the risks here are that you end up paying a lot more than you should or agreeing to terms which could limit the opportunities for your business in the future. For example, if you sign very broad 'undertakings' to not use a particular word or phrase in your business you may contractually limit yourself to a greater extent than you need to. There is also a risk that the case escalates to litigation more quickly and you lose the opportunity to reach a settlement without getting embroiled in litigation. Even if you have instructed a lawyer, sometimes a business-to-business approach further down the line, once everyone has put their cards on the table, can lead to a quicker resolution.

If the amount in dispute is low (so it would not be worth them suing you) or you think they are just 'trying it on' you could decide to do nothing or potentially just withdraw the item from sale or simply stop whatever activity they are complaining about. This is obviously the cheapest option but if you have not resolved the underlying issue it can lead to a lot of sleepless nights and a legal claim popping up in the future. If the claim is a simple money claim, you can simply pay up and avoid the dispute. The settlement amount which is likely to be acceptable varies between jurisdictions and depends on the extent of the infringement (both in terms of the number of products sold and how closely they infringe). It is also common for the settlement sum to include an amount in relation to the legal costs incurred. The amount that it is reasonable to request can vary substantially between jurisdictions.

22 Taxation and logistics

Tax is rarely the driving force behind the decision to set up a fashion business. However, it can be crucial in determining your business' success. Identifying and taking advantage of tax reliefs and operating in the most tax efficient way for your business makes sense. The consequences of getting tax wrong can be huge whether overpaying and losing shareholder profits or underpaying and being hit with a substantial tax liability not to mention the potential reputational damage.

Tax is an entire topic in itself and this chapter does not pretend to come close to everything you need to know or do. However, it does touch on some of the most relevant taxes for the fashion industry and the sorts of issues you need to be aware of when operating your business.

22.1 Tax and public relations

 Various high-profile scandals regarding taxes paid by European businesses have highlighted the importance of getting tax right.[1] Bear in mind that as your business grows, expands and changes, so too does your tax liability. No business is immune from these issues and it is well worth taking the time to work out exactly how your business operates and what you need to do to be tax efficient without tax evasion.

22.1.1 The Dolce and Gabbana example

The Italian Supreme Court, Criminal Division[2] relatively recently acquitted the designers Domenico Dolce and Stefano Gabbana for tax

---

1 See, e.g.: https://www.theguardian.com/fashion/2017/dec/04/gucci-offices-raided-suspected-tax-evasion-prada-dolce-gabbana.

2 Cass. Pen., Sezione III, decision n° 43809, dated 30/10/2015.

evasion under the Italian Law.[3] This decision came after the Milan Court of Appeal had previously found the famous fashion duo liable and sentenced them to 18 months in prison for omitted tax returns by Gado SARL in 2004 and 2005. Gado is a Luxembourg company which was assigned ownership of two valuable trade marks for D&G and DOLCE AND GABBANA. These marks were previously owned by Gado's Italian holding company D&G S.r.l.

The prosecution accused Dolce and Gabbana of not paying approximately €200 million of taxable income on the basis that the use of the Luxembourg company fell within the Italian legal concept of *Esterovestizione* (or 'Relocation Abroad'). This involves setting up a company in a country, in this case, Luxembourg, which has a more favourable tax regime than your main country of business, Italy, with the aim of claiming the income made as taxable in the foreign country rather than in Italy. Usually the income invested abroad consists of the capital gains resulting from the transfer of stocks.

The factors considered by the lower courts when they decided to convict the designers included that the Luxembourg company did not hire any personnel following the company's creation and Italy was the place where the main corporate decisions were taken and consequently the 'place of effective management' of the company.

This concept of the 'place of effective management of the company' was essential to the decision. It set out the criteria to be used in order to determine the fiscal residence of the corporation under investigation (i.e., Gado). The Italian courts considered the Italy-Luxembourg Treaty on the double taxation that has been ratified in Italy[4] and which precisely defines such term as the place of corporate business, the place where the directors reside or the place where the shareholders' meetings occur.

On its second appeal, the Italian Supreme Court reversed the previous two decisions and acquitted the designers. In particular, the Supreme Court noted that just because a company has been incorporated under the laws of another Member State with a more favourable tax regime, does not immediately give rise to the presumption of a fiscal fraud. The court clarified that it is unlawful and constitutes *'abuso del diritto di*

---

3 Art. 5 Legislative Decree 74/2000 – omission of tax returns filing.
4 Law No.747/1982.

stabilimento nel caso di esterovestizione' (i.e., misuse of the company's right of establishment) if no transfer has occurred and where the corporate creation was a wholly artificial arrangement.

Because Gado was a foreign subsidiary of the Italian parent company, the Italian Supreme Court held that the company's place of effective management cannot be the only criteria to consider in order to determine the existence or not of the fiscal fraud. This may give more opportunities for creative corporate structure charts or may simply lead to this loophole being blocked by the Italian Government.

 The point is that taxation is complicated and even large multinational brands can get it wrong (or risk doing so). Although Dolce and Gabbana were subsequently acquitted they had to endure several years of stress with the threat of imprisonment hanging over then. This is not in anyone's interests! Make sure you appoint a good tax adviser and auditors and if some advice sounds too good to be true, get a second opinion.

22.2   Customs and international trade

As for all businesses involved in the manufacture and transport of goods around the world, Customs can present a range of issues for the fashion industry. Goods in the fashion industry can have very high duty rates imposed on both the materials used to manufacture the products and on the material itself. The value of your brand can also create tax issues as it is a valuable asset which needs to be taken into account when pricing the goods.

There are various means of pricing goods which are acceptable for Customs. The easiest and preferred method is the transaction value (i.e., the amount for which the goods will be sold to the end consumer). This can present problems. For example, the duty paid on goods tends to be linked to the base price of the goods ignoring any deductions or similar which may be made on the goods prior to sale. Further, it cannot apply to items such as samples which will not be sold.

In theory all methods of calculation should lead to the same ultimate tax figure but in practice it can be difficult to get the correct information such as the cost of materials as many factories are unwilling to provide precise information.

Royalties and licence fees present specific challenges which are outside the scope of this book but many of the tax scandals have the royalty and licence value at their heart so bear in mind that even if you fall the right side of the line as far as the tax authorities are concerned, you still risk being damned in the court of public opinion.

The classification of goods is an important part of the Customs form- filling process. As fashion trends such as gender neutral clothing continue, this process can be considerably more complicated as it can be hard to determine into which box your goods fit. The form is based on both the type of good and the gender and age of the ultimate wearer of the goods. If you face major uncertainty, you can request a classification ruling from Customs before importing the goods.

22.2.1   Incoterms

An important part of any shipping process is deciding which incoterm will apply to the shipment. Incoterms set out when responsibility (and consequently risk) for the goods passes. The International Chamber of Commerce has defined incoterms[5] and often a shipping contract will simply refer to one of these incoterms by their three letter acronym. They range from the most onerous (EXW) to the least onerous (DDP).

EXW or Ex Works means that the goods are available to be picked up from the seller's factory and from there responsibility for shipping the goods and complying with all Customs procedures and tariffs rests with the buyer.

DDP or Delivered Duty Paid means, as the name suggests, that the goods are delivered to the buyer with all shipping and Customs formalities sorted out. This is much easier for the buyer but typically comes at a price.

22.3   The European Union Customs Union

The European Union Customs Union (the Customs Union) consists of all EU Member States plus Monaco and various UK territories such as Guernsey and Jersey which are not part of the EU. In addition, the EU

---

5 The current list was updated in 2010 and is available from the ICC website, at: https://iccwbo.org/resources-for-business/incoterms-rules/incoterms-rules-2010/.

has separate customs unions with Andorra, San Marino, and Turkey. Members of the Customs Union impose a common external tariff (i.e., tax) on all goods entering the union. Once goods have entered one of the Customs Union's member states, no further customs duties (i.e., taxes) are levied on goods while they remain in the Customs Union.

The European Commission negotiates for and on behalf of the Customs Union as a whole in international trade deals such as those with the World Trade Organization. This puts members of the Customs Union in a much stronger negotiating position.

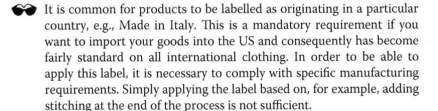 Customs audits in theory happen on a regular basis – at least every three years as this is the statute of limitation for customs duties and import VAT (although this limit can be extended where there is fraudulent behaviour). However, the administrative burden of a three year audit is very high so voluntary risk assessments and disclosures have become common. Risk assessments are linked to the annual import volume, sensitivity of import goods, applicable duty rates and any customs irregularities which have occurred in the past.

22.4   VAT

No matter what you are selling, Value Added Tax or VAT will be added to the price when you sell most products in Europe. The precise amount varies between countries. Some products are rated 0 per cent for VAT such as children's clothes (i.e., VAT is applied but the percentage rate is 0 per cent). This is different to no VAT being applied. Payments of import VAT and the distribution of VAT between member states of the Customs Union are based on a special agreement.

22.5   Product labelling

It is common for products to be labelled as originating in a particular country, e.g., Made in Italy. This is a mandatory requirement if you want to import your goods into the US and consequently has become fairly standard on all international clothing. In order to be able to apply this label, it is necessary to comply with specific manufacturing requirements. Simply applying the label based on, for example, adding stitching at the end of the process is not sufficient.

Complying with the correct country of origin labelling is important for two reasons. First, it affects the level of duty applied to the goods. Secondly, if the country of origin labelling is incorrect you risk a claim for false advertising either from the relevant regulator or (less likely in Europe) a class action from a consumer group.

When importing temporary goods such as samples or archive works, the Customs issues become even more complex because they are one-off items. In these sorts of situation it is even more important to get specialist advice to avoid goods being detained or an unjustifiably high levy being applied.[6]

Customs also plays a very important role in combating counterfeits and preventing the import of parallel goods which originated outside the EEA. This is discussed in more detail in Chapter 24.

22.6   What might the future hold?

The European Commission plans to stop cross-border tax schemes where at least one of the countries involved is within the EU. How this will work in practice remains to be seen.

On 21 June 2017, the European Commission proposed new transparency rules for intermediaries (such as tax advisers, accountants, banks and lawyers) who design and promote tax planning schemes for their clients. The aim is to create a more cautious approach to tax planning. The proposals follow in the wake of the recent leaks from various offshore advisers such as the Panama papers.

The European Commission intends for the new reporting requirements to enter into force on 1 January 2019, with EU Member States obliged to exchange information every three months after that.[7]

---

6 For a fascinating insight into the fine line between whether or not something is classified as 'art' by Customs and the economic consequences of this classification, see E. Burstein and S. Wagner (eds), *Taxing Art: When Objects Travel* Gestalten, Berlin 2011.

7 See at: http://europa.eu/rapid/press-release_IP-17-1663_en.htm.

23 Selling up

A business goes through many stages as it evolves and grows and it is very rare for a large business' founder to remain the sole or even the majority owner over the medium to long term. The whole of the business may be sold or some equity may be sold in return for investment and expertise (for example, under the private equity or venture capital model). You may even float the business on a stock exchange.

This decision may be made in order to help your business go to the next step or to help you move on to new projects or possibly even retire. Whatever the motivation, there are many decisions which you can make in advance which will put you in the best possible position when it comes to selling up. Conversely, you may decide to grow your business by buying up another business which is strategically beneficial for your longer term growth. Although this chapter is geared toward the sale of your business, the same issues apply if you are purchasing another business.

This chapter talks you through the basics of the sale process and discusses some of things to think about in advance of sale.

23.1   Your business or your brand?

 There are essentially two options when it comes to sale or acquisition. You can sell or purchase some or all of the business' (1) shares or (2) assets. A share sale tends to be simpler as you simply transfer the shares from one person or legal entity to another. Once the company has a new corporate owner, they then own all of the company's assets including stock, cash, employees and the brand. An asset purchase is far more specific, it involves identifying particular assets which you would like to purchase and paying a fixed amount of money for the privilege of purchasing the goods.

There is a lot of flexibility to suit both the seller and the buyer. For example, you may be offered an 'earn out'. This is a chance to stay on with the business and essentially increase the purchase price provided the business meets certain targets over the next one to three years. Some deals may involve a mixture of cash, a swap of your shares for shares in the newly formed larger corporate group and/or debt in the form of a loan note.

23.2   The corporate sale process

First, you need to identify whether it is a share or asset purchase and think about the broad structure that is likely to be adopted and timings. It is important to be realistic about the time frame, it is better to allow plenty of time rather than rushing to complete a sale. Exceptions to this general rule may apply where there is an auction or some other regulatory or tax deadline. If time is likely to be a factor, make sure you do not leave the decision until the last minute. Even if you are not sure whether now is the right time, there is a huge benefit to you in getting your records up to date and thinking about where the relevant documents are stored. The more streamlined and efficient you can make this, the cheaper the corporate transaction and quicker the overall process.

Then you need to start working with your legal team. There are three important documents which tend to be created in parallel:

1.   The sale and purchase agreement (or asset purchase agreement if an asset purchase).

2.   The disclosure list.

3.   The due diligence report.

The legal process is essentially about identifying potential risk areas in the business which may affect the purchase price and either disclosing them or giving a contractual promise (known as a warranty or an indemnity) that there is not an issue. If the promise turns out to be broken, usually within a fixed period of time (potentially a couple of years), the buyer has the opportunity to claim back some of the money they paid (if an escrow account has been used) and in extreme cases may decide to sue for breach of contract.

There are important differences between warranties and indemnities. Put simply, a breach of warranty requires more work for the buyer if they want to claim against it in the future as they need to show both that the warranty was breached and that the effect of that breach was to reduce the value of the company or the asset, as appropriate. By contrast, an indemnity is more like a guarantee where you promise to compensate the buyer for their full losses if a particular event or liability arises. As you can imagine, this means that sellers are reluctant to grant indemnities and if they do so, they are typically on specific issues rather than on a general basis. Whether you can maintain this position when you're selling depends on the strength of your negotiating position.

In order to determine what promises to make, it is usually necessary for lawyers to review the relevant documents that your business relies on in order to trade. This includes:

1. Contracts with suppliers and distributors.

2. Leases.

3. Employment and freelancer contracts.

4. Data protection processes including contracts with your data processor(s).

5. Licences and assignments of intellectual property rights.

6. Registered intellectual property rights.

7. Details of any litigation which is threatened or ongoing.

8. Evidence of ownership of other unregistered intellectual property rights.

You could limit this review to key documents but it is important that you are careful about what you share, particularly if you doing a deal with a competitor. This is because you are in effect telling, at least, their lawyers exactly how your business works. There are various technological solutions to this issue including via an online 'data room' where the key legal documents are uploaded by you, reviewed by your lawyers and, if relevant, disclosed to the purchaser's lawyers on the basis that they can only review the agreement and cannot provide copies to the purchaser.

This process is known as 'due diligence' and it is very important as it allows the purchaser to determine whether or not the amount they have proposed to pay is in line with the actual value of the company and in more extreme cases, whether the risks associated with purchasing the company mean that they should not purchase the business at all.

The review of documents will ultimately result in a disclosure report being prepared by the seller's lawyers and a due diligence report being prepared by the purchaser's lawyers. They should identify all of the potential issues and then it is a question of deciding to what extent the seller should be warranting aspects of the business and/or whether the purchase terms should be changed.

The same issues apply to the early stage funding rounds albeit in a slightly simplified form. For example, you will likely be required to give a warranty that your business owns the key intellectual property rights, particularly unregistered rights which cannot be checked against a register.

Both funders and buyers generally may also require that key individu- als remain with the company for a period of time.

23.3   Intellectual property ownership

In a fashion business, your brand is often the primary value in your business. In intellectual property terms, this means your registered trade marks and designs as well as unregistered rights such as the goodwill you have generated in your brand, any unregistered design right and copyright in patterns, your website and any other advertising. As explained in Chapter 10, it is common for issues to arise where ownership of rights has been assumed on the basis that they have been paid for but in fact, they still belong to the creator. This is particularly a problem if you have heavily relied on freelancers. If you identify any potential issues, the normal course is to either rectify them or disclose against them and try to agree an appropriate warranty or reduction in the purchase price.

Good record keeping and regular audits can help to reduce your risks, save time and money and put you in the strongest possible position when it comes to sale.

It is possible to buy or sell a company without any due diligence but there are risks on both sides for taking this approach. If you are selling, it may mean that you cannot secure the favourable price that your business deserves. If you are buying, you face the prospect of paying money for a business which is in fact worth a lot less and may come with a whole host of liabilities attached. These issues can to a large extent be controlled contractually via the sale and purchase agreement but a promise to pay from someone with no money is not worth very much.

23.4 Change of control clauses

Some of your key commercial contracts will likely contain 'change of control clauses.' They sometimes state that the contract can be terminated immediately upon a change of control of your company. As mentioned in Chapter 9, it is important to avoid these terms where possible when signing contracts and to disclose them early on in the sale process if they exist. Where they exist you have to decide when to give notice to the other party (be they a supplier, distributor or customer). This is particularly important where you have a valuable contract which may affect the sale price.

23.5 Practical issues

23.5.1 Management of the website and key social media accounts

The login details for your website's content management system and social media accounts are an important feature of any transition process. You must make sure that you do not lose access to the accounts in the transition. It is wise to retain the personnel in charge of the website and any other online marketing in order to assist with the transition.

You will also need to make sure that any potential new brands following a merger or acquisition are registered on all relevant social media accounts (and as trade marks and domain names) as quickly as possible. There are many enterprising individuals out there who have been known to swoop on these rights, usually trade marks and domain names, at the first sign of a potential merger. This can create an expensive legal mess or the prospect of a ransom payment in order to resolve the issue. Before you publicise a potential new business, make sure you have applied to register a trade mark somewhere so you can secure your six-month priority period. See Chapter 3 for details.

23.5.2   Avoiding future trade mark conflicts

As mentioned in Chapter 3, disputes can often occur when you name your business after yourself. If you sell your business, you are also selling the right to trade under your business' name in the future. Consequently, selling up can potentially be very limiting on your ability to trade under your name in the future. It is a good idea to agree the parameters under which you can use a variation on your name for a future fashion business, or potentially, in a different industry. If you go into this transaction with your eyes open you can minimise the potential for future disappointment.

23.5.3   Employee protection

Employees are protected throughout the sale process in the EU. The legislation comes from an EU Directive and consequently varies in the way in which it is implemented across the EU.[1] For convenience, the UK acronym for the process, TUPE, will be used. The Directive requires that employees in the EU retain continuity of employment when their employer is sold. In other words, their employment contract and any associated accrued rights automatically transfer to a new employer. This is important as many employment rights such as the right to compensation in the event of unfair dismissal and the right to payment in the event of redundancy only apply after you have worked for an employer for a certain amount of time. The number of years of employment also affects the amount an employee is entitled to in a redundancy.

---

1 Council Directive 2001/23/EC of 12 March 2001 on the approximation of the laws of the Member States relating to the safeguarding of employees' rights in the event of transfers of undertakings, businesses or parts of undertakings or businesses. For example, in the UK, this has become the Transfer of Undertakings (Protection of Employment) Regulations 2006.

In most Member States[2] there is no minimum number of employees involved in the transfer for TUPE to apply. In many instances,[3] there is a mandatory consultation process either with employees or with the works council (if relevant).

23.5.4   Asset sales and intellectual property

If there is an asset sale, there can be extensive time tied up after purchase in transferring the assets. This is a particular issue with large portfolios of registered intellectual property rights in multiple jurisdictions. Typically this means trade marks, designs, patents and, in some circumstances, copyright but there are other rights such as certification marks and related licences which may also need to be updated.

It is usually necessary to instruct a specialist in each territory to comply with the intellectual property transfer formalities. They will likely require a power of attorney (often an original document) and may require further formalities to be followed such as the use of a notary or similar. The entire process can take a very long time, particularly in the Middle East, and can be very expensive and hard to manage as you are usually instructing several different law firms. The best approach is to instruct a single law firm to be the point of contact and manage the process internationally.

---

2 Italy is a notable exception, the *Traserferimento d'Azienda* only applies where there are more than 15 employees.

3 In Germany, for example, mandatory written information must be provided to employees but it is only necessary to have a consultation if there is a works council.

24 Combating counterfeits

If you become successful, counterfeiting is inevitable. This is a somewhat backhanded compliment! There are different theories on the economic impact of counterfeiting. The more generous theories suggest that it can be beneficial on the basis that it raises awareness of your brand and provides access to the brand to consumers who would not otherwise purchase your product. This tends to be an oversimplification of the myriad issues associated with counterfeiting.

First, some nomenclature. Knock-offs, counterfeits and duplicates or replicas are often used interchangeably but they have slightly different meanings. A counterfeit is the most serious form of copying, where an exact copy is made of the original including the branding, product labels and swing tags. Counterfeit products are deliberately designed to give consumers the impression that they are the original product. Despite this, many counterfeits include quite glaring differences in product quality or wording. For example, typos in brand names are common, e.g., Prado or Guccy.

Knock-offs are closely inspired by the original product but tend to copy the product design and remove the branding. As discussed in Chapters 3–7, just because a product has not copied a brand name or logo does not mean that it has not infringed any intellectual property rights. A duplicate or replica is very similar to a counterfeit and a knock-off in that it is a copy of the original but it could fall anywhere on the copying scale from a perfect imitation to an inspired similar product. For convenience, the rest of this chapter will use 'counterfeit' as a catch all term.

The most significant impact from counterfeiting is the damage to brand reputation which is notoriously hard to quantify. Counterfeits can vary substantially in quality from items which are so poorly made that you would hope they are immediately recognisable as fakes to fairly good quality replicas which have skimped corners on less visible aspects such as the waterproof nature of the material. Bags tend to be the main counterfeiting problem for the fashion industry but a wide range of things can be counterfeited from clothes (particularly branded clothing) to jewellery. If consumers see these items in the street, the quality is usually sufficiently poor that it is inevitable that they will damage your brand's reputation.

Further counterfeit goods tend to skip corners as far as, at least, the following issues are concerned: the standards of manufacture; use of dangerous or banned substances; use of labour including child labour; payment of tax, particularly sales tax; and sustainability. If consumers associate the counterfeiters' failure with regard to any of these issues with your brand this causes further reputational damage.

Although it is still common for counterfeit goods to be sold from physical premises and markets, the Internet has quickly become the dominant means for distributing counterfeits. Many items are sold in small parcels which makes them very difficult to track and what began as primarily an eBay or Amazon problem has now ballooned in size and scope including sales on social media and via the dark web. That said, the various enforcement options are now catching up with the new technology and there are plenty of options at your disposal to combat counterfeits.

24.1   Customs

 An oldie but a goodie – the various Customs authorities are one of the most efficient means of removing counterfeit goods from the marketplace as they stop them long before the goods get on to the street. Each country has a designated customs authority and while the associated rules tend to follow a broadly similar process, there can be major differences. In most instances, in order to improve the likelihood of the relevant Customs authority seizing counterfeits (and not seizing your legitimate goods) it is necessary to file a Customs 'recordal' or 'notification.' This document will typically set out your registered rights, particularly trade marks, and potentially unregistered rights such as copyright and may also list your authorised distributors, factories and similar. As you can imagine, this information can change on a regular basis and it is important that it is kept up to date.

Some regions, notably the European Union, allow you to file a Customs notification which covers a large geographic area (such as the whole of the EU) provided that the rights you are registering are pan-European (i.e., EU trade marks or Community designs). The EU Customs Regulation[1] also provides for Customs registration on a national basis.

In order to file an EU customs recordal or 'application for action,' you must include full details of your genuine goods including photographs of the products and any security features such as holograms, RFID chips, 2D barcodes, etc. Bear in mind that the more accurate and complete your recordal, the easier it will be for Customs to identify and stop counterfeit goods. It is important that you include a point of contact who can respond within the very tight timeframes set by the EU Customs Regulation. This responsibility can be outsourced to a legal adviser. If this point of contact is a legal representative, you will also need to file a Power of Attorney (commonly abbreviated to a 'POA'). Once your recordal has been accepted, the information is shared with Customs authorities across the EU via a centralised database.

Although on paper EU Customs has a unified procedure and process, in practice the level of rigour applied by Customs authorities can vary across the EU. Bear in mind that because the EEA allows for free movement of goods, once the goods have entered the EEA, they will typically not be checked and detained again. This can cause issues with countries such as Norway which are part of the EEA but not part of the Customs Union. In this instance, Norwegian goods can be traded on a tariff-free basis to the rest of the EEA but products which enter the Customs Union from Norway (but originated elsewhere) are subject to further checks.

24.1.1   The simplified procedure

The major change which was brought about by the EU Customs Regulation is introducing the 'simplified procedure' and 'super simplified procedure' to all EU Member States. Under the simplified procedure, when Customs identifies potentially infringing goods, both the brand owner and the importer are notified. It is possible for the brand owner to request a sample of the detained item in order to assess whether it is infringing. In addition, both parties can inspect the consignment.

---

1 EU Regulation No 608/2013.

Any goods which are detained by Customs are automatically destroyed if you (i.e., the brand owner) confirm that the goods are infringing and the importer does not contest the detention within ten working days. If the importer *does* contest the detention, you have ten working days in which to start court proceedings otherwise the goods are released. You are entitled to request samples of the detained goods in order to determine if they are counterfeit and to assist if you need to file a court action.

The 'super simplified procedure' applies to very small consignments of goods (i.e., three units or less or with a combined weight of less than 2 kg). If you elect to join the super simplified procedure when filing your EU Customs recordal, then any goods which meet these requirements will automatically be detained and destroyed and you will only be notified if the importer contests the detention within the ten working day time period.

24.2   Practical points

Timing is very important when dealing with Customs both in the EU and elsewhere. There are very tight deadlines and extensions will not be granted. It is important that Customs knows who to contact and that person is able to quickly respond when notified. This is particularly important around public holidays. Ideally there should be a dedicated email address which is automatically sent to several designated people.

You can dramatically improve the prospects of having a successful relationship with Customs if you take the time to build up a positive relationship via regular training and contact with the key individuals involved in each territory.

While Customs does not apply to parallel or 'grey' goods, in practice these goods will likely be detained at some point and the details on the detention can be very useful in terms of identifying issues in your supply chain. Bear in mind that if goods which enter the EU have an ultimate destination which is outside the EU, i.e., 'goods in transit,' you cannot detain them because they are not intended to be put onto the market in the EU.

Make sure that you keep all Customs information up to date. This both increases the likelihood that Customs will detain counterfeits and reduces the risk of Customs incorrectly detaining genuine goods. In any event, many Customs recordals or notifications need to be renewed on a regular basis (e.g., annually).

It is also possible to sue a counterfeiter in the court of the relevant country(ies) in which the infringement occurred. The different options which are available in terms of civil proceedings are set out in Chapters 19 and 20. They include court orders:

1. Against ISPs (or similar intermediaries) who may have information on the counterfeiters.

2. Against landlords who allow counterfeit goods to be sold on their property.

3. To search the counterfeiters' premises and seize infringing goods and incriminating information.

4. For interim injunctions to prevent further trade in counterfeit goods pending trial.

5. For a term of imprisonment, a fine, or both (via the criminal justice system or a private prosecution).

24.3   Sales in physical marketplaces

If counterfeit goods make it past Customs and into the EU, they may be sold either online or via the more traditional route of the market stall. These stalls may appear at temporary markets or are often located in front of legitimate shops which deny all knowledge or connection to the infringing activity when challenged.

As discussed in Chapter 19, it is possible to get various forms of order which, provided you can convince the court to grant them, enable the search and seizure of infringing goods from the marketplace and any associated locations such as storage facilities. In order for this to be effective, it is wise to engage investigators to gather as much information as possible about the potential ringleaders and supply chain before taking action. An English search and seizure order will typically include all relevant digital records including any apps or similar. This can enable you to build up an accurate picture of the entire supply chain – but comes with a hefty price tag. For that reason, it is common for brand owners to work together when tackling particularly prolific counterfeiters. One recent spanner in the works of investigation concerns the impact of the GDPR on the accessibility of WHOIS information on the people and businesses behind domain names.[2]

 All of the remedies discussed in Chapter 19 are available against counterfeiters. This includes delivery up of infringing products and damages or an account of profits. The difficulty with these kinds of cases tends to be identifying the relevant people including their legal name and contact details. This is yet another reason why the investigation phase is crucial.

24.4   The Internet and counterfeits

As discussed in Chapter 19, there are now many options available to stop online infringement, from utilising the takedown processes on online marketplaces such as eBay, Amazon and Alibaba to blocking injunctions against large swathes of infringing websites.

Social media and other online activity can be a fantastic source of information on counterfeiters both in terms of identifying counterfeit goods being sold online and investigating the counterfeiters themselves. The data from social media is particularly useful in terms of identifying counterfeit networks around the world.

 However, social media has brought its own set of problems. The sale of counterfeit goods via closed social media groups is currently a major problem without an easy solution. For the time being, they require time to investigate and while each seller tends to be small scale they add up to a substantial problem. A combination of investigation, making test purchases and sending takedown notices as well as sending cease and desist letters can help to manage this activity but it will not fundamentally change without the cooperation of the various social media platforms.

---

2 For a more detailed review of this issue see Ingram, Elliot 'Is GDPR The Catalyst to Replace the Broken WHOIS System?' 1 June 2018, at https://www.linkedin.com/pulse/gdpr-catalyst-replace-br oken-whois-system-elliott-ingram/.

24.5   3D printing

Finally, there has been a lot of speculation that 3D printing will be a game-changing technology and make counterfeiting much more common and harder to stop. 3D printing, also known as additive manufacturing, is essentially the ability to create more or less any shape of object from raw materials either using lasers to join small particles together or a 'printer' to build up layers of the material. Often this material is PLA – a biodegradable type of plastic. This is a very simplified description and if you are unfamiliar with the concept, it is definitely worth more detailed investigation. 3D printing can save significant amounts of time and money in prototyping and open up new creative opportunities, particularly in terms of jewellery design and other accessories including buttons and clasps.

There was a lot of panic about the impact of 3D printing when it first came on the scene and the worry was that counterfeiters would either be able to manufacture specific items such as branded plates to be added to unbranded bags or in the case of jewellery, manufacture and sell precise copies from scratch in a highly portable fashion. So far these fears have not proven well-founded. This is in part because 3D printing is currently much more expensive and often lower quality than traditional mass manufacturing methods. Consequently, it is still worth counterfeiters taking the risk of sending multiple counterfeit branded plates through the post rather than 3D printing them within a jurisdiction. While customised fan versions of products may be created using 3D printing and sold on a small scale, true counterfeits are less of a problem for the time being.

25 Managing the supply chain

Understanding and controlling your supply chain is important from day one. It avoids any reputation-destroying revelations and makes it easier to manage costs, scale up and work with Customs. Supply chain management is not necessarily the reason you entered the fashion industry but if it is not the thing that gets you up in the morning, either find someone who specialises in it to help you or look into it in more detail. Supply chain management involves a wide range of cultural, environmental and legal issues each of which is fascinating and extremely important to get right. There are no excuses for burying your head in the sand about the origin of your goods.

25.1   Ethical fashion

Quite apart from the strong moral reasons for making ethics an integral part of your supply chain, there are significant legal motivations ranging from laws about modern slavery to corporate manslaughter which are particularly prevalent at an EU Level. For example, a recent EU Directive[1] requires large businesses to disclose diversity data and other non-financial information. As this is a Directive, it has been implemented by each Member State in national legislation such as the 2016 French Corporate Duty of Vigilance Law and the English Groups (Accounts and Non-Financing Reporting) Regulations 2016.

An ethical approach to business also has an impact on the bottom line. In the short term, low prices may win out but longer term brand loyalty comes from people believing and investing in a brand. If your only differentiator is price, you will not have to wait long for a competitor to come along and undercut you with a new and nimbler business model.

---

1   Directive 2014/95/EU of the European Parliament and of the Council of 22 October 2014 amending Directive 2013/34/EU as regards disclosure of non-financial and diversity information by certain large undertakings and groups.

Taking an ethical approach is not only the right thing to do but has huge business upsides too.

For example, in the 1980s through to the early 2000s, the American footwear giant, Nike, took advantage of sourcing on a global scale to produce products at a lower cost. Nike's business model meant that they reinvested these savings into marketing campaigns and product development which resulted in a high return in terms of brand growth over the decades. However, these apparent savings also resulted in several serious reputational and public relations concerns involving underpaid workers, use of child labour and poor working conditions across developing countries. Each scandal tarnished the brand's image. Since the mid-2000s, Nike has worked hard to review its practices and is now considered one of the most sustainable international companies in terms of environmental impact improvements, transparency and working conditions. This shows that it is possible to turn it around – but why create the problem and the negative environmental and social impact in the first place?

Nike's historic problems can be traced back to its practices such as offshore sourcing and outsourcing – both are a common part of the fashion supply chain. These practices not only pose potential strategic and logistical issues, but also create risk in respect of social and environmental responsibility. In this context, it is not surprising that corporate and social responsibility ('CSR') is growing in importance within the fashion sector.

The fashion industry's initial commitment to CSR may have been for PR and marketing purposes only (at least if Absolutely Fabulous is an accurate representation of the state of the industry in the 1990s).[2] This has changed over time and many major brands such as Stella McCartney have helped to lead the way.

The introduction of the voluntary international standard ISO 26000 on Social Responsibility in 2010 has provided guidance to help understand social responsibility and allows businesses and organisations (regardless of their size or location) to incorporate best practices into their local and international operations.

The international standard centres around seven key areas: (i) internal organisation and governance; (ii) human rights; (iii) labour practices;

---

2 See at: https://en.wikipedia.org/wiki/Absolutely_Fabulous.

(iv) the environment; (v) fair operating practices; (vi) consumer issues; and (vii) community involvement and development. Each of these elements has a direct link with the activities of fashion retailers.

London-based international retailer, Marks & Spencer (M&S), has long led the way on these issues and famously integrated the standard into their company CSR policies, so that responsible sourcing, environmental and social sustainability form a key part of its supply chain.

In Europe generally, there has also been a move to local manufacturing which both gives more control over the factories and their associated working conditions and significantly reduces the environmental impact. A famous recent example of this in the UK is Hiut Denim which has revitalised the denim industry in Cardigan Bay, Wales.[3]

In addition to the PR effect, these companies are able to supply robust evidence as part of their external reporting on ethical issues, which evidences transparency, avoids time consuming and distracting audits and results in long-term reputational benefits with current and potential customers.

 This points at an increasing movement toward 'the circular economy' with the recyclability of fashion items becoming an important selling point. At the Fifth Copenhagen Fashion Summit of 2017, 20 brands including Asos, Adidas, H&M and the Kering Group undertook to meet circular economy targets by 2020.

The Global Fashion Agenda, a global forum on fashion sustainability founded in 2016, further aims to ensure that all fashion brands and retailers adhere to similar commitments as part of its 'Call to Action' campaign. Concrete steps towards achieving these goals have already been taken by some retailers. For example, Adidas Sport's Infinity Shoes are entirely recyclable, and in 2013, the H&M Group launched its Garment Collecting service, which has collected in excess of 40,000 tonnes of garments to date. The garments collected are re-worn as second hand clothing, reused to create new garments or other goods, or recycled into textile fibres for other uses, such as for insulation. These examples demonstrate how the fashion industry is changing

---

3 See at: https://hiutdenim.co.uk/blogs/story/5156362-our-town-is-going-to-make-jeans-again.

its approach towards manufacturing as well as how fashion items are produced and consumed.

Another interesting trend is around the use of charitable giving being hardwired into the business model. For example, Bottletop feeds 20 per cent of its profits into its charitable foundation which funds selected projects. Meanwhile, Ninety Percent goes considerably further and gives its customers the opportunity to choose which charity will receive its donation of, as you may have guessed, 90 per cent of its profits.

Although major developments have been made in recent years, the  intense pressure of retail, particularly those larger businesses with many legacy stores and large pension commitments means that there is a risk of CSR falling down the priority list. For example, many large retailers delayed renewal of the Bangladesh Accord on fire and building safety which was set up in the wake of the Rana Plaza disaster where a Bangladesh textile factory collapsed in 2013 killing 1,135 people.[4]

25.2   One Belt One Road

One of the big issues with international manufacturing is the time and 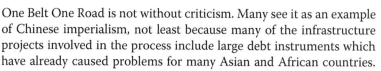 pollution involved in shipping the goods around the world, particularly from China. The Chinese Government has come up with a solution to the first issue; six new train and maritime routes which will link Mainland China with Europe. This initiative is known as One Belt One Road (and also as the Belt and Road Initiative). It is aimed at being a 21st century version of the Silk Road. The initiative connects more than 60 countries in Asia, Europe and Australasia.

One Belt One Road is not without criticism. Many see it as an example of Chinese imperialism, not least because many of the infrastructure projects involved in the process include large debt instruments which have already caused problems for many Asian and African countries. Long term, this initiative will transform international trade.

---

4 See at: https://www.theguardian.com/uk-news/2018/jan/29/ms-john-lewis-sainsburys-bangladesh
  -factory-safety-accord.

25.3   Fair Trade materials

 In addition to the working conditions, the origin of the raw textile materials and the manufacturing processes used are all important in terms of meeting ethical standards. There are various organisations who are looking at ethical standards in fashion. The following examples give a flavour of the many learning and licensing opportunities that are available.[5]

25.3.1   The World Fair Trade Organization

The World Fair Trade Organization (WFTO) represents over 350 organisations around the world which are committed to creating market access to Fair Trade goods through policy, advocacy, campaigning, marketing and monitoring. WFTO is focused on improving the situation of women, child labour, working conditions, the environment and the payment of a fair price. This is achieved by a combination of transparency and accountability for the supply chain. The WFTO provides a list of vetted members which may be useful when identifying potential partners around the world.

25.3.2   Fair Trade Labelling Organization

Fair Trade labels for seed cotton (i.e., raw cotton) were launched in France, Switzerland and the UK in 2005 following the introduction of standards in 2004. These labels certify that cotton producers have received a fair deal for their work.[6] Although the standard only covers the cotton production phase, the label does require a social compliance assessment covering the processing and manufacturing of the ultimate garment. The Fair Trade Labelling Organization is developing a label which covers the whole garment production process from start to finish.

25.3.3   The Ethical Trading Initiative

The Ethical Trading Initiative (ETI) is a British alliance of businesses, NGOs and trade union organisations. ETI's aim is to promote and improve the implementation of corporate codes of practice which

---

5 You can read more about the different options from the Ethical Fashion Forum, at: http://www. ethicalfashionforum.com/the-issues/standards-labelling.

6 See the Fairtrade Standards for Seed Cotton from the (FLO) website at: www.fairtrade.net.

cover supply chain working conditions. A number of large high street retailers in the fashion sector are members of the ETI. Compliance is achieved via self-assessment and monitoring.

25.3.4   Eco-labelling

The textile and clothing industry has around 100 different labels that address either environmental or social sustainability, or consumers' health. Two of the most common European Eco-Labels are the Oko-Tex standard 100 mark, which focuses on health standards, and the European Eco-Label for Textile Products, which focuses on water pollution.

25.3.5   GOTS

The Global Organic Textile Standard (GOTS)[7] is a German originated initiative which sets an international processing standard for textiles made from organic fibres. In order to become GOTS certified, your textile products must contain a minimum of 70 per cent organic fibres and all chemicals used in the manufacturing process, including dyes, must meet set environmental and toxicological criteria. There are also requirements over water usage. GOTS controls the types of businesses which can use its name and logo via its registered trade mark. It has also made a recent application to register the GOTS logo as a certification mark.[8] Other labels which certify organic standards in clothing include the Soil Association and EKO.

25.3.6   European Laws

There is a specific EU Regulation for textiles used in clothing,[9] and an EU Directive which makes the laws on the information provided to consumers regarding the different materials used in footwear consistent across the Member States.[10]

The Textile Regulation means that there is now a consistent approach across the EU for the naming, labelling and marking of the fibre

7 You can read more about the standard at: http://www.global-standard.org/.
8 The application for an EU certification mark was made on 2 October 2017, the day after the law changed and it became possible to do so. Details of the mark are available at: https://euipo.europa. eu/eSearch/#details/trademarks/017283128.
9 Textile Regulation (EU) No 1007/2011.
10 Directive 94/11/EC on labelling of materials used in footwear. You can read more about it at: https://ec.europa.eu/growth/sectors/fashion/footwear/legislation_en.

composition of textile products. This Regulation includes a general obligation to state the full fibre composition of textile products as well as minimum technical requirements for applications for a new fibre name and a requirement to indicate the presence of non-textile parts of animal origin. There is an exemption for customised products made by self-employed tailors.[11]

The Footwear Directive is more straightforward and simply requires clear information to be provided to consumers regarding the composition of the top, sole and lining of the relevant shoe. Pictograms can be used to avoid translation into multiple European languages.

There are also European standards for materials such as leather (which currently has 143 different standards) and the European Commission is considering introducing a similar European level labelling system to textiles.[12]

25.4 Modern slavery

Retail as an industry involves a lot of opportunities for potential abuse in the supply chain. As a result of continued issues with the origins of employees working both in factories, warehouses and on the shop floor, there has been a move toward 'anti-slavery' legislation in many jurisdictions worldwide. In the UK, this takes the form of the Modern Slavery Act 2015.

The Act requires retailers with an annual turnover of £36 million or more (including franchisees who meet that threshold in their own right) to monitor their supply chains and publish an annual statement which sets out the steps they have taken to ensure that slave labour is not used in their supply chains.

There is no prescribed format for the published statements but the UK government suggests that they cover the following six areas:

1. the organisation's structure, its business and its supply chains;

2. its policies in relation to slavery and human trafficking;

---

11 You can read more about it at: https://ec.europa.eu/growth/sectors/fashion/textiles-clothing/legislation_en.

12 More details are available at: https://ec.europa.eu/growth/sectors/fashion/leather_en.

3. its due diligence processes in relation to slavery and human trafficking in its business and supply chains;

4. the parts of its business and supply chains where there is a risk of slavery and human trafficking taking place, and the steps it has taken to assess and manage that risk;

5. its effectiveness in ensuring that slavery and human trafficking are not taking place in its business or supply chains, measured against such performance indicators as it considers appropriate; and

6. the training and capacity building about slavery and human trafficking available to its staff.

The government requires the organisations to paint a detailed picture of all the steps it has taken to address and remedy modern slavery, and the effectiveness of all such steps.[13]

Unlike the legislation for bribery, corruption and money laundering, the Modern Slavery Act does not carry a prison sentence. However, it is seen as a good start in terms of creating good working practices and the annual nature of the publication ensures that there are regular audits and that consideration is given to the issue at board level on a regular basis.

25.4.1   International equivalents to the Modern Slavery Act

The closest equivalent in France concerns the obligations set out in the Non-Financial Reporting Directive in 2016.[14] This Directive is aimed at improving corporate transparency. It strengthened the French Corporate Duty of Vigilance Law 2016 which imposes obligations in respect of human rights, the environment and fundamental freedoms on large companies in France and abroad. The Directive also strengthened the requirements set out in the English Modern Slavery Act.

It is now expressly stated under French law that large companies not only need to be vigilant on labour and human rights matters in

---

13 For the UK Government guidance, see at: https://www.gov.uk/government/uploads/system/ uploads/attachment_data/file/649906/Transparency_in_Supply_Chains_A_Practical_Guide _2017.pdf.
14 Directive 2014/95/EU.

respect of themselves, but need to ensure this is the case regarding 'the subcontractors or suppliers with whom [the company] maintains an established commercial relationship, when such operations derive from this relationship'.[15]

The Dutch Child Labour Due Diligence Law ('Wet Zorgplicht Kinderarbeid') will apply from 1 January 2020 and covers similar ground. Again, this law is a result of the EU Directive.

25.5   Anti-bribery legislation

The Non-Financial Reporting Directive is also relevant to the fraught issue of bribery. In recent decades, and in the wake of various scandals, the laws on bribery have been greatly strengthened in many jurisdictions, particularly the UK[16] and US.[17] This might not seem like an obvious issue for the fashion industry but if the manufacture or sale of your goods is occurring in a high-risk territory, it is perfectly conceivable that you could fall on the wrong side of the line without intending to do so.

The bribery offences include bribing another person,[18] being bribed,[19] a function or activity to which bribe relates[20] (including in the course of employment), bribery of foreign public officials[21] and failure of commercial organisations to prevent bribery.[22]

The UK Bribery Act includes any activities which 'ha[ve] no connection with the United Kingdom, and [are] performed in a country or territory outside the United Kingdom.'[23] The penalties include up to a year's imprisonment for individuals involved, including company directors, and a fine.

---

15 See Art. L. 225-102-4. – I of the French Commercial Code.
16 The Bribery Act 2010.
17 The Foreign Corrupt Practices Act 1977 15 U.S.C. § 78dd-1, et seq.
18 Bribery Act 2010, s. 1.
19 Ibid., s. 2.
20 Ibid., s. 3.
21 Ibid., s. 6.
22 Ibid., s. 7.
23 See e.g., ibid., s. 3(6).

25.6   Blockchain

Blockchain has been touted as a means of solving many supply chain issues (and other issues such as trade mark management). Blockchain is a type of distributed ledger technology which creates a secure and indisputable record of events. This record includes the nature and sequence of the events. For example, it could track a particular component, such as a fabric or button, leaving one factory and arriving at the next factory. The record of the component's journey to the second factory would be permanently maintained on the blockchain ledger including the relevant times, businesses involved and method of transport. This is important for keeping track of the supply chain including data such as the carbon footprint. The blockchain could also be updated from employee ID cards to create and retain a record of who worked on what when.

The big difference between records which are stored on a blockchain and more normal centralised records and databases is that for a centralised database there is one single 'true' copy to which everyone refers. Where the records are de-centralised there can be a near infinite number of copies each of which is identical and 'true' (i.e., accurate). This is very useful from a security point of view because even if you are able to change a large number of the de-centralised records, changing them all is so challenging as to be essentially impossible. This makes the blockchain far more secure than a centralised database (although it can also be more expensive to set up and maintain).

The records which are stored in a blockchain can be kept anonymous and only made available to people who have the correct digital 'key' to access them with. Because the blockchain builds on top of existing records, once a record has been added to the database, it cannot be removed in the future (i.e., it is irreversible, although an incorrect entry can be updated, the record of the incorrect entry and subsequent change will remain in the blockchain). The digital key is essentially a very long sequence of numbers which is unique to the owner and so long as to be impossible to duplicate.

Blockchain is most commonly associated with bitcoin which is a public blockchain, however, it is possible to have a private blockchain where only a few people have access and permission to add new events to the ledger. Alternatively you could have a public database which is decentralised for security reasons but where the authority over what can be added is centralised (or at least limited to a handful of people). Even if a ledger is public, the information referred to in the ledger (e.g., the identity of a particular factory, textile fabric or employee) can remain confidential if you do not include this information in the public ledger. For example, the bitcoin ledger is public so everyone with access to the ledger can see that money was transferred from Person A to Person B on X date. However, the identities of Person A and Person B are not recorded in the ledger and therefore remain confidential.

It is also possible to execute what are confusingly known as 'smart contracts' via the blockchain. These are predetermined events which are carried out as soon as one or more conditions are fulfilled. For example, when a particular shipment clears Customs, money transfers to Company A and ownership of goods transfers to Company B.

Blockchain is commonly used in connection with supply chain management via the use of RFID or NFC chips or QR codes.[24] RFID and NFC chips can be easily scanned and are commonly added to swing tags or care labels. Be careful about the stage at which they are added as they may get damaged if added too early in the production process. The downside of using a QR code is that they can fade over time and consequently cannot be scanned.

In addition to complying with ethical codes of conduct, having an immutable record of the supply chain reduces the cost of audits and helps in proving the country(ies) of origin and whether or not goods are genuine or the rights in them have been exhausted.[25]

Although a blockchain solution involves significant upfront investment, the long-term savings in compliance and audit control should eventually lead to significant savings and enable much greater transparency.[26]

---

24 RFID (Radio Frequency Identification) chips use radio waves to automatically identify and track tags attached to objects (e.g., clothing or accessories). QR (Quick Response) codes are static barcodes that consist of a series of small black boxes within one larger box. They are sometimes referred to as 2D barcodes and are commonly added to product packaging and care labels. When scanned by a smartphone, QR codes can provide access to data, such as product care information.

25 See Chapter 20 for more information on the principle of the exhaustion of intellectual property rights.

26 For more information on the Blockchain opportunities for the fashion industry see R. Burbidge, 'The Blockchain is in Fashion', 107(6) The Trademark Reporter 1262–7.

26 What's next?

Both fashion and law are in a state of flux at the moment and it is hard to predict what the future will hold with anything remotely resembling accuracy. However, there are a few known unknowns to which it is worth giving some thought as you plan your business' strategy and set your legal budget. This chapter will start with the obvious political changes such as Brexit and move on to the more technological changes.

26.1 Brexit and IP

There has been a lot of panic about the impact of Brexit (the UK's non-binding referendum regarding whether the UK should remain a member of the EU). As a result of this vote, the UK is heading toward complete constitutional upheaval. At the time of writing, there is still no certainty about what will happen after the UK leaves the EU as a deal has not been finalised (indeed a no-deal scenario remains a possibility). As an earlier draft of this section has since become obsolete, I do not intend to opine too much on this issue!

Intellectual property was one of the areas of law which had been made most consistent across the EU in the last 40 or so years. Consequently, it is particularly likely to change significantly after Brexit. Many of these changes may incur legal and/or official fees.

26.1.1 Exhaustion of rights

The principles relating to exhaustion of rights are introduced in 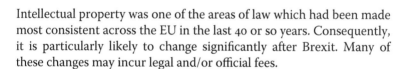 Chapter 20. Before the UK joined the EU, it allowed worldwide exhaustion of goods. In other words, once a branded product was put on sale anywhere in the world, a trade mark owner could not prevent its resale in another territory. In the US, this is known as the first sale doctrine. Following its entry into the EU, the UK limited exhaustion to goods from the European Economic Area (essentially the EU plus Liechtenstein, Norway and Iceland). After Brexit, the UK may return to international exhaustion or could agree to a much more limited exhaustion based on trade deals.

This is important because prices can vary substantially across territories and it is possible for third party retailers to purchase and sell branded products purchased in one much cheaper territory and resell them in a more expensive territory. This is known as parallel importing. Parallel imports can damage your brand as you cannot control the conditions for resale and the goods may be sold for less than the official distributors.

Exhaustion of rights and parallel imports are discussed in more detail in Chapter 20.

26.1.2   Contractual terms

The other major risk area is around contracts. As mentioned in Chapter 9, it is important to properly define the EU on the basis of your actual intention. In other words, do you intend the agreement to cover the EU Member States on a particular date or is your intention that the definition will change as EU membership changes.

Many businesses are still drafting contracts which define the territory as the 'European Union.' There are many more contracts out there which include these sorts of clauses and may be continually renewed based on a course of dealing or have a long fixed term. If your business has signed this sort of contract, it is worth finding out now and varying the terms to include some Brexit proof wording in line with your actual intentions for the contract (i.e., do you want it to cover the UK post Brexit or not).

26.1.3   Other issues

 There are many other lesser known pan-EU rights such as Protected Designations of Origin and their close cousins, Geographical Indications. These geographical focused rights mean that you do not see English Champagne or Dutch Stilton on the shelves. This could all change in the English supermarkets of the future. In many instances there are parallel trade mark rights e.g., Scotch whisky, but this can still pose problems when the trade mark owner has not got the right sort of licence scheme in place.

Other issues include the status of pan-EU injunctions, settlement agreements and co-existence agreements which are based on EU rights may no longer cover the UK etc.

26.1.4   What can you do?

Although the outcome of Brexit is still somewhat up in the air, by reviewing your trade mark and design portfolio and European contracts, you can at least identify known problems and be primed to act once you have confirmation of exactly what is going to happen when.

26.2   Data

The political controversies in, at least, the UK and US regarding the use of Facebook data coupled with the introduction of the General Data Protection Regulation (GDPR) in May 2018 show that data is now central to modern business and it is imperative that it is handled carefully, securely and no more than is absolutely necessary.

If you have not carried out a data audit and ensured that you have satis- factory processes in place to comply with GDPR, now is the time to do so. You can read more about GDPR and data protection in Chapter 14.

26.3   Virtual reality

What shopping will look like in ten years' time is still an open ques- tion. E-commerce has fundamentally changed retail and many town centres across Europe have been subject to significant change as a result. Will augmented and/or virtual reality change things again? Who knows!

If the last 20 years has taught anything it is that technological changes can happen extremely quickly and have far-reaching and often unintended consequences. Regardless of whether it goes mainstream or not, fashion is often at the forefront of technological change and it pays to keep track of what is happening at the cutting edge of technology.

26.4   It's not the end

As mentioned in the introduction, one of the intentions of this book is to start a conversation around European fashion law. It is obviously impossible to cover every single aspect of fashion law in detail but the book should have given you a helpful flavour of many common issues which face the fashion industry on a regular basis. Please do sign up to and contribute to the website at www.europeanfashionlaw.com.

The ultimate aim of this book is to provide an accessible overview of the legal issues facing the fashion industry and hopefully head off any expensive legal problems or at least give you an idea of the different options which are available. If there are any issues you have faced which have not been considered or any issues on which you would like more detail, please do get in touch. You never know, there may be a second edition!

Index